PRENTICE HALL MATHEMATICS

PRE-ALGEBRA

ALL-IN-ONE
Student Workbook
VERSION A

PEARSON

Prentice
Hall

Boston, Massachusetts
Upper Saddle River, New Jersey

ISBN 0-13-165717-8

17 18 19 20 V039 17 16 15 14

Practice, Guided Problem Solving, Vocabulary

Chapter 3 Decimals and Equations

Chapter 4 Factors, Fractions, and Exponents

Chapter 5 Operations With Fractions

Chapter 10 Area and Volume

Chapter 11 Right Triangles in Algebra

Chapter 12 Data Analysis and Probability

Chapter 13 Nonlinear Functions and Polynomials

A Note to the Student:

This section of your workbook contains notetaking pages for each lesson in your student edition. They are structured to help you take effective notes in class. They will also serve as a study guide as you prepare for tests and quizzes.

Lesson 1-1

Variables and Expressions

Lesson Objectives	**NAEP 2005 Strand:** Algebra
▼ Identify variables, numerical expressions, and variable expressions	**Topic:** Variables, Expressions, and Operations
▼ Write variable expressions for word phrases	**Local Standards:** _____

Vocabulary

A variable is _____

A variable expression is _____

_____

$$\text{variable} \rightarrow \quad m \quad \leftarrow \text{ miles on 10 gallons}$$
$$\text{variable expression} \rightarrow \quad m \div 10 \quad \leftarrow \text{ miles per gallon}$$

Examples

❶ Identifying Expressions Identify each expression as a *numerical expression* or a *variable expression*. For a variable expression, name the variable.

a. 7×3

[ ] expression

b. $4t$

[ ] expression

[ ] is the variable.

❷ Writing Variable Expressions Write a variable expression for the cost of p pens priced at 29¢ each.

Words [29¢] times [number of pens]

Let [p] = number of pens.

Expression [ ] · [ ]

The variable expression [ ], or [ ], describes the cost of p pens.

Daily Notetaking Guide

Name_____ Class_____ Date _____

Quick Check

1. Identify each expression as a *numerical expression* or a *variable expression*. For a variable expression, name the variable.

   a. $8 \div x$ **b.** 100×6 **c.** $d + 43 - 9$

   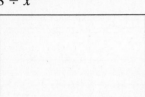   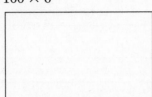

2. **a.** Bagels cost $.50 each. Write a variable expression for the cost of b bagels.

   b. Measurement Write a variable expression for the number of hours in m minutes.

3. Write a variable expression for each word phrase.

Word Phrase	Variable Expression
Nine more than a number y	
4 less than a number n	
A number z times three	
A number a divided by 12	
5 times the quantity 4 plus a number c	

Lesson 1-2

The Order of Operations

Lesson Objectives	NAEP 2005 Strand: Number Properties and Operations
V Use the order of operations	**Topic:** Properties of Number and Operations
2 Use grouping symbols	**Local Standards:** _____

Key Concepts

Order of Operations

1. Work inside [   ] symbols.

2. [   ] and [   ] in order from left to right.

3. [   ] and [   ] in order from left to right.

Examples

❶ Simplifying Expressions Simplify $8 - 2 \cdot 2$.

$8 - 2 \cdot 2$

$8 - $ [   ]   **First multiply.**

[   ]   **Then subtract.**

❷ Using the Order of Operations Simplify $12 \div 3 - 1 \cdot 2 + 1$.

$12 \div 3 - 1 \cdot 2 + 1$

[   ] $-$ [   ] $+ 1$ **Multiply and divide from left to right.**

[   ] $+ 1$ **Add and subtract from left to right.**

[   ]   **Add.**

Quick Check

1. Simplify each expression.

a. $2 + 5 \times 3$

b. $12 \div 3 - 1$

c. $10 - 1 \cdot 7$

Name_____ Class_____ Date _____

❸ **Simplifying With Grouping Symbols** Simplify $20 - 3[(5 + 2) - 1]$.

$20 - 3[(5 + 2) - 1]$

$20 - 3[\boxed{} - 1]$ **Add within parentheses.**

$20 - 3[\boxed{}]$ **Subtract within brackets.**

$20 - \boxed{}$ **Multiply.**

$\boxed{}$ **Subtract.**

Quick Check

2. Simplify each expression.

   a. $4 - 1 \cdot 2 + 6 \div 3$

   b. $5 + 6 \cdot 4 \div 3 - 1$

3. Simplify each expression.

   a. $2[(13 - 4) \div 3]$

   b. $1 + \dfrac{10 - 2}{4}$

Lesson 1-3

Writing and Evaluating Expressions

Lesson Objectives	NAEP 2005 Strand: Algebra
▼ Evaluate variable expressions	**Topic:** Variables, Expressions, and Operations
▼ Solve problems by evaluating expressions	**Local Standards:** _____

Vocabulary

To evaluate an expression is _____

_____

Examples

❶ Evaluating a Variable Expression Evaluate $18 + 2g$ for $g = 3$.

$18 + 2g = 18 + 2\left(\boxed{}\right)$ **Replace the variable.**

$\qquad = 18 + \boxed{}$ **Multiply.**

$\qquad = \boxed{}$ **Add.**

❷ Replacing More Than One Variable Evaluate $2ab - \frac{c}{3}$ for $a = 3, b = 4,$ and $c = 9$.

$2ab - \frac{c}{3} = 2 \cdot \boxed{} \cdot \boxed{} - \frac{\boxed{}}{3}$ **Replace the variables.**

$\qquad = 2 \cdot 3 \cdot 4 - \boxed{}$ **Work within grouping symbols.**

$\qquad = \boxed{} \cdot 4 - 3$ **Multiply from left to right.**

$\qquad = \boxed{} - 3$ **Multiply.**

$\qquad = \boxed{}$ **Subtract.**

Quick Check

1. Evaluate each expression.

a. $63 - 5x$, for $x = 7$

b. $4(t + 3) + 1$, for $t = 8$

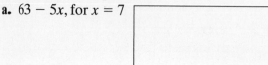

c. $6(g + h)$,
for $g = 8$ and $h = 7$

d. $2xy - z$,
for $x = 4, y = 3,$ and $z = 1$

e. $\frac{r + s}{2}$,
for $r = 13$ and $s = 11$

Examples

❸ The Omelet Café buys cartons of 36 eggs.

   a. Write a variable expression for the number of cartons the café should buy for x eggs.

      An expression for x eggs is $\boxed{}$.

   b. Evaluate the expression for 180 eggs.

$$\frac{x}{36} = \frac{\boxed{}}{36} \quad \textbf{Evaluate for } x = 180.$$

$$= \boxed{} \quad \textbf{Divide.}$$

   The Omelet Café should buy $\boxed{}$ cartons to get 180 eggs.

❹ The One Pizza restaurant makes only one kind of pizza, which costs $16. The delivery charge is $2. Write a variable expression for the cost of having pizzas delivered. Evaluate the expression to find the cost of having five pizzas delivered.

Table

Number of Pizzas	Cost of Pizza	Delivery	Total Cost
1	1 · ☐	☐	1 · ☐ + ☐
2	2 · ☐	☐	2 · ☐ + ☐
4	4 · ☐	☐	4 · ☐ + ☐

Expression $\boxed{} \cdot \boxed{} + \boxed{}$

Evaluate the expression for $p = 5$

$$16 \cdot p + 2 = 16 \cdot \boxed{} + 2$$

$$= \boxed{} + 2$$

$$= \boxed{}$$

It costs $\boxed{}$ to have five pizzas delivered.

Quick Check

2. The café in Example 3 pays $21 for each case of bottled water. Write a variable expression for the cost of c cases. Evaluate the expression to find the cost of 5 cases.

$\boxed{}$

3. Evaluate the expression in Example 4 to find the cost of ordering 8 pizzas.

$\boxed{}$

Name_____

Integers and Absolute Value

Lesson 1-4

Lesson Objectives
▼ Represent, graph, and order intege~~~~
values
▼ Find opposites and ~~~~

NAEP 2005 Strand: Number Properties and Operations

Topic: Number Sense

Local Standards: _____

~~~~osites are _____

_____

Integers are _____

_____

An absolute value is _____

_____

Example

❶ Representing Negative Numbers Write a number to represent the temperature shown by the thermometer.

The thermometer shows ☐ degrees Celsius below zero, or ☐.

Quick Check

1. Temperature Seawater freezes at about 28°F, or about 2 degrees Celsius below zero. Write a number to represent the Celsius temperature.

_____

Name_____ Class_____ Date _____

Examples

❷ **Graphing on a Number Line** Graph 2, −2, and −3 on a number line.
Compare the numbers and order the numbers from least to greatest.

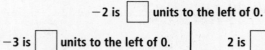

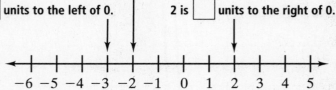

−3 is to the left of −2, and −2 is to the left of 2, so −3 < −2 < 2 .

The numbers from least to greatest are [   ], [   ], [   ].

❸ **Finding Absolute Value** Use a number line to find |−5| and |5|.

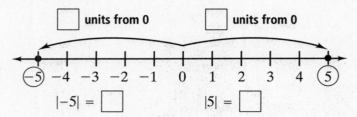

Quick Check

2. Graph 0, 2, and −6 on a number line. Compare the numbers and order them
from least to greatest.

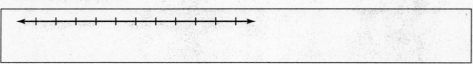

−6 < 0 < 2

The numbers from least to greatest are [   ], [   ], [   ].

3. Write |−10| in words. Then find |−10|.

Lesson 1-5   **Adding Integers**

Lesson Objectives	**NAEP 2005 Strand:** Number Properties and Operations
▼ 1 Use models to add integers ▼ 2 Use rules to add integers	**Topic:** Number Operations **Local Standards:** _____

Key Concepts

Addition of Opposites

The sum of an integer and its opposite is [   ].

<table>
<tr><th>Arithmetic</th><th>Algebra</th></tr>
<tr><td>$1 + (-1) = \boxed{}$</td><td>$x + (-x) = \boxed{}$</td></tr>
<tr><td>$-1 + 1 = \boxed{}$</td><td>$-x + x = \boxed{}$</td></tr>
</table>

Adding Integers

Same Sign The sum of two positive integers is [   ]. The sum of two

negative integers is [   ].

Different Signs To add two integers with different signs, find the difference

of their [   ]. The sum has the sign of the integer with the

[   ] absolute value.

Example

❶ **Using Tiles to Add Integers** Use tiles to find $(-7) + 3$.

 **Model the sum.**

 **Group and remove zero pairs.**

There are [   ] **negative tiles left.**

$(-7) + 3 = \boxed{}$

Quick Check

1. Use tiles to find each sum.

a. $-1 + 4$

■ + ☐☐☐☐

[   ]

b. $7 + (-3)$

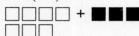

[   ]

c. $-2 + (-2)$

[   ]

Name_____ Class_____ Date _____

Examples

❷ Using a Number Line From the surface, a diver goes down 20 feet and then comes back up 4 feet. Find $-20 + 4$ to find where the diver is.

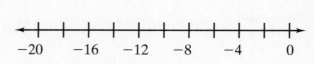

Start at 0. To represent -20, move

left [ ] units. To add positive 4,

move right [ ] units to [ ].

$-20 + 4 =$ [ ]

The diver is [ ] feet below the surface.

❸ Using the Order of Operations Find $-7 + (-4) + 13 + (-5)$.

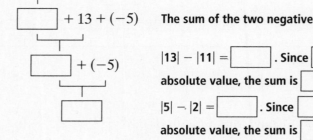

$-7 + (-4) + 13 + (-5)$ **Add from left to right.**

[ ] $+ 13 + (-5)$ **The sum of the two negative integers is** [ ]**.**

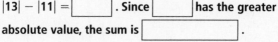

[ ] $+ (-5)$ $|13| - |11| =$ [ ] **. Since** [ ] **has the greater**

absolute value, the sum is [ ]**.**

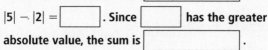

[ ] $|5| - |2| =$ [ ] **. Since** [ ] **has the greater**

absolute value, the sum is [ ]**.**

$-7 + (-4) + 13 + (-5) =$ [ ]**.**

Quick Check

2. Use this number line to find each sum.

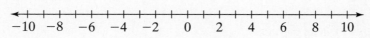

a. $2 + (-6)$ **b.** $-4 + 9$ **c.** $-5 + (-1)$

[   ]   [   ]   [   ]

3. a. $1 + (-3) + 2 + (-10)$ **b.** $-250 + 200 + (-100) + 220$

[   ]   [   ]

4. Geography An earthquake monitor in Hockley, Texas, is located in a salt mine at an elevation of -416 m. The elevation of an earthquake monitor in Piñon Flat, California, is 1,696 m higher than the monitor in Hockley. Find the elevation of the monitor in Piñon Flat.

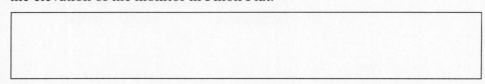

Lesson 1-6   Subtracting Integers

Lesson Objectives	NAEP 2005 Strand: Number Properties and Operations
▼ Use models to subtract integers ▼ Use a rule to subtract integers	Topic: Number Operations Local Standards: _____

Key Concepts

Subtracting Integers

To subtract an integer, add its [   ].

Arithmetic	**Algebra**
$2 - 5 = 2 + (\boxed{}) = -3$	$a - b = a + (\boxed{})$
$2 - (\boxed{}) = 2 + 5 = 7$	$a - (\boxed{}) = a + b$

Examples

❶ **Using Tiles to Subtract Integers** Find $-7 - (-5)$.

  Start with 7 negative tiles.

  Take away 5 negative tiles. There
are [ ] negative tiles left.

$-7 - (-5) = \boxed{}$

❷ **Using Zero Pairs to Subtract Integers** Find $2 - 8$.

□□ Start with 2 positive tiles.

□□ + ■■■■■■ / □□□□□□ There are not enough positive tiles to take
away 8. Add [ ] zero pairs.

 Take away 8 positive tiles. There are
[ ] negative tiles left.

$2 - 8 = \boxed{}$

Name_____ Class_____ Date _____

❸ Using a Rule to Subtract Integers An airplane left Houston, Texas, where the temperature was 42°F. When the airplane landed in Anchorage, Alaska, the temperature was 50°F lower. What was the temperature in Anchorage?

$42 - 50$ **Write an expression.**

$42 - 50 = 42 + \left(\boxed{} \right)$ **To subtract 50, add its** $\boxed{}$.

$ = \boxed{}$ **Simplify.**

The temperature in Anchorage was $\boxed{}$.

Quick Check

1. Use tiles to find each difference.

  a. $-7 - (-2)$ **b.** $-4 - (-3)$ **c.** $-8 - (-5)$

    $-7 - (-2) = \boxed{}$ $-4 - (-3) = \boxed{}$ $-8 - (-5) = \boxed{}$

2. Use tiles to find each difference.

  a. $4 - 8$ **b.** $-1 - 5$ **c.** $-2 - (-7)$

    $4 - 8 = \boxed{}$ $-1 - 5 = \boxed{}$ $-2 - (-7) = \boxed{}$

3. Find each difference.

  a. $32 - (-3)$

  b. $-40 - 66$

  c. $2 - 48$

  d. Weather The lowest temperature ever recorded on the moon was about $-170°C$. The lowest temperature ever recorded in Antarctica was $-89°C$. Find the difference in the temperatures.

Lesson 1-7   **Inductive Reasoning**

Lesson Objectives	**NAEP 2005 Strand:** Algebra
▼ Write rules for patterns	**Topic:** Patterns, Relations, and Functions
② Make predictions and test conjectures	**Local Standards:** _____

Vocabulary

Inductive reasoning is _____

_____

A conjecture is _____

_____

A counterexample is _____

_____

Examples

❶ **Reasoning Inductively** Use inductive reasoning. Make a conjecture about the next figure in the pattern. Then draw the figure.

Observation: The circles are rotating [_____] within the square.

Conjecture: The next figure will have a shaded circle at the

[_____].

❷ **Writing Rules for Patterns** Write a rule for each number pattern.

a. $0, -4, -8, -12, \ldots$ Start with 0 and [_____] repeatedly.

b. $4, -4, 4, -4, \ldots$ Alternate [___] and its [_____].

c. $1, 2, 4, 8, 10, \ldots$ Start with [___]. Alternate [_____]

and [_____].

❸ Extending a Pattern Write a rule for the number pattern 110, 100, 90, 80,.... Find the next two numbers in the pattern.

110, 100, 90, 80,   **The first number is 110.**
  ⌣   ⌣   ⌣
 −10 −10 −10   **The next numbers are found by subtracting 10.**

The rule is *Start with* [   ] *and* [   ] *repeatedly.* The next two

numbers in the pattern are 80 − [   ] = [   ] and [   ] − [   ] = [   ].

❹ Analyzing Conjectures Is the conjecture correct or incorrect? If it is incorrect, give a counterexample.

Every triangle has three sides of equal length.

The conjecture is [   ]. The figure to the right is a triangle but

[   ]

Quick Check

1. Make a conjecture about the next figure in the pattern at the right. Then draw the figure.

[   ]

2. Write a rule for each pattern.

   a. 4, 9, 14, 19, … [   ]

   b. 3, 9, 27, 81, … [   ]

   c. 1, 1, 2, 3, 5, 8, … [   ]

3. Write a rule for the pattern 1, 3, 5, 7, …. Find the next two numbers in the pattern.

[   ]

4. Is each conjecture correct or incorrect? If it is incorrect, give a counterexample.

   a. The last digit of the product of 5 and a whole number is 0 or 5.

   [   ]

   b. A number and its absolute value are always opposites.

   [   ]

   c. The next figure in the pattern has 25 dots.

   [   ]

     1   4   9   16

Lesson 1-8

Look for a Pattern

Lesson Objective	NAEP 2005 Strand: Algebra
▼ Find number patterns	**Topic:** Patterns, Relations, and Function
	Local Standards: _____

Example

❶ Each student on a committee of five students shakes hands with every other committee member. How many handshakes will there be in all?

Understand the Problem How many hands does each committee member shake?

_____

Make and Carry Out a Plan Make a table to organize the numbers. Then look for a pattern.

The pattern is to add the number of new handshakes to the number of handshakes already made.

☐   **the number of handshakes by 1 student**

4 + ☐ = ☐   **the number of handshakes by 2 students**

Make a table to extend the pattern to 5 students.

Student	1	2	3	4	5
Number of original handshakes	4	3	2	☐	☐
Total number of handshakes	4	4 + ☐ = ☐	7 + ☐ = ☐	9 + ☐ = ☐	10 + ☐ = ☐

There will be ☐ handshakes in all.

Check the Answer One way to check a solution is to solve the problem by another method. You can use a diagram to show the pattern visually.

There are ☐ diagonals in the pentagon, so there will be ☐ handshakes in all.

Daily Notetaking Guide

Name_____ Class_____ Date _____

Quick Check

1. Suppose that the committee is made up of six people. How many handshakes would there be?

2. **a.** **Information** News spreads quickly at Riverdell High. Each student who hears a story repeats it 15 minutes later to two students who have not heard it yet, and then tells no one else. Suppose one student hears some news at 8:00 A.M. How many students will know the news at 9:00 A.M.?

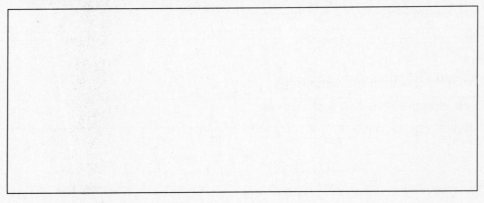

b. Suppose each student who hears the story repeats it in 10 minutes. How many students will know the news at 9:00 A.M.?

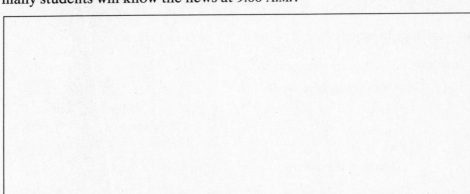

Lesson 1-9

Multiplying and Dividing Integers

Lesson Objectives	NAEP 2005 Strand: Number Properties and Operations
▼ Multiply integers using repeated addition, patterns, and rules ② Divide integers using rules	**Topic:** Number Operations **Local Standards:** _____

Key Concepts

Multiplying Integers

The product of two integers with the same sign is [   ].

The product of two integers with different signs is [   ].

The product of zero and any integer is [   ].

Examples

$3(4) =$ [   ] $3(-4) =$ [   ]

$-3(-4) =$ [   ] $-3(4) =$ [   ]

$3(0) =$ [   ] $-4(0) =$ [   ]

Dividing Integers

The quotient of two integers with the same sign is [   ].

The quotient of two integers with different signs is [   ].

Remember that division by zero is [   ].

Examples

$12 \div 3 =$ [   ] $12 \div (-3) =$ [   ]

$-12 \div (-3) =$ [   ] $-12 \div 3 =$ [   ]

Examples

❶ **Using Patterns to Multiply Integers** Use a pattern to find each product.

a. $-2(7)$ **b.** $-2(-7)$

$2(7) =$ [   ]   ← Start with products you know. → $2(-7) =$ [   ]

$1(7) =$ [   ] $1(-7) =$ [   ]

$0(7) =$ [   ] $0(-7) =$ [   ]

$-1(7) =$ [   ]   ←   Continue the pattern.   → $-1(-7) =$ [   ]

$-2(7) =$ [   ] $-2(-7) =$ [   ]

❷ Using Rules to Multiply Integers Multiply $(6)(-2)(-3)$.

$6(-2)(-3) = \left(\boxed{}\right)(-3)$ **Multiply from left to right. The product of a positive integer and a negative integer is** $\boxed{}$**.**

$= \boxed{}$ **Multiply. The product of two negative integers is** $\boxed{}$**.**

❸ Currency Use the table to find the average of the differences in the values of a Canadian dollar and a U.S. dollar for 1994–1997.

Value of Dollars (U.S. cents)

Year	Canadian Dollar	U.S. Dollar	Difference
1994	73	100	−27
1995	73	100	−27
1996	74	100	−26
1997	72	100	−28

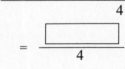

Sᴏᴜʀᴄᴇs: Bank of Canada; *The World Almanac*

$$\dfrac{-27 + (-27) + \left(\boxed{}\right) + \left(\boxed{}\right)}{4}$$ **Write an expression for the average.**

$= \dfrac{\boxed{}}{4}$ **Use the order of operations.**
The fraction bar acts as a $\boxed{}$ **symbol.**

$= \boxed{}$ **The quotient of a negative integer and a positive integer is** $\boxed{}$**.**

For 1994 to 1997, the average difference was $\boxed{}$.

Quick Check

1. Patterns Use a pattern to simplify $-3(-4)$.

$\boxed{}$

2. Simplify each product.

   a. $2(-6) = \boxed{}$ **b.** $4(-3) = \boxed{}$ **c.** $7(-2) = \boxed{}$

   d. $-4 \cdot 8 \,(-2) = \boxed{}$ **e.** $6(-3)(5) = \boxed{}$ **f.** $-7 \cdot (-14) \cdot 0 = \boxed{}$

3. Simplify each quotient.

   a. $-32 \div 8 = \boxed{}$ **b.** $-48 \div (-6) = \boxed{}$ **c.** $-56 \div (-4) = \boxed{}$

   d. Find the average of $4, -3, -5, 2,$ and -8.

$\boxed{}$

Lesson 1-10

The Coordinate Plane

Lesson Objectives	**NAEP 2005 Strand:** Algebra
▼ Name coordinates and quadrants in the coordinate plane ▼ Graph points in the coordinate plane	**Topic:** Algebraic Representations **Local Standards:** _____

Vocabulary

A coordinate plane is _____

The *x*-axis is _____

The *y*-axis is _____

Quadrants are _____

The origin is _____

An ordered pair is _____

An *x*-coordinate is _____

A *y*-coordinate is _____

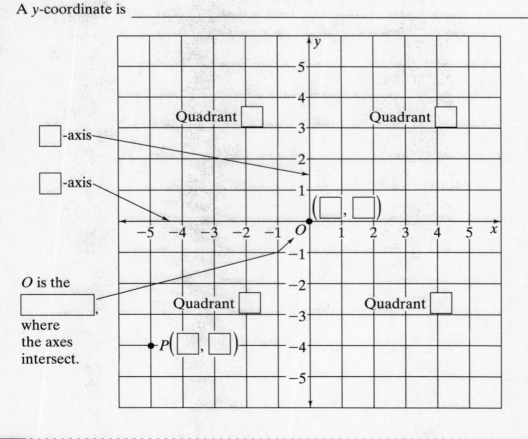

Name_____ Class_____ Date _____

Examples

➊ Naming Coordinates and Quadrants Write the coordinates of point *G*. In which quadrant is point *G* located?

Point *G* is located ▢ units to the left of the *y*-axis. So the *x*-coordinate is ▢. The point is ▢ units below the *x*-axis. So the *y*-coordinate is ▢.

The coordinates of point *G* are (▢ , ▢). Point *G* is located in Quadrant ▢.

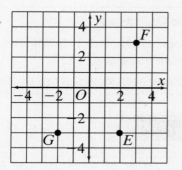

➋ Graphing Points Graph point $M(-3, 3)$.

Step 1
Start at the origin.

Step 2
Move ▢ units to the ▢.

Step 3
Move ▢ units up.
Draw a dot.
Label it ▢.

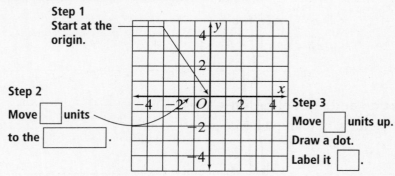

Quick Check

1. a. Use the graph in Example 1. Write the coordinates of *E* and *F*.

b. Identify the quadrants in which *E* and *F* are located.

2. Graph these points on one coordinate plane: $K(3, 1)$, $L(-2, 1)$, and $M(-2, -4)$. Then describe the figure that is formed by connecting points *K*, *L*, and *M*.

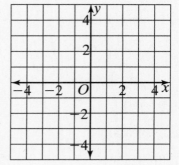

Daily Notetaking Guide   *Pre-Algebra* Lesson 1-10   **21**

Lesson 2-1

Properties of Numbers

Lesson Objectives	NAEP 2005 Strand: Number Properties and Operations
▼ Identify properties of addition and multiplication ✔ Use properties to solve problems	Topic: Properties of Number and Operations Local Standards: _____

Key Concepts

Properties of Addition and Multiplication

Commutative Properties of Addition and Multiplication Changing the

[____] of the values you are adding or multiplying does not change the

sum or product.

Arithmetic	**Algebra**
$6 + 4 = \boxed{} + \boxed{}$	$a + b = \boxed{} + \boxed{}$
$9 \cdot 5 = \boxed{} \cdot \boxed{}$	$a \cdot b = \boxed{} \cdot \boxed{}$

Associative Properties of Addition and Multiplication Changing the

[____] of the values you are adding or multiplying does not change

the sum or product.

Arithmetic	**Algebra**
$(2 + 7) + 3 = 2 + \boxed{}$	$(a + b) + c = a + \boxed{}$
$(9 \cdot 4)5 = 9\boxed{}$	$(ab)c = a\boxed{}$

Identity Properties of Addition and Multiplication The sum of any

number and [____] is the original number. The product of any number

and [__] is the original number.

Arithmetic	**Algebra**
$12 + \boxed{} = 12$	$a + \boxed{} = a$
$10 \cdot \boxed{} = 10$	$a \cdot \boxed{} = a$

The additive identity is $\boxed{}$. The multiplicative identity is $\boxed{}$.

Examples

❶ **Identifying Properties** Name each property shown.

a. $17 + x + 3 = 17 + 3 + x$ [_____] Property of Addition

b. $(36 \times 2)10 = 36(2 \times 10)$ [_____] Property of Multiplication

c. $km = km \cdot 1$ [_____] Property of Multiplication

❷ Using Mental Math With Addition Suppose you buy school supplies costing \$.45, \$.65, and \$1.55. Use mental math to find the cost of these supplies.

$0.45 + 0.65 + 1.55$

$= 0.65 + 0.45 + 1.55$ Use the [_____] **Property of Addition.**

$= 0.65 + (0.45 + 1.55)$ Use the [_____] **Property of Addition.**

$= 0.65 +$ [_____]   **Add within parentheses.**

$= 2.65$ **Add.**

The cost of the school supplies is [_____].

❸ Using Mental Math With Multiplication Use mental math to simplify $(20 \cdot 13) \cdot 5$.

$(20 \cdot 13) \cdot 5 = (13 \cdot 20) \cdot 5$ Use the [_____] **Property of Multiplication.**

$= 13 \cdot (20 \cdot 5)$ Use the [_____] **Property of Multiplication.**

$= 13 \cdot$ [_____]   **Multiply within parentheses.**

$=$ [_____]   **Multiply.**

Quick Check

1. You spend \$6 for dinner, \$8 for a movie, and \$4 for popcorn. Find your total cost. Explain which property or properties you used.

2. Name each property shown.

  a. $3 + 6 = 6 + 3$ **b.** $8 = 1 \cdot 8$ **c.** $(3z)m = (3zm)$

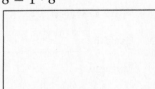 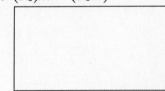

3. Use mental math to simplify each expression.

  a. $5 + 12 + 18 + 5$ **b.** $19 + (-30) + 21$

Lesson 2-2

The Distributive Property

Lesson Objectives	**NAEP 2005 Strand:** Number Properties and Operations
▼ Use the Distributive Property with numerical expressions	**Topic:** Properties of Number and Operations
▼ Use the Distributive Property with algebraic expressions	**Local Standards:** _____

Key Concepts

Distributive Property

To multiply a sum or difference, multiply each number within the parentheses by the number outside the parentheses.

Arithmetic

$3(2 + 6) = 3(\boxed{}) + 3(\boxed{})$

$(2 + 6)3 = 2(\boxed{}) + 6(\boxed{})$

$6(7 - 4) = 6(\boxed{}) - 6(\boxed{})$

$(7 - 4)6 = 7(\boxed{}) - 4(\boxed{})$

Algebra

$a(b + c) = a(\boxed{}) + a(\boxed{})$

$(b + c)a = b(\boxed{}) + c(\boxed{})$

$a(b - c) = a(\boxed{}) - a(\boxed{})$

$(b - c)a = b(\boxed{}) - c(\boxed{})$

Examples

❶ **Using the Distributive Property I** Find 15(110) mentally.

$15(110) = 15(\boxed{} + \boxed{})$ **Write 110 as (100 + 10).**

$= 15 \cdot \boxed{} + 15 \cdot \boxed{}$ **Use the** $\boxed{}$ **Property.**

$= \boxed{} + \boxed{}$ **Multiply.**

$= \boxed{}$ **Add.**

❷ Ms. Thomas gave 5 pencils to each of her 37 students. What is the total number of pencils she gave to the students?

$(37)5 = (\boxed{} - \boxed{})5$ **Write 37 as (40 − 3).**

$= \boxed{} \cdot 5 - \boxed{} \cdot 5$ **Use the** $\boxed{}$ **Property.**

$= \boxed{} - \boxed{}$ **Multiply.**

$= \boxed{}$ **Subtract.**

Ms. Thomas gave the students $\boxed{}$ pencils.

Quick Check

1. Find each product mentally.

   a. $(53)50 = \boxed{}$ **b.** $30 \cdot 104 = \boxed{}$ **c.** $9 \cdot 199 = \boxed{}$

Name_____ Class_____ Date _____

Examples

❸ Using the Distributive Property II Simplify $11(23) + 11(7)$.

$11(23) + 11(7) = 11\left(\boxed{} + \boxed{}\right)$ Use the $\boxed{}$ Property.

$= 11\left(\boxed{}\right)$ Add within parentheses.

$= \boxed{}$ Multiply.

❹ Using Tiles to Multiply Use algebra tiles to multiply $4(3x - 4)$.

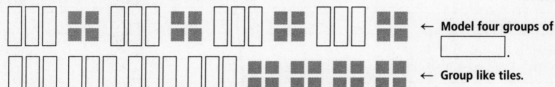

← Model four groups of $\boxed{}$.

← Group like tiles.

So $4(3x - 4) = \boxed{}$.

❺ Using the Distributive Property III Simplify each expression.

a. $-9(2 - 8y) = -9\left(\boxed{}\right) - (-9)\left(\boxed{}\right)$ Use the $\boxed{}$ Property.

$= \boxed{} - \left(\boxed{}\right)$ Multiply.

$= \boxed{} + \boxed{}$ Simplify.

b. $(5m + 6)11 = \left(\boxed{}\right)11 + \left(\boxed{}\right)11$ Use the $\boxed{}$ Property.

$= \boxed{} + \boxed{}$ Multiply.

Quick Check

2. Your club sold calendars for \$7. Club members sold 204 calendars. How much money did they raise?

$\boxed{}$

3. Simplify each expression.

a. $7(21) + 7(9) = \boxed{}$ **b.** $12(52) - 12(62) = \boxed{}$ **c.** $(16)7 - (11)7 = \boxed{}$

4. Use algebra tiles to multiply.

a. $4(2x - 3)$ **b.** $3(x + 4)$ **c.** $(3x + 1)2$

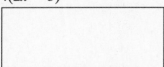 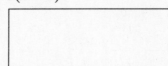

5. Multiply.

a. $2(7 - 3d) = \boxed{}$ **b.** $(6m + 1)(3) = \boxed{}$ **c.** $-3(5t - 2) = \boxed{}$

Lesson 2-3

Simplifying Variable Expressions

Lesson Objectives	NAEP 2005 Strand: Algebra
▼ 1 Identify parts of a variable expression	**Topic:** Variables, Expressions, and Operations
▼ 2 Simplify expressions	**Local Standards:** _____

Vocabulary

A term is _____

_____

A constant is _____

_____

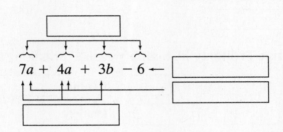

Like terms have _____

_____

A coefficient is _____

_____

You simplify a variable expression by _____

_____

Deductive reasoning is _____

_____

Examples

❶ Identifying Parts of an Expression Name the coefficients, the like terms, and the constants in $7x + y - 2x - 7$.

Coefficients: 7, ☐ , ☐

Like terms: $7x$, ☐

Constant: ☐

❷ Using Tiles to Simplify Simplify $9 + 4f + 3 + 2f$.

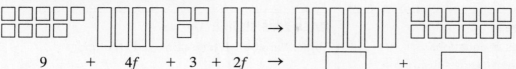

$$9 \quad + \quad 4f \quad + \quad 3 \quad + \quad 2f \quad \rightarrow \quad \boxed{} \quad + \quad \boxed{}$$

❸ Combining Like Terms Simplify $2b + b - 4$.

$2b + b - 4 = \boxed{}b + \boxed{}b - 4$ **Use the Identity Property of Multiplication.**

$ = (\boxed{} + \boxed{})b - 4$ **Use the Distributive Property.**

$ = \boxed{}b - 4$ **Simplify.**

❹ Using Deductive Reasoning Simplify $(7 - 3x)5 + 20x$.

$(7 - 3x)5 + 20x = 35 - 15x + 20x$ **Use the** $\boxed{}$ **Property.**

$ = 35 + (\boxed{}x + \boxed{}x)$ **Use the** $\boxed{}$ **Property of Addition.**

$ = 35 + (\boxed{} + \boxed{})x$ **Use the** $\boxed{}$ **Property to combine like terms.**

$ = 35 + \boxed{}x$ **Simplify.**

Quick Check

1. Name the coefficients, the like terms, and the constants.

   a. $6 + 2s + 4s$ $\boxed{}$

   b. $-4x$ $\boxed{}$

   c. $9m + 2r - 2m + r$ $\boxed{}$

2. Use tiles to simplify $3a + 2 + 4a - 1$.

3. Simplify each expression.

   a. $3b - b$ **b.** $-4m - 9m$ **c.** $p + 6p - 4p$

4. Simplify each expression. Justify each step.

   a. $6y + 4m - 7y + m$ **b.** $4x + 3 - 2(5 + x)$

Lesson 2-4   **Variables and Equations**

Lesson Objectives	**NAEP 2005 Strand:** Algebra
▼ Classify types of equations ▼ Check equations using substitution	**Topic:** Variables, Expressions, and Operations **Local Standards:** _____

Vocabulary

An equation is _____

An open sentence is _____

_____

A solution of an equation is _____

_____

Examples

❶ **Classifying Equations** State whether each equation is *true*, *false*, or an *open sentence*. Explain.

    a. $3(b - 8) = 12$

           [   ] , because there is a variable.

    b. $7 - (-6) = 1$

           [   ] , because $13 \neq 1$.

    c. $-9 + 5 = -4$

           [   ] , because $-4 = -4$.

❷ **Writing an Equation** Write an equation for *Six times a number added to the number is the opposite of forty-two*. State whether the equation is *true*, *false*, or an *open sentence*. Explain.

Words	six times the number	added to	the number	is	the opposite of 42.
	[ ]	added to	[ ]	is	[ ]
Equation	[ ]	+	[ ]	=	[ ]

The equation is [   ] , because there is a variable.

Quick Check

1. State whether each equation is *true*, *false*, or an *open sentence*. Explain.

    a. $9 - 7 = 3$ **b.** $8 + x = 2$ **c.** $4 \cdot 5 = 20$

    [   ]   [   ]   [   ]

Examples

❸ Substituting to Check Is 45 a solution of the equation $120 + x = 75$?

$120 + x = 75$

$120 +$ ☐ $\overset{?}{=} 75$ **Substitute** ☐ **for x.**

☐ $\neq 75$

☐ , 45 ☐ a solution of the equation.

❹ A gift pack must hold 20 lb of food. Apples weigh 9 lb and cheese weighs 5 lb. Can the jar of jam that completes the package weigh 7 lb?

Words | weight of apples | plus | weight of cheese | plus | weight of jam | is | 20 lb |

Let | j | = weight of jam.

Equation ☐ $+$ ☐ $+$ ☐ $=$ ☐

$9 + 5 + j = 20$

$14 + j = 20$ **Add.**

$14 +$ ☐ $\overset{?}{=} 20$ **Substitute** ☐ **for the variable.**

21 ☐ 20

☐ , the jar of jam cannot weigh 7 lb.

Quick Check

2. Write an equation for *Twenty minus x is three*. Is the equation *true*, *false*, or an *open sentence*? Explain.

☐

3. Is the given number a solution of the equation?
  a. $8 + t = 2t; 1$ **b.** $9 - m = 3; 6$

 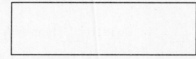

4. A tent weighs 6 lb. Your backpack and the tent weigh 33 lb. Use an equation to find whether the backpack weighs 27 lb.

Lesson 2-5

Solving Equations by Adding or Subtracting

Lesson Objectives	NAEP 2005 Strand: Algebra
☑ Solve one-step equations using subtraction	**Topic:** Equations and Inequalities
☑ Solve one-step equations using addition	**Local Standards:** _____

Vocabulary and Key Concepts

Subtraction Property of Equality

You can subtract the same number from each side of an equation.

Arithmetic	**Algebra**
$10 = 2(5)$	If $a = b$,
$10 - 5 = 2(5) - \boxed{}$	then $a - c = b - \boxed{}$

Addition Property of Equality

You can add the same number to each side of an equation.

Arithmetic	**Algebra**
$8 = 2(4)$	If $a = b$,
$8 + 3 = 2(4) + \boxed{}$	then $a + c = b + \boxed{}$

Inverse operations are operations that _____

_____

Examples

❶ **Subtracting to Solve an Equation** Solve $y + 5 = 13$.

Method 1

$$y + 5 = 13$$
$$y + 5 - \boxed{} = 13 - \boxed{} \quad \leftarrow \text{Subtract } \boxed{} \text{ from each side.} \rightarrow$$
$$y = \boxed{} \quad \leftarrow \text{Simplify.} \rightarrow$$

Method 2

$$y + 5 = \quad 13$$
$$\underline{- \boxed{}} = \underline{- \boxed{}}$$
$$y = \boxed{}$$

❷ **Adding to Solve an Equation** Solve $c - 23 = -40$.

$$c - 23 = -40$$
$$c - 23 + \boxed{} = -40 + \boxed{} \qquad \text{Add } \boxed{} \text{ to each side.}$$
$$c = \boxed{} \qquad \text{Simplify.}$$

③ Larissa wants to increase the number of books in her collection to 327 books. She has 250 books now. Find the number of books she needs to buy.

Words | target number | is | 250 | plus | number to buy |

Let | x | = number to buy.

Equation | | = | | + | |

$327 = 250 + x$

$327 = x + 250$ **Use the** | | **Property of Addition.**

$327 -$ | | $= x + 250 -$ | | **Subtract** | | **from each side.**

| | $= x$ **Simplify.**

Larissa needs to buy | | more books.

④ Marcy's CD player cost $113 less than her DVD player. Her CD player cost $78. About how much did her DVD player cost?

Round to numbers that are easy to compute.

$113 \approx 110$

$78 \approx 80$

$80 = t - 110$ **Write an equation.**

$80 +$ | | $= t - 110 +$ | | **Add** | | **to each side.**

| | $= t$ **Simplify.**

Marcy's DVD player cost about | |.

Quick Check

1. Solve each equation.

a. $x + 8 = 3$

b. $5 = d + 1$

c. $c + (-4) = -5$

d. $y - 5 = 8$

e. $p - 30 = 42$

f. $98 = x - 14$

2. Cora measures her heart rate at 123 beats per minute. This is 55 beats more than her resting heart rate r. Write and solve an equation to find Cora's resting heart rate.

3. A softcover book costs $17 less than its hardcover edition. The softcover costs $5. Write and solve an equation to find the cost h of the hardcover book.

Lesson 2-6

Solving Equations by Multiplying or Dividing

Lesson Objectives	NAEP 2005 Strand: Algebra
▼ Solve one-step equations using division	**Topic:** Equations and Inequalities
▼ Solve one-step equations using multiplication	**Local Standards:** _____

Key Concepts

Division Property of Equality

If you divide each side of an equation by the same nonzero number, the two sides remain equal.

Arithmetic	**Algebra**
$6 = 3(2)$	If $a = b$ and $c \neq 0$,
$\dfrac{6}{3} = \dfrac{3(2)}{\boxed{}}$	$\dfrac{a}{c} = \dfrac{b}{\boxed{}}$

Multiplication Property of Equality

You can multiply each side of an equation by the same number.

Arithmetic	**Algebra**
$12 = 3(4)$	If $a = b$,
$12 \cdot 2 = 3(4) \cdot \boxed{}$	then $ac = \boxed{}$.

Examples

❶ Dividing to Solve an Equation Solve $-2v = -24$.

$$-2v = -24$$

$$\frac{-2v}{\boxed{}} = \frac{-24}{\boxed{}} \qquad \text{Divide each side by } \boxed{}.$$

$$v = \boxed{} \qquad \text{Simplify.}$$

Check $\qquad -2v = -24$

$$-2\left(\boxed{}\right) \overset{?}{=} -24 \qquad \text{Replace } v \text{ with } \boxed{}.$$

$$\boxed{} = -24 \checkmark$$

❷ A total of 288 pens are boxed by the dozen. How many boxes are needed?

Words | number of pens | is | 12 | times | number of boxes |

Let $\boxed{b}$ = number of boxes

Equation $\boxed{}$ = $\boxed{}$ · $\boxed{}$

$288 = 12b$

$\dfrac{288}{\boxed{}} = \dfrac{12b}{\boxed{}}$ **Divide each side by** $\boxed{}$.

$\boxed{} = b$ **Simplify.**

$\boxed{}$ boxes are needed.

Check Is the answer reasonable?

$\boxed{}$ times the number of boxes is the number of pens.

Since $12 \times 24 = \boxed{}$, the answer is reasonable.

❸ **Multiplying to Solve an Equation** Solve $\frac{x}{8} = -5$.

$\dfrac{x}{8} = -5$

$\boxed{}\dfrac{x}{8} = \boxed{}(-5)$ **Multiply each side by** $\boxed{}$.

$x = \boxed{}$ **Simplify.**

Quick Check

1. Solve each equation.

a. $4x = 84$

b. $91 = 7y$

c. $12w = 108$

d. $-3b = 24$

e. $96 = -8n$

f. $-4d = -56$

g. $\frac{r}{-5} = 10$

h. $\frac{s}{6} = 54$

i. $-30 = \frac{t}{20}$

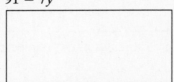

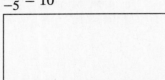

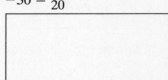

Lesson 2-7

Guess, Check, Revise

Lesson Objective	**Local Standards:** _____
▼ Solve a problem using the Guess, Check, Revise strategy	

Example

❶ During the intermission of a play, the Theater Club sold cups of popcorn and soda. The club sold 79 cups of popcorn and 96 sodas for a total of $271. If the selling prices for popcorn and soda were in whole dollars, what was the selling price of a cup of popcorn? Of a soda?

(Understand the Problem)

Look at the information given to make an informed conjecture.

1. How many cups of [____] and [____] did the club sell? [____]

2. How much money did the club raise from sales of [____] and [____]? [____]

(Make and Carry Out a Plan) Make a conjecture, and then test it. Use what you learn from your conjecture to make a better second conjecture.

3. When you make a conjecture for the selling prices of a cup of popcorn and a cup of soda, how can you use your conjecture to find the actual selling prices of a cup of popcorn and a cup of soda?

[_____]

4. By what numbers do you multiply your conjecture for the selling prices of a cup of popcorn and a cup of soda to find the amount of money the club would have raised by selling popcorn and soda at those selling prices?

[_____]

You can organize conjectures in a table. As a first conjecture, try both with a price of $1.

Popcorn Price	Soda Price	Total Price	
$1	$1	$79([__]) + 96([__]) = [__] + [__] = [__]$	The total is too [__]. Increase the price of the popcorn only.
$2	$1	$79([__]) + 96([__]) = [__] + [__] = [__]$	The total is too [__]. Increase the price of the soda.

Continue your table until the total is correct.

Name_____ Class_____ Date _____

$2	$2	$79(□) + 96(□) = □ + □ = □		
$1	$2	$79(□) + 96(□) = □ + □ = □		

The total is too □.
Decrease the price of
the popcorn only.

The total is correct.

The popcorn price was □ , and the soda price was □ .

Check Your Answer Is it possible to solve the problem in another way?
Consider using logical reasoning.

- We know the prices must be in whole dollars. Since $271 \div 96 \approx 2.8229$, the soda would cost at most $2.
- If the price of the soda were $2, then the theater club would earn $96 \cdot \$2$, or $192, from the sale of sodas.
- At a cost of $2 per soda, that would leave $271 − $192, or $79, for sales from popcorn.
- Since 79 cups of popcorn were sold, the price of a cup of popcorn could be $1.
- Therefore, the solution of $2 for soda and $1 for a cup of popcorn is correct.

Quick Check

1. Suppose the club sold the same number of cups of popcorn and soda as in Example 1, but raised $446. What would have been the selling prices of a cup of popcorn and a cup of soda?

Popcorn Price	Soda Price	Total Price		
□	□	79(□) + 96(□) = □ + □ = □		
□	□	79(□) + 96(□) = □ + □ = □		
□	□	79(□) + 96(□) = □ + □ = □		
□	□	79(□) + 96(□) = □ + □ = □		

The popcorn price would have been □ , and the soda price would
have been □ .

Lesson 2-8

Inequalities and Their Graphs

Lesson Objectives	NAEP 2005 Strand: Algebra
▼ Graph inequalities ▼ Write inequalities	**Topic:** Equations and Inequalities **Local Standards:** _____

Vocabulary

An inequality is _____

_____

A solution of an inequality is _____

_____

Examples

❶ Graphing Solutions of Inequalities Graph the solutions of each inequality on a number line.

a. $x > -2$

An ⬚ dot shows that -2 is not a solution.

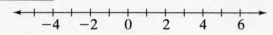

Shade all points to the ⬚ of -2.

b. $w \geq -5$

A ⬚ dot shows that -5 is a solution.

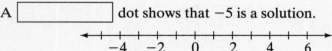

Shade all points to the ⬚ of -5.

c. $k \leq 4$

A ⬚ dot shows that 4 is a solution.

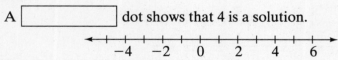

Shade all points to the ⬚ of 4.

d. $y < 6$

An ⬚ dot shows that 6 is not a solution.

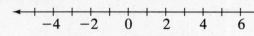

Shade all points to the ⬚ of 6.

❷ **Writing Inequalities to Describe Graphs** Write the inequality shown in each graph.

a.

b.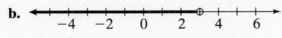

❸ **Writing Inequalities** Food can be labeled *very low sodium* only if it meets the requirements established by the federal government. Use the table to write an inequality for this requirement.

Label	Definition
Sodium-free food	Less than 5 mg per serving
Very low sodium food	At most 35 mg per serving
Low-sodium food	At most 140 mg per serving

Words | a serving of very low sodium | | has at most | | 35 mg sodium |

Let ⬚ v = the number of milligrams of sodium in a serving of very low sodium food.

Inequality ⬚   ⬚   ⬚

Quick Check

1. Graph the solutions of each inequality.

a. $z < -2$

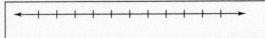

b. $4 > t$

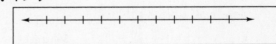

c. $a \le -5$

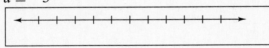

d. $2 \ge c$

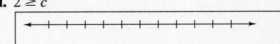

2. Write an inequality for the graph.

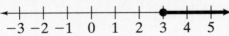

3. Use the table from Example 3. A food is labeled sodium-free. Write an inequality for n, the number of milligrams of sodium in a serving of sodium-free food.

Lesson 2-9

**Solving One-Step Inequalities
by Adding or Subtracting**

Lesson Objectives	NAEP 2005 Strand: Algebra
☑ Solve one-step inequalities using subtraction	**Topic:** Equations and Inequalities
☑ Solve one-step inequalities using addition	**Local Standards:** _____

Key Concepts

Subtraction Property of Inequality

You can subtract the same number from each side of an inequality.

Arithmetic	**Algebra**
$7 > 4$, so $7 - 3 > 4 - \boxed{}$	If $a > b$, then $a - c > b - \boxed{}$.
$6 < 9$, so $6 - 2 < 9 - \boxed{}$	If $a < b$, then $a - c < b - \boxed{}$.

Addition Property of Inequality

You can add the same number to each side of an inequality.

Arithmetic	**Algebra**
$7 > 3$, so $7 + 4 > 3 + \boxed{}$	If $a > b$, then $a + c > b + \boxed{}$.
$2 < 5$, so $2 + 6 < 5 + \boxed{}$	If $a < b$, then $a + c < b + \boxed{}$.

Examples

❶ Subtracting to Solve an Inequality Solve each inequality. Graph the solutions.

a. $4 + s < 12$

$$4 + s < 12$$
$$4 + s - \boxed{} < 12 - \boxed{} \quad \textbf{Subtract } \boxed{} \textbf{ from each side.}$$
$$s < \boxed{} \quad \textbf{Simplify.}$$

b. $-16 \geq y - 14$

$$-16 \geq y - 14$$
$$-16 + \boxed{} \geq y - 14 + \boxed{} \quad \textbf{Add } \boxed{} \textbf{ to each side.}$$
$$\boxed{} \geq y \text{ or } y \leq \boxed{} \quad \textbf{Simplify.}$$

Name_____ Class_____ Date _____

❷ Computers Suppose your computer's hard drive has a capacity of 6 gigabytes (GB). The files you have stored on the hard drive occupy at least 2 GB. How much storage space is left for other files?

Words

| storage space for your files | plus | storage space left | is less than or equal to | total space |

Let $\boxed{s}$ = storage space available.

Inequality $\boxed{}$ + $\boxed{}$ ≤ $\boxed{}$

$2 + s \le 6$

$2 - \boxed{} + s \le 6 - \boxed{}$ **Subtract** $\boxed{}$ **from each side.**

$s \le \boxed{}$ **Simplify.**

No more than $\boxed{}$ GB are left.

❸ Adding to Solve an Inequality Solve $-10 < -13 - q$.

$-10 < -13 + q$

$-10 + \boxed{} < -13 + \boxed{} + q$ **Add** $\boxed{}$ **to each side.**

$\boxed{} < q$ **Simplify.**

Quick Check

1. Solve each inequality. Graph the solutions.

a. $8 + t < 15$ $\boxed{}$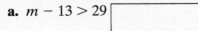

b. $-3 \le x + 7$ $\boxed{}$

2. An airline lets you check up to 65 lb. of luggage. One suitcase weighs 37 lb. How much can the other suitcase weigh?

$\boxed{}$

3. Solve each inequality. Graph the solutions.

a. $m - 13 > 29$ $\boxed{}$

b. $t - 5 \ge 11$ $\boxed{}$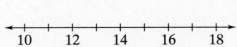

Lesson 2-10

Lesson Objectives	NAEP 2005 Strand: Algebra
▼ Solve one-step inequalities using division	**Topic:** Equations and Inequalities
② Solve one-step inequalities using multiplication	**Local Standards:** _____

Key Concepts

Division Properties of Inequality

If you divide each side of an inequality by a positive number, you leave the direction of the inequality symbol unchanged.

Arithmetic	**Algebra**
$3 < 6$, so $\frac{3}{3}$ ☐ $\frac{6}{3}$	If $a < b$ and c is positive, then $\frac{a}{c}$ ☐ $\frac{b}{c}$.
$8 > 2$, so $\frac{8}{2}$ ☐ $\frac{2}{2}$	If $a > b$ and c is positive, then $\frac{a}{c}$ ☐ $\frac{b}{c}$.

If you divide each side of an inequality by a negative number, you *reverse the direction of the inequality symbol.*

Arithmetic	**Algebra**
$6 < 12$, so $\frac{6}{-3}$ ☐ $\frac{12}{-3}$	If $a < b$ and c is negative, then $\frac{a}{c}$ ☐ $\frac{b}{c}$.
$16 > 8$, so $\frac{16}{-4}$ ☐ $\frac{8}{-4}$	If $a > b$ and c is negative, then $\frac{a}{c}$ ☐ $\frac{b}{c}$.

Multiplication Properties of Inequality

If you multiply each side of an inequality by a positive number, you leave the direction of the inequality symbol unchanged.

Arithmetic	**Algebra**
$3 < 4$, so $3(5)$ ☐ $4(5)$	If $a < b$ and c is positive, then ac ☐ bc.
$7 > 2$, so $7(6)$ ☐ $2(6)$	If $a > b$ and c is positive, then ac ☐ bc.

If you multiply each side of an inequality by a negative number, you *reverse the direction of the inequality symbol.*

Arithmetic	**Algebra**
$6 < 9$, so $6(-2)$ ☐ $9(-2)$	If $a < b$ and c is negative, then ac ☐ bc.
$7 > 5$, so $7(-3)$ ☐ $5(-3)$	If $a > b$ and c is negative, then ac ☐ bc.

Name_____ Class_____ Date _____

Examples

① **Dividing to Solve an Inequality** A 1-ton truck has the ability to haul 1 ton, or 2,000 lb. At most, how many television sets can the truck carry if each TV set weighs 225 lb?

Words | number of televisions | times | 225 lb | is less than or equal to | 2,000 lb |

Let $\boxed{x}$ = number of televisions.

Inequality $\boxed{}$ · $\boxed{}$ ≤ $\boxed{}$

$$255x \le 2{,}000$$

$$\frac{255x}{\boxed{}} \le \frac{2{,}000}{\boxed{}}$$ **Divide each side by** $\boxed{}$.

$$x \le \boxed{}$$ **Simplify.**

At most, the truck can carry $\boxed{}$ television sets.

Check Is the answer reasonable?
The total weight of 8 television sets is $8\left(\boxed{}\right) = \boxed{}$ lbs, which is less than 2,000 lb but so close that another television set could not be carried. The answer is reasonable.

② **Multiplying to Solve an Inequality** Solve $\frac{z}{-8} \le -2$.

$$\frac{z}{-8} \le -2$$

$$\boxed{}\left(\frac{z}{-8}\right) \ge \boxed{}(-2)$$ **Multiply each side by** $\boxed{}$.

$$z \ge \boxed{}$$ **Simplify.**

Quick Check

1. Solve each inequality.

a. $4x > 40$

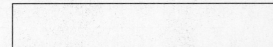

b. $-21 > 3m$

c. $36 > -9t$

d. $\frac{m}{4} \ge 2$

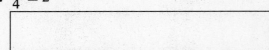

e. $\frac{t}{-3} > 7$

f. $5 < \frac{r}{7}$

Lesson 3-1

Rounding and Estimating

Lesson Objectives	NAEP 2005 Strand: Number Properties and Operations
▼ Round decimals	**Topic:** Estimation
▼ Estimate sums and differences	**Local Standards:** _____

Examples

❶ Rounding Decimals

a. Round 8.7398 to the nearest tenth.

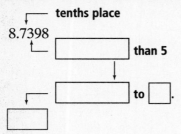

b. Round 8.7398 to the nearest integer.

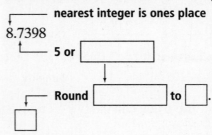

❷ Rounding to Estimate Estimate to find whether each answer is reasonable.

Calculation		Estimate
$115.67	≈	$ ⬚
$ 83.21	≈	$ ⬚
+ $ 59.98	≈	+ $ ⬚
$258.86		$ ⬚

The answer ⬚ close to the estimate. It is ⬚.

Calculation		Estimate
$176.48	≈	$ ⬚
− $ 39.34	≈	− $ ⬚
$107.14		$ ⬚

The answer ⬚ close to the estimate. It is ⬚.

Quick Check

1. Identify the underlined place. Then round each number to that place.

a. 38.<u>4</u>1

b. <u>0</u>.7772

c. 7,098.<u>5</u>6

d. 274.94<u>3</u>4

e. 5.<u>0</u>25

f. 9.8<u>5</u>1

2. Estimate by rounding.

a. 355.302 + 204.889

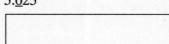

b. 453.56 − 230.07

Daily Notetaking Guide

Name_____ Class_____ Date _____

Examples

❸ **Using Front-End Estimation** You are buying some fruit. The bananas cost $1.32, the apples cost $2.19, and the avocados cost $1.63. Use front-end estimation to estimate the total cost of the fruit.

$$\begin{array}{ccc} 1.32 & \to & \boxed{} \\ \textbf{Add the front-end digits.} \quad 2.19 & \to & \boxed{} \\ \underline{+1.63} & \to & \boxed{} \end{array} \left. \begin{array}{c} \\ \\ \\ \end{array} \right\} \quad \textbf{Estimate by rounding.}$$

$$\boxed{} \quad + \quad \boxed{} \quad = \quad \boxed{}$$

The total cost is about $\boxed{}$.

❹ **Using Clustering to Estimate** Estimate the total electricity cost: March $81.75; April: $79.56; May: $80.89.

3 Months
↓

The values cluster around $\boxed{}$. → $\boxed{} \cdot 3 = \boxed{}$

The total electricity cost is about $\boxed{}$.

Quick Check

3. Estimate using front-end estimation.

a. $6.75 + 2.2 + 9.58$

b. $1.07 + $2.49 + $7.40

4. Estimate using clustering.

a. $4.50 + $5.50 + $5.55

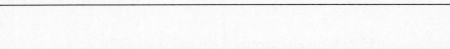

b. $26.7 + 26.2 + 24.52 + 23.9$

Name_____ Class_____ Date_____

Lesson 3-2   **Estimating Decimal Products and Quotients**

Lesson Objectives	**NAEP 2005 Strand:** Number Properties and Operations
Estimate products	**Topic:** Estimation
Estimate quotients	**Local Standards:** _____

Vocabulary

Compatible numbers are _____

_____

Examples

❶ **Estimating the Product** Estimate 6.43 · 4.7.

$6.43 \approx$ ☐ $4.7 \approx$ ☐   **Round to the nearest integer.**

☐ · ☐ = ☐   **Multiply.**

$6.43 \cdot 4.7 \approx$ ☐

❷ Joshua bought 3 yd of fabric to make a flag. The fabric cost $5.35/yd. The clerk said his total was $14.95 before tax. Did the clerk make a mistake? Explain.

$5.35 \approx$ ☐   **Round to the nearest dollar.**

$5 \cdot 3 =$ ☐   **Multiply** ☐ **times** ☐ **, the number of yards of fabric.**

The sales clerk ☐_____. Since 5.35 ☐ 5, the actual cost

should be more than the estimate. The clerk should have charged Joshua

more than ☐ before tax.

Quick Check

1. Estimate each product.
   a. 4.72 · 1.8   **b.** 17.02 · 3.78   **c.** 8.25 · 19.8

   ☐   ☐   ☐

2. **Photography** You buy 8 rolls of film for your camera. Each roll costs $4.79. Estimate the cost of the film before tax.

   ☐

❸ Estimating the Quotient The cost to ship one yearbook is $3.12. The total cost for a shipment was $62.40. Estimate how many books were in the shipment.

$3.12 \approx$ ☐ **Round the divisor.**

$62.40 \approx$ ☐ **Round the dividend to a multiple of** ☐ **that is close to 62.40.**

$60 \div 3 =$ ☐ **Divide.**

The shipment is made up of about ☐ books.

❹ Estimating to Determine Reasonableness Is 3.29 a reasonable quotient for $31.423 \div 5.94$?

$5.94 \approx$ ☐ **Round the divisor.**

$31.423 \approx$ ☐ **Round the dividend to a multiple of** ☐ **that is close to 31.423.**

$30 \div 6 =$ ☐ **Divide.**

Since 3.29 is not close to ☐, it is not reasonable.

Quick Check

3. Estimate each quotient.

a. $38.9 \div 1.79$

b. $11.95 \div 2.1$

c. $82.52 \div 4.25$

4. Use estimation. Is each quotient reasonable? Explain.

a. $1.564 \div 2.3 = 0.68$

b. $26.0454 \div 4.98 = 10.12$

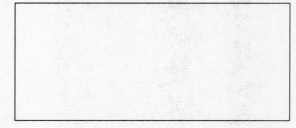

Lesson 3-3

Mean, Median, and Mode

Lesson Objectives	**NAEP 2005 Strand:** Data Analysis and Probability
▼ Find mean, median, and mode of a set of data	**Topic:** Characteristics of Data Sets
② Choose the best measure of central tendency	**Local Standards:** _____

Vocabulary

Three measures of central tendency are [_____], [_____], and [_____].

A mean is _____

_____

A median is _____

_____

If there is an even number of data values, the median is _____

_____

A mode is _____

An outlier is _____

_____

Examples

❶ Finding the Mean, Median, and Mode Six elementary students are participating in a one-week Readathon to raise money for a good cause. Use the graph to find the (a) mean, (b) median, and the (c) mode of the data if you leave out the number of pages Latana has read.

a. Mean $= \dfrac{\text{sum of data values}}{\text{number of data values}}$

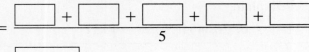

$= \dfrac{\boxed{}}{5}$

$= \boxed{}$

The mean is $\boxed{}$.

b. Median: 40   45   48   50   50   **Write the data in order.**

The median is the $\boxed{}$ number, or $\boxed{}$.

c. Mode: Find the data value that occurs most often.
40   45   48 ⎣50   50⎦

The mode is $\boxed{}$.

REApATHON
(PAGES READ)

❷ Identifying Outliers Use the data 7%, 4%, 10%, 33%, 11%, 12%.

a. Which data value is an outlier? The data value ⬚ is an outlier.
It is an outlier because it is much ⬚ than the other data values.

b. How does the outlier affect the mean?

$\frac{77}{6} \approx$ ⬚   **Find the mean with the outlier.**

$\frac{44}{5} \approx$ ⬚   **Find the mean without the outlier.**

⬚ − ⬚ = ⬚

The outlier raises the mean by about ⬚ points.

❸ Identifying the Best Measure Which measure of central tendency best describes each situation? Explain.

a. the monthly amount of rain for a year

⬚ ; since the average monthly amount of rain for a year is

not likely to have an outlier, ⬚ is the appropriate measure.

When the data have no outliers, use the ⬚ .

b. the most popular color of shirt

⬚ ; since the data are not numerical, the ⬚ is

the appropriate measure. When determining the most frequently chosen

item, or when the data are not numerical, use the ⬚ .

c. time student leaves home to get to school

⬚ ; since a few students may leave much earlier or much

later than most of the studetns, the ⬚ is the appropriate

measure. When an outlier may significantly influence the mean, use

the ⬚ .

Quick Check

1. Find the mean, median, and mode of each group of data.

a. 2.3   4.3   3.2   2.9   2.7   2.3

mean = ⬚ , median = ⬚ , mode = ⬚

b. $20 $26 $27 $28 $21 $42 $18 $20

mean = ⬚ , median = ⬚ , mode = ⬚

2. Find an outlier in each group of data below and tell how it affects the mean.

a. 9   10   12   13   8   9   31   9   b. 1   17.5   18   19.5   16   17.5

⬚   ⬚

Lesson 3-4

Using Formulas

Lesson Objectives	NAEP 2005 Strand: Algebra
▼ Substitute into formulas	**Topic:** Equations and Inequalities
▼ Use the formula for the perimeter of a rectangle	**Local Standards:** _____

Vocabulary

A formula is _____

_____

Perimeter is _____

_____

Example

1 **Using a Formula** Suppose you ride your bike 18 miles in 3 hours. Use the formula $d = rt$ to find your average speed.

$d = rt$ **Write the formula.**

$\boxed{} = (r)\left(\boxed{}\right)$ **Substitute** $\boxed{}$ **for d and** $\boxed{}$ **for t.**

$\dfrac{18}{\boxed{}} = \dfrac{3r}{\boxed{}}$ **Divide each side by** $\boxed{}$.

$\boxed{} = r$ **Simplify.**

Your average speed is $\boxed{}$ mi/h.

Quick Check

1. Use the formula $d = rt$. Find d, r, or t.

   a. $d = 273$ mi, $t = 9.75$ h

   b. $d = 540.75$ in., $r = 10.5$ in./yr

Name_____ Class_____ Date _____

Examples

2 Use the formula $F = \frac{n}{4} + 37$, where n is the number of chirps a cricket makes in one minute, and F is the temperature in degrees Fahrenheit. Estimate the temperature when a cricket chirps 76 times in a minute.

$F = \frac{n}{4} + 37$ **Write the formula.**

$F = \dfrac{\boxed{}}{4} + 37$ **Replace _n_ with** $\boxed{}$.

$F = \boxed{} + 37$ **Divide.**

$F = \boxed{}$ **Add.**

The temperature is $\boxed{}$.

3 **Finding Perimeter** Find the perimeter of a rectangular tabletop with a length of 14.5 in. and width of 8.5 in. Use the formula for the perimeter of a rectangle, $P = 2\ell + 2w$.

$P = 2\ell + 2w$ **Write the formula.**

$P = 2\left(\boxed{}\right) + 2\left(\boxed{}\right)$ **Replace** ℓ **with** $\boxed{}$ **and _w_ with** $\boxed{}$.

$P = \boxed{} + \boxed{}$ **Multiply.**

$P = \boxed{}$ **Add.**

The perimeter of the tabletop is $\boxed{}$ in.

Quick Check

2. Use the formula $F = \frac{n}{4} + 37$ to estimate the temperature in degrees Fahrenheit for each situation.

a. 96 chirps/min   **b.** 88 chirps/min   **c.** 66 chirps/min

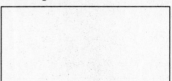 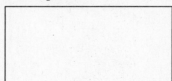 

3. Find the perimeter of each rectangle.

a.

16.8 cm

27.3 cm

b.
8.6 in.

17.4 in.

Lesson 3-5

Solving Equations by Adding or Subtracting Decimals

Lesson Objectives	NAEP 2005 Strand: Algebra
▼1 Solve one-step decimal equations involving addition	Topic: Equations and Inequalities
▼2 Solve one-step decimal equations involving subtraction	Local Standards: _____

Examples

❶ Subtracting to Solve an Equation Solve $6.8 + p = -9.7$.

$$6.8 + p = -9.7$$

$6.8 - \boxed{} + p = -9.7 - \boxed{}$ **Subtract** $\boxed{}$ **from each side.**

$p = \boxed{}$ **Simplify.**

Check $6.8 + p = -9.7$

$6.8 + \left(\boxed{}\right) \stackrel{?}{=} -9.7$ **Replace p with** $\boxed{}$.

$\boxed{} = -9.7$ ✔

❷ Solving a One-Step Equation by Subtracting Ping has a board that is 14.5 ft long. She saws off a piece that is 8.75 ft long. Find the length left over.

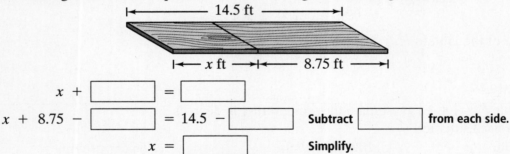

$x + \boxed{} = \boxed{}$

$x + 8.75 - \boxed{} = 14.5 - \boxed{}$ **Subtract** $\boxed{}$ **from each side.**

$x = \boxed{}$ **Simplify.**

The length of the piece that is left is $\boxed{}$ ft.

Quick Check

1. Solve each equation.

   a. $x + 4.9 = 18.8$

   b. $14.73 = -24.23 + b$

2. **Retail** A store's cost plus markup is the price you pay for an item. Suppose a pair of shoes costs a store $35.48. You pay $70. Write and solve an equation to find the store's markup.

Examples

❸ **Adding to Solve an Equation** Solve $-23.34 = q - 16.99$.

$$-23.34 = q - 16.99$$

$-23.34 + \boxed{} = q - 16.99 + \boxed{}$ **Add** $\boxed{}$ **to each side.**

$\boxed{} = q$ **Simplify.**

❹ **Solving a One-Step Equation by Adding** Alejandro wrote a check for $49.98. His new account balance is $169.45. What was his previous balance?

Words | previous balance | minus | check | is | new balance

Let $\boxed{p}$ = previous balance.

Equation $\boxed{p}$ $-$ $\boxed{}$ $=$ $\boxed{}$

$$p - 49.98 = 169.45$$

$p - 49.98 + \boxed{} = 169.45 + \boxed{}$ **Add** $\boxed{}$ **to each side.**

$p = \boxed{}$ **Simplify.**

Alejandro had $\boxed{}$ in his account before he wrote the check.

Quick Check

3. Solve each equation.

   a. $n - 5.85 = 15.25$

   b. $-10 = c - 2.6$

4. **Shopping** You spent $14.95 for a new shirt. You now have $12.48. Write and solve an equation to find how much money you had before you bought the shirt.

Lesson 3-6

Lesson Objectives	NAEP 2005 Strand: Algebra
▼ Solve one-step decimal equations involving multiplication	**Topic:** Equations and Inequalities
▼ Solve one-step decimal equations involving division	**Local Standards:** _____

Examples

① Solving a One-Step Equation by Dividing Every day the school cafeteria uses about 85.8 gallons of milk. About how many days will it take for the cafeteria to use the 250 gallons in the refrigerator?

Words

daily milk consumption	times	number of days	equals	250 gallons

Let $\boxed{x}$ = number of days.

Equation $\boxed{} \cdot \boxed{x} = \boxed{}$

$85.8x = 250$

$\dfrac{85.8x}{\boxed{}} = \dfrac{250}{\boxed{}}$ **Divide each side by** $\boxed{}$.

$x = \boxed{}$ **Simplify.**

$x \approx \boxed{}$ **Round to the nearest whole number.**

The school will take about $\boxed{}$ days to use 250 gallons of milk.

② Multiplying to Solve an Equation Solve $-37.5 = \dfrac{c}{-1.2}$

$-37.5 = \dfrac{c}{-1.2}$

$-37.5\left(\boxed{}\right) = \dfrac{c}{-1.2}\left(\boxed{}\right)$ **Multiply each side by** $\boxed{}$.

$\boxed{} = c$ **Simplify.**

Check $-37.5 = \dfrac{c}{-1.2}$

$-37.5 \overset{?}{=} \dfrac{\boxed{}}{-1.2}$ **Replace c with** $\boxed{}$.

$-37.5 = -37.5$ ✔   **Simplify.**

Name_____ Class_____ Date _____

❸ Solving a One-Step Equation by Multiplying A little league player was at bat 15 times and had a batting average of 0.133 (rounded to the nearest thousandth). The batting average formula is $a = \frac{h}{n}$, where a is the batting average, h is the number of hits, and n is the number of times at bat. Use the formula to find the number of hits she made.

$$a = \frac{h}{n}$$

$$\boxed{} = \frac{h}{\boxed{}}$$ **Replace a with** $\boxed{}$ **and n with** $\boxed{}$.

$$0.133\left(\boxed{}\right) = \frac{h}{15}\left(\boxed{}\right)$$ **Multiply each side by** $\boxed{}$.

$$\boxed{} = h$$ **Simplify.**

$$\boxed{} \approx h$$ **Since h (hits) represents an integer, round to the nearest integer.**

The little league player made $\boxed{}$ hits.

Quick Check

1. Solve each equation. Check the solution.

   a. $0.8x = -1.6$

   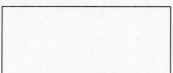

   b. $1.15 = 2.3x$

   c. $-81.81 = -0.9n$

   d. $\frac{r}{-6.0} = 0.5$

   e. $\frac{s}{2.5} = 5$

   f. $-80 = \frac{t}{4.5}$

2. **Postage** You paid $7.70 to mail a package that weighed 5.5 lb. Write and solve an equation to find the cost per pound.

3. Suppose your batting average is 0.222. You have batted 54 times. How many hits do you have?

Lesson 3-7

Using the Metric System

Lesson Objectives	NAEP 2005 Strand: Measurement
▼ Identify appropriate metric measures	**Topic:** System of Measurement
▼ Convert metric units	**Local Standards:** _____

Key Concepts

Metric Units of Measurement

	Unit	Reference Example
	millimeter (☐)	about the thickness of a dime
	centimeter (☐)	about the width of a thumbnail
	meter (☐)	about the distance from a doorknob to the floor
	kilometer (☐)	a little more than one half mile
	milliliter (☐)	about 5 drops of water
	liter (☐)	a little more than a quart of milk
	milligram (☐)	about the mass of a speck of sawdust
	gram (☐)	about the mass of a paper clip
	kilogram (☐)	about one half the mass of your math book

Examples

❶ Estimating With Metric Units Choose a reasonable estimate. Explain your choice.

a. capacity of a drinking glass: 500 L or 500 mL

[   ] ; a drinking glass holds less than a quart of milk.

b. mass of a pair of hiking boots: 1kg or 1g

[   ] ; the mass is about one half the mass of your math book.

❷ Converting Between Metric Units Complete each statement.

a. 7,603 mL = L

7,603 ÷ [   ] = [   ]   **To convert from milliliters to liters, divide by** [   ].

7,603 mL = [   ]

b. 4.57 m = [▨] cm

4.57 × [   ] = [   ] cm   **To convert meters to centimeters, multiply by** [   ].

4.57 m = [   ]

❸ Converting Lengths A blue whale caught in 1931 was about 2,900 cm long. What was its length in meters?

Words ⬇

length in centimeters	÷	centimeters per meter	=	length in meters

Equation [   ] ÷ [   ] = [   ]

The whale was about [   ] m long.

Quick Check

1. Choose a reasonable estimate. Explain your choice.

   a. distance between two cities: 50 mm or 50 km

   [   ]

   b. amount of liquid that an eyedropper holds: 10 mL or 10 L

   [   ]

2. Complete each statement.

   a. 35 mL = [   ] L   **b.** [   ] g = 250 kg   **c.** [   ] cm = 60 m

3. a. The record for the highest a kite has flown is 3.8 km. Find the height of the kite in meters.

   [   ]

   b. Number Sense You have a recipe that requires 0.25 L of milk. Your measuring cup is marked only in milliliters. How many milliliters of milk do you need?

   [   ]

Lesson 3-8

Act It Out

Lesson Objective	Local Standards: _____
▼ Solve problems by acting them out	

Example

❶ Currency Marta gives her sister one penny on the first day of October, two pennies on the second day, and four pennies on the third day. She continues to double the number of pennies each day. On what date will Marta give her sister $10.24 in pennies?

Understand the Problem Marta needs to give her sister pennies worth

$[   ]. Marta gives her [   ] penny on the first day. She

[   ] the number of pennies every day.

1. How many pennies does Marta's sister get on the first day? [   ]

2. How many pennies does Marta's sister get on the second day? [   ]

3. How many pennies does Marta's sister get on the third day? [   ]

Make and Carry Out a Plan Act out the problem. Keep track of the amount given each day in a chart.

Days After the First	Number of Pennies	Amount
0	1	$.01
1	2	$.02
2	$2 \cdot 2 =$ [ ]	
3	$4 \cdot 2 =$ [ ]	
4	$8 \cdot 2 =$ [ ]	
5	$16 \cdot 2 =$ [ ]	

You can tell from the pattern in the chart that you just need to count the number of 2's multiplied until you reach [   ], which is $[   ] in pennies.

$2 \cdot 2 \cdot 2 \cdot 2 \cdot 2 \cdot 2 \cdot 2 \cdot 2 \cdot 2 \cdot 2 =$ [   ]

[   ] twos = [   ] days after the first penny is given

Marta will give her sister $10.24 in pennies on [   ].

Name_____ Class_____ Date _____

Quick Check

1. Complete the chart to check your answer to Example 1.

Days After the First	Number of Pennies	Amount
0	1	$.01
1	2	$.02
2	$2 \cdot 2 = \boxed{}$	
3	$4 \cdot 2 = \boxed{}$	
4	$8 \cdot 2 = \boxed{}$	
5	$16 \cdot 2 = \boxed{}$	

Lesson 4-1

Divisibility and Factors

Lesson Objectives	**NAEP 2005 Strand:** Number Properties and Operations
▼ 1 Use divisibility tests ▼ 2 Find factors	**Topic:** Properties of Number and Operations **Local Standards:** _____

Vocabulary and Key Concepts

Divisibility Rules for 2, 5, and 10

An integer is divisible by

- ☐ if it ends in 0, 2, 4, 6, or 8.

- ☐ if it ends in 0 or 5.

- ☐ if it ends in 0.

☐ numbers end in 0, 2, 4, 6, or 8 and are divisible by ☐.

☐ numbers end in 1, 3, 5, 7, or 9 and are not divisible by 2.

Divisibility Rules for 3 and 9

An integer is divisible by

- ☐ if the sum of its digits is divisible by 3.

- ☐ if the sum of its digits is divisible by 9.

One integer is divisible by another if _____

_____

One integer is a factor of another integer if _____

_____

Examples

❶ Divisibility by 2, 5, and 10 Is the first number divisible by the second?

a. 1,028 by 2

☐ ; 1,028 ends in ☐.

b. 572 by 5

☐ ; 572 doesn't end in ☐ or ☐.

c. 275 by 10

☐ ; 275 doesn't end in ☐.

❷ **Divisibility by 3 and 9** Is the first number divisible by the second?

a. 1,028 by 3 　　　[　　]; 1 + 0 + 2 + 8 = 11; 11 is not divisible by [　].

b. 522 by 9 　　　[　　]; 5 + 2 + 2 = 9; 9 is divisible by [　].

❸ **Using Factors** Ms. Washington's class is having a class photo taken. Each row must have the same number of students. There are 35 students in the class. How can Ms. Washington arrange the students in rows if there must be at least 5 students, but no more than 10 students, in each row?

Find pairs of factors of 35: 1 · [　　], 5 · [　　]

There can be 5 rows of [　] students, or 7 rows of [　] students.

Quick Check

1. Is the first number divisible by the second? Explain.

a. 160 by 5

[　　　　　　　　　　　　　　　　　　　　]

b. 56 by 10

[　　　　　　　　　　　　　　　　　　　　]

c. 53 by 2

[　　　　　　　　　　　　　　　　　　　　]

d. 1,118 by 2

[　　　　　　　　　　　　　　　　　　　　]

e. 64 by 9

[　　　　　　　　　　　　　　　　　　　　]

f. 472 by 3

[　　　　　　　　　　　　　　　　　　　　]

g. 174 by 3

[　　　　　　　　　　　　　　　　　　　　]

h. 43,542 by 9

[　　　　　　　　　　　　　　　　　　　　]

2. List the positive factors of each number.

a. 10 [　　　　　　　　　]　　**b.** 21 [　　　　　　　　　]

c. 24 [　　　　　　　　　]　　**d.** 31 [　　　　　　　　　]

3. What are the possible arrangements for Example 3 if there are 36 students in Ms. Washington's class?

[　　　　　　　　　　　　　　　　　　　　]

Lesson 4-2

Exponents

Lesson Objectives	NAEP 2005 Strand: Algebra
▼ Use exponents ▼ Use the order of operations with exponents	**Topic:** Variables, Expressions, and Operations **Local Standards:** _____

Vocabulary and Key Concepts

Order of Operations

1. Work inside [   ] symbols.

2. Simplify any terms with [   ].

3. [   ] and [   ] in order from left to right.

4. [   ] and [   ] in order from left to right.

Exponents are used to show _____

_____

A *power* has two parts, a [   ] and an [   ].

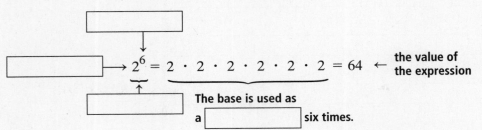

$2^6 = 2 \cdot 2 \cdot 2 \cdot 2 \cdot 2 \cdot 2 = 64$ ← **the value of the expression**

The base is used as a [   ] **six times.**

Examples

❶ Using an Exponent Write using exponents.

a. $(-11)(-11)(-11)(-11)$

$\left([-11]\right)^{[4]}$ **Include the negative sign within parentheses.**

b. $-5 \cdot x \cdot x \cdot y \cdot y \cdot x$

$-5 \cdot x \cdot x \cdot x \cdot y \cdot y$ **Rewrite the expression using the** [Commutative]

and [   ] **Properties.**

$-5x^{[3]}y^{[2]}$ **Write** $x \cdot x \cdot x$ **and** $y \cdot y$ **using exponents.**

Daily Notetaking Guide

❷ **Science** Suppose a certain star is 10^4 light-years from Earth. How many light-years is that?

$10^4 = \boxed{10 \cdot 10 \cdot 10 \cdot 10}$ ← The exponent indicates that the base $\boxed{10}$ is used as a factor $\boxed{4}$ times.

$\qquad = \boxed{10,000}$ light-years **Multiply.**

❸ **Using the Order of Operations**

a. Simplify $3(1 + 4)^3$.

$3(1 + 4)^3 = 3\left(\boxed{5}\right)^3$ **Work within parentheses first.**

$\qquad = 3 \cdot \boxed{5 \cdot 5 \cdot 5}$ **Simplify 5^3.** $\begin{array}{r}125 \\ \times 3 \\ \hline 375\end{array}$

$\qquad = \boxed{375}$ **Multiply.**

b. Evaluate $7(w + 3)^3 + z$, for $w = -5$ and $z = 6$.

$7(w + 3)^3 + z = 7\left(\boxed{} + 3\right)^3 + \boxed{}$ **Replace w with -5 and z with 6.**

$\qquad = 7\left(\boxed{}\right)^3 + \boxed{}$ **Work within parentheses.**

$\qquad = 7\left(\boxed{}\right) + \boxed{}$ **Simplify $(-2)^3$.**

$\qquad = \boxed{} + \boxed{}$ **Multiply from left to right.**

$\qquad = \boxed{}$ **Add.**

Quick Check

1. Write using exponents.

   a. $6 \cdot 6 \cdot 6$

   b. $4 \cdot y \cdot x \cdot y$

   c. $(-3)(-3)(-3)(-3)$

2. a. Simplify 6^2.

   b. Evaluate $-a^4$ and $(-a)^4$, for $a = 2$.

   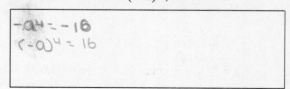
   $-a^4 = -16$
   $(-a)^4 = 16$

3. a. Simplify $2 \cdot 5^2 + 4 \cdot (-3)^3$.

   b. Evaluate $3a^2 + 6$, for $a = -5$.

   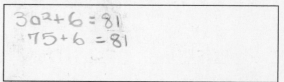
   $3a^2 + 6 = 81$
   $\cdot 75 + 6 = 81$

Lesson 4-3

Lesson Objectives	NAEP 2005 Strand: Number Properties and Operations
▼ Find the prime factorization of a number	Topic: Properties of Number and Operations
▼ Find the greatest common factor (GCF) of two or more numbers	Local Standards: _____

Vocabulary

A prime number is _a positive integer, greater than 1, with exactly two factors_

A composite number is _a positive integer, greater than 1, with more than 2 factors_

The prime factorization of a number is _____
_____

The greatest common factor (GCF) is _____
_____

Examples

❶ Prime or Composite? State whether each number is *prime* or *composite*. Explain.

a. 46

    Composite ; 46 has more than two factors, 1, 2 , 23 , and 46 .

b. 13

    Prime ; 13 has exactly two factors, 1 and 13 .

❷ Writing the Prime Factorization Use a factor tree to write the prime factorization of 273.

273

Prime ③ · 91   **Start with a prime factor.
Continue branching.**

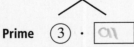

Primes 7 · 13   **Stop when all factors
are prime.**

273 = 7 · 13 · 3   **Write the prime factorization.**

Name_____ Class_____ Date _____

❸ Finding the GCF Find the GCF of each pair of numbers and expressions.

a. 24 and 30

$24 = \boxed{2}^3 \cdot \boxed{3}$

$30 = \boxed{2} \cdot \boxed{3} \cdot \boxed{5}$ Write the prime factorizations.

$GCF = \boxed{2} \cdot \boxed{3}$ Find the common factors. Use the lesser power of the common factors.

$= \boxed{6}$

The GCF of 24 and 30 is $\boxed{6}$.

b. $36ab^2$ and $81b$

$36ab^2 = 2^2 \cdot 3^2 \cdot a \cdot b^2$ Write the prime factorizations.
$81b = 3^4 \cdot b$ Find the common factors.

$GCF = \boxed{} \cdot \boxed{}$ Use the lesser power of the common factors.

$= \boxed{}$

The GCF of $36ab^2$ and $81b$ is $\boxed{}$.

Quick Check

1. a. Which numbers from 10 to 20 are prime?

b. Which are composite?

2. Write the prime factorization of each number.

a. 72   **b.** 121   **c.** 225   **d.** 236

3. Use prime factorizations to find each GCF.

a. 8, 20   **b.** 12, 87   **c.** $12r^3, 8r$ **d.** $15m^2n, 45m$

  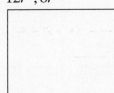

Lesson 4-4

Simplifying Fractions

Lesson Objectives	NAEP 2005 Strand: Number Properties and Operations
▼ Find equivalent fractions ▼ Write fractions in simplest form	Topic: Number Operations Local Standards: _____

Vocabulary

Two fractions are equivalent if _____

_____

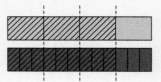

$\frac{3}{4}$ of the bar is shaded.

$\frac{9}{12}$ of the bar is shaded.

$$\frac{3}{4} = \frac{3 \cdot \boxed{}}{4 \cdot \boxed{}} = \frac{9}{12}$$

A fraction is in simplest form when _____

_____

Example

❶ **Finding an Equivalent Fraction** Find two fractions equivalent to $\frac{18}{21}$.

a. $\frac{18}{21} = \dfrac{18 \cdot \boxed{}}{21 \cdot \boxed{}}$

b. $\frac{18}{21} = \dfrac{18 \div \boxed{}}{21 \div \boxed{}}$

$= \dfrac{\boxed{}}{\boxed{}}$

$= \dfrac{\boxed{}}{\boxed{}}$

The fractions $\dfrac{\boxed{}}{\boxed{}}$ and $\dfrac{\boxed{}}{\boxed{}}$ are both equivalent to $\frac{18}{21}$.

Quick Check

1. Find two fractions equivalent to each fraction.

a. $\frac{5}{15}$

b. $\frac{10}{12}$

c. $\frac{14}{20}$

Daily Notetaking Guide

Examples

❷ You learn that 21 out of the 28 students in a class, or $\frac{21}{28}$, buy their lunches in the cafeteria. Write this fraction in simplest form.

$\frac{21}{28} = \dfrac{21 \div \boxed{}}{28 \div \boxed{}}$ **Divide the numerator and denominator by the GCF, $\boxed{}$.**

$= \dfrac{\boxed{}}{\boxed{}}$ **Simplify.**

$\dfrac{\boxed{}}{\boxed{}}$ of the students in the class buy their lunches in the cafeteria.

❸ Simplifying a Fraction Write in simplest form.

a. $\dfrac{p}{2p} = \dfrac{p\boxed{}}{2p\boxed{}}$ **Divide the numerator and denominator by the common factor $\boxed{}$.**

$= \dfrac{\boxed{}}{\boxed{}}$ **Simplify.**

b. $\dfrac{14q^2rs^3}{8qrs^2} = \dfrac{2 \cdot 7 \cdot q \cdot q \cdot r \cdot s \cdot s \cdot s}{2 \cdot 2 \cdot 2 \cdot q \cdot r \cdot s \cdot s}$ **Write as a product of prime factors.**

$= \dfrac{2^{\boxed{}} \cdot 7 \cdot \cancel{q}^{\boxed{}} \cdot q \cdot \cancel{r}^{\boxed{}} \cdot \cancel{s}^{\boxed{}} \cdot \cancel{s}^{\boxed{}} \cdot s}{2^{\boxed{}} \cdot 2 \cdot 2 \cdot \cancel{q}^{\boxed{}} \cdot \cancel{r}^{\boxed{}} \cdot \cancel{s}^{\boxed{}} \cdot \cancel{s}^{\boxed{}}}$ **Divide the numerator and denominator by the common factors.**

$= \dfrac{\boxed{} \cdot \boxed{} \cdot \boxed{}}{\boxed{} \cdot \boxed{}}$ **Simplify.**

$= \dfrac{\boxed{}}{\boxed{}}$ **Simplify.**

Quick Check

2. Write each fraction in simplest form.

a. $\dfrac{6}{8} = \dfrac{6 \div \boxed{}}{8 \div \boxed{}} = \dfrac{\boxed{}}{\boxed{}}$

b. $\dfrac{9}{12} = \dfrac{9 \div \boxed{}}{12 \div \boxed{}} = \dfrac{\boxed{}}{\boxed{}}$

c. $\dfrac{28}{35} = \dfrac{28 \div \boxed{}}{35 \div \boxed{}} = \dfrac{\boxed{}}{\boxed{}}$

d. $\dfrac{b}{abc} = \dfrac{\boxed{}}{\boxed{}}$

e. $\dfrac{2mn}{6m} = \dfrac{\boxed{}}{\boxed{}}$

f. $\dfrac{24x^2y}{8xy} = \dfrac{\boxed{}}{\boxed{}}$

Lesson 4-5

Lesson Objective	NAEP 2005 Strand: Algebra
▼ Solve complex problems by first solving simpler cases	**Topic:** Patterns, Relations, and Functions
	Local Standards: _____

Example

❶ Aaron, Chris, Maria, Sonia, and Ling are on a class committee. They want to choose two members to present their conclusions to the class. How many different groups of two members can they form?

Understand the Problem

1. What do you need to find?

2. How many people are there in all?

3. How many people will present their conclusions?

Make and Carry Out a Plan

To make sure that you account for every pair of committee members, make an organized list.

Solve a simpler problem. Change the problem to a simpler one based on three committee members, and then try four members to see if there is a pattern.

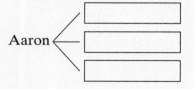

Three Members	Four Members
(Aaron, Chris, Maria)	(Aaron, Chris, Maria, Sonia)

Aaron < [ ] [ ]

Aaron < [ ] [ ] [ ]

Chris —— Maria

Chris < [ ] [ ]

Maria —— [ ]

(Chris has already been paired with [ ].)

(Maria has already been paired with [ ] and [ ].)

Example

4. What pattern do you see?

5. How many different groups of two committee members are there?

Look Back and Check

Another way to solve this problem is to use a diagram. Draw line segments to represent the number of different groups of two members that can be formed.

Aaron
●

Maria ●   ● Chris

●   ●
Sonia   Ling

There are [   ] line segments. The answer checks. ✔

Quick Check

1. Suppose there were eight people on the committee. How many different groups of two committee members would there be?

Lesson 4-6

Lesson Objectives	NAEP 2005 Strands: Number Properties and Operations; Algebra
❶ Identify and graph rational numbers ❷ Evaluate fractions containing variables	Topics: Number Sense; Variables, Expressions, and Operations Local Standards: _____

Vocabulary

A rational number is _____

_____

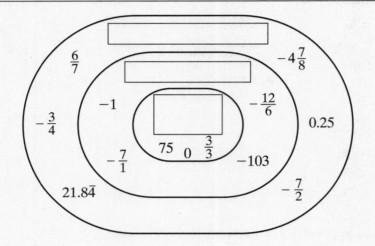

Example

❶ **Writing Equivalent Fractions** Write two lists of fractions equivalent to $\frac{2}{3}$.

$\frac{2}{3} = \frac{\boxed{}}{6} = \frac{\boxed{}}{9} = \cdots$ **Numerators and denominators are positive.**

$\frac{2}{3} = \frac{\boxed{}}{-3} = \frac{\boxed{}}{-6} = \cdots$ **Numerators and denominators are negative.**

Quick Check

1. Write three fractions equivalent to each fraction.

a. $\frac{1}{3} = \boxed{} = \boxed{} = \boxed{}$

b. $\frac{5}{8} = \boxed{} = \boxed{} = \boxed{}$

c. $-\frac{4}{5} = \boxed{} = \boxed{} = \boxed{}$

d. $-\frac{1}{2} = \boxed{} = \boxed{} = \boxed{}$

Examples

❷ **Graphing a Rational Number** Graph each rational number on the number line below.

a. $-\frac{3}{4}$ **b.** 0.5   **c.** 0   **d.** $\frac{1}{3}$

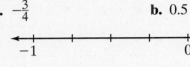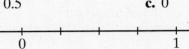

❸ **Science** A fast sports car can accelerate from a stop to 90 ft/s in 5 seconds. What is its acceleration in feet per second per second (ft/s^2)? Use the formula $a = \frac{f - i}{t}$, where a is acceleration, f is final speed, i is initial speed, and t is time.

$a = \dfrac{f - i}{t}$ **Use the acceleration formula.**

$= \dfrac{\boxed{} - \boxed{}}{\boxed{}}$ **Substitute.**

$= \dfrac{\boxed{}}{\boxed{}}$ **Subtract.**

$= \boxed{}$ **Write in simplest form.**

The car's acceleration is $\boxed{}$ ft/s^2.

Quick Check

2. Graph each rational number on the number line below.

a. $-\frac{1}{2}$ **b.** $-\frac{4}{10}$ **c.** -2 **d.** 0.9

3. Evaluate each expression for $a = 6$ and $b = -5$. Write in simplest form.

a. $\dfrac{a + b}{-3}$ **b.** $\dfrac{7 - b}{3a}$ **c.** $\dfrac{a + 9}{b}$

Lesson 4-7

Exponents and Multiplication

Lesson Objectives	NAEP 2005 Strand: Algebra
▼ Multiply powers with the same base	**Topic:** Variables, Expressions, and Operations
▼ Find a power of a power	**Local Standards:** _____

Key Concepts

Multiplying Powers with the Same Base

To multiply numbers or variables with the same base, ☐ the exponents.

Arithmetic

$2^3 \cdot 2^4 = 2^{\Box + \Box} = 2^{\Box}$

Algebra

$a^{\Box} \cdot a^{\Box} = a^{\Box + \Box}$, for positive integers m and n.

Finding a Power of a Power

To find a power of a power, ☐ the exponents.

Arithmetic

$(2^3)^4 = 2^{\Box \cdot \Box} = 2^{\Box}$

Algebra

$(a^m)^n = a^{\Box \cdot \Box}$, for positive integers m and n.

Example

❶ **Multiplying Powers** Simplify each expression.

a. $5^2 \cdot 5^3 = 5^{\Box + \Box}$ 　　　☐ the exponents of powers with the same base.

   $= 5^{\Box}$ 　　**Simplify the exponent.**

   $= \boxed{}$ 　　**Simplify.**

b. $x^5 \cdot x^7 \cdot y^2 \cdot y = x^{\Box + \Box} \cdot y^{\Box + \Box}$ 　☐ the exponents of powers with the same base.

   $= x^{\Box} y^{\Box}$ 　　**Simplify.**

Quick Check

1. Simplify each expression.

   a. $2^2 \cdot 2^3$

   b. $m^5 \cdot m^7$

   c. $x^2 \cdot x^3 \cdot y \cdot y^4$

Name_____ Class_____ Date _____

Examples

2 **Using the Commutative Property** Simplify $3a^3 \cdot -5a^4$.

$3a^3 \cdot -5a^4 = 3 \cdot -5 \cdot a^3 \cdot a^4$ Use the [_____] **Property** **of Multiplication.**

$= -15a^{\square + \square}$ [_____] **the exponents.**

$= $ [_____]   **Simplify.**

3 **Simplifying Powers of Powers** Simplify each expression.

a. $(2^3)^3 = (2)^{\square \cdot \square}$ [_____] **the exponents.**

$= (2)^{\square}$ **Simplify the exponent.**

$= $ [_____]   **Simplify.**

b. $(g^5)^4 = g^{\square \cdot \square}$ [_____] **the exponents.**

$= (g)^{\square}$ **Simplify the exponent.**

Quick Check

2. Simplify each expression.

a. $6a^3 \cdot 3a$

b. $-5c^2 \cdot -3c^7$

c. $4x^2 \cdot 3x^4$

3. Simplify each expression.

a. $(2^4)^2$

b. $(c^5)^4$

c. $(m^3)^2$

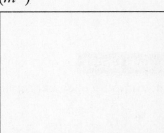

Lesson 4-8

Exponents and Division

Lesson Objectives	NAEP 2005 Strand: Algebra
▼ Divide expressions containing exponents ❷ Simplify expressions with integer exponents	**Topic:** Variables, Expressions, and Operations **Local Standards:** _____

Key Concepts

Dividing Powers With the Same Base

To divide numbers or variables *with the same nonzero base,* [   ]
the exponents.

Arithmetic

$$\frac{4^5}{4^2} = 4^{\boxed{} - \boxed{}} = 4^{\boxed{}}$$

Algebra

$$\frac{a^m}{a^n} = a^{\boxed{} - \boxed{}}, \text{ for } a \neq 0 \text{ and positive integers } m \text{ and } n.$$

Zero as an Exponent

Arithmetic

$$3^0 = \boxed{}$$

Algebra

$$a^0 = \boxed{}, \text{ for } a \neq 0.$$

Negative Exponents

Arithmetic

$$3^{-2} = \frac{1}{3^2}$$

Algebra

$$a^{-n} = \frac{1}{a^n}, \text{ for } a \neq 0.$$

Example

❶ Dividing a Power by a Power Simplify each expression.

a. $\dfrac{4^{12}}{4^8} = 4^{\boxed{} - \boxed{}}$ [   ] the exponents.

$= 4^{\boxed{}}$ **Simplify the exponent.**

$= \boxed{}$ **Simplify.**

b. $\dfrac{w^{18}}{w^{13}} = w^{\boxed{} - \boxed{}}$ [   ] the exponents.

$= w^{\boxed{}}$ **Simplify the exponent.**

Quick Check

1. Simplify each expression.

a. $\dfrac{10^7}{10^4}$

b. $\dfrac{x^{25}}{x^{18}}$

c. $\dfrac{12m^5}{3m}$

Examples

❷ Simplifying When Zero is an Exponent Simplify each expression.

a. $\dfrac{(-12)^{73}}{(-12)^{73}} = (-12)^{\boxed{} - \boxed{}}$ $\boxed{}$ the exponents.

$= (-12)^{\boxed{}}$ **Simplify.**

$= \boxed{}$ **Simplify.**

b. $\dfrac{8s^{20}}{32s^{20}} = \dfrac{\boxed{}}{\boxed{}} s^{\boxed{}}$ $\boxed{}$ the exponents. Simplify $\dfrac{8}{32}$.

$= \dfrac{1}{4} \cdot \boxed{}$ **Simplify s^0.**

$= \dfrac{\boxed{}}{\boxed{}}$ **Multiply.**

❸ Using Positive Exponents Simplify $\dfrac{z^4}{z^{15}}$.

$\dfrac{z^4}{z^{15}} = z^{\boxed{} - \boxed{}}$ **Subtract the exponents.**

$= z^{\boxed{}}$

$= \dfrac{1}{z^{\boxed{}}}$ **Write with a positive exponent.**

❹ Using Negative Exponents Write $\dfrac{a^2b^3}{ab^{15}}$ without a fraction bar.

$\dfrac{a^2b^3}{ab^{15}} = a^{\boxed{} - \boxed{}} b^{\boxed{} - \boxed{}}$ **Use the rule for dividing powers with the same base.**

$= ab^{\boxed{}}$ **Subtract the exponents.**

Quick Check

2. Simplify each expression.

a. $\dfrac{5^2x^6}{5x^6} = \boxed{} = \boxed{}$ **b.** $\dfrac{4^5}{4^7} = \boxed{} = \boxed{}$ **c.** $\dfrac{3y^8}{9y^{12}} = \boxed{} = \boxed{}$

3. Write each fraction without a fraction bar.

a. $\dfrac{b^3}{b^9} = \boxed{}$ **b.** $\dfrac{m^3n^2}{m^6n^8} = \boxed{}$ **c.** $\dfrac{xy^5}{x^5y^3} = \boxed{}$

Lesson 4-9 Scientific Notation

Lesson Objectives	NAEP 2005 Strand: Number Properties and Operations
▼ Write and evaluate numbers in scientific notation ▼ Calculate with scientific notation	Topic: Number Sense Local Standards: _____

Vocabulary

Scientific notation is _____

_____

$$7,500,000,000,000 = 7.5 \times 10^{\boxed{}}$$

Second factor is a power of $\boxed{}$.

First factor is greater than or equal to $\boxed{}$, but less than $\boxed{}$.

You can change numbers from scientific notation to $\boxed{}$ by simplifying the product of the two factors.

Examples

❶ Writing in Scientific Notation

a. About 6,300,000 people visited the Eiffel Tower in the year 2000. Write this number in scientific notation.

6,300,000   Move the decimal point to get a decimal greater than $\boxed{}$ but less than $\boxed{}$.

$\boxed{}$ places

6.3   Drop the zeros after the 3.

$6.3 \times 10^{\boxed{}}$ You moved the decimal point $\boxed{}$ places. The number is large. Use $\boxed{}$ as the exponent of 10.

b. Write 0.00037 in scientific notation.

0.00037   Move the decimal point to get a decimal greater than $\boxed{}$ but less than $\boxed{}$.

$\boxed{}$ places

3.7   Drop the zeros after the 3.

$3.7 \times 10^{\boxed{}}$ You moved the decimal point $\boxed{}$ places. The number is small. Use $\boxed{}$ as the exponent of 10.

Examples

❷ **Writing in Standard Notation** Write each number in standard notation.

a. 3.6×10^4

3.6000

Write zeros while moving the decimal point.

Rewrite in standard notation.

b. 7.2×10^{-3}

007.2

❸ **Chemistry** One mole of any element contains about 6.02×10^{23} atoms. If each hydrogen atom has a mass of approximately 1.67×10^{-27} kg, what is the approximate mass of one mole of hydrogen atoms?

$(6.02 \times 10^{23})(1.67 \times 10^{-27})$ **Multiply the number of atoms by the mass of each atom.**

$= 6.02 \times 1.67 \times 10^{23} \times 10^{-27}$ **Use the** _____ **Property of Multiplication.**

$\approx \boxed{} \times 10^{23} \times 10^{-27}$ **Multiply 6.02 and 1.67.**

$= 10.1 \times 10^{\boxed{}}$ $\boxed{}$ **the exponents.**

$= 1.01 \times 10^{\boxed{}} \times 10^{\boxed{}}$ **Write 10.1 as $1.01 \times 10^{\boxed{}}$.**

$= 1.01 \times 10^{\boxed{}}$ $\boxed{}$ **the exponents.**

One mole of hydrogen atoms has a mass of approximately $\boxed{}$ kg.

Quick Check

1. Write each number in scientific notation.
   a. 54,500,000

   b. 0.00021

2. Write each number in standard notation.
   a. 3.21×10^7

   b. 5.9×10^{-8}

3. Multiply $(7.1 \times 10^{-8})(8 \times 10^4)$. Express the result in scientific notation.

4. **Chemistry** A hydrogen atom has a mass of 1.67×10^{-27} kg. What is the mass of 6×10^3 hydrogen atoms? Express the result in scientific notation.

Lesson 5-1

Comparing and Ordering Rational Numbers

Lesson Objectives	NAEP 2005 Strand: Number Properties and Operations
▼ Find the least common multiple	Topic: Number Sense
▼ Compare fractions	Local Standards: _____

Vocabulary

A multiple is _____

_____

A least common multiple (LCM) is _____

_____

A least common denominator (LCD) is _____

_____

Examples

❶ Using the LCM Today, the school's baseball and soccer teams had games. The baseball team plays every 7 days. The soccer team plays every 3 days. When will the teams have games on the same day again?

7, 14, ☐, ☐, ☐, ☐, . . .   **List the multiples of 7.**

3, 6, ☐, ☐, ☐, ☐, ☐, . . .   **List the multiples of 3.**

The LCM is ☐. In ☐ days both teams will have games on the same day again.

❷ Using Prime Factorization Find the LCM of 16 and 36.

$16 =$ ☐   **Write the prime factorizations.**

$36 =$ ☐ · ☐

$LCM =$ ☐ · ☐   **Use the greatest power of each factor.**

$=$ ☐   **Multiply.**

The LCM of 16 and 36 is ☐.

❸ Finding the LCM of Variable Expressions Find the LCM of $5a^4$ and $15a$.

$5a^4 = 5 \cdot$ ☐

$15a =$ ☐ · ☐ · a **Write the prime factorizations.**

$LCM =$ ☐ · ☐ · ☐   **Use the greatest power of each factor.**

$=$ ☐   **Multiply.**

The LCM of $5a^4$ and $15a$ is ☐.

Name_____ Class_____ Date _____

4 **Ordering Fractions** Order $-\frac{3}{7}, -1, \frac{1}{4},$ and $\frac{2}{3}$ from least to greatest.

All [____] numbers are less than all [____] numbers, so $-\frac{3}{7}$ and -1
are both less than $\frac{1}{4}$ and $\frac{2}{3}$. Compare each pair.

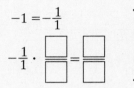

$-1 = -\frac{1}{1}$

$-\frac{1}{1} \cdot \dfrac{\square}{\square} = \dfrac{\square}{\square}$

Change -1 to a fraction by using 1 as its denominator.
The LCM of 1 and 7 is [__]. Use [__] as the common
denominator.

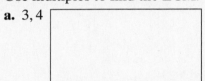

$\dfrac{1}{4} = \dfrac{1 \cdot \square}{4 \cdot \square} = \dfrac{\square}{\square}$

The LCM of 7, 4, and 3 is [____].
Use [____] as the common denominator.

$\dfrac{2}{3} = \dfrac{2 \cdot \square}{3 \cdot \square} = \dfrac{\square}{\square}$

$-\dfrac{7}{7} \,\square\, -\dfrac{3}{7}$ and $\dfrac{21}{84} \,\square\, \dfrac{56}{84},$ so $-1 \,\square\, -\dfrac{3}{7} \,\square\, \dfrac{1}{4} \,\square\, \dfrac{2}{3}.$

Quick Check

1. Use multiples to find the LCM.
   a. $3, 4$ [____]   **b.** $4, 5$ [____]   **c.** $3, 4, 5$ [____]

2. Use prime factorization to find the LCM.
   a. $6, 16$ [____]   **b.** $9, 15$ [____]   **c.** $12, 15, 18$ [____]

3. Find the LCM.
   a. $12x, 15xy$ **b.** $8m^2, 14m^4$ **c.** $25y^2, 15x$

[____]

4. Compare the fractions in each pair.
   a. $\dfrac{6}{7} \,\square\, \dfrac{4}{5}$ **b.** $\dfrac{2}{3} \,\square\, \dfrac{3}{4}$ **c.** $-\dfrac{3}{4} \,\square\, -\dfrac{7}{10}$

5. Order from least to greatest.
   a. $\dfrac{2}{3}, \dfrac{1}{6}, \dfrac{5}{12}$ [____]   **b.** $\dfrac{3}{10}, \dfrac{1}{5}, \dfrac{1}{2}, \dfrac{7}{12}$ [____]

Lesson 5-2   **Fractions and Decimals**

Lesson Objectives	NAEP 2005 Strand: Number Properties and Operations
▼ Write fractions as decimals ▼ Write terminating and repeating decimals as fractions	Topic: Number Sense Local Standards: _____

Vocabulary

A terminating decimal is _____

A repeating decimal is _____

Examples

❶ **Writing Fractions as Decimals** Write each fraction as a decimal. State the block of digits that repeats.

a. $\frac{5}{6}$ $5 \div 6 =$ [   ]   **Divide.**

                    $=$ [   ]   **Place a bar over the digit that repeats.**

         $\frac{5}{6} =$ [   ]; the digit that repeats is [   ].

b. $\frac{7}{11}$ $7 \div 11 =$ [   ]   **Divide.**

                    $=$ [   ]   **Place a bar over the block of digits that repeats.**

         $\frac{7}{11} =$ [   ]; the block of digits that repeats is [   ].

❷ **Writing a Decimal as a Fraction** Write 1.72 as a mixed number in simplest form.

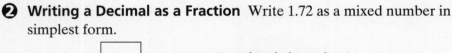

$1.72 = 1\dfrac{\boxed{}}{\boxed{}}$ **Keep the whole number 1.**
Write seventy-two hundredths as a fraction.

$= 1\dfrac{\boxed{} \div \boxed{}}{\boxed{} \div \boxed{}}$ **Divide the numerator and denominator.**
of the fraction by the GCF, [   ].

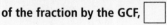

$= \boxed{}\dfrac{\boxed{}}{\boxed{}}$ **Simplify.**

Name_____ Class_____ Date _____

Example

❸ Writing a Repeating Decimal as a Fraction Write $0.\overline{18}$ as a fraction in simplest form.

$$n = 0.\overline{18}$$

Let the variable *n* equal the decimal.

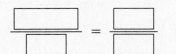 $n = $ ☐

Because ☐ digits repeat, multiply each side by 10^2, or ☐ .

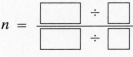 $n = $ ☐

$$-n = -0.\overline{18}$$

☐ = ☐

The Subtraction Property of Equality lets you subtract the same value from each side of the equation. So, subtract to eliminate $0.\overline{18}$.

Divide each side by ☐ .

$$n = \frac{☐ \div ☐}{☐ \div ☐}$$

Divide the numerator and denominator by the GCF, ☐ .

$$= \frac{☐}{☐}$$

Simplify.

As a fraction in simplest form, $0.\overline{18} = \dfrac{☐}{☐}$.

Quick Check

1. Write each fraction as a decimal. State whether the decimal is *terminating* or *repeating*. If the decimal repeats, state the block of digits that repeats.

   a. $\frac{7}{9}$ [   ]   **b.** $\frac{21}{22}$ [   ]

   c. $\frac{11}{8}$ [   ]   **d.** $\frac{8}{11}$ [   ]

2. Write as a fraction or a mixed number in simplest form.
   a. 1.75    **b.** 0.65

3. Write each decimal as a fraction in simplest form.
   a. $0.\overline{7}$    **b.** $0.\overline{54}$ [   ]

Lesson 5-3

Adding and Subtracting Fractions

Lesson Objectives	**NAEP 2005 Strand:** Number Properties and Operations
▼ Add and subtract fractions	**Topic:** Number Operations
▼ Add and subtract mixed numbers	**Local Standards:** _____

Examples

① **Like Denominators** Find each sum or difference. Simplify if possible.

a.
$$\frac{4}{9} + \frac{2}{9} = \frac{\boxed{} + \boxed{}}{9}$$ **Add the numerators.**

$$= \frac{\boxed{}}{\boxed{}}$$ **Simplify.**

$$= \frac{\boxed{}}{\boxed{}}$$ **Write in simplest form.**

b.
$$\frac{12}{b} - \frac{5}{b} = \frac{\boxed{} - \boxed{}}{\boxed{}}$$ **Subtract the numerators.**

$$= \frac{\boxed{}}{\boxed{}}$$ **Simplify.**

② **Unlike Denominators** Simplify each difference.

a.
$$\frac{1}{6} - \frac{3}{4} = \frac{\boxed{} \cdot \boxed{} - \boxed{} \cdot \boxed{}}{\boxed{} \cdot \boxed{}}$$ **Rewrite using a common denominator.**

$$= \frac{\boxed{} - \boxed{}}{\boxed{}}$$ **Use the Order of Operations to simplify.**

$$= \frac{\boxed{}}{\boxed{}}$$ **Simplify.**

$$= -\frac{\boxed{}}{\boxed{}}$$ **Write in simplest form.**

b.
$$\frac{2}{y} - \frac{5}{16} = \frac{\boxed{} \cdot \boxed{} - \boxed{} \cdot \boxed{}}{\boxed{} \cdot \boxed{}}$$ **Rewrite using a common denominator.**

$$= \frac{\boxed{} - \boxed{}}{\boxed{}}$$ **Simplify.**

Quick Check

1. Find the sum or difference. Simplify if possible.

a. $\dfrac{3}{7} + \dfrac{1}{7} = \boxed{}$ **b.** $\dfrac{2}{k} + \dfrac{3}{k} = \boxed{}$ **c.** $\dfrac{11}{y} + \left(-\dfrac{5}{y}\right) = \boxed{}$

Name_____ Class_____ Date _____

Example

③ Adding Mixed Numbers Suppose one day you rode a bicycle for $3\frac{1}{2}$ hours and jogged for $1\frac{1}{4}$ hours. How many hours did you exercise?

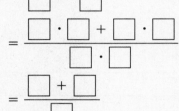

Write mixed numbers as improper fractions.

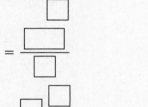

Rewrite using a common denominator.

Use the Order of Operations to simplify.

Add.

Write as a mixed number.

Simplify.

You exercised for ⬜ hours.

Quick Check

2. Simplify each sum or difference.

a. $\frac{2}{3} - \frac{1}{5}$

b. $-\frac{7}{8} + \frac{3}{4}$

c. $\frac{3}{7} - \frac{2}{m}$

d. $5\frac{3}{4} + \frac{7}{8}$

e. $5\frac{2}{3} - 3\frac{1}{6}$

f. $2\frac{3}{8} + \frac{7}{8}$

3. A recipe for punch calls for $1\frac{1}{2}$ qt of orange juice, $1\frac{1}{4}$ qt of ginger ale, and $\frac{3}{4}$ qt of cranberry juice. How many quarts of punch will the recipe make?

Lesson 5-4

Multiplying and Dividing Fractions

Lesson Objectives	**NAEP 2005 Strand:** Number Properties and Operations
▼ Multiply fractions ▼ Divide fractions	**Topic:** Number Operations **Local Standards:** _____

Vocabulary

Reciprocals are _____

_____

Example

1 Multiplying Fractions

a. Find $\frac{3}{4} \cdot \frac{2}{3}$.

b. Find $\frac{5}{w} \cdot \frac{3w}{17}$.

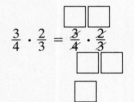

$$\frac{3}{4} \cdot \frac{2}{3} = \frac{\cancel{3}}{4} \cdot \frac{\cancel{2}}{\cancel{3}}$$

Divide common factors.

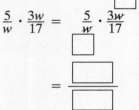

$$\frac{5}{w} \cdot \frac{3w}{17} = \frac{5}{\cancel{w}} \cdot \frac{3\cancel{w}}{17}$$

$$= \frac{\square}{\square}$$

Multiply.

$$= \frac{\square}{\square}$$

Quick Check

1. Find each product. Simplify if possible.

a. $\frac{2}{3} \cdot \frac{6}{7}$

b. $-\frac{5}{15} \cdot \frac{21}{25}$

c. $\frac{2x}{9} \cdot \frac{3}{4}$

d. $3\frac{3}{4} \cdot \frac{2}{5}$

e. $\frac{2}{3} \cdot 1\frac{2}{7}$

f. $\left(-2\frac{5}{6}\right) \cdot 1\frac{3}{5}$

Name_____ Class_____ Date _____

Examples

❷ Dividing Fractions

a. Find $\frac{3}{5} \div \frac{7}{10}$.

$\frac{3}{5} \div \frac{7}{10} = \frac{3}{5} \cdot \frac{\boxed{}}{\boxed{}}$ **Multiply by the reciprocal of the divisor.**

$= \frac{3}{\boxed{}\!\!5} \cdot \frac{10^{\boxed{}}}{7}$ **Divide the common factors.**

$= \frac{\boxed{}}{\boxed{}}$ **Multiply. Simplify if necessary.**

b. Find $\frac{27}{8m} \div \frac{9}{4m}$.

$\frac{27}{8m} \div \frac{9}{4m} = \frac{27}{8m} \cdot \frac{\boxed{}}{\boxed{}}$

$= \frac{27^{\boxed{}}}{8m_{\boxed{}}} \cdot \frac{4m^{\boxed{}}}{9_{\boxed{}}}$

$= \frac{\boxed{}}{\boxed{}}, \text{ or } \boxed{}\frac{\boxed{}}{\boxed{}}$

❸ Dividing Mixed Numbers Find $4\frac{1}{2} \div \left(-3\frac{3}{8}\right)$.

$4\frac{1}{2} \div \left(-3\frac{3}{8}\right) = \frac{9}{2} \div \left(-\frac{\boxed{}}{\boxed{}}\right)$ **Change to improper fractions.**

$= \frac{9}{2} \cdot \left(-\frac{\boxed{}}{\boxed{}}\right)$ **Multiply by** $-\dfrac{\boxed{}}{\boxed{}}$**, the reciprocal of** $-\frac{27}{8}$**.**

$= \frac{9^{\boxed{}}}{2_{\boxed{}}} \cdot -\frac{8^{\boxed{}}}{27_{\boxed{}}}$ **Divide the common factors.**

$= -\frac{\boxed{}}{\boxed{}}, \text{ or } -\boxed{}\frac{\boxed{}}{\boxed{}}$ **Simplify.**

Quick Check

2. Find each quotient. Simplify if possible.

a. $-\frac{1}{4} \div \frac{1}{2}$

b. $\frac{5a}{8} \div \frac{2}{3}$

c. $\frac{3b}{7} \div \frac{6}{7}$

d. $1\frac{1}{3} \div \frac{5}{6}$

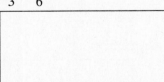

e. $-1\frac{3}{5} \div 1\frac{1}{5}$

f. $12\frac{1}{2} \div 1\frac{2}{3}$

Lesson 5-5

Using Customary Units of Measurement

Lesson Objectives	NAEP 2005 Strand: Measurement
▼ Identify appropriate customary units	**Topic:** Systems of Measurement
▼ Convert customary units	**Local Standards:** _____

Vocabulary

Dimensional analysis is _____

_____

Customary Units of Measure

Type	Length	Capacity	Weight
Unit	Inch (in.) Foot (ft) Yard (yd) Mile (mi)	Fluid ounce (fl oz) Cup (c) Pint (pt) Quart (qt) Gallon (gal)	Ounce (oz) Pound (lb) Ton (t)
Equivalents	1 ft = ☐ in. 1 yd = ☐ ft 1 mi = ☐ ft = ☐ yd	1 c = ☐ fl oz 1 pt = ☐ c 1 qt = ☐ pt 1 gal = ☐ qt	1 lb = ☐ oz 1 t = ☐ lb

Example

❶ Choosing a Unit of Measure Choose an appropriate unit of measure.
Explain your choice.

a. weight of a hummingbird

Measure its weight in [   ] because a hummingbird is very light.

b. length of a soccer field

Measure its length in [   ] because it is too long to measure in

[   ] or [   ] and too short to measure in [   ].

Quick Check

1. Choose an appropriate unit of measure. Explain.

   a. length of a swimming pool   **b.** capacity of an eyedropper

Name_____ Class_____ Date _____

Examples

❷ **Using Dimensional Analysis** Use dimensional analysis to convert 68 fluid ounces to cups.

$68 \text{ fl oz.} = \dfrac{68 \text{ fl oz.}}{1} \cdot \dfrac{1 \text{ c}}{\boxed{} \text{ fl oz.}}$ **Use a conversion factor that changes fluid ounces to cups.**

$= \dfrac{68 \text{ fl oz.} \cdot 1 \text{ c}}{8 \text{ fl oz.}}$ **Divide the common factors and units.**

$= \dfrac{\boxed{}}{\boxed{}} \text{ c}$ **Simplify.**

$= \boxed{} \dfrac{\boxed{}}{\boxed{}} \text{ c}$ **Write as a mixed number.**

There are $\boxed{}$ c in 68 fl oz.

❸ Fred's Fruit stand sells homemade lemonade in $6\frac{1}{2}$-pint bottles for $1.99. Jill's fruit stand sells homemade lemonade in $3\frac{1}{2}$-qt containers for the same price. At which stand do you get more lemonade for your money?

$3\frac{1}{2} \text{ qt} = \dfrac{7}{2} \text{ qt} \cdot \dfrac{\boxed{} \text{ pt}}{1 \text{ qt}}$ **Use a conversion factor that changes quarts to pints.**

$= \dfrac{7 \text{ qt}}{2} \cdot \dfrac{2 \text{ pt}}{1 \text{ qt}}$ **Divide the common factors and units.**

$= \boxed{} \text{ pt}$ **Multiply.**

Since $\boxed{}$ pints $\boxed{}$ $6\frac{1}{2}$ pints, you get more lemonade for your money at $\boxed{}$ stand.

Quick Check

2. Complete each equation.

a. 14 oz = $\boxed{}$

= $\boxed{}$ lb

b. 14 in. = $\boxed{}$

= $\boxed{}$ ft

c. $3\frac{1}{2}$ yd = $\boxed{}$

= $\boxed{}$ ft

d. $3\frac{1}{2}$ pt = $\boxed{}$

= $\boxed{}$ c

Lesson 5-6

Work Backward

Lesson Objective	NAEP 2005 Strand: Number Properties and Operations
▼ Solve problems by working backward	Topic: Number Operations
	Local Standards: _____

Example

1 **Travel** Your flight leaves the airport at 10:00 A.M. You must arrive 2 hours early to check your luggage. The drive to the airport takes about 90 minutes. A stop for breakfast takes about 30 minutes. It will take about 15 minutes to park and get to the terminal. At what time should you leave home?

Understand the Problem

Think about the information you are given.

1. What do you want to find?

2. What is your arrival time?

3. How much time will you spend driving to the airport?

4. How much time will you spend eating breakfast?

5. How much time will you spend parking and getting to the terminal?

Make and Carry Out a Plan

You know that the series of events must end at 10:00 A.M. Work backward to find when the events must begin.

Redraw the hands of the clock to find the time you should leave home.

Write the starting time for each event.

Flight leaves

Arrive at airport

Park

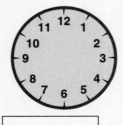

_____ A.M.   _____ A.M.   _____ A.M.

Daily Notetaking Guide

Name_____ Class_____ Date _____

Breakfast   Leave home

   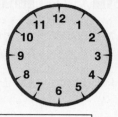

[_____] A.M.   [_____] A.M.

You should leave home at [_____]

(Check the Answer)

Check the departure time. Find the total time needed.

90 min + 30 min + 15 min + 120 min = [_____] min

Add [_____] minutes to your departure time.

5:45 + 0:255 = 5: 300

5:[_____]   [_____] min = [_____] h

5:[_____] = [_____] hours after 5:00, or [_____]

Since your flight leaves at 10:00 A.M., your departure time is correct.

Quick Check

1. Suppose you find out the night before that the flight is delayed until 11:15 A.M. What time should you leave home?

[   ]

Lesson 5-7

Solving Equations by Adding or Subtracting Fractions

Lesson Objectives	NAEP 2005 Strand: Number Properties and Operations
▼ Solve equations by subtracting fractions ▼ Solve equations by adding fractions	**Topic:** Number Operations **Local Standards:** _____

Example

① **Solving by Subtracting** One school recycles about $\frac{1}{3}$ of its waste paper. The student council set a goal of recycling $\frac{3}{4}$ of the school's waste paper by the end of the year. By how much does the school need to increase its paper recycling to reach the goal?

Words ⟶ | fraction school recycles | plus | the increase | is | student goal |

Let $\boxed{n}$ = the increase.

Equation $\dfrac{\square}{\square} \quad + \quad \boxed{n} \quad = \quad \dfrac{\square}{\square}$

$$\frac{1}{3} + n = \frac{3}{4}$$

$\dfrac{1}{3} - \dfrac{\square}{\square} + n = \dfrac{3}{4} - \dfrac{\square}{\square}$ **Subtract** $\dfrac{\square}{\square}$ **from each side.**

$n = \dfrac{3 \cdot \square - \square \cdot 4}{\square \cdot \square}$ **Use** $\square \cdot \square$ **as the common denominator.**

$n = \dfrac{\square - \square}{\square}$ **Use the Order of Operations.**

$n = \dfrac{\square}{\square}$ **Simplify.**

To meet the student council goal, the school needs to recycle $\dfrac{\square}{\square}$ more of its waste paper.

Check Is the answer reasonable? The present fraction of paper waste that is recycled plus the increase must equal the goal. Since

$$\frac{1}{3} + \frac{5}{12} = \frac{4}{12} + \frac{5}{12} = \boxed{} = \boxed{} \text{, the answer is}$$

reasonable.

Example

❷ **Solving by Adding** Solve $q - 6\frac{1}{2} = -1\frac{3}{5}$.

$$q - 6\frac{1}{2} = -1\frac{3}{5}$$

$q - 6\frac{1}{2} + \boxed{}\dfrac{\boxed{}}{\boxed{}} = -1\frac{3}{5} + \boxed{}\dfrac{\boxed{}}{\boxed{}}$ **Add** $\boxed{}\dfrac{\boxed{}}{\boxed{}}$ **to each side.**

$q = -\dfrac{\boxed{}}{\boxed{}} + \dfrac{\boxed{}}{\boxed{}}$ **Write mixed numbers as improper fractions.**

$q = \dfrac{-8 \cdot \boxed{} + 5 \cdot \boxed{}}{\boxed{} \cdot \boxed{}}$ **Use** $\boxed{} \cdot \boxed{}$ **as the common denominator.**

$q = \dfrac{\boxed{} + \boxed{}}{\boxed{}}$ **Use the Order of Operations.**

$q = \dfrac{\boxed{}}{\boxed{}}$ **Simplify.**

$q = \boxed{}\dfrac{\boxed{}}{\boxed{}}$ **Write as a mixed number.**

Quick Check

1. Solve and check each equation.

a. $y + \frac{8}{9} = \frac{5}{9}$

b. $\frac{2}{3} = u + \frac{3}{5}$

c. $a - \frac{3}{5} = \frac{1}{5}$

d. $\frac{6}{7} = x - \frac{2}{7}$

e. $c - 2\frac{1}{6} = 5\frac{1}{4}$

f. $3\frac{7}{18} = z + 1\frac{1}{3}$

Lesson 5-8   Solving Equations by Multiplying Fractions

Lesson Objectives	NAEP 2005 Strand: Algebra
▼ Solve equations by multiplying fractions	Topic: Equations and Inequalities
② Solve equations by multiplying mixed numbers	Local Standards: _____

Examples

❶ Multiplying by a Reciprocal Solve $7y = \frac{1}{3}$.

$$7y = \frac{1}{3}$$

$$\frac{\square}{\square} \cdot (7y) = \frac{\square}{\square} \cdot \frac{1}{3}$$ **Multiply each side by** $\frac{\square}{\square}$**, the reciprocal of 7.**

$$y = \frac{\square}{\square}$$ **Simplify.**

❷ Multiplying by the Negative Reciprocal Solve $-\frac{20}{27}c = \frac{4}{9}$.

$$-\frac{20}{27}c = \frac{4}{9}$$

$$-\frac{\square}{\square}\left(-\frac{20}{27}c\right) = -\frac{\square}{\square}\left(\frac{4}{9}\right)$$ **Multiply each side by** $-\frac{\square}{\square}$**, the reciprocal of** $-\frac{20}{27}$**.**

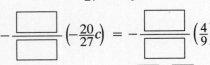

$$c = -\frac{27 \cdot 4}{20 \cdot 9}$$ **Divide common factors.**

$$c = -\frac{\square}{\square}$$ **Simplify.**

Quick Check

1. Solve each equation.

    a. $2y = \frac{7}{9}$ **b.** $3a = \frac{4}{5}$ **c.** $\frac{2}{9}t = \frac{5}{6}$

Example

❸ Using Mixed Numbers How many $2\frac{1}{2}$-t trucks can you place on a rail car

that has a carrying capacity of 15 t?

Words

| weight of each truck | times | the number of trucks | is | carrying capacity |

Let $\boxed{n}$ = the number of trucks.

Equation $\cdot$ $\boxed{n}$ = $\boxed{}$

$2\frac{1}{2} \cdot n = 15$

$\dfrac{\boxed{}}{\boxed{}} n = 15$ **Write $2\frac{1}{2}$ as improper fraction.**

$\dfrac{\boxed{}}{\boxed{}} \cdot \dfrac{5}{2}n = \dfrac{\boxed{}}{\boxed{}} \cdot 15$ **Multiply each side by $\dfrac{\boxed{}}{\boxed{}}$, the reciprocal of $\dfrac{5}{2}$.**

$n = \dfrac{2 \cdot \cancel{15}^{\boxed{}}}{\cancel{5}_{\boxed{}} \cdot 1}$ **Divide common factors.**

$n = \boxed{}$ **Simplify.**

You can place $\boxed{}$ trucks on the rail car.

Quick Check

2. Solve each equation.

   a. $-\frac{6}{7}r = \frac{3}{4}$ **b.** $-\frac{10}{13}b = -\frac{2}{3}$ **c.** $-6n = \frac{3}{7}$

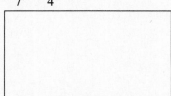   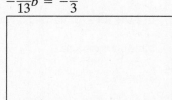 

   d. $3\frac{1}{2}n = 28$ **e.** $-\frac{7}{20} = 1\frac{1}{6}r$ **f.** $-2\frac{3}{4}h = -12\frac{1}{2}$

Lesson 5-9

Powers of Products and Quotients

Lesson Objectives	NAEP 2005 Strand: Algebra
▼ Find powers of products	**Topic:** Variables, Expressions, and Operations
▼ Find powers of quotients	**Local Standards:** _____

Key Concepts

Raising a Product to a Power

To raise a product to a power, raise each factor to the power.

Arithmetic

$(5 \cdot 3)^4 = 5^{\boxed{}} \cdot 3^{\boxed{}}$

Algebra

$(ab)^m = a^{\boxed{}} b^{\boxed{}}$ for any positive integer m

Raising a Quotient to a Power

To raise a quotient to a power, raise both the numerator and denominator to the power.

Arithmetic

$\left(\dfrac{2}{3}\right)^4 = \dfrac{2^{\boxed{}}}{3^{\boxed{}}}$

Algebra

$\left(\dfrac{a}{b}\right)^m = \dfrac{a^{\boxed{}}}{b^{\boxed{}}}$, for $b \neq 0$ and any positive integer m

Example

1 **Simplifying a Power of a Product** Simplify $(3z^5)^4$.

$(3z^5)^4 = 3^{\boxed{}} \cdot \left(\boxed{}\right)^{\boxed{}}$ **Raise each factor to the fourth power.**

$= 3^4 \cdot z^{\boxed{}} \cdot \boxed{}$ **Use the Rule for Raising a Power to a Power.**

$= 3^4 \cdot \boxed{}$ **Multiply exponents.**

$= \boxed{}$ **Simplify.**

Quick Check

1. Simplify each expression.

a. $(2(3))^3$ **b.** $(2p)^4$ **c.** $(xy^2)^5$ **d.** $(5x^3)^2$

          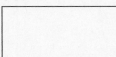   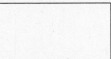

Name_____ Class_____ Date _____

Examples

❷ Working With a Negative Sign

a. Simplify $(-3a)^4$.

$(-3a)^4 = (-3)^{\square}(a)^{\square}$

$\qquad = \boxed{}$

b. Simplify $-(3a)^4$.

$-(3a)^4 = (-1)(3a)^{\square}$

$\qquad = (-1)(3)^{\square}(a)^{\square}$

$\qquad = \boxed{}$

❸ Geometry Find the area of a square with side length $\frac{x}{4}$.

$A = s^2 \qquad\qquad$ **s = length of a side.**

$\quad = \left(\frac{x}{4}\right)^2 \qquad$ **Substitute $\dfrac{\square}{\square}$ for s.**

$\quad = \dfrac{\square}{\square}$

$\quad = \dfrac{\square}{\square}$

The area of the square is $\boxed{}$ square units.

Quick Check

2. Simplify each expression.

a. $(-2y)^4$

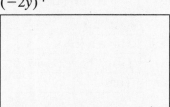

b. $-(2y)^4$

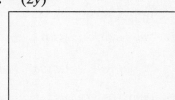

c. $(-5a^2b)^3$

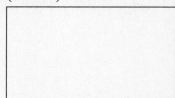

3. Simplify each expression.

a. $\left(\frac{1}{2}\right)^3$

b. $\left(-\frac{2}{3}\right)^4$

c. $\left(\frac{2x^2}{3}\right)^3$

Lesson 6-1

Ratios and Unit Rates

Lesson Objectives	**NAEP 2005 Strand:** Number Properties and Operations
▼ 1 Write and simplify ratios	**Topic:** Ratios and Proportional Reasoning
▼ 2 Find rates and unit rates	**Local Standards:** _____

Vocabulary and Key Concepts

Ratio

A ratio is _____

_____

	Arithmetic			**Algebra**		
10 to 15	[____]	$\dfrac{}{}$		[____]	[____]	$\dfrac{a}{b}$, for $b \neq 0$

A rate is _____

_____

A unit rate is _____

_____

Examples

❶ **Surveys** A survey asks students whether they had after-school jobs. Write each ratio as a fraction in simplest form.

After-School Jobs

Response	Number
Have a job	40
Don't have a job	60
Total	100

a. all students surveyed to students without jobs

$$\frac{\text{all students surveyed}}{\text{students without jobs}} = \frac{100}{\boxed{}}$$

$$= \frac{\boxed{}}{\boxed{}}$$

b. all students surveyed to students with jobs.

$$\frac{\text{all students surveyed}}{\text{students with jobs}} = \frac{100}{\boxed{}}$$

$$= \frac{\boxed{}}{\boxed{}}$$

Name_____ Class_____ Date _____

❷ Unit Cost The table shows prices for different packages of index card. What size has the lowest unit cost?

Size (cards)	Price
100	$2.70
50	$1.30
25	$.75

100 cards: $\dfrac{\text{price}}{\text{number of cards}}$ → $\dfrac{270}{100 \text{ cards}} = \dfrac{¢27}{\text{card}}$

50 cards: $\dfrac{\text{price}}{\text{number of cards}}$ → $\dfrac{1.30}{50 \text{ cards}} = \dfrac{¢25}{\text{card}}$ **Find the unit costs.**

25 cards: $\dfrac{\text{price}}{\text{number of cards}}$ → $\dfrac{.75}{25 \text{ cards}} = \dfrac{\boxed{}}{\text{card}}$

The $\boxed{}$-card pack has the lowest unit cost.

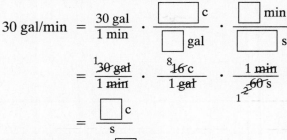

❸ Converting a Rate Convert 30 gal/min to cups/second.

$30 \text{ gal/min} = \dfrac{30 \text{ gal}}{1 \text{ min}} \cdot \dfrac{\boxed{}\,c}{\boxed{}\,gal} \cdot \dfrac{\boxed{}\,min}{\boxed{}\,s}$ **Use conversion factors that convert gallons to cups and minutes to seconds.**

$= \dfrac{\overset{1}{\cancel{30 \text{ gal}}}}{1 \cancel{\text{ min}}} \cdot \dfrac{\overset{8}{\cancel{16}}\,c}{1 \cancel{\text{ gal}}} \cdot \dfrac{1 \cancel{\text{ min}}}{\underset{2}{\cancel{60}}\,s}$ **Divide the common factors and units.**

$= \dfrac{\boxed{}\,c}{s}$ **Simplify.**

30 gal/min equals $\boxed{}$ c/s.

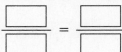

Quick Check

1. Using the data from Example 1, write each ratio as a fraction in simplest form.

   a. students with jobs to all students surveyed

$$\dfrac{\boxed{}}{\boxed{}} = \dfrac{\boxed{}}{\boxed{}}$$

   b. students without jobs to students with jobs

$$\dfrac{\boxed{}}{\boxed{}} = \dfrac{\boxed{}}{\boxed{}}$$

2. Find each unit rate.

   a. Two liters of spring water cost $1.98.

   b. A car goes 425 mi on 12.5 gal of gas.

3. Complete each statement.

   a. 3.5 qt/min = $\boxed{}$ gal/h

   b. 12 cm/s = $\boxed{}$ m/h

Lesson 6-2

Proportions

Lesson Objectives	NAEP 2005 Strand: Number Properties and Operations
▼ Solve proportions	**Topic:** Ratios and Proportional Reasoning
▼ Use proportions to solve problems	**Local Standards:** _____

Vocabulary and Key Concepts

Cross Products

In a proportion, the cross products are [   ].

Arithmetic   **Algebra**

$6 \cdot$ [   ] $= 9 \cdot$ [   ] $=$ [   ] $ad =$ [   ]

A proportion is _____

The cross products of the proportion $\frac{a}{b} = \frac{c}{d}$ are [   ] and [   ].

Examples

❶ Multiplying to Solve a Proportion Solve $\frac{2}{7} = \frac{y}{14}$.

Method 1 Multiplication Property of Equality

$$\frac{2}{7} = \frac{y}{14}$$

$\frac{2}{7} \cdot$ [   ] $= \frac{y}{14} \cdot 14$ **Multiply each side by** [   ].

$\dfrac{[\ \ ]}{[\ \ ]} = y$ **Multiply.**

[   ] $= y$ **Simplify.**

Method 2 Cross Products

$$\frac{2}{7} = \frac{y}{14}$$

$2 \cdot$ [   ] $= 7 \cdot$ [   ]   **Write cross products.**

$28 = 7y$ **Multiply.**

$\dfrac{28}{[\ \ ]} = \dfrac{7y}{[\ \ ]}$ **Divide each side by** [   ].

[   ] $= y$ **Simplify.**

Name_____ Class_____ Date _____

❷ Testing for a Proportion Do the ratios $\frac{3}{5}$ and $\frac{21}{35}$ form a proportion? Explain.

$\frac{3}{5} \overset{?}{=} \frac{21}{35}$ **Test by writing as a proportion.**

$3 \cdot$ [____] $\overset{?}{=} 5 \cdot$ [____]   **Write cross products.**

[____] $=$ [____]   **Simplify.**

The ratios [____] form a proportion. The [____] are equal.

❸ Measurement One hundred rods is about 275 fathoms. To the nearest fathom, how many fathoms is 25 rods?

Let d = distance in fathoms.

$$\frac{\text{length in rods} \;\rightarrow}{\text{length in fathoms} \;\rightarrow} \frac{[\quad]}{[\quad]} = \frac{[\quad]}{[\quad]} \begin{array}{l} \leftarrow \;\text{distance in rods} \\ \leftarrow \;\text{distance in fathoms} \end{array}$$

$100d = 275(25)$ **Write cross products.**

$d = \dfrac{275(25)}{[\quad]}$ **Divide each side by** [____].

$d \approx$ [____]   **A calculator may be useful.**

25 rods is about [____] fathoms.

Quick Check

1. Solve each proportion.

    a. $\frac{h}{9} = \frac{2}{3}$ **b.** $\frac{4}{5} = \frac{t}{55}$ **c.** $\frac{22}{d} = \frac{6}{21}$

   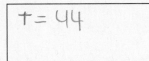 $t = 44$ 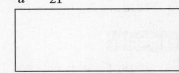

2. Tell whether the two ratios form a proportion. Explain.

    a. $\frac{6}{9}, \frac{4}{6}$ **b.** $\frac{15}{20}, \frac{5}{7}$ **c.** $\frac{7}{12}, \frac{17.5}{30}$

   yes      no   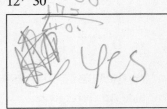   yes

3. To the nearest rod, about how many rods is 100 fathoms?

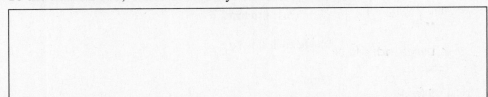

Lesson 6-3

Similar Figures and Scale Drawings

Lesson Objectives	**NAEP 2005 Strands:** Geometry; Measurement
▼ Solve problems that involve similar figures	**Topics:** Transformation of Shapes and Preservation of Properties; Systems of Measurement
❷ Solve problems that involve scale drawings	**Local Standards:** _____

Vocabulary and Key Concepts

Similar Figures

Similar figures have two properties:

- The corresponding angles have ⟨same/equal⟩ measures.

- The lengths of corresponding sides are in ⟨proportions⟩

Similar figures have _the same shape but not the same size_

Indirect measurement is _a process that involves using similar figures to compute distances that are difficult to measure_

A scale drawing is _____

The symbol ~ means _similar (□abcd ~ □efgh)_

Examples

❶ **Using Similar Figures** Trapezoid $ABCD$ ~ trapezoid $EFGH$. Find the value of k.

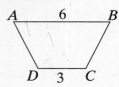   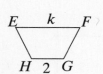

Write a proportion for corresponding sides.

Side $\overline{AB}$ corresponds to side ⟨ef⟩ . $\dfrac{6}{\boxed{k}} = \dfrac{3}{\boxed{2}}$ **Side $\overline{CD}$ corresponds to side** ⟨HG⟩ .

$6 \cdot \boxed{2} = k \cdot \boxed{3}$ **Write cross products.**

$\dfrac{6 \cdot 2}{\boxed{3}} = \dfrac{3k}{\boxed{3}}$ **Divide each side by** ⟨3⟩ .

$\boxed{4} = k$ **Simplify.**

Name_____ Class_____ Date _____

❷ A flagpole casts a shadow 5 ft long. At the same time, a yardstick casts a
shadow 1.5 ft long. The triangle shown for the flagpole and its shadow is
similar to the triangle shown for the yardstick and its shadow. How tall
is the flagpole?

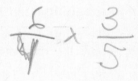

3 ft

1.5 ft   5 ft

$$\frac{1.5}{\boxed{5}} = \frac{3}{\boxed{x}}$$ **Corresponding sides of similar triangles
are in** $\boxed{1.5 \times 3 \times 5}$.

$$\boxed{1.5}\, x = \boxed{3} \cdot \boxed{5}$$ **Write cross products.**

$$\frac{1.5x}{\boxed{1.5}} = \frac{5 \cdot 3}{\boxed{1.5}}$$ **Divide each side by** $\boxed{1.5}$.

$$x = \boxed{10}$$ **Simplify.**

The flagpole is $\boxed{10}$ ft tall.

❸ **Scale Drawings** The scale of a map is 1 in. : 24 mi. About how far is it
between two cities that are 3 in. apart on the map?

$$\begin{array}{c}\text{map (in.)} \rightarrow \\ \text{actual (mi)} \rightarrow\end{array} \frac{1}{\boxed{24}} = \frac{3}{\boxed{d}} \begin{array}{c}\leftarrow \text{map (in.)} \\ \leftarrow \text{actual (mi)}\end{array}$$ **Write a proportion.**

$$1 \cdot d = \boxed{24} \cdot \boxed{3}$$ **Write cross products.**

$$d = \boxed{72}$$ **Simplify.**

It is about $\boxed{72}$ mi between the two cities.

$\frac{6}{4} \times \frac{3}{5}$

30

Quick Check

1. Trapezoid *KLMN* is similar to trapezoid *ABCD* in Example 1.
Find the value of *y*.

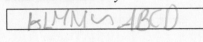
KLMN ∾ ABCD   y = 10

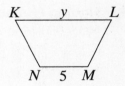
K   *y*   *L*

N   5   *M*

2. A building 70 ft high casts a 150-ft shadow. A nearby flagpole casts a 60-ft
shadow. Draw a diagram. Use similar triangles to find the height of the
flagpole.

3. The distance from Atlanta to Macon is about 75 mi. On a map whose scale
is the same as the scale in Example 3, what is the approximate map distance
between these two cities?

$\frac{1}{24} \times \frac{x}{75}$

Lesson 6-4   Probability

Lesson Objectives	NAEP 2005 Strand: Data Analysis and Probability
▼ 1 Find probability	Topic: Probability
▼ 2 Find odds	Local Standards: _____

Vocabulary

Outcomes are _____

An event is _____

The probability of an event $= P(\text{event}) = \dfrac{\text{number of } \boxed{} \text{ outcomes}}{\text{number of } \boxed{} \text{ outcomes}}$

An impossible event has probability $\boxed{0}$. A certain event has probability $\boxed{1}$.

The complement of an event is _____

A part/part ratio, called odds, describes _____

Examples

❶ Finding Probability Find $P(\text{rolling a prime number})$ with one number cube.

$\dfrac{\text{number of favorable outcomes}}{\text{number of possible outcomes}} \quad \begin{array}{l} \rightarrow \ 3 \ \leftarrow \text{3 prime-number outcomes (2, 3, 5)} \\ \rightarrow \ 6 \ \leftarrow \text{6 possible outcomes} \end{array}$

$P(\text{rolling a prime number}) = \dfrac{\boxed{}}{\boxed{}}, \text{or } \dfrac{\boxed{}}{\boxed{}}.$

❷ Finding Probability The probability that a child is an identical twin is 4 in 1,000. Find $P(\text{not an identical twin})$.

$P(\text{not an identical twin}) + P(\text{identical twin}) = \boxed{}$ **Write an equation.**

$P(\text{not an identical twin}) + \dfrac{\boxed{}}{\boxed{}} = 1$ **Substitute.**

$P(\text{not an identical twin}) + \dfrac{4}{1,000} - \dfrac{\boxed{}}{\boxed{}} = 1 - \dfrac{\boxed{}}{\boxed{}}$ **Subtract** $\dfrac{\boxed{}}{\boxed{}}$ **from each side.**

$P(\text{not an identical twin}) = \dfrac{\boxed{}}{1,000}$ **Simplify.**

$= \dfrac{\boxed{}}{\boxed{}}$

The probability that a child is not an identical twin is $\dfrac{\boxed{}}{\boxed{}}$.

❸ **Odds** You have five different coins in your pocket: a penny, a nickel, a dime, a quarter, and a half-dollar. You pull out one coin at random. What are the odds in favor of the coin being worth less than ten cents?

odds in favor $= \dfrac{\boxed{}\ \leftarrow\ \boxed{}}{\boxed{}\ \leftarrow\ \boxed{}}$ **are worth less than ten cents.**

are not.

The odds are $\dfrac{\boxed{}}{\boxed{}}$, or $\boxed{}$ to $\boxed{}$, in favor of the coin being worth less than ten cents.

Quick Check

1. Find each probability for one roll of a number cube.

a. $P(\text{odd number})$ **b.** $P(2)$ **c.** $P(5 \text{ or } 6)$

 $\dfrac{3}{6} = \dfrac{1}{2}$ $\dfrac{1}{6}$ $\dfrac{2}{6} = \dfrac{1}{3}$

2. a. When you roll a number cube, what is $P(\text{not } 2)$?

 $\dfrac{5}{6}$

b. Reasoning What is the complement of an impossible event?

 1

3. You choose one coin at random from the five coins in Example 3 above.

a. What are the odds that it is silver?

b. What are the odds that it is not silver?

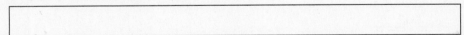

c. Consider the event that the coin is worth more than 15 cents.

i. What are the odds in favor of the event?

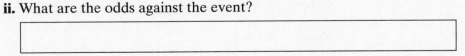

ii. What are the odds against the event?

Lesson 6-5

Fractions, Decimals, and Percents

Lesson Objectives	**NAEP 2005 Strand:** Number Properties and Operations
▼ Write percents as fractions and decimals	**Topic:** Number Sense
▼ Write decimals and fractions as percents	**Local Standards:** _____

Vocabulary

A percent is _____

Examples

❶ **Writing a Percent as a Fraction** Write each percent as a fraction or a mixed number.

a. 30%

$$\frac{30}{\boxed{100}}$$ **Write as a fraction with a denominator of** $\boxed{100}$.

$$\frac{\boxed{3}}{\boxed{10}}$$ **Simplify.**

b. 175%

$$\frac{175}{\boxed{100}}$$ **Write as a fraction with a denominator of** $\boxed{100}$.

$$\frac{\boxed{35}}{\boxed{20}}$$ **Simplify.**

$$\boxed{1}\frac{\boxed{13}}{\boxed{20}}$$ **Write as a mixed number.**

❷ **Writing a Percent as a Decimal** Express 7.3% as a decimal.

$$7.3\% = \frac{7.3}{\boxed{}}$$ **Write as a fraction with a denominator of** $\boxed{}$.

$$= 0\underset{\smile}{07}.3$$ **Divide a decimal by 100 by moving the decimal point** $\boxed{}$ **places to the left. You may need to write one or more zeros.**

$$= \boxed{}$$

❸ **Writing a Decimal as a Percent** Express 0.412 as a percent.

Method 1 Rewrite as a fraction.

$$0.412 = \frac{412}{\boxed{}}$$

$$= \frac{412 \div \boxed{}}{1{,}000 \div \boxed{}}$$ **Divide the numerator and the denominator by** $\boxed{}$ **to get a denominator of** $\boxed{}$.

$$= \frac{\boxed{}}{100}$$ **Simplify.**

$$= \boxed{}\%$$ **Write as a percent.**

Method 2 Move the decimal point.

$$0.\underset{\smile}{412} = \boxed{}\%$$ **Move the decimal point** $\boxed{}$ **places to the right to multiply by 100.**

Name_____ Class_____ Date _____

❹ Writing a Fraction as a Percent Four out of seven members of the chess club are boys. What percent of the chess club members are boys?

       Write a fraction.

$4 \div 7 \approx$ 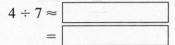   **Divide the numerator by the denominator.**

= [_____]   **Write as a percent.**

About [_____] of the chess club members are boys.

Quick Check

1. Write each percent as a fraction or mixed number in simplest form.

   a. 58%   **b.** 72%   **c.** 144%

      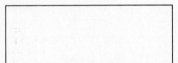   

2. Write each percent as a decimal.

   a. 16%   **b.** 62.5%   **c.** 120%

   d. Reasoning About 45% of the people in the United States have type O blood. Write this percent as a decimal and as a fraction in simplest form.

   .45   9/20

3. Write each decimal as a percent.

   a. 0.4   **b.** 0.023   **c.** 1.75

      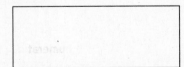   

4. Three out of eleven families in the United States own cats. To the nearest percent, what percent of families own cats?

   .27̄   27%

Lesson 6-6

Proportions and Percents

Lesson Objectives	NAEP 2005 Strand: Number Properties and Operations
▼ 1 Find a part of a whole and a percent	**Topic:** Ratios and Proportional Reasoning
▼ 2 Find a whole amount	**Local Standards:** _____

Key Concepts

Percents and Proportions

Finding the Percent

What percent of 40 is 6?

$$\frac{n}{100} = \frac{\boxed{}}{\boxed{}} \begin{array}{l} \leftarrow \text{part} \\ \\ \leftarrow \text{whole} \end{array}$$

Finding the Part

What number is 15% of 40?

$$\frac{15}{100} = \frac{\boxed{}}{\boxed{}} \begin{array}{l} \leftarrow \text{part} \\ \\ \leftarrow \text{whole} \end{array}$$

Finding the Whole

6 is 15% of what number?

$$\frac{15}{100} = \frac{\boxed{}}{\boxed{}} \begin{array}{l} \leftarrow \text{part} \\ \\ \leftarrow \text{whole} \end{array}$$

Examples

❶ Finding Part of a Whole Find 23% of 158.

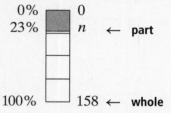

$$\frac{23}{100} = \frac{\boxed{}}{\boxed{}}$$ **Write a proportion.**

 **Write cross products.**

$$\frac{23(158)}{\boxed{}} = \frac{100n}{\boxed{}}$$ **Divide each side by** $\boxed{}$.

$$\boxed{} = n$$ **Simplify.**

23% of 158 is $\boxed{}$.

❷ Finding a Percent What percent of 34 is 28? Round to the nearest tenth of a percent.

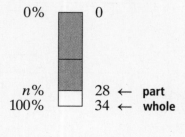

$$\frac{n}{100} = \frac{\boxed{}}{\boxed{}}$$ **Write a proportion.**

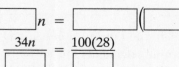 **Write cross products.**

$$\frac{34n}{\boxed{}} = \frac{100(28)}{\boxed{}}$$ **Divide each side by** $\boxed{}$.

$$n = \boxed{}$$ **Simplify.**

$$\approx \boxed{}$$ **Round to the nearest tenth.**

28 is approximately $\boxed{}$ % of 34.

Name_____ Class_____ Date _____

❸ Finding the Whole A tile floor has 90 blue tiles, which is 15% of all the tiles in the floor. How many tiles are in the floor in all?

$$\frac{15}{100} = \frac{\boxed{}}{\boxed{}}$$ **Write a proportion.**

$$\boxed{}\, x = \boxed{}\left(\boxed{}\right)$$ **Write cross products.**

$$\frac{15x}{\boxed{}} = \frac{100(90)}{\boxed{}}$$ **Divide each side by $\boxed{}$.**

$$x = \boxed{}$$ **Simplify.**

The floor has $\boxed{}$ tiles in all.

Check Is the answer reasonable? The problem says the number of blue tiles is 15%. 10% of 600 is $\boxed{}$, so 5% of 600 is $\boxed{}$, and 15% is $60 + 30 = \boxed{}$. The answer is reasonable.

Quick Check

1. **Draw a model and write a proportion. Then solve.**

   a. 25% of 124 is $\boxed{}$.

   b. 43% of 230 is $\boxed{}$.

   c. 12.5% of 80 is $\boxed{}$.

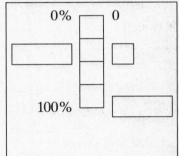
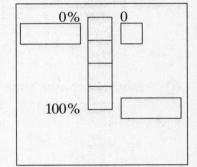

2. **Round to the nearest tenth.**

   a. What percent of 250 is 138?

   b. 14 is what percent of 15?

   c. 19 is 75% of what?

3. **Entertainment** In 2000, the number of drive-in movie screens was about 20.1% of the number in 1980. If there were 717 drive-in movie screens in 2000, about how many drive-in movie screens were there in 1980?

Lesson 6-7

Percents and Equations

Lesson Objectives	**NAEP 2005 Strand:** Number Properties and Operations
▼ Write and solve percent equations ▼ Use equations in solving percent problems	**Topic:** Ratios and Proportional Reasoning **Local Standards:** _____

Vocabulary and Key Concepts

Percent Equations

Finding the Percent	**Finding the Part**	**Finding the Whole**
What percent of 40 is 6?	What is 15% of 40?	6 is 15% of what?
$n \cdot 40 = \boxed{}$	$n = \boxed{} \cdot 40$	$\boxed{} = 0.15 \cdot n$

Commission is _____

Examples

❶ Solving a Percent Equation What is 35% of 84?

$n = \boxed{} \cdot \boxed{}$ **Write an equation. Write the percent as a decimal.**

$n = \boxed{}$ **Simplify.**

35% of 84 is $\boxed{}$.

❷ Percents Greater Than 100% What percent of 26 is 65?

$n \cdot \boxed{} = \boxed{}$ **Write an equation.**

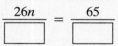 $\dfrac{26n}{\boxed{}} = \dfrac{65}{\boxed{}}$ **Divide each side by $\boxed{}$.**

 $n = \boxed{}$ **Simplify.**

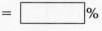 $= \boxed{}\%$ **Change the decimal to a percent.**

65 is $\boxed{}$% of 26.

Quick Check

Write and solve an equation.

1a. 0.96 is what percent of 10?   **b.** 19.2 is 32% of what?   **2.** What is 145.5% of 20?

Examples

❸ **Sales and Commission** A car salesman makes a 6.5% commission on each car he sells. How much does he make on the sale of a car for $35,000?

Words | Amount of commission | is | 6.5% | of | $35,000 |

Let $\boxed{c}$ = amount of commission.

Equation $\boxed{}$ = $\boxed{}$ · $\boxed{}$

$c = 0.065 \cdot 35{,}000$

$= \boxed{}$

The salesman's commission is $\boxed{}$.

❹ **Surveys** During a telephone survey, 414 people, or 46% of those called, said they were watching station RFGT at the time of the call. How many people were called?

Words | 414 | is | 46% | of | people called |

Let $\boxed{n}$ = number of people called.

Equation $\boxed{}$ = $\boxed{}$ · $\boxed{}$

$0.46n = 414$

$\dfrac{0.46n}{\boxed{}} = \dfrac{414}{\boxed{}}$

$n = \boxed{}$

$\boxed{}$ people were called.

Quick Check

3. **Royalties** A singer receives a 5% royalty on each CD sale. To the nearest cent, find his royalty for a CD that sells for $16.99.

4. In a survey, 952 people, or 68%, preferred smooth peanut butter to crunchy. How many people were surveyed?

Lesson 6-8

Percent of Change

Lesson Objectives	NAEP 2005 Strand: Number Properties and Operations
▼ Find percent of increase ▼ Find percent of decrease	**Topic:** Ratios and Proportional Reasoning **Local Standards:** _____

Vocabulary

The percent of change is _____

_____

Example

① **Finding Percent of Increase** Find the percent of increase from 8 to 9.6.

amount of increase = ⬚ − ⬚ = ⬚

percent of increase = $\dfrac{\boxed{}}{\boxed{}}$ **Write an equation.**

= $\dfrac{\boxed{}}{\boxed{}}$ **Substitute.**

= ⬚   **Simplify.**

= ⬚ %   **Write as a percent.**

The percent of increase from 8 to 9.6 is ⬚.

Check Understanding

1. Find each percent of increase.

a. from 100 to 114

b. from 2.0 to 3.2

c. from 4,000 to 8,500

Daily Notetaking Guide

Examples

❷ Rainfall In a given year, Hillsboro had a total of 7.5 in. of rain by March 1 and a total of 22.5 in. by July 1. Find the percent of increase from 7.5 to 22.5.

amount of increase = ☐ – ☐ = ☐

percent of increase = $\dfrac{\boxed{}}{\boxed{}}$

$= \dfrac{\boxed{}}{\boxed{}}$

$= \boxed{}$

$= \boxed{}$ %

The percent increase from March 1 to July 1 was $\boxed{}$.

❸ Finding Percent of Decrease Find the percent of decrease from 1,250 to 1,120.

amount of decrease = ☐ – ☐ = ☐

percent of decrease = $\dfrac{\boxed{}}{\boxed{}}$

$= \dfrac{\boxed{}}{\boxed{}}$

$= \boxed{}$

$= \boxed{}$ %

The percent of decrease from 1,250 to 1,120 is $\boxed{}$.

Check Understanding

2. In the same year as in Example 2 above, Hillsboro had a total of 10.5 inches of rain by April 1. Find the percent of increase from 7.5 to 10.5.

$\boxed{}$

3. Find each percent of decrease.
  a. from 9.6 to 4.8   **b.** from 202 to 192   **c.** from 854.5 to 60.6

$\boxed{}$ $\boxed{}$ $\boxed{}$

Name_____ Class_____ Date_____

Lesson 6-9   Markup and Discount

Lesson Objectives	**NAEP 2005 Strand:** Number Properties and Operations
Find markups	**Topic:** Ratios and Proportional Reasoning
Find discounts	**Local Standards:** _____

Vocabulary

Markup is _____

Percent increase is _____

Discount is _____

Percent of discount is _____

Examples

❶ Finding Markup A grocery store has a 20% markup on a can of soup. The can of soup costs the store $1.25. Find the markup.

markup = [＿＿＿＿＿＿＿] · [＿＿＿＿＿＿＿]

        = [＿＿＿] · [＿＿＿]

        = [＿＿＿]

The markup is [＿＿＿].

❷ Finding Selling Price A bookstore pays $4.50 for a novel. The percent markup is 45%. Find the novel's selling price.

[＿＿＿] · [＿＿＿] = [＿＿＿]   **Multiply to find the markup.**

4.50 + [＿＿＿] = [＿＿＿]   store's cost + [＿＿＿＿＿] = [＿＿＿＿＿]

The selling price is [＿＿＿].

❸ Finding Discount A camera that regularly sells for $210 is on sale for 30% off. Find the discount.

discount = [＿＿＿＿＿＿＿] · [＿＿＿＿＿＿＿]

        = [＿＿＿] · [＿＿＿]

        = [＿＿＿]

The discount is [＿＿＿].

❹ Finding Sale Price A video game that regularly sells for $39.95 is on sale for 20% off. What is the sale price?

Method 1 Find the discount. Then find the sale price.

discount = [   ] · [   ]

= [   ] · [   ]

= [   ]

sale price = [   ] − [   ]

= 39.95 − [   ]

= [   ]

The sale price is [   ].

Method 2 Find the sale price directly. The sale price equals 100% of the regular price minus 20% of the regular price.

sale price = ([   ]% − [   ]%) · regular price

= [   ] · regular price

= [   ](39.95)

= [   ]

The sale price is [   ].

Quick Check

1. A clothing store pays $56 for a jacket. The store's percent markup is 75%. Find the markup for the jacket.

2. A $5 cap has a 70% markup. Find the selling price.

3. Pants priced at $21.99 are marked 15% off. Find the discount.

4. Find the sale price of the video game from Example 4 if the percent discount is 25%. Round to the nearest cent.

Lesson 6-10

Make a Table

Lesson Objective	NAEP 2005 Strand: Number Properties and Operations
▼ Solve problems by making a table	**Topic:** Ratios and Proportional Reasoning
	Local Standards: _____

Example

1 Martin had 100 trees in his orchard the first year. Each year after that, he increased the number of trees in his orchard by 10%, rounded to the nearest whole number. How many trees did he have in his orchard in the sixth year?

(Understand the Problem) Read the problem carefully.

1. What information are you given?

Martin had ⬚ trees in his orchard the first year. Each year after

that, he increased the number of trees in his orchard by ⬚.

2. What information are you asked to find?

(Make and Carry Out a Plan) Decide on a strategy. You can use the percent of increase to predict the increase in the number of trees in the orchard each year for six years. You can make a table to organize your predictions for each year.

3. How can you find the increase in the number of trees in the orchard from the beginning of the first year to the end of the first year?

4. How can you find the number of trees in the orchard at the beginning of the second year?

5. The percent of increase is the same each year. Does that mean that the increase in the number of trees in the orchard will be the same each year? Explain your reasoning.

Name_____ Class_____ Date _____

Complete the table below.

6. Find the numbers for Column 4 by multiplying the numbers in Columns 2 and 3. Round to the nearest whole number.

7. Find the numbers for Column 5 by adding the numbers in Columns 2 and 4.

1	2	3	4	5
Year	Tree Count at Beginning of Year	Rate of Increase (10%)	Increase in Tree Count	Tree Count at Beginning of Next Year
1	100	0.1	10	110
2	110	0.1		
3		0.1		
4		0.1		
5		0.1		

8. What is your prediction for the number of trees in the orchard at the beginning of the sixth year?

(**Check the Answer**) Your friend says that she knows a quicker way to find the answer. Simply multiply 100 · 0.1 · 6 to find the increase for the six-year period. Do you agree with your friend's approach? Explain your reasoning.

Quick Check

1. Suppose the annual increase in the number of trees in the orchard is 15%. At that rate, how many trees will Martin have in the orchard at the beginning of the sixth year?

Lesson 7-1

Solving Two-Step Equations

Lesson Objectives	NAEP 2005 Strand: Algebra
▼ Solve two-step equations	**Topic:** Equations and Inequalities
▼ Use two-step equations to solve problems	**Local Standards:** _____

Example

① Undoing an Operation Solve $5v - 12 = 8$.

$$5v - 12 = 8$$

$5v - 12 + \boxed{} = 8 + \boxed{}$ **Add** $\boxed{}$ **to each side.**

$5v = \boxed{}$ **Simplify.**

$\dfrac{5v}{\boxed{}} = \dfrac{\boxed{}}{\boxed{}}$ **Divide each side by** $\boxed{}$.

$v = \boxed{}$ **Simplify.**

Check $5v - 12 = 8$

$5\left(\boxed{}\right) - 12 \stackrel{?}{=} 8$ **Replace** *v* **with** $\boxed{}$.

$\boxed{} - 12 \stackrel{?}{=} 8$ **Multiply.**

$\boxed{} = 8$ ✓ **Simplify.**

Quick Check

1. Solve each equation.

a. $15x + 3 = 48$

b. $\frac{t}{4} - 10 = -6$

c. $\frac{b}{3} + 13 = 11$

d. $9g + 11 = 2$

Examples

2 **Negative Coefficients** Solve $7 - 3b = 1$.

$$7 - 3b = 1$$

$\boxed{} + 7 - 3b = \boxed{} + 1$ **Add** $\boxed{}$ **to each side.**

$\boxed{} - 3b = \boxed{}$ **Simplify.**

$-3b = \boxed{}$ $0 - 3b = \boxed{}$

$\dfrac{-3b}{\boxed{}} = \dfrac{\boxed{}}{\boxed{}}$ **Divide each side by** $\boxed{}$.

$b = \boxed{}$ **Simplify.**

3 **Using Two-Step Equations** You borrow $350 to buy a bicycle. You agree to pay $100 the first week, and then $25 each week until the balance is paid off. To find how many weeks w it will take you to pay for the bicycle, solve $100 + 25w = 350$.

$$100 + 25w = 350$$

$100 + 25w - \boxed{} = 350 - \boxed{}$ **Subtract** $\boxed{}$ **from each side.**

$25w = \boxed{}$ **Simplify.**

$\dfrac{25w}{\boxed{}} = \dfrac{\boxed{}}{\boxed{}}$ **Divide each side by** $\boxed{}$.

$w = \boxed{}$ **Simplify.**

It will take you $\boxed{}$ weeks to pay for the bicycle.

Quick Check

2. Solve each equation.

a. $-a + 6 = 8$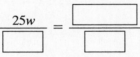

b. $-9 - \dfrac{y}{7} = -12$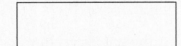

c. $13 - 6f = 31$

3. Jacob bought four begonias in 6-in. pots and a $19 fern at a fundraiser. He spent a total of $63. Solve the equation $4p + 19 = 63$ to find the price p of each begonia.

Lesson 7-2

Solving Multi-Step Equations

Lesson Objectives	**NAEP 2005 Strand:** Algebra
▼ Combine like terms to simplify an equation	**Topic:** Equations and Inequalities
▼ Use the Distributive Property to simplify an equation	**Local Standards:** _____

Vocabulary and Key Concepts

Steps for Solving a Multi-Step Equation

    Step 1 Use the Distributive Property, if necessary.

    Step 2 Combine like terms.

    Step 3 Undo addition or subtraction.

    Step 4 Undo multiplication or division.

Consecutive integers are _____

_____

Example

❶ **Finding Consecutive Integers** The sum of three consecutive integers is 42. Find the integers.

Words

    | sum of three consecutive integers | is | 42 |

    Let $\boxed{n}$ = the least integer.

    Then $\boxed{}$ = the second integer,

    and $\boxed{}$ = the third integer.

Equation

$$\boxed{} + \boxed{} + \boxed{} = \boxed{}$$

$$\boxed{} + \left(\boxed{}\right) + \left(\boxed{}\right) = \boxed{}$$

$$\left(\boxed{} + \boxed{} + \boxed{}\right) + \left(\boxed{} + \boxed{}\right) = 42 \qquad \text{Use the } \boxed{} \text{ and } \boxed{}$$

Properties of Addition to group like terms together.

$$\boxed{} + \boxed{} = 42 \qquad \text{Combine like terms.}$$

$$\boxed{} + \boxed{} - \boxed{} = 42 - \boxed{} \qquad \text{Subtract } \boxed{} \text{ from each side.}$$

$$3n = \boxed{} \qquad \text{Simplify.}$$

$$\frac{3n}{\boxed{}} = \frac{\boxed{}}{\boxed{}} \qquad \text{Divide each side by } \boxed{}.$$

$$n = \boxed{} \qquad \text{Simplify.}$$

If $n = \boxed{}$, then $n + 1 = \boxed{}$, and $n + 2 = \boxed{}$. The three integers

are $\boxed{}$, $\boxed{}$, and $\boxed{}$.

Daily Notetaking Guide

❷ Using the Distributive Property Solve $44 = -5(r - 4) - r$.

$$44 = -5(r - 4) - r$$

$44 = \boxed{} + \boxed{} - r$ **Use the** $\boxed{}$ **Property.**

$44 = \boxed{} + 20$ **Combine like terms.**

$44 - \boxed{} = -6r + 20 - \boxed{}$ **Subtract** $\boxed{}$ **from each side.**

$\boxed{} = -6r$ **Simplify.**

$\dfrac{\boxed{}}{\boxed{}} = \dfrac{-6r}{\boxed{}}$ **Divide each side by** $\boxed{}$**.**

$\boxed{} = r$ **Simplify.**

Quick Check

1. **Basketball Scores** One basketball team defeated another by 13 points. The total number of points scored by both teams was 171. Solve the equation $p + p - 13 = 171$ to find the number of points p scored by the winning team.

2. **a. Number Sense** Find four consecutive integers with a sum of 358.

   b. For *consecutive even integers*, the first is n, and the second is $n + 2$. Find two consecutive even integers with a sum of 66.

3. Solve each equation.
   a. $-3(m - 6) = 4$

   b. $3(x + 12) - x = 8$

Lesson 7-3

Multi-Step Equations With Fractions and Decimals

Lesson Objectives	NAEP 2005 Strand: Algebra
▼ Solve multi-step equations with fractions	**Topic:** Equations and Inequalities
▼ Solve multi-step equations with decimals	**Local Standards:** _____

Examples

❶ Using the Reciprocal Solve $\frac{3}{4}p - 7 = 11$.

$$\frac{3}{4}p - 7 = 11$$

$\frac{3}{4}p - 7 + \boxed{} = 11 + \boxed{}$ **Add** $\boxed{}$ **to each side.**

$\frac{3}{4}p = \boxed{}$ **Simplify.**

$\dfrac{\boxed{}}{\boxed{}} \cdot \frac{3}{4}p = \boxed{} \cdot \dfrac{\boxed{}}{\boxed{}}$ **Multiply each side by** $\dfrac{\boxed{}}{\boxed{}}$**, the reciprocal of** $\frac{3}{4}$**.**

$1p = \dfrac{4 \cdot 18^{\boxed{}}}{3} $ **Divide common factors.**

$p = \boxed{}$ **Simplify.**

Check $\frac{3}{4}p - 7 = 11$

$\frac{3}{4}\left(\boxed{} \right) - 7 \overset{?}{=} 11$ **Replace** p **with** $\boxed{}$**.**

$\dfrac{3 \cdot 24^{\boxed{}}}{4} - 7 \overset{?}{=} 11$ **Divide common factors.**

$\boxed{} - 7 \overset{?}{=} 11$ **Simplify.**

$\boxed{} = 11 ✓$

❷ Using the LCM Solve $\frac{1}{2}y + 3 = \frac{2}{3}$.

$$\frac{1}{2}y + 3 = \frac{2}{3}$$

$\boxed{}\left(\frac{1}{2}y + 3 \right) = \boxed{}\left(\frac{2}{3} \right)$ **Multiply each side by** $\boxed{}$**, the** $\boxed{}$ **of 2 and 3.**

$\boxed{} \cdot \frac{1}{2}y + \boxed{} \cdot 3 = 6\left(\frac{2}{3} \right)$ **Use the** $\boxed{}$ **Property.**

$\boxed{}y + \boxed{} = 4$ **Simplify.**

$3y = \boxed{}$ **Subtract** $\boxed{}$ **from each side. Simplify.**

$\dfrac{3y}{\boxed{}} = \dfrac{-14}{\boxed{}}$ **Divide each side by** $\boxed{}$**.**

$y = -\boxed{}\dfrac{\boxed{}}{\boxed{}}$ **Simplify.**

❸ Solving Multi-Step Equations With Decimals Suppose your cell phone
plan is $30 per month plus $.05 per minute. Your bill is $36.75. Use the
equation $30 + 0.05x = 36.75$ to find the number of minutes on your bill.

$$30 + 0.05x = 36.75$$

$30 - \boxed{} + 0.05x = 36.75 - \boxed{}$ **Subtract** $\boxed{}$ **from each side.**

$0.05x = \boxed{}$ **Simplify.**

$$\frac{0.05x}{\boxed{}} = \frac{6.75}{\boxed{}}$$ **Divide each side by** $\boxed{}$ **.**

$x = \boxed{}$ **Simplify.**

There are $\boxed{}$ minutes on your bill.

Quick Check

1. Use a reciprocal to solve each equation.

   a. $-\frac{7}{10}k + 14 = -21$ **b.** $\frac{2}{3}(m - 6) = 3$

2. Use the LCM to solve each equation.

   a. $-\frac{7}{12} + y = \frac{1}{6}$ **b.** $\frac{1}{3}b - 1 = \frac{5}{6}$

3. Solve each equation.

   a. $1.5x - 3.6 = 2.4$ **b.** $1.06p - 3 = 0.71$

Lesson 7-4

Write an Equation

Lesson Objective	NAEP 2005 Strand: Algebra
▼ Write an equation to solve a problem	Topic: Equations and Inequalities
	Local Standards: _____

Example

1 Van Rental A moving van rents for $29.95 a day plus $.12 a mile. Mr. Reynolds's bill was $137.80 and he drove the van 150 mi. For how many days did he have the van?

Understand the Problem

1. What is the goal of this problem?

[ ]

2. How many miles did Mr. Reynolds drive?

[ ]

3. What does the van cost without mileage?

[ ]

4. What is the mileage charge?

[ ]

Make and Carry Out a Plan

Write an equation.

Words $\boxed{\text{number of days}}$ · $29.95/d + $.12/mi · $\boxed{150 \text{ mi}}$ = $\boxed{\$137.80}$

Let $\boxed{d}$ = the number of days Mr. Reynolds had the van.

Equation $\boxed{}$ · 29.95 + 0.12 · $\boxed{}$ = $\boxed{}$

Solve the equation.

$d \cdot 29.95 + 0.12 \cdot 150 = 137.80$

$29.95d + \boxed{} = 137.80$ **Multiply 0.12 and 150.**

$29.95d + 18 - \boxed{} = 137.80 - \boxed{}$ **Subtract** $\boxed{}$ **from each side.**

$29.95d = \boxed{}$ **Simplify.**

$\dfrac{29.95d}{\boxed{}} = \dfrac{119.80}{\boxed{}}$ **Divide each side by** $\boxed{}$.

$d = \boxed{}$ **Simplify.**

Mr. Reynolds had the van for $\boxed{}$ days.

Check the Answer

You can estimate to check the reasonableness of the answer.

$29.95 \approx 30$
$0.12 \approx 0.1$ } **Round each number.**
$137.80 \approx 140$

$4 \cdot 30 + 0.1 \cdot 140 = 120 + 14$
$= 134$

Since $134 \approx 137.80$, 2 days is a reasonable answer.

Quick Check

1. Suppose that Mr. Reynold's bill was \$161.80 and he drove the van 350 mi.
   a. How would the equation change?

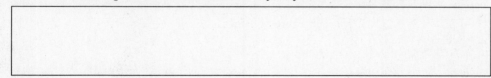

   b. Solve the new equation to find how many days he rented the van.

   c. Estimate to check the reasonableness of your answer to part (b).

Lesson 7-5

Lesson Objectives	**NAEP 2005 Strand:** Algebra
▼ Solve equations with variables on both sides	**Topic:** Equations and Inequalities
▼ Use equations with variables on both sides	**Local Standards:** _____

Example

❶ Collecting the Variable on One Side Solve $4c + 3 = 15 - 2c$.

$$4c + 3 = 15 - 2c$$

$4c + \boxed{} + 3 = 15 - 2c + \boxed{}$ **Add** $\boxed{}$ **to each side.**

$6c + 3 = 15$ **Combine like terms.**

$6c + 3 - \boxed{} = 15 - \boxed{}$ **Subtract** $\boxed{}$ **from each side.**

$6c = \boxed{}$ **Simplify.**

$\dfrac{6c}{\boxed{}} = \dfrac{12}{\boxed{}}$ **Divide each side by** $\boxed{}$.

$c = \boxed{}$ **Simplify.**

Check $4c + 3 = 15 - 2c$

$4\left(\boxed{}\right) + 3 \stackrel{?}{=} 15 - 2\left(\boxed{}\right)$ **Substitute** $\boxed{}$ **for** c.

$\boxed{} + 3 \stackrel{?}{=} 15 - \boxed{}$ **Multiply.**

$\boxed{} = \boxed{}$ ✓

Quick Check

1. Solve and check each equation.

a. $4x + 4 = 2x + 36$

b. $-15 + 6b = -8b + 13$

Example

❷ Using Equations Steve types at a rate of 15 words/min and Jenny types at a rate of 20 words/min. Steve and Jenny are both typing the same document, and Steve starts 5 min before Jenny. How long will it take Jenny to catch up with Steve?

words Jenny types = words Steve types

Words   20 words/min · $\boxed{\text{Jenny's time}}$ = 15 words/min · $\boxed{\text{Steve's time}}$

Let $\boxed{x}$ = Jenny's time.

Then $\boxed{}$ = Steve's time.

Equation   20 · $\boxed{}$ = 15 · $\boxed{}$

$20x = 15(x + 5)$

$20x = \boxed{} + \boxed{}$ **Use the** $\boxed{}$ **Property.**

$20x - \boxed{} = 15x - \boxed{} + 75$ **Subtract** $\boxed{}$ **from each side.**

$\boxed{} = 75$ **Combine like terms.**

$\dfrac{5x}{\boxed{}} = \dfrac{75}{\boxed{}}$ **Divide each side by** $\boxed{}$.

$x = \boxed{}$ **Simplify.**

Jenny will catch up to Steve in $\boxed{}$ min.

Check Test the result.

At 20 words/min for $\boxed{}$ min, Jenny types 300 words. Steve's time is 5 min longer. He types for 20 min. At 15 words/min for 20 min, Steve types 300 words. Since Jenny and Steve each type 300 words, the answer checks.

Quick Check

2. **Travel Time** Car A leaves Eastown traveling at a steady rate of 50 mi/h. Car B leaves Eastown 1 h later following Car A. It travels at a steady rate of 60 mi/h. How long after Car A leaves Eastown will Car B catch up?

Name_____ Class_____ Date_____

Lesson 7-6

Solving Two-Step Inequalities

Lesson Objectives	**NAEP 2005 Strand:** Algebra
▼ Solve two-step inequalities	**Topic:** Equations and Inequalities
▼ Use two-step inequalities to solve problems	**Local Standards:** _____

Example

① **Undoing Operations** Solve and graph $7g + 11 > 67$.

$$7g + 11 > 67$$

$7g + 11 - \boxed{} > 67 - \boxed{}$ **Subtract** $\boxed{}$ **from each side.**

$7g > \boxed{}$ **Simplify.**

$\dfrac{7g}{\boxed{}} > \dfrac{56}{\boxed{}}$ **Divide each side by** $\boxed{}$.

$g > \boxed{}$ **Simplify.**

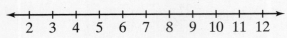

② **Reversing the Inequality Symbol** Solve $6 \le -\frac{2}{3}r - 6$.

$$6 \le -\tfrac{2}{3}r - 6$$

$6 + \boxed{} \le -\tfrac{2}{3}r - 6 + \boxed{}$ **Add** $\boxed{}$ **to each side.**

$12 \le -\tfrac{2}{3}r$ **Simplify.**

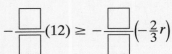 **Multiply each side by** $-\dfrac{\boxed{}}{\boxed{}}$.
Reverse the direction of the inequality symbol.

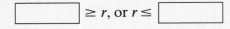 **Simplify.**

Quick Check

1. Solve and graph each inequality.

   a. $5a - 9 > 11$ **b.** $-10 \ge \frac{1}{2}x - 6$ **c.** $17 + \frac{1}{2}c < 14$

Daily Notetaking Guide

Examples

❸ Using Inequalities Dale has $25 to spend at a carnival. If the admission to the carnival is $4 and the rides cost $1.50 each, what is the greatest number of rides Dale can go on?

Words $4 admission + $1.50/ride · number of rides is less than or equal to $25

Let r = number of rides Dale goes on.

Inequality ☐ + ☐ · ☐ ≤ ☐

$$4 + 1.5r \leq 25$$

$4 + 1.5r -$ ☐ $\leq 25 -$ ☐ **Subtract** ☐ **from each side.**

$1.5r \leq 21$ **Simplify.**

$\dfrac{1.5r}{\boxed{}} \leq \dfrac{21}{\boxed{}}$ **Divide each side by** ☐ .

$r \leq$ ☐ **Simplify.**

The greatest number of rides Dale can go on is ☐ .

Quick Check

2. Solve and graph each inequality.

a. $-2m + 4 \leq 34$

b. $6 - x > 3$

c. $8.3 < -0.5b - 2.7$

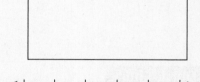

3. Commissions A stereo salesperson earns a salary of $1,200 per month, plus a commission of 4% of sales. The salesperson wants to maintain a monthly income of at least $1,500. How much must the salesperson sell each month?

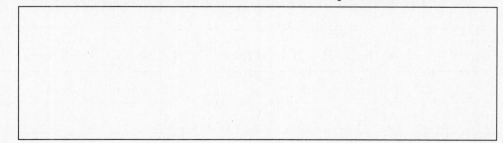

Lesson 7-7

Transforming Formulas

Lesson Objectives	NAEP 2005 Strand: Algebra
▼ Solve a formula for a given variable ▼ Use formulas to solve problems	**Topic:** Equations and Inequalities **Local Standards:** _____

Examples

1 **Transforming in One Step** Solve the circumference formula $C = 2\pi r$ for r.

$$C = 2\pi r$$

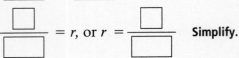 **Use the Division Property of Equality.**

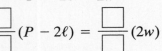 $= r$, or $r =$  **Simplify.**

2 **Using More Than One Step** Solve the perimeter formula $P = 2\ell + 2w$ for w.

$$P = 2\ell + 2w$$

$P -$ ☐ $= 2\ell + 2w -$ ☐   **Subtract** ☐ **from each side.**

$P - 2\ell = 2w$ **Simplify.**

$\dfrac{\square}{\square}(P - 2\ell) = \dfrac{\square}{\square}(2w)$ **Multiply each side by** $\dfrac{\square}{\square}$**.**

$\dfrac{\square}{\square}\square - \square = w$ **Use the Distributive Property and simplify.**

Quick Check

1. Solve for the indicated variable.

a. Solve $p = s - c$ for s.

b. Solve $h = \frac{k}{j}$ for k.

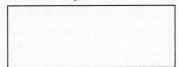

c. Solve $I = prt$ for p.

d. Solve $5a + 7 = b$ for a.

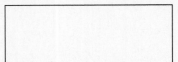

e. Solve $P = 2l + 2w$ for w.

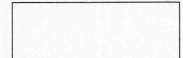

f. Solve $y = \frac{x}{3} + 8$ for x.

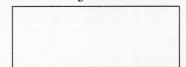

Example

❸ **Using Formulas** You plan a 600-mi trip to New York City. You estimate your trip will take about 10 hours. To estimate your average speed, solve the distance formula $d = rt$ for r. Then substitute to find the average speed.

$$d = rt$$

$$\frac{d}{\boxed{}} = \frac{rt}{\boxed{}} \qquad \textbf{Divide each side by } \boxed{}.$$

$$\frac{d}{t} = r, \text{ or } r = \frac{d}{t} \qquad \textbf{Simplify.}$$

$$r = \frac{\boxed{}}{\boxed{}} \qquad \textbf{Replace } d \textbf{ with } \boxed{} \textbf{ and } t \textbf{ with } \boxed{}.$$

$$r = \boxed{} \qquad \textbf{Simplify.}$$

❹ **Using Formulas** The high temperature one day in San Diego was 32°C. Solve $C = \frac{5}{9}(F - 32)$ for F. Then substitute to find the temperature in degrees Fahrenheit.

$$C = \frac{5}{9}(F - 32)$$

$$\frac{\boxed{}}{\boxed{}}(C) = \frac{\boxed{}}{\boxed{}}\left[\frac{5}{9}(F - 32)\right] \qquad \textbf{Multiply each side by } \frac{\boxed{}}{\boxed{}}.$$

$$\frac{9}{5}C = F - 32 \qquad \textbf{Simplify.}$$

$$\frac{9}{5}C + \boxed{} = F - 32 + \boxed{} \qquad \textbf{Add } \boxed{} \textbf{ to each side.}$$

$$\frac{9}{5}C + 32 = F, \text{ or } F = \frac{9}{5}C + 32 \qquad \textbf{Simplify and rewrite.}$$

$$F = \frac{9}{5}\left(\boxed{}\right) + 32 = \boxed{} \qquad \textbf{Replace } C \textbf{ with } \boxed{}. \textbf{ Simplify.}$$

$$32°\text{C is } \boxed{} °\text{F}.$$

Quick Check

2. Assume that in Example 3 your average speed is 50 mi/h. Solve the distance formula for the new t.

3. Solve the batting average formula, $a = \frac{h}{n}$, for h. Find the number of hits h a batter needs in 40 times at bat n to have an average of 0.275.

Lesson 7-8

Simple and Compound Interest

Lesson Objectives	NAEP 2005 Strand: Algebra
▼ Solve simple-interest problems ② Solve compound-interest problems	**Topic:** Equations and Inequalities **Local Standards:** _____

Vocabulary and Key Concepts

Simple-Interest Formula

$$I = prt,$$

where I is the [_____], p is the [_____],

r is the [_____] per year, and t is [_____] in years.

Compound-Interest Formula

$$B = p(1 + r)^n,$$

where B is the [_____], p is the [_____],

r is the [_____] for each interest period, and

n is the [_____].

The principal is _____

Interest is _____

The interest rate is _____

_____

Simple interest is _____

Compound interest is _____

_____

Balance is _____

Examples

❶ **Finding Simple Interest** Suppose you deposit $1,000 in a savings account that earns 3% per year. Find the interest earned in two years. Find the total of principal plus interest.

$I = prt$ **Use the simple interest formula.**

$I =$ [_____] · [_____] · [___]   **Replace p with [_____], r with [_____], and t with [___].**

$I =$ [_____]   **Simplify.**

total = 1,000 + [_____] = [_____]   **Find the total.**

The account will earn [_____] in two years. The total of principal plus interest will be [_____].

❷ Finding Compound Interest You deposit $400 in an account that earns 5% interest compounded annually (once per year). The balance after the first four years is $486.20. What is the balance in your account after another 4 years, a total of 8 years? Round to the nearest cent.

Principal at Beginning of year	Interest	Balance
Year 5: $486.20	$486.20 \cdot 0.05 = $ ☐	$486.20 + 24.31 = $ ☐
Year 6: $ ☐	☐ $\cdot 0.05 = $ ☐	☐ $+ 25.53 = $ ☐
Year 7: $ ☐	☐ $\cdot 0.05 = $ ☐	☐ $+ 26.80 = $ ☐
Year 8: $ ☐	☐ $\cdot 0.05 = $ ☐	☐ $+ 28.14 = $ ☐

After four more years, a total of 8 years, the balance is $ ☐ .

❸ Finding a Balance Find the balance on a deposit of $2,500 that earns 3% interest compounded semiannually for 4 years.

The interest rate r for compounding semiannually is $0.03 \div 2$, or ☐ .

The number of payment periods n is 4 years × 2 interest periods per year, or ☐ .

$B = p(1 + r)^n$ Use the ☐ interest formula.

$B = $ ☐ $\left(1 + \right.$ ☐ $\left.\right)^{☐}$ Replace p with ☐ , r with ☐ , and n with ☐ .

$B \approx$ ☐   Use a calculator. Round to the nearest cent.

The balance is ☐ .

Quick Check

1. Find the simple interest.

  a. principal = $250, interest rate = 4%
    time = 3 years

  b. principal = $250, interest rate = 3.5%
    time = 6 months

2. Make a table to find the balance. The interest is compounded annually.

principal = $500
interest rate = 3%
time = 2 years

Bal. at Yr. Start	Interest	Bal. at Yr. End

3. Find the balance for the account.

Amount deposited: $900, annual interest: 2%, time: 3 years

  a. compounding annually

  b. compounding semiannually

Lesson 8-1

Relations and Functions

Lesson Objectives	NAEP 2005 Strand: Measurement
▼ Determine whether a relation is a function	**Topic:** Algebraic Representations
▼ Graph relations and functions	**Local Standards:** _____

Vocabulary

A relation is _____

The domain of a relation is _____

_____

The range of a function is _____

_____

A function is a relation for which _____

_____

The vertical-line test is a test that determines _____

Examples

❶ Identifying a Function Is each relation a function? Explain.

a. $\{(0,5), (1,5), (2,6), (3,7)\}$

Domain   Range

There is [   ] range value for each domain value.

The relation is a function.

b. $\{(0,5), (0,6), (1,6), (2,7)\}$

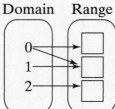

Domain   Range

There are [   ] range values for the domain value 0.

The relation is not a function.

❷ Is the time needed to mow a lawn a function of the size of the lawn? Explain.

[   ] ; two lawns of the same size ([   ] value) can require different

lengths of time ([   ] values) for mowing.

Name_____ Class_____ Date _____

Example

❸ **Using the Vertical-Line Test**

a. Graph the relation shown in the table.

Domain Value	Range Value
−3	5
−5	3
3	5
5	3

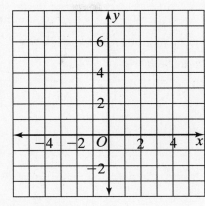

Graph the ordered pairs (−3,5), (−5,3), (3,5) and (5,3).

b. Use the vertical-line test. Is the relation a function? Explain.

Quick Check

1. Is each relation a function? Explain.

a. $\{(-2, 3), (2, 2), (2, -2)\}$

b. $\{(-5, -4), (0, -4), (5, -4)\}$

2. a. For the United States Postal Service, is package weight a function of the postage paid to mail the package? Explain.

b. For the United States Postal Service, is the cost of postage a function of package weight? Explain.

3. **Algebra** Graph the relation shown in each table. Use the vertical-line test. Is the relation a function? Explain.

a.

x	y
−6	−5
−3	−2
0	−2
1	0
4	3
5	7

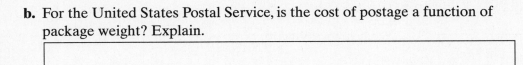

b.

x	y
−7	4
−2	6
−1	−1
−1	3
0	5
1	5

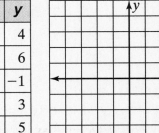

Lesson 8-2

Equations With Two Variables

Lesson Objectives	**NAEP 2005 Strand:** Measurement
▼ Find solutions of linear equations with two variables	**Topic:** Algebraic Representations
▼ Graph linear equations with two variables	**Local Standards:** _____

Vocabulary

A solution of an equation with two variables is _____

_____

A linear equation is _____

_____

Examples

① **Finding a Solution** Find the solution of $y = 4x - 3$ for $x = 2$.

$y = 4x - 3$

$y = 4(\boxed{}) - 3$ **Replace x with** $\boxed{}$.

$y = 8 - 3$ **Multiply.**

$y = \boxed{}$ **Subtract.**

A solution of the equation is $\boxed{}$.

Quick Check

1. Find the solution of each equation for $x = -3$.

  a. $y = 2x + 1$ **b.** $y = -4x + 3$ **c.** $y = 0x - 4$

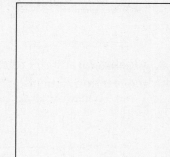

2. **Meteorology** The equation $t = 21 - 0.01n$ models the normal low temperature in degrees Celsius at Mount Rushmore, South Dakota. In the equation, t is the temperature at n meters above the base of the mountain. Find the normal low July temperature at 700 m above the base of Mount Rushmore.

Daily Notetaking Guide

Examples

❷ Graphing _y_ = _a_ and _x_ = _b_ Graph each equation. Is the equation a function?

a. $y = -3$

For every value of $x, y = -3$.

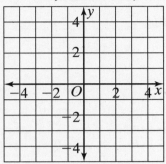

This is a [   ] line. The equation $y = -3$ is a function.

b. $x = 4$

For every value of $y, x = 4$.

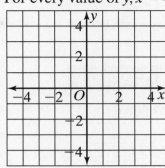

This is a [   ] line. The equation $x = 4$ is not a function.

❸ Graphing by solving for _y_ Solve $y - x = 3$ for y. Then graph the equation.

Solve the equation for y.

$$y - x = 3$$

$y - x +$ [   ] $= 3 +$ [   ]   **Add** [   ] **to each side.**

$y =$ [   ] $+$ [   ]   **Simplify.**

Make a table of values.

x	$x + 3$	(x, y)
-1	$-1 + 3 =$ [ ]	$\left(-1, \boxed{}\right)$
0	$0 + 3 =$ [ ]	$\left(0, \boxed{}\right)$
1	$1 + 3 =$ [ ]	$\left(1, \boxed{}\right)$

Graph the ordered pairs.

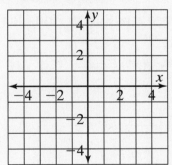

Quick Check

3. Graph each linear equation. Is it a function?

a. $y = 2x + 1$ [   ]

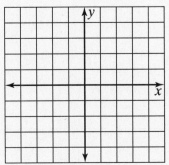

b. $y + \frac{1}{2}x = 4$ [   ]

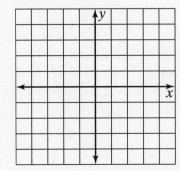

c. $x = 1$ [   ]

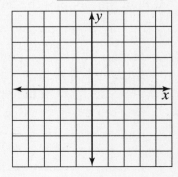

Lesson 8-3

Slope and *y*-intercept

<table>
<tr><td>

Lesson Objectives

▼ Find the slope of a line

② Use slope-intercept form in graphing a linear equation

</td><td>

NAEP 2005 Strand: Algebra

Topic: Equations and Inequalities

Local Standards: _____

</td></tr>
</table>

Vocabulary and Key Concepts

Slope-intercept Form

The equation [_____] is the slope-intercept form. In this form,

m is the [_____] of the line, and *b* is the [_____] .

$$\text{slope} = \frac{\boxed{} \text{ change}}{\boxed{} \text{ change}} = \boxed{}$$

The *y*-intercept of a line is _____

Example

❶ **Using Rise and Run to Find Slope** Find the slope of the line.

$$\text{slope} = \frac{\text{rise}}{\text{run}} = \frac{\boxed{}}{\boxed{}} = \boxed{}$$

down 6 units

rise = [____]

right 3 units

run = [____]

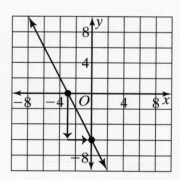

Quick Check

1. Find the slope of the line.

$$\text{slope} = \frac{\text{rise}}{\text{run}} = \frac{\boxed{}}{\boxed{}} = \boxed{}$$

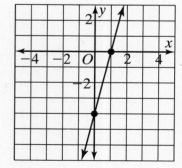

Name_____ Class_____ Date _____

Examples

❷ Using Coordinates to Find Slope Find the slope of the line through $E(7, 5)$ and $F(-2, 0)$.

$$\text{slope} = \frac{\text{difference in } \boxed{}\text{-coordinates}}{\text{difference in } \boxed{}\text{-coordinates}} = \frac{\boxed{} - \boxed{}}{\boxed{} - \boxed{}} = \frac{\boxed{}}{\boxed{}} = \frac{\boxed{}}{\boxed{}}$$

❸ A ramp slopes from a warehouse door down to a street. The function $y = -\frac{1}{5}x + 4$ models the ramp, where x is the distance in feet from the bottom of the door and y is the height in feet above the street. Graph the equation.

Step 1 Since the y-intercept is $\boxed{}$, graph the point $\boxed{}$.

Step 2 Since the slope is $\boxed{}$, move $\boxed{}$ unit down from $(0, 4)$.

Then move $\boxed{}$ units right to graph a second point.

Step 3 Draw a line though the points.

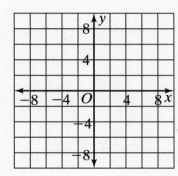

Quick Check

2. Find the slope of the line through each pair of points.

    a. $V(8, -1), Q(0, -7)$ **b.** $S(-4, 3), R(-10, 9)$

3. Graph each equation.

    a. $y = 2x - 3$ **b.** $y = -x + 4$

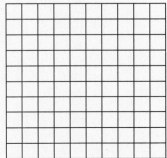 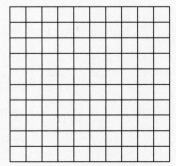

Lesson 8-4

Writing Rules for Linear Functions

Lesson Objectives	NAEP 2005 Strand: Algebra
▼ Write a function rule for a word relationship ▼ Write a function rule by analyzing a table or graph	Topic: Patterns, Relationships, and Functions Local Standards: _____

Vocabulary

A function can be written in function notation using $\boxed{f(x)}$ instead of *y*.
You read $f(x)$ as *f* of *x*.

A function rule is _____

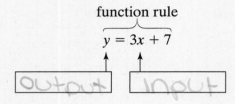

$$y = 3x + 7$$

output   input

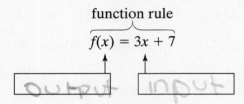

$$f(x) = 3x + 7$$

output   input

Example

1 A long-distance company charges its customers a monthly fee of $4.95 plus 9¢ for each minute of a long-distance call. Find the total monthly bill if the customer made 90 minutes of long-distance calls.

Step 1 Write a function rule that relates the total monthly bill to the number of minutes a customer spent on long-distance calls.

Words | $\boxed{\text{total bill}}$ is $4.95 plus 9¢ times $\boxed{\text{number of minutes}}$

Let $\boxed{m}$ = the number of minutes.

Let $\boxed{t(m)}$ = total bill, a function of the number of minutes

Rule | $\boxed{t(m)}$ = $\boxed{4.95}$ + $\boxed{.09}$ · $\boxed{90}$

$t(m) = 4.95 + .09 · 90$

A rule for the function is $\boxed{}$.

Step 2 Evaluate the function for $m = 90$.

$t(m) = 4.95 + 0.09m$

$t(\boxed{m}) = 4.95 + 0.09(\boxed{90})$ **Replace *m* with** $\boxed{90}$.

$t(90) = 4.95 + \boxed{8.10}$ **Multiply.**

$t(90) = \boxed{13.05}$ **Add.**

The total monthly bill for 90 minutes of long-distance calls is $\boxed{13.05}$.

Name_____ Class_____ Date _____

Examples

② Writing a Function Rule From a Table Write a rule for the linear function in the table below.

x	f(x)
2	3
0	−5
−2	−13
−4	−21

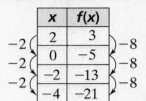

As the *x* values decrease by 2, the *f(x)* values decrease by $\boxed{8}$.

So $m = \dfrac{\boxed{8}}{\boxed{2}} = \boxed{4}$.

When $x = 0$, $f(x) = \boxed{4}$. So $b = \boxed{-5}$.

A rule for the function is $\boxed{y = 4x - 5}$.

$Y = 4(2) + b$

③ Writing a Function Rule From a Graph Write a rule for the linear function in the graph below.

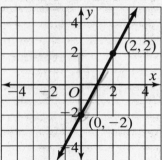

slope $= \dfrac{\boxed{2} - \boxed{-2}}{\boxed{2} - \boxed{0}} = \dfrac{\boxed{4}}{\boxed{2}} = \boxed{2}$

y-intercept $= \boxed{-2}$

A rule for the function is $f(x) = $ ~~_____~~

$y = 2x - 2$

Quick Check

1. Scrumptious Snack Mix is sold by mail order. It costs \$3/lb, plus \$4 for shipping and handling. Write a function rule for the total cost $c(p)$ based on the number of pounds p bought. Use your function to find the total cost of 5 lb of snack mix.

$3p + \$4$
$3p + \$4$

2. Write a rule for each linear function.

a.

x	f(x)
−3	6
0	0
3	−6
6	−12

b.

x	y
−6	−11
−4	−7
−2	−3
0	1

3. Write a rule for the function graphed at right.

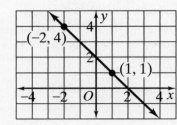

Lesson 8-5

Scatter Plots

Lesson Objectives	NAEP 2005 Strand: Data Analysis and Probability
▼ Interpret and draw scatter plots	Topic: Data Representations
▼ Use scatter plots to find trends	Local Standards: _____

Vocabulary

A scatter plot is _____

_____

	correlation

As one set of values
increases, the other
set tends to increase.

	correlation

As one set of values
increases, the other
set tends to decrease.

	correlation

The values show
no relationship.

Example

❶ The scatter plot shows education and income data.

a. Describe the person represented by the point with
coordinates (10, 30).

This person has ☐ years of education and earns
☐☐☐☐☐ each year.

b. How many people have exactly 14 years of education?
What are their incomes?

The points (14, ☐), (14, ☐), and (14, ☐)
have education coordinate 14. The three people they
represent earn ☐☐☐☐ , ☐☐☐☐☐ , and
☐☐☐☐☐ , respectively.

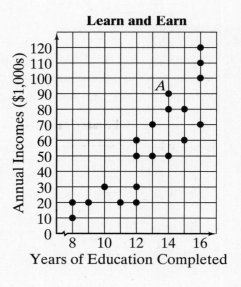

Learn and Earn

c. Is there a *positive correlation*, a *negative correlation*, or *no correlation* between education
and income? Explain.

As the years of education ☐☐☐☐☐ , annual income ☐☐☐☐☐ .
There is a ☐☐☐☐ correlation.

Name_____ Class_____ Date _____

Example

2 Use the table to make a scatter plot of the elevation and precipitation data.

Elevation and Precipitation

City	Elevation Above Sea Level (ft)	Mean Annual Precipitation (in.)
Atlanta, GA	1,050	51
Boston, MA	20	42
Chicago, IL	596	36
Honolulu, HI	18	22
Miami, FL	11	56
Phoenix, AZ	1,072	8
Portland, ME	75	44
San Diego, CA	40	10
Wichita, KS	1,305	29

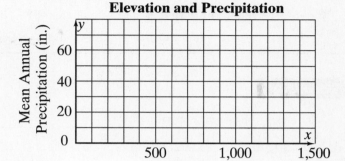

Elevation and Precipitation

Quick Check

1. a. Use the information in Example 1 to describe the person represented by point *A*.

b. How many people have exactly 12 years of education?

2. Use the table at the right. Make a scatter plot of the latitude and precipitation data.

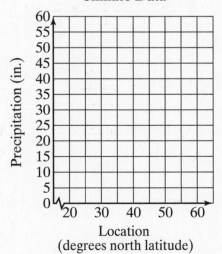

Climate Data

Climate Data

City	Location (degrees north latitude)	Mean Annual Precipitation (inches)
Atlanta, GA	34	51
Boston, MA	42	42
Chicago, IL	42	36
Duluth, MN	47	30
Honolulu, HI	21	22
Houston, TX	30	46
Juneau, AK	58	54
Miami, FL	26	56
Phoenix, AZ	33	8
Portland, ME	44	44
San Diego, CA	33	10
Wichita, KS	38	29

SOURCES: *The World Almanac* and *The Statistical Abstract of the United States*. Go to **www.PHSchool.com** for a data update. Web Code: adg-2041

Lesson 8-6

Solve by Graphing

Lesson Objective	NAEP 2005 Strand: Data Analysis and Probability
▼ Solve problems by graphing	Topic: Data Representation
	Local Standards: _____

Vocabulary

The trend line on a scatter plot _____

Example

1 Use the data in the table below. Suppose this year there are 12 wolves on the island. Predict how many moose are on the island.

Isle Royale Populations

Year	Wolf	Moose	Year	Wolf	Moose	Year	Wolf	Moose
1982	14	700	1988	12	1,653	1994	15	1,800
1983	23	900	1989	11	1,397	1995	16	2,400
1984	24	811	1990	15	1,216	1996	22	1,200
1985	22	1,062	1991	12	1,313	1997	24	500
1986	20	1,025	1992	12	1,600	1998	14	700
1987	16	1,380	1993	13	1,880	1999	25	750

SOURCE: Isle Royale National Park Service

Understand the Problem

1. What are the two variables?

2. What are you trying to predict?

Make and Carry Out a Plan   You can graph the data in a scatter plot. If the points show a correlation, you can draw a trend line. You can use the line to predict other data values.

Step 1   Make a scatter plot by graphing the (wolf, moose) ordered pairs. Use the x-axis for [_____] and the y-axis for [_____].

Step 2   Sketch a trend line. The line should be as close as possible to each data point. There should be about as many points above the trend line as below it.

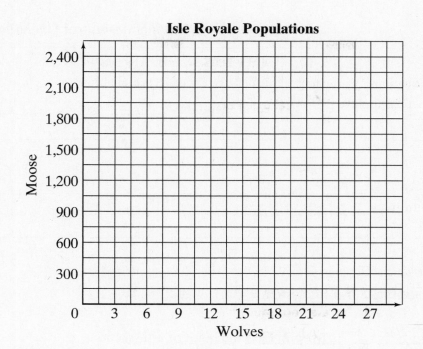

Isle Royale Populations

Step 3 To predict the number of moose when there are 12 wolves, find
12 along the [ ] axis. Look up to find the point on
the trend line that corresponds to 12 wolves. Then look across to
the value on the [ ] axis, which is about [ ].

There are about [ ] moose on the island.

[**Check the Answer**] You can write an equation for a trend line. You can use
the equation to make predictions.

Quick Check

1. a. What is the *y*-intercept of the trend line above?

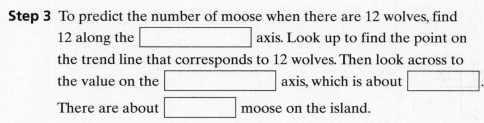

b. Locate one other point on the trend line. Then find the slope
of the trend line.

c. Write an equation for the trend line in slope-intercept form.

d. Use the equation you wrote in part (c). Find the solution of the equation
when $x = 12$.

Lesson 8-7   **Solving Systems of Linear Equations**

Lesson Objectives	**NAEP 2005 Strand:** Algebra
▼ Solve systems of linear equations by graphing	**Topic:** Algebraic Representations
▼ Use systems of linear equations to solve problems	**Local Standards:** _____

Vocabulary

A system of linear equations is _____

_____

Example

① **Solve a System by Graphing** Solve the system $y = x - 7$ and $y = 4x + 2$ by graphing.

Step 1 Graph each line.

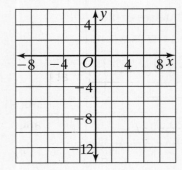

Step 2 Find the point of intersection.

The lines intersect at one point, [   ].

The solution is [   ].

Check See whether $(-3, -10)$ makes both equations true.

$y = x - 7$ **Replace *x* with** [   ] $y = 4x + 2$

[   ] $\overset{?}{=}$ [   ] $- 7$ **and *y* with** [   ].   [   ] $\overset{?}{=} 4($ [   ] $) + 2$

[   ] $=$ [   ] ✔   **The solution checks.**   [   ] $=$ [   ] ✔

Quick Check

1. Solve each system of equations by graphing. Check the solution.

   a. $y = x - 6$ and $y = -2x$

   [   ]

   b. $y = 3x - 3$ and $x + y = 1$

   [   ]

a.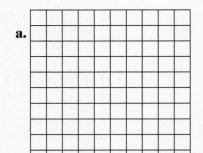

b.

Name_____ Class_____ Date _____

Examples

❷ **Solving Special Systems** Solve each system of equations by graphing.

a. $27x + 9y = 36; y = 4 - 3x$

b. $8 = 4x + 2y; 2x + y = 5$

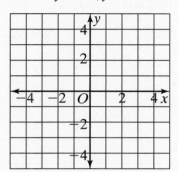

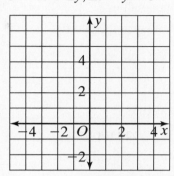

The lines are the same line. There are

[   ] many solutions.

The lines are [   ]. They do

not intersect. There is [   ] solution.

❸ **Using a System of Equations** Find two numbers with a sum of 10 and a difference of 2.

Step 1 Write equations.

Let x = the greater number.

Let y = the lesser number.

Equation 1 Sum is 10.

[   ] + [   ] = [   ]

Equation 2 Difference is 2.

[   ] − [   ] = [   ]

Step 2 Graph the equations.

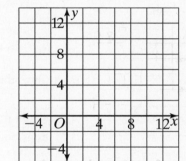

The lines intersect

at [   ].

The numbers are

[   ] and [   ].

Quick Check

2. Solve each system of equations by graphing.

a. $y = x - 6;$
$x - y = 6$

b. $y = x + 4;$
$y = x$

3. Find two numbers with a difference of 2 and a sum of −8.

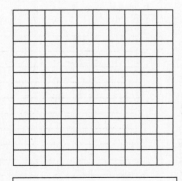

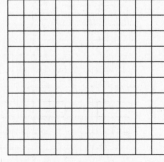

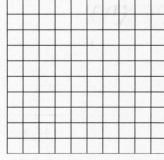

Lesson 8-8
Graphing Linear Inequalities

Lesson Objectives	NAEP 2005 Strand: Algebra
▼ Graph linear inequalities	Topic: Variables, Expressions, and Operations
▼ Graph systems of linear inequalities	Local Standards: _____

Vocabulary

A linear inequality is _____

_____

A system of linear inequalities is _____

Example

1 **Graphing a Linear Inequality** Graph the inequality $y > 2x + 1$ on a coordinate plane.

Step 1 Graph the boundary line.

Points on the boundary line do not make $y > 2x + 1$ true. Use a ☐ line.

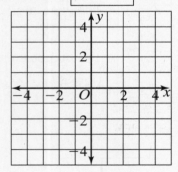

Step 2 Test a point not on the boundary line. Test $(0, 0)$ in the inequality.

$y > 2x + 1$

$\boxed{} \overset{?}{>} 2\left(\boxed{}\right) + 1$ **Substitute.**

$0 \overset{?}{>} 0 + 1$

$0 > 1$ ✗   **false**

Since the inequality is ☐ for (0, 0), shade the region that does not contain (0, 0).

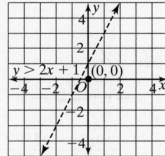

Quick Check

1. Graph each inequality.

a. $y \geq 3x - 1$ **b.** $y > -x + 3$ **c.** $y < 2x - 4$

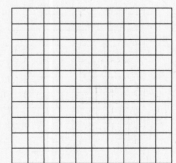   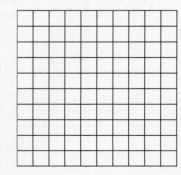   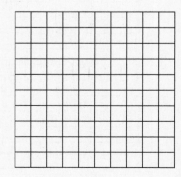

Examples

❷ Cashews cost $2/lb. Pecans cost $4/lb. You plan to spend no more than $20. Write an inequality to represent the number of pounds of each you can buy.

Words | cost of cashews | plus | cost of pecans | | is at most | | twenty dollars |

Let ⬚y = number of pounds of cashews.

Let ⬚x = number of pounds of pecans.

Inequality ⬚ + ⬚ ⬚ ⬚

❸ **Solving a System of Linear Inequalities** Solve the system $y \geq x + 1$ and $y < 2x + 3$ by graphing.

Step 1 Graph $y \geq x + 1$ and shade in one color.

Step 2 Graph $y < 2x + 3$ and shade in second color.

The solutions are the coordinates of all the points in the region that is shaded in both colors.

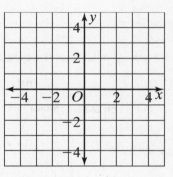

Quick Check

2. Adult tickets to the school play cost $4. Children's tickets cost $2. Your goal is to sell tickets worth at least $30. Let x be the number of children's tickets and y be the number of adult tickets. Write a linear inequality to show how many of each type of ticket you must sell to reach your goal.

3. Solve each system by graphing.

a. $y \leq -2x - 5$
   $y < \frac{1}{2}x$

b. $y > x - 1$
   $y < 3x + 4$

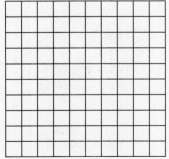

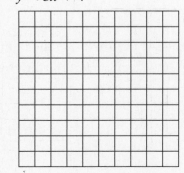

Lesson 9-1

**Introduction to Geometry:
Points, Lines and Planes**

Lesson Objectives

▼ Name basic geometric figures

▼ Recognize intersecting lines, parallel lines and skew lines

NAEP 2005 Strand: Geometry

Topic: Relationships Among Geometric Figures

Local Standards: _____

Vocabulary

Basic Geometric Figures

Sample	Symbolic Name	Description
•A	Point A	A point is a location in space. It has no size.
A B n	$\overleftrightarrow{AB}$, $\overleftrightarrow{BA}$, or n	A line is a series of points that extends in opposite directions without end. A lowercase letter can name a line.
A B M D C	ABCD or M	A plane is a flat surface with no thickness. It contains many lines and extends without end in the directions of all its lines.
Q P	$\overline{PQ}$, or $\overline{QP}$	A segment is a part of a line. It has two endpoints. PQ represents the length of $\overline{PQ}$.
C R	$\overrightarrow{CR}$	A ray is a part of a line. It has exactly one endpoint. Name its endpoint first.

Parallel lines are lines that are in the same plane that never intersect eachother

Skew lines are lines that are not in the same plane, are not parallel and do not intersect

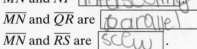

$\overline{MN}$ and $\overline{NP}$ intersecting

$\overline{MN}$ and $\overline{QR}$ are parallel.

$\overline{MN}$ and $\overline{RS}$ are skew.

Examples

❶ **Naming Geometric Figures** Use the figure to name each of the following.

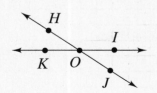

a. four different segments

$\overline{OI}$, $\overline{OJ}$, $\overline{OK}$, and $\overline{OH}$,

Name a segment by its endpoints.

b. five different rays

$\overrightarrow{OI}$, $\overrightarrow{OJ}$, $\overrightarrow{OK}$, and $\overrightarrow{OH}$,

The first letter names the endpoint.

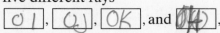

Name_____ Class_____ Date _____

❷ Relationships of Lines You are looking at a picture frame. Name each of the following.

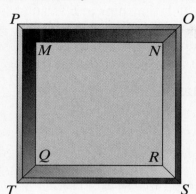

a. four segments that intersect $\overline{PT}$

[___] , [___] , [___] , and [___]

b. three segments parallel to $\overline{PT}$

[___] , [___] , and [___]

c. four segments skew to $\overline{PT}$

[___] , [___] , [___] , and [___]

❸ Drawing Lines Draw two intersecting lines. Then draw a segment that is parallel to one of the intersecting lines.

Use the lines on notebook paper or graph paper. First draw the lines that intersect. Then draw a segment that is parallel to one of the lines.

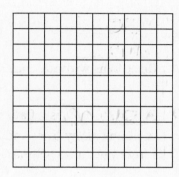

Quick Check

1. Name each figure in the diagram.

a. two segments [___] , [___]

b. two rays [___] , [___]

2. Use the picture in Example 2 to name each of the following:

a. four segments that intersect $\overline{QR}$

[___] , [___] ,

[___] , and [___]

b. Three segments parallel to $\overline{QR}$

[___] , [___] ,

and [___]

c. four segments that are skew to $\overline{QR}$

[___] , [___] ,

[___] , and [___]

3. Use the grid to draw the figures indicated.

a. three parallel segments

b. a ray that intersects the parallel segments of part (a)

c. a segment, $\overline{AB}$

d. a ray, $\overrightarrow{QR}$

e. a line, $\overleftrightarrow{LM}$

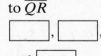

Lesson 9-2

Angle Relationships and Parallel Lines

Lesson Objectives	NAEP 2005 Strand: Geometry
▼ Identify adjacent and vertical angles	**Topic:** Relationships Among Geometric Figures
▼ Relate angles formed by parallel lines and a transversal	**Local Standards:** _____

Vocabulary

Angles 1 and 2 are [adjacent] angles. They share a [vertex] and a side.

Angles 1 and 4 are [verticle] angles. They are formed by two [intersecting] lines.

Line *n* is a [transversal]. It [intersects] lines ℓ and *m*.

Angles 1 and 5 are [corresponding] angles.

Angles 3 and 6 are [alternate interior] angles.

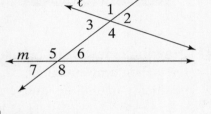

∠*ABC* and ∠*CBD* are [complimentry] angles. The sum of their measures is [90°].

∠*ABD* and ∠*DBE* are [supplementary] angles. The sum of their measures is [180°].

Examples

① **Finding the Measure of an Angle** Find the measure of ∠3 if *m*∠4 = 110°.

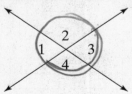

$m\angle 3 + m\angle 4 =$ [180]   ∠**3 and** ∠**4 are** [supplementary]

$m\angle 3 +$ [110] $= 180°$ **Replace** *m*∠**4 with** [110].

$m\angle 3 + 110° -$ [110] $= 180° -$ [110]   **Solve for** *m*∠**3.**

$m\angle 3 =$ [70]

Daily Notetaking Guide

❷ Identifying Congruent Angles In the diagram, $p \parallel q$. Identify each of the following.

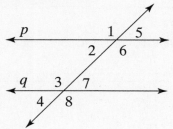

a. congruent corresponding angles

☐ ≅ ☐ , ☐ ≅ ☐ , ☐ ≅ ☐ , ☐ ≅ ☐

b. congruent alternate interior angles

☐ ≅ ☐ , ☐ ≅ ☐

Quick Check

1. If $m\angle 8 = 20°$, find the measures of $\angle 5$, $\angle 6$, and $\angle 7$.

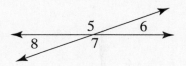

$m\angle 5 =$ ☐

$m\angle 6 =$ ☐

$m\angle 7 =$ ☐

2. In the diagram, $a \parallel b$.

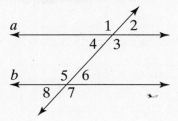

a. Name four pairs of congruent corresponding angles.

☐ ≅ ☐ , ☐ ≅ ☐ , ☐ ≅ ☐ , ☐ ≅ ☐

b. Name two pairs of congruent alternate interior angles.

☐ ≅ ☐ , ☐ ≅ ☐

Name_____ Class_____ Date_____

Lesson 9-3

Classifying Polygons

Lesson Objectives	**NAEP 2005 Strand:** Algebra
▼ Classify triangles	**Topic:** Equations and Inequalities
▼ Classify quadrilaterals	**Local Standards:** _____

Vocabulary

A polygon is _____

_____

A regular polygon is _____

_____

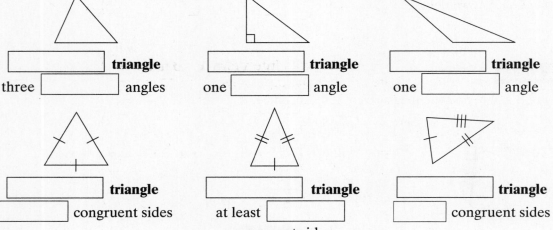

☐ **triangle**	☐ **triangle**	☐ **triangle**
three ☐ angles	one ☐ angle	one ☐ angle

☐ **triangle**	☐ **triangle**	☐ **triangle**
☐ congruent sides	at least ☐ congruent sides	☐ congruent sides

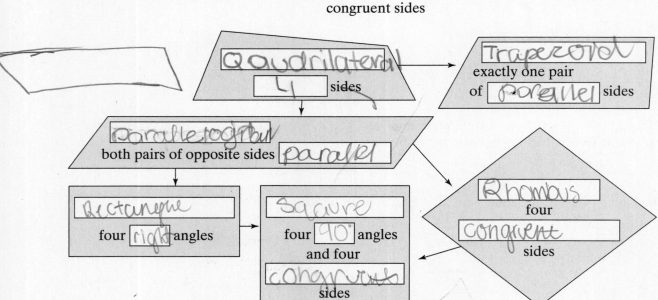

Qaudrilateral
4 sides

Trapezoid
exactly one pair of Parallel sides

Parallelogram
both pairs of opposite sides parallel

Rhombus
four congruent sides

Rectangle
four right angles

Square
four 90° angles
and four congruent sides

Daily Notetaking Guide

Name_____ Class_____ Date _____

Examples

❶ Classifying a Triangle Classify the triangle by its sides and angles.

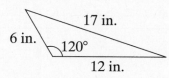

The triangle has [   ] congruent
sides and one [   ] angle.

The triangle is a scalene obtuse triangle.

❷ Classifying Quadrilaterals Name the types of quadrilaterals that have at least one pair of parallel sides.

All [   ] and [   ] have at least one pair of

parallel sides. Parallelograms include [   ] and [   ].

❸ Construction A contractor is framing the wooden deck shown below in the shape of a regular dodecagon (12 sides). Write a formula to find the perimeter of the deck. Evaluate the formula for a side length of 3 ft.

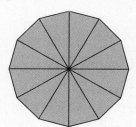

To write a formula, let x = the length of each side.
The perimeter of the regular dodecagon is
$P = x + x + x + x + x + x + x + x + x + x + x + x$.
Therefore a formula for the perimeter is [   ].

$P = 12x$ **Write the formula.**

$= 12([   ])$ **Substitute** [   ] **for** x.

$= [   ]$ **Simplify.**

For a side length of 3 ft, the perimeter is [   ] ft.

Quick Check

1. Judging by appearance, classify each triangle by its sides and angles.

a.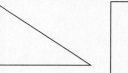

b.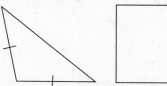

2. Name the two types of quadrilaterals that have four right angles.

[   ] and [   ]

3. a. Write a formula to find the perimeter of a regular hexagon. [   ]

    b. Use the formula to find the perimeter if one side is 16 cm. [   ]

Name_____ Class_____ Date_____

Lesson 9-4

Draw a Diagram

Lesson Objective	
▼ Draw a diagram	**Local Standards:** _____

Example

1 **Diagonals** How many diagonals does a nonagon have?

(Understand the Problem)

In reading the problem, make sure you understand the meanings of all the terms.

1. What is a nonagon?

a ninesided ~~figure~~

2. What is a diagonal?

a segment that connects to non-consecutive verticies

(Make and Carry Out a Plan)

One strategy for solving this problem is to draw a diagram and count the diagonals. A nonagon has [nine] sides. You can draw [6] diagonals from one vertex of a nonagon.

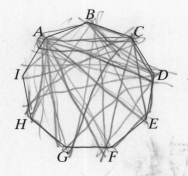

$\overline{AH}, \overline{AG}, \overline{AF}, \overline{AE}, \overline{AD},$ and $\overline{AC}$ are some of the diagonals.

54 diagnols in all

You can organize your results as you count the diagonals. Do not count the same diagonal twice. (The diagonal from A to C is the same as the one from C to A.) Then find the sum of the numbers of diagonals.

Vertex	A	B	C	D	E	F	G	H	I	Total
Number of Diagonals	6	6	5	3	2	1	0	0		27

A nonagon has [27] diagonals.

Check the Answer

Counting the diagonals after they have all been drawn is not an easy task. To check your results, you may want to try a different approach.

Start with figures with fewer sides and see whether there is a pattern to the total numbers of diagonals as you increase the number of sides.

Figure	Number of Sides	Number of Diagonals
Triangle	3	0
Quadrilateral	4	2
Pentagon	5	5
Hexagon	6	9

Notice that the total number of diagonals increases as you increase the number of sides of the polygon. First the number increases by 2, then by 3, and then by 4. Continue the pattern to check your results.

Figure	Number of Sides	Number of Diagonals
____	7	14
____	8	20
____	9	27

Quick Check

1. How many diagonals does a dodecagon have?

Lesson 9-5

Congruence

Lesson Objectives	NAEP 2005 Strand: Geometry
▼ Identify corresponding parts of congruent triangles ▼ Determine whether triangles are congruent	**Topic:** Transformation of Shapes and Preservation of Properties **Local Standards:** _____

Vocabulary and Key Concepts

Congruent figures are _____

_____

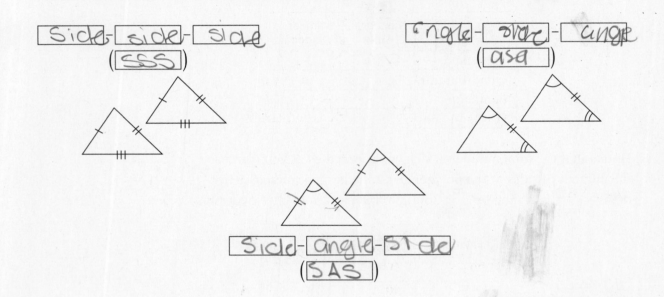

Side - side - side
(SSS)

angle - ava - unge
(asa)

Side - angle - side
(SAS)

Examples

❶ **Identifying Congruent Parts** In the figure, $\triangle TUV \cong \triangle WUX$.

a. Name the corresponding congruent angles.

$\angle V \cong \angle \boxed{X}$, $\angle T \cong \angle \boxed{W}$, $\angle TUV \cong \angle \boxed{WUX}$

b. Name the corresponding congruent sides.

$\overline{TV} \cong \boxed{WX}$, $\overline{TU} \cong \boxed{WU}$, $\overline{VU} \cong \boxed{XU}$

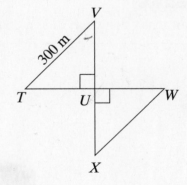

c. Find the length of $\overline{WX}$.

Since $\overline{WX} \cong \boxed{TV}$ and $TV = 300$ m, $WX = \boxed{300}$ m.

② **Identifying Congruent Triangles** List the congruent corresponding parts of each pair of triangles. Write a congruence statement for the triangles.

a.

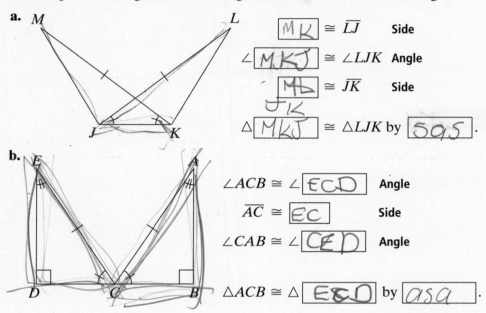

$\overline{MK}$ ≅ $\overline{LJ}$ **Side**

∠MKJ ≅ ∠LJK **Angle**

$\overline{MJ}$ ≅ $\overline{JK}$ **Side**

△MKJ ≅ △LJK by SAS.

b.

∠ACB ≅ ∠ECD **Angle**

$\overline{AC}$ ≅ $\overline{EC}$ **Side**

∠CAB ≅ ∠CED **Angle**

△ACB ≅ △ECD by asa.

Quick Check

1. △ABC ≅ △DEC. Judging by appearance, list all pairs of congruent corresponding sides and angles. Then find AC.

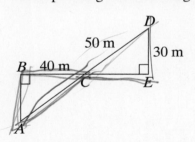

$\overline{AB}$ ≅ $\overline{ED}$, $\overline{BC}$ ≅ $\overline{EC}$, $\overline{AC}$ ≅ $\overline{DC}$,

∠A ≅ ∠D , ∠B ≅ ∠E ,

∠BCA ≅ ∠ECD; AC = 50 m

2. For the two triangles, list the congruent corresponding parts. Write a congruence statement (and reason) for the triangles.

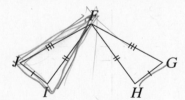

$\overline{FJ}$ ≅ $\overline{FG}$, $\overline{JI}$ ≅ $\overline{GH}$, $\overline{FI}$ ≅ $\overline{FH}$;

△JFI ≅ △GFH by SSS

Lesson 9-6

Circles

Lesson Objectives	NAEP 2005 Strand: Measurement
▼ Find circumferences	Topic: Measuring Physical Attributes
▼ Find central angles and make circle graphs	Local Standards: _____

Vocabulary and Key Concepts

Circumference of a Circle

The circumference of a circle is π times the diameter.

$C = \boxed{} \cdot \boxed{}$

$C = 2\boxed{} \cdot \boxed{}$

A circle is _____

A central angle is _____

_____

A $\boxed{}$ is a segment that has one endpoint at the center and the other point on the circle.

A $\boxed{}$ is a chord that passes through the center of a circle.

$\boxed{}$ is the distance around the circle.

A $\boxed{}$ is a segment whose endpoints are on the circle.

Examples

① Finding Circumference Find the circumference of the circle.

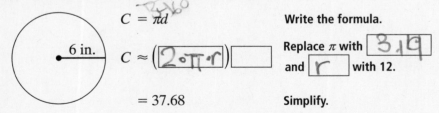

6 in.

$C = \pi d$ — Write the formula.

$C \approx \left(\boxed{2 \cdot \pi \cdot r}\right)\boxed{}$ — Replace π with $\boxed{3.19}$ and $\boxed{r}$ with 12.

$= 37.68$ — Simplify.

The circumference of the circle is about $\boxed{}$ in.

Daily Notetaking Guide

❷ Making a Circle Graph Make a circle graph for Jackie's weekly budget. Use proportions to find the measures of the central angles.

Jackie's Weekly Budget	
Entertainment (e)	20%
Food (f)	20%
Transportation (t)	10%
Savings (s)	50%

$$\dfrac{\boxed{}}{100} = \dfrac{e}{360} \qquad \dfrac{\boxed{}}{100} = \dfrac{f}{360}$$

$$e = \boxed{} \qquad\qquad f = \boxed{}$$

$$\dfrac{\boxed{}}{100} = \dfrac{t}{360} \qquad \dfrac{\boxed{}}{100} = \dfrac{s}{360}$$

$$t = \boxed{} \qquad\qquad s = \boxed{}$$

Use a compass to draw a circle. Draw the central angles with a protractor. Label each section. Add a title.

Jackie's Weekly Budget

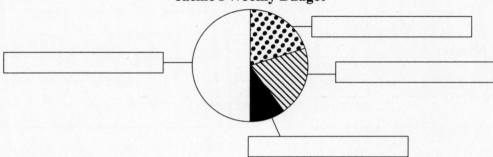

Quick Check

1. Find the circumference of a circle with a diameter of $2\frac{4}{5}$ in.

2. Make a circle graph for the data. Round the measure of each central angle to the nearest degree.

Blood Types of Population

Type A	Type B	Type AB	Type O
40%	12%	5%	43%

Blood Types of Population

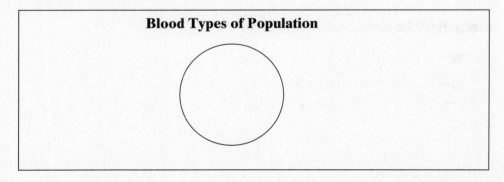

Lesson 9-7

Constructions

Lesson Objectives	NAEP 2005 Strand: Geometry
▼ Construct a segment or an angle congruent to a given segment or angle	**Topic:** Relationships Among Geometric Figures
▼ Construct segment bisector and angle bisectors	**Local Standards:** _____

Vocabulary

Perpendicular lines, segments, or rays _____

_____

A segment bisector is _____

_____

A perpendicular bisector is _____

_____

An angle bisector is _____

_____

Examples

❶ **Constructing a Perpendicular Bisector** Construct the perpendicular bisector of $\overline{WX}$.

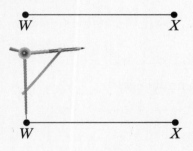

Step 1 Open the compass to more than half the length of $\overline{WX}$. Put the compass tip at W. Draw an arc intersecting $\overline{WX}$. With the same compass setting, repeat from point X.

Step 2 Label the points of intersection S and T. Draw $\overleftrightarrow{ST}$. Label the intersection of $\overleftrightarrow{ST}$ and $\overline{WX}$ point M.

$\overline{ST}$ is ⬚ to $\overline{WX}$ and $\overline{ST}$ ⬚ $\overline{WX}$.

❷ Constructing a Congruent Angle Construct an angle congruent to ∠*W*.

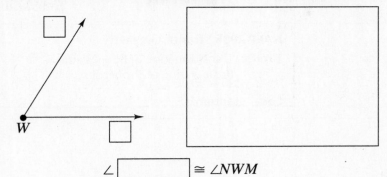

∠ [   ] ≅ ∠*NWM*

Step 1 Draw a ray with endpoint *A*.

Step 2 With the compass point at *W*, draw an arc that intersects the sides of ∠*W*. Label the intersection points *M* and *N*.

Step 3 With the *same* compass setting, put the compass tip on *A*. Draw an arc that intersects the ray at point *B*.

Step 4 Open the compass to the length of $\overline{MN}$. Using this setting, put the compass tip at *B*. Draw an arc to determine the point *C*. Draw $\overrightarrow{AC}$.

Quick Check

1. Construct the perpendicular bisector of $\overline{CD}$.

C   D

2. Construct an angle congruent to ∠*A*.

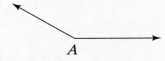

A

Name_____ Class_____ Date_____

Lesson 9-8

Translations

<table>
<tr><td>

Lesson Objectives

▼ Graph translations

▼ Describe translations

</td><td>

NAEP 2005 Strand: Geometry

Topics: Transformation of Shapes and Preservation of Properties

Local Standards: _____

</td></tr>
</table>

Vocabulary

A transformation is _____

A translation is _____

An image is _____

Example

❶ **Translating a Figure** Graph the image of $\triangle BCD$ after a translation 3 units to the left and 4 units down.

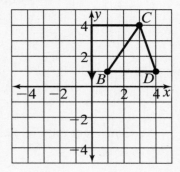

Quick Check

1. On a coordinate plane, draw $\triangle BCD$ from Example 1. Graph the image of $\triangle BCD$ after a translation of $\triangle BCD$ four units to the left.

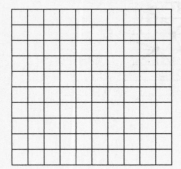

Examples

❷ Using Arrow Notation Use arrow notation to describe the translation of X to X'.

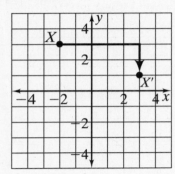

The point moves from $X(-2, 3)$ to $X'(3, 1)$, so the translation is [   ] → [   ].

❸ Writing a Rule Write a rule to describe the translation of $\triangle RST$ to $\triangle R'S'T'$.

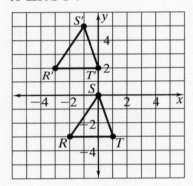

Use $R(-2, -3)$ and its image $R'(-3, 2)$ to find the horizontal and vertical translations.

Horizontal translation: $-3 - \left(\boxed{} \right) = \boxed{}$

Vertical translation: $2 - \left(\boxed{} \right) = \boxed{}$

The rule is $(x, y) \to (x - \boxed{}, y + \boxed{})$.

Quick Check

2. Use arrow notation to describe a translation of $B(-1, 5)$ to $B'(3, 1)$.

[   ]

3. Write a rule to describe the translation of quadrilateral $ABCD$ to quadrilateral $A'B'C'D'$.

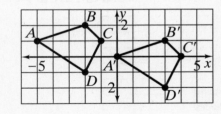

Lesson 9-9

Symmetry and Reflections

Lesson Objectives	NAEP 2005 Strand: Geometry
▼ Identify a line of symmetry	**Topic:** Transformation of Shapes and Preservation of Properties
▼ Graph a reflection of a geometric figure	**Local Standards:** _____

Vocabulary

Reflectional symmetry is _____

_____

A line of symmetry is _____

_____

A reflection is _____

_____

A line of reflection is _____

_____

Example

1 **Finding Lines of Symmetry** Draw the lines of symmetry. Tell how many lines there are.

a.

b.

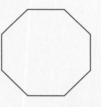

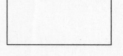

☐ lines of symmetry   ☐ lines of symmetry

Quick Check

1. Draw all lines of symmetry for each figure.

a.

b.

Examples

❷ **Reflecting Over an Axis** Graph the image of △*EFG* after a reflection over the *x*-axis.

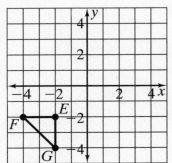

Since *F* is ☐ units below the *x*-axis,

F' is ☐ units above the *x*-axis.

Reflect the other vertices.
Draw △*E'F'G'*.

❸ **Reflecting Over a Line** Graph the image of △*EFG* after a reflection over $y = -1$.

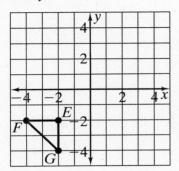

Graph $y = -1$.

Since *F* is ☐ unit below the line,

F' is ☐ unit above the line.

Reflect the other vertices.
Draw △*E'F'G'*.

Quick Check

2. Graph the image of △*EFG* after a reflection over the *y*-axis.

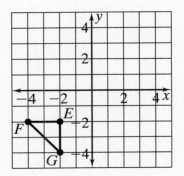

3. Graph △*ABC* with vertices $A(3, 0)$, $B(2, 3)$, and $C(5, -1)$ and its image after a reflection over the line $x = 2$.

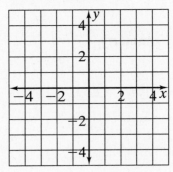

Pre-Algebra Lesson 9-9   **163**

Lesson 9-10

Rotations

Lesson Objectives	NAEP 2005 Strand: Geometry
▼ Graph rotations	**Topic:** Transformation of Shapes and Preservation of Properties
✔ Identify rotational symmetry	**Local Standards:** _____

Vocabulary

A rotation is _____

_____

A center of rotation is _____

_____

An angle of rotation is _____

_____

A figure has rotational symmetry if the _____

_____

Examples

❶ Finding a Rotation Image Find the vertices of the image of △RST after a rotation of 90° about the origin.

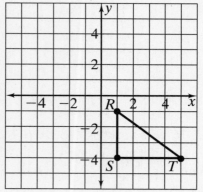

Step 1 Use a blank transparency sheet. Trace △RST, the x-axis, and the y-axis. Then fix the tracing in place at the origin.

Step 2 Rotate the tracing 90° counterclockwise. Make sure the axes line up. Label the vertices R′, S′, and T′. Connect the vertices of the rotated triangle.

The vertices of the image are R′(☐, ☐), S′(☐, ☐), and T′(☐, ☐).

❷ Finding Rotational Symmetry Judging from appearance, tell whether the star has rotational symmetry. If so, what is the angle of rotation?

The star can match itself in ☐ positions.

The pattern repeats in ☐ equal intervals.

$360° ÷ ☐ = ☐$

The figure ☐☐☐☐☐☐☐☐ rotational symmetry.

The angle of rotation is ☐ .

Quick Check

1. Draw the image of △*RST* in Example 1 after a rotation of 180° about the origin. Name the coordinates of the vertices of the image.

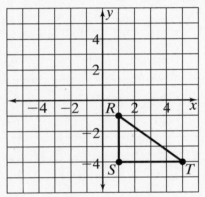

The vertices of the image are *R*′(☐, ☐), *S*′(☐, ☐), and *T*′(☐, ☐).

2. Judging from appearance, tell whether each figure has rotational symmetry. If so, what is the angle of rotation?

a.

b.

c.

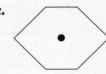

Lesson 10-1

Area: Parallelograms

Lesson Objectives	NAEP 2005 Strand: Measurement
▼ Find areas of rectangles ❷ Find areas of parallelograms	Topic: Measuring Physical Attributes; Systems of Measurement
	Local Standards: _____

Vocabulary and Key Concepts

Area of a Parallelogram

The area of a parallelogram is the product of any base length b and the corresponding height h.

$$A = \boxed{} \cdot \boxed{}$$

The area of a figure is _____

An altitude is _____

_____

Examples

❶ **Finding Area of a Rectangle** Find the area of the rectangle.

4 m

150 cm

Step 1 Change the units so they are the same.

150 cm = $\boxed{}$ m **Change 150 centimeters to meters.**

Step 2 Find the area.

$A = bh$ **Use the formula for area of a rectangle.**

$= (\boxed{})(\boxed{})$ **Replace b and h with the dimensions** $\boxed{}$ **and** $\boxed{}$.

$= \boxed{}$ **Simplify.**

The area of the rectangle is $\boxed{}$ m^2.

❷ Finding Area of a Parallelogram Find the area of each parallelogram.

a.

$A = bh$ **area formula**

$= ($ ☐ $)($ ☐ $)$ **Substitute.**

$= $ ☐   **Simplify.**

The area is ☐ m².

b.

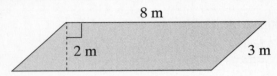

6 in.

$A = bh$ **area formula**

$= ($ ☐ $)($ ☐ $)$ **Substitute.**

$= $ ☐   **Simplify.**

2.5 in.

The area is ☐ in.².

Quick Check

1. Find the area of each rectangle.

a.

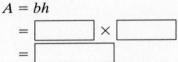

1 m

10 cm

$A = bh$

$= $ ☐ $\times$ ☐

$= $ ☐

The area is ☐ cm².

b.

2 yd

2 ft

$A = bh$

$= $ ☐ $\times$ ☐

$= $ ☐

The area is ☐ ft².

2. Find the area of each parallelogram.

a.

3 m

2 m

$A = bh$

$= $ ☐ $\times$ ☐

$= $ ☐

The area is ☐ m².

b.

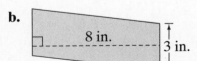

8 in.

3 in.

$A = bh$

$= $ ☐ $\times$ ☐

$= $ ☐

The area is ☐ in.².

Lesson 10-2

Area: Triangles and Trapezoids

<table>
<tr><td>

Lesson Objectives

▼ Find areas of triangles

▼ Find areas of trapezoids
</td><td>

NAEP 2005 Strand: Measurement

Topics: Measuring Physical Attributes;
Systems of Measurement

Local Standards: _____
</td></tr>
</table>

Vocabulary and Key Concepts

Area of a Triangle

The area of a triangle equals half the product of any base length b and the corresponding height h.

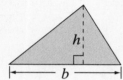

$$A = \frac{\square}{\square} \square \square$$

Area of a Trapezoid

The area of a trapezoid is half the product of the height and the sum of the lengths of the bases.

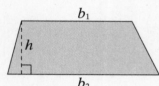

$$A = \frac{\square}{\square} \square \left(\square + \square \right)$$

An altitude of a triangle is _____

_____

Examples

❶ Finding Area of a Triangle Find the area of the triangle.

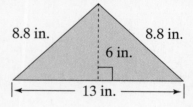

$A = \dfrac{\square}{\square}\ \square$ Use the formula for area of a triangle.

$= \dfrac{1}{2} \cdot \square \cdot \square$ Replace b with $\square$ and h with $\square$.

$= \square$ Simplify.

The area is $\square$ in.^{2}.

❷ Finding Area of a Trapezoid Suppose that, through the years, a layer of silt and mud settled in the bottom of the Erie Canal. Below is the resulting cross section of the canal. Find the area of the trapezoidal cross section.

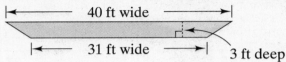

$A = \dfrac{\square}{\square}\,\square(\square + \square)$ **Use the formula for area of a trapezoid.**

$A = \dfrac{1}{2} \cdot \square(\square + \square)$ **Replace *h* with** $\square$ **, b_1 with** $\square$ **, and b_2 with** $\square$ **.**

$\quad = \dfrac{1}{2} \cdot 3(\square)$ **Add.**

$\quad = \dfrac{1}{2} \cdot \square$ **Multiply.**

$\quad = \boxed{}$ **Simplify.**

The area of the cross section is $\boxed{}$ ft^2.

Quick Check

1. Find the area of each figure.

a.
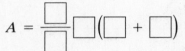

$A = \dfrac{1}{2}bh$

$\quad = \dfrac{1}{2}\left(\boxed{} \times \boxed{}\right)$

$\quad = \boxed{}$

The area is $\boxed{}$ ft^2.

b.
5 m

2 m

5.4 m

$A = \dfrac{1}{2}bh$

$\quad = \dfrac{1}{2}\left(\boxed{} \times \boxed{}\right)$

$\quad = \boxed{}$

The area is $\boxed{}$ m^2.

c.
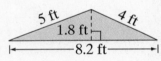

$A = \dfrac{1}{2}h(b_1 + b_2)$

$\quad = \dfrac{1}{2}\boxed{}\left(\boxed{} + \boxed{}\right)$

$\quad = \boxed{}$

The area is $\boxed{}$ ft^2.

Lesson 10-3

Area: Circles

Lesson Objectives	NAEP 2005 Strand: Measurement
Find areas of circles **2** Find area of irregular figures that include parts of circles	**Topics:** Estimation; Measuring Physical Attributes **Local Standards:** _____

Key Concepts

Area of a Circle

The area of a circle equals the product of π and the square of the radius r.

 $A = \boxed{}\boxed{}^2$

Examples

1 **Finding Area of a Circle** Find the exact area of a circle with diameter 20 in.

$A = \boxed{}$ **Use the formula for area of a circle.**

$ = \pi\left(\boxed{}\right)^2$ $r = \frac{1}{2}d; r = \boxed{}$

$ = \boxed{}$ **Simplify.**

The area is $\boxed{}$ in.^{2}.

2 **Using a Decimal Approximation of π** A TV station's weather radar can detect precipitation in a circular region having a diameter of 100 mi. Find the area of the region.

$A = \boxed{}$ **Use the formula for area of a circle.**

$ = \pi\left(\boxed{}\right)^2$ $r = \frac{1}{2}d; r = \boxed{}$

$ = 2{,}500\pi$ **exact area**

$ \approx 2{,}500\left(\boxed{}\right)$ **Use** $\boxed{}$ **for π.**

$ = \boxed{}$ **approximate area**

The area of the region is about $\boxed{}$ mi^2.

Name_____ **Class**_____ **Date** _____

❸ Finding Areas of Irregular Figures A pound of grass seed covers approximately 675 ft². Find the area of the lawn below. Then find the number of bags of grass seed you need to buy to cover the lawn. Grass seed comes in 3-lb bags.

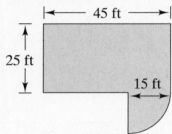

Area of region that is one fourth of a circle:

area of a circle = $\boxed{}\boxed{}^2$

area of a quarter circle = $\dfrac{\boxed{}}{\boxed{}}\boxed{}\boxed{}^2$

$A \approx \dfrac{1}{4}\left(\boxed{}\right)\left(\boxed{}\right)^2$ **Replace π with** $\boxed{}$ **and** *r* **with** $\boxed{}$.

= $\boxed{}$ ft²

Area of region that is a rectangle:

area of a rectangle = $\boxed{}$

$A \approx \boxed{} \cdot \boxed{}$ **Replace** *b* **with** $\boxed{}$ **and** *h* **with** $\boxed{}$.

= $\boxed{}$ ft²

The area of the lawn is about $\boxed{}$ ft² + $\boxed{}$ ft² = $\boxed{}$ ft².

You need to buy $\boxed{}$ 3-lb bag of grass seed.

Quick Check

1. Find the exact area of a circle with radius 50 in.

$\boxed{}$

2. Find the approximate area of a circle with radius 6 mi.

$\boxed{}$

3. Find the area of the shaded figure to the nearest tenth.

10 cm

5 cm

2.5 cm

$\boxed{}$

Lesson 10-4

Space Figures

Lesson Objectives	**NAEP 2005 Strand:** Geometry
▼ Identify common space figures	**Topic:** Dimension and Shape
▼ Identify space figures from nets	**Local Standards:** _____

Vocabulary

A space figure is _____

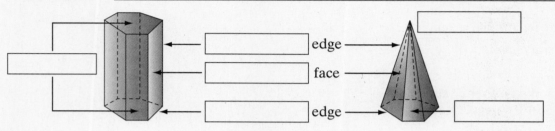

edge

face

edge

A pyramid has _____

The lateral faces are [_____] .

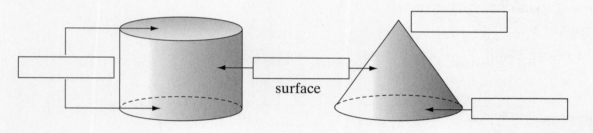

surface

A cylinder has _____

A cone has _____

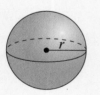

A sphere is _____

_____

A net is _____

Examples

❶ Naming Space Figures For each figure, describe the bases and name the figure.

a.

The bases are ⬚⬚⬚⬚⬚ . The figure is a ⬚⬚⬚⬚⬚ .

b.

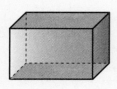

The bases are ⬚⬚⬚⬚⬚ .

The figure is a ⬚⬚⬚⬚⬚ .

❷ Naming Space Figures From Nets Name the space figure you can form from each net.

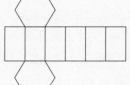

a. With two ⬚⬚⬚⬚⬚ bases and ⬚⬚⬚⬚⬚ sides,
you can form a ⬚⬚⬚⬚⬚ .

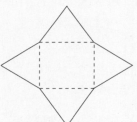

b. With a ⬚⬚⬚⬚⬚ base and ⬚⬚⬚⬚⬚ sides,
you can form a ⬚⬚⬚⬚⬚ .

Quick Check

1. Name each figure.

a.

⬚⬚⬚⬚⬚⬚⬚⬚⬚⬚

b.

⬚⬚⬚⬚⬚⬚⬚⬚⬚⬚

2. Name the space figure you can form from each net.

a.

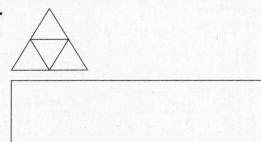

b.

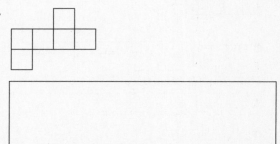

Lesson 10-5

Surface Area: Prisms and Cylinders

Lesson Objectives	NAEP 2005 Strand: Measurement
1 Find surface area of prisms	**Topic:** Measuring Physical Attributes
2 Find surface area of cylinders	**Local Standards:** _____

Vocabulary and Key Concepts

Surface Area of a Prism

The lateral area of a prism is the product of the perimeter of the base and the height.

L.A. = [ ]

Surface Area of a Cylinder

The lateral area of a cylinder is the product of the circumference of the base and the height of the cylinder.

L.A. = [ ]

The surface area of a cylinder is the sum of the lateral area and the areas of the two bases.

S.A. = L.A. + [ ]

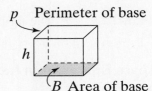

Surface area (S.A.) is _____

_____

Lateral area (L.A.) of a prism is _____

Examples

1 **Using a Net** Find the surface area of the rectangular prism using a net.

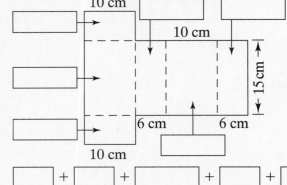

10 cm

10 cm

15 cm

6 cm   6 cm

10 cm

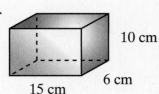

10 cm

15 cm

6 cm

Draw and label a net.

Find the area of each rectangle in the net.

[ ] + [ ] + [ ] + [ ] + [ ] + [ ] = [ ]   **Add the areas.**

The surface area is [ ] cm².

② **Using Formulas** Find the surface area of the cylindrical water tank.

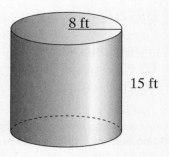

Step 1 Find the lateral area.

L.A. = [   ]   **Use the formula for lateral area.**

≈ 2(3.14)([   ])([   ])

≈ [   ]

Step 2 Find the surface area.

S.A. = [   ] + [   ]   **Use the formula for surface area.**

= L.A. + 2([   ])

≈ [   ] + 2(3.14)([   ])^2

= [   ]

The surface area of the water tank is about [   ] ft^2.

Quick Check

1. Find the surface area of each prism.

a.

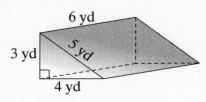

b.

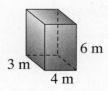

2. Find the surface area of a can with radius 5 cm and height 20 cm.

Lesson 10-6

**Surface Area: Pyramids,
Cones, and Spheres**

Lesson Objectives	NAEP 2005 Strand: Measurement
▼ Find surface area of pyramids	**Topic:** Measuring Physical Attributes
▼ Find surface area of cones and spheres	**Local Standards:** _____

Vocabulary and Key Concepts

Surface Area of a Pyramid

The lateral area of a pyramid is one-half the product of
the perimeter of the base and the slant height.

L.A. = $\dfrac{\square}{\square}$ $\square$ $\square$ S.A. = L.A. + $\square$

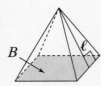

Surface Area of a Cone

The surface area of a cone is the sum of the lateral area
and base area.

L.A. = $\square$ $\square$ $\square$ S.A. = L.A. + $\square$

Surface Area of a Sphere

S.A. = $\square$ $\square$ $\square$

The slant height is _____

Examples

① Finding Surface Area of a Pyramid Find the surface area of the square pyramid.

Step 1 Find the lateral area.

L.A. = $\dfrac{\square}{\square}$ $\square$ **Use the formula for lateral area.**

= $\dfrac{1}{2}$ · $\square$ · $\square$ $p = 4\left(\square\right)$ and $\ell = \square$.

= 80

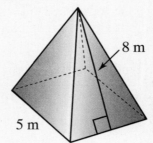

8 m

5 m

Step 2 Find the surface area.

S.A. = L.A. + B

= 80 + $\square$ **Lateral area = $\square$ and B = $\square$.**

= 80 + 25 = $\square$

The surface area of the pyramid is $\square$ m².

❷ Finding Surface Area of a Cone Find the surface area of the cone.

Step 1 Find the lateral area.

L.A. = ▯▯▯   **Use the formula for lateral area.**

≈ (3.14)(▯)(▯) $r =$ ▯ and $\ell =$ ▯.

≈ ▯

7 m

3 m

Step 2 Find the surface area.

S.A. = L.A. + B **Use the formula for surface area.**

≈ ▯ + (3.14)(▯)²   **L.A.** ≈ ▯ and $B = \pi($▯$)^2$.

= 65.94 + 28.26

= ▯

The surface area of the cone is about ▯ m².

❸ Finding Surface Area of a Sphere Earth has an approximate radius of 3,963 mi. What is the Earth's approximate surface area to the nearest 1,000 mi²? Assume the Earth is a sphere.

S.A. = ▯▯▯²   **Use the formula for surface area.**

≈ 4(3.14)(▯)² $r ≈$ ▯

= 197,259,434.64   **Multiply.**

≈ ▯   **Round to the nearest 1,000.**

The surface area of the Earth is about ▯ mi².

⊢— 7,926 mi —⊣

Quick Check

1. A pyramid has a square base with edge 20 ft. The slant height is 8 ft. Find its surface area.

▯

2. A cone has lateral height 39 ft and radius 7 ft. Find its surface area.

▯

3. A sphere has a radius of 6 cm. Find its surface area.

▯

Lesson 10-7

Volume: Prisms and Cylinders

Lesson Objectives	NAEP 2005 Strand: Measurement
▼ Find volumes of prisms ✔ Find volumes of cylinders	**Topic:** Measuring Physical Attributes **Local Standards:** _____

Vocabulary and Key Concepts

Volume of a Prism

The volume V of a prism is the product of the base area B and height h.

$V = \boxed{}\boxed{}$

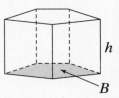

Volume of a Cylinder

The volume V of a cylinder is the product of the base area B and height h.

$V = \boxed{}\boxed{}$.

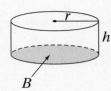

The volume of a three-dimensional figure is _____

_____

A cubic unit is _____

_____

Examples

❶ **Finding Volume of a Prism** Find the volume of the triangular prism.

$V = \boxed{}$ **Use the formula for volume.**

$ = \boxed{} \cdot 20$ $B = \frac{1}{2} \cdot \boxed{} \cdot \boxed{} = \boxed{}$ cm^2

$ = \boxed{}$ **Simplify.**

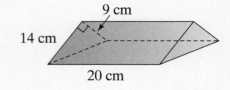

The volume is $\boxed{}$ cm^3.

Name_____ Class_____ Date _____

❷ Find the volume of the juice can to the nearest cubic centimeter.

3.4 cm

16 cm

$V = \boxed{}$ **Use the formula for volume.**

$V = \boxed{}\,h$ $B = \boxed{}$

$\approx 3.14 \cdot \boxed{}^2 \cdot \boxed{}$ **Replace *r* with** $\boxed{}$ **and *h* with** $\boxed{}$.

$= \boxed{}$ **Simplify.**

The volume is about $\boxed{}$ cm³.

Quick Check

1. Find the volume of the triangular prism.

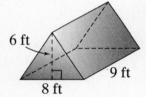

6 ft

9 ft

8 ft

2. Find the volume of the cylinder to the nearest cubic foot.

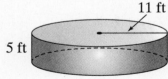

11 ft

5 ft

Lesson 10-8

Make a Model

Lesson Objective	Local Standards: _____
▼ Make a model	

Example

1 **Packaging** A can company rolls rectangular pieces of metal that measure 8 in. by 10 in. to make the sides of cans. Which height, 8 in. or 10 in., will make a can with the greater volume?

8 in.

10 in.

Understand the Problem

1. What is the goal of the problem?

2. What information do you have to help you build a model?

Make and Carry Out a Plan

You must find the height that gives you the greatest volume. Build two cans using 8 in-by-10 in. pieces of paper. You do not need to make the bases, just the sides.

10 in.

8 in.

3. Measure your models to find approximate radii.

    a. Radius of 10-in. = high can is approximately [   ] in.

    b. Radius of 8-in. = high can is approximately [   ] in.

    Find the volumes.

$V = $ [   ] $V = $ [   ]

$\approx (3.14)\left([\quad]^2\right)\left([\quad]\right)$ $\approx (3.14)\left([\quad]^2\right)\left([\quad]\right)$

$= $ [   ] $= $ [   ]

The volume is [   ] in.^{3}.   The volume is [   ] in.^{3}.

The can with the greater volume is the can whose height is [   ].

Check the Answer

A table is another way to organize your information and solve the problem.

4. List the height of each can, and then find the radius and the volume of the can.

Height	Radius	Volume
8 in.		
10 in.		

Quick Check

1. Suppose the company uses rectangular pieces of metal that measure 7 in. by 9 in. to form the cans. Build two models to determine which height, 7 in. or 9 in., will make the can with greater volume. Use the table below to organize your information.

Height	Radius	Volume

The can with the greater volume is the can whose height is [   ].

Lesson 10-9

Volume: Pyramids, Cones, and Spheres

Lesson Objectives	NAEP 2005 Strand: Measurement
▼ Find volumes of pyramids and cones ❷ Find volumes of spheres	**Topic:** Measuring Physical Attributes
	Local Standards: _____

Key Concepts

Volume of a Cone and of a Pyramid

The volume V of a cone or a pyramid is $\frac{1}{3}$ the product of the base area B and the height h.

$V = \boxed{}$

Volume of a Sphere

The volume V of a sphere with radius r is $\frac{4}{3}\pi$ times the cube of the radius.

$V = \boxed{}$

Examples

❶ **Finding Volume of a Cone** Find the volume of the cone.

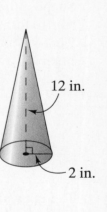

12 in.

2 in.

$V = \dfrac{\boxed{}}{\boxed{}}\boxed{}$ **Use the formula for volume.**

$= \frac{1}{3}\boxed{}h$ $B = \boxed{}$

$\approx \frac{1}{3}(3.14)\left(\boxed{}\right)^2\left(\boxed{}\right)$ **Replace r with $\boxed{}$, and h with $\boxed{}$. Use 3.14 for π.**

$= \boxed{}$ **Simplify.**

The volume of the cone is about $\boxed{}$ in.^{3}.

Name_____ Class_____ Date _____

❷ Finding Volume of a Pyramid Find the volume of the square pyramid.

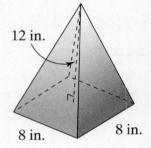

12 in.

8 in.   8 in.

$V = \dfrac{\boxed{}}{\boxed{}}\boxed{}$ **Use the formula for volume.**

$= \dfrac{1}{3}\boxed{}h$ $B = \boxed{}$

$= \dfrac{1}{3}\left(\boxed{}\right)^2\left(\boxed{}\right)$ **Replace *s* with $\boxed{}$, and *h* with $\boxed{}$.**

$= \boxed{}$ **Simplify.**

The volume of the pyramid is $\boxed{}$ in.^{3}.

❸ Finding Volume of a Sphere Earth has an average radius of 3,963 mi. What is Earth's approximate volume to the nearest 1,000,000 mi^3? Assume that Earth is a sphere.

$V = \dfrac{\boxed{}}{\boxed{}}\boxed{}$ **Use the volume formula.**

$\approx \dfrac{4}{3}(3.14)\left(\boxed{}\right)^3$ **Replace *r* with $\boxed{}$. Use 3.14 for π.**

$= \boxed{}$ **Simplify.**

The volume of Earth is about $\boxed{}$ mi^3.

Quick Check

1. Find the volume, to the nearest cubic unit, of a cone with height 5 cm and radius of base 2 cm.

2. Find the volume of a square pyramid that has a side of 5 ft and a height of 20 ft.

3. Find the volume of each sphere to the nearest whole number. Use 3.14 for π.

   a. radius = 15 m   **b.** diameter = 7 mi

Lesson 11-1

Square Roots and Irrational Numbers

Lesson Objectives	**NAEP 2005 Strand:** Number Sense
▼ Find square roots of numbers	**Topic:** Estimation
▼ Classify real numbers	**Local Standards:** _____

Vocabulary

A perfect square is _____

_____

Finding a square root is _____

_____

An irrational number is a number that _____

_____

Examples

❶ **Simplifying Square Roots** Simplify each square root.

a. $\sqrt{144}$

$\sqrt{144} = \boxed{}$

b. $-\sqrt{81}$

$-\sqrt{81} = \boxed{}$

❷ **Estimating Square Roots** You can use the formula $d = \sqrt{1.5h}$ to estimate the distance d, in miles, to a horizon line when your eyes are h feet above the ground. Estimate the distance to the horizon seen by a lifeguard whose eyes are 20 feet above the ground.

$d = \sqrt{1.5h}$	**Use the formula.**
$d = \sqrt{1.5\left(\boxed{}\right)}$	**Replace h with** $\boxed{}$.
$d = \sqrt{30}$	**Multiply.**
$\sqrt{25} < \sqrt{30} < \sqrt{36}$	**Find the perfect squares close to 30.**
$\sqrt{25} = \boxed{}$	**Find the square root of the closest perfect square.**

The lifeguard can see about $\boxed{}$ miles to the horizon.

Name_____ Class_____ Date _____

❸ Identifying Irrational Numbers Use a Calculator. Identify each number as rational or irrational. Explain.

Ir = irrational
r = ration

a. $\sqrt{49}$

rational

b. 0.16

r

c. $\sqrt{3}$

ir

d. 0.3333…

r

e. $-\sqrt{15}$

ir

f. 12.69

r

g. 0.1234567…

ir

Quick Check

1. Simplify each square root.

a. $\sqrt{100}$ ☐   **b.** $-\sqrt{100}$ ☐   **c.** $\sqrt{16}$ ☐   **d.** $-\sqrt{16}$ ☐

2. Estimate to the nearest integer.

a. $\sqrt{27}$ **b.** $-\sqrt{72}$ **c.** $\sqrt{50}$ **d.** $-\sqrt{22}$

3. Identify each number as rational or irrational. Explain.

a. $\sqrt{2}$ **b.** $-\sqrt{81}$

c. 0.53   **d.** $\sqrt{42}$

Lesson 11-2

The Pythagorean Theorem

Lesson Objectives	NAEP 2005 Strand: Geometry
▼ Use the Pythagorean Theorem ❷ Identify right triangles	Topic: Relationships Among Geometric Figures Local Standards: _____

Vocabulary and Key Concepts

Pythagorean Theorem

In any right triangle, the sum of the squares of the lengths of the legs is equal to the square of the length of the hypotenuse.

$$\boxed{a}^2 + \boxed{b}^2 = \boxed{c}^2$$

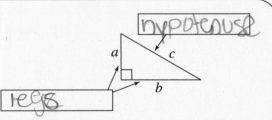

The legs of a right triangle are the shortest sides of a right triangle

The hypotenuse is the longest side & opposite the legs

Example

❶ **Using the Pythagorean Theorem** Find c, the length of the hypotenuse.

$c^2 = \boxed{}^2 + \boxed{}^2$ **Use the Pythagorean Theorem.**

$c^2 = \boxed{}^2 + \boxed{}^2$ **Replace a with** $\boxed{}$ **and b with** $\boxed{}$.

$c^2 = \boxed{}$ **Simplify.**

$c^2 = \sqrt{1,225} = \boxed{}$ **Find the positive square root of each side.**

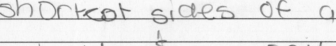

The length of the hypotenuse is $\boxed{}$ cm.

Quick Check

1. The lengths of two sides of a right triangle are given. Find the length of the third side.

a. legs: 3 ft and 4 ft

b. leg: 12 m; hypotenuse: 15 m

Name_____ Class_____ Date _____

Examples

❷ Finding an Approximate Length The carpentry terms *span*, *rise*, and *rafter length* are illustrated in the diagram. A carpenter wants to make a roof that has a span of 20 ft and a rise of 10 ft. What should the rafter length be?

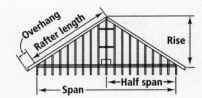

$c^2 = \boxed{}^2 + \boxed{}^2$ — Use the Pythagorean Theorem.

$c^2 = \boxed{}^2 + \boxed{}^2$ — Replace *a* with $\boxed{}$ (half the span), and *b* with 10.

$c^2 = \boxed{} + \boxed{}$ — Square 10.

$c^2 = \boxed{}$ — Add.

$c = \sqrt{\boxed{}}$ — Find the positive square root.

$c \approx \boxed{}$ — Round to the nearest tenth.

The rafter length should be about $\boxed{}$ ft.

❸ Finding a Right Triangle Is a triangle with sides 10 cm, 24 cm, and 26 cm a right triangle?

$a^2 + b^2 = c^2$ — Write the equation for the Pythagorean Theorem.

$\boxed{}^2 + \boxed{}^2 \stackrel{?}{=} \boxed{}^2$ — Replace *a* and *b* with the shorter lengths and *c* with the longest length.

$\boxed{} + \boxed{} \stackrel{?}{=} \boxed{}$ — Simplify.

$\boxed{} = 676$ ✔ — Add.

The triangle $\boxed{}$ a right triangle.

Quick Check

2. a. In a right triangle, the length of the hypotenuse is 15 m and the length of a leg is 8 m. What is the length of the other leg, to the nearest tenth of a meter?

$\boxed{}$

b. Carpentry What is the rise of a roof if the span is 22 feet and the rafter length is 14 feet? Round to the nearest tenth of a foot.

$\boxed{}$

3. Can you form a right triangle with the three lengths given? Explain.

a. 7 in., 8 in., $\sqrt{113}$

b. 5 mm, 6 mm, 10 mm

Lesson 11-3

Distance and Midpoint Formulas

Lesson Objectives	**NAEP 2005 Strand:** Measurement
▼ Find the distance between two points using the Distance Formula	**Topic:** Measuring Physical Attributes
❷ Find the midpoint of a segment using the Midpoint Formula	**Local Standards:** _____

Vocabulary and Key Concepts

Distance Formula

The distance d between any two points (x_1, y_1) and (x_2, y_2) is

$$d = \sqrt{(\boxed{x_2} - \boxed{x_1})^2 + (\boxed{y_2} - \boxed{y_1})^2}$$

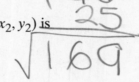

Midpoint Formula

The midpoint M of a line segment with endpoints $A(x_1, y_1)$ and $B(x_2, y_2)$ is

$$M\left(\frac{\boxed{y_1} + x_2}{2}, \frac{\boxed{x_1} + y_2}{2}\right)$$

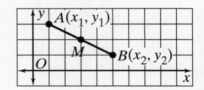

The midpoint of segment $\overline{AB}$ is _____

_____

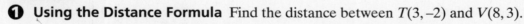

Example

❶ **Using the Distance Formula** Find the distance between $T(3, -2)$ and $V(8, 3)$.

$$d = \sqrt{(x_2 - x_1)^2 + (y_2 - y_1)^2}$$ Use the Distance Formula.

$$d = \sqrt{(\square - \square)^2 + (\square - (\square))^2}$$ Replace (x_2, y_2) with $(\boxed{\ }, \boxed{\ })$ and (x_1, y_1) with $(\boxed{\ }, \boxed{\ })$.

$$d = \sqrt{\square^2 + \square^2}$$ Simplify.

$$d = \sqrt{\square}$$ Find the exact distance.

$$d \approx \boxed{\ }$$ Round to the nearest tenth.

The distance between T and V is about $\boxed{\ }$ units.

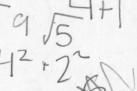

Quick Check

1. Find the distance between the two points in each pair. Round to the nearest tenth.

   a. $(3, 8), (2, 4)$

   b. $(10, -3), (1, 0)$

   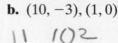

Name_____ Class_____ Date _____

Example

❷ Finding the Midpoint of a Segment Find the midpoint of $\overline{TV}$.

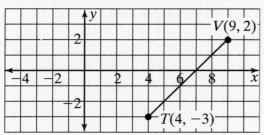

$$\left(\frac{x_1 + x_2}{2}, \frac{y_1 + y_2}{2}\right)$$ **Use the Midpoint Formula.**

$$= \left(\frac{\boxed{} + \boxed{}}{2}, \frac{\boxed{} + \boxed{}}{2}\right)$$ **Replace (x_1, y_1) with $\left(\boxed{}, \boxed{}\right)$ and (x_2, y_2) with $\left(\boxed{}, \boxed{}\right)$.**

$$= \left(\frac{\boxed{}}{2}, \frac{\boxed{}}{2}\right)$$ **Simplify the numerators.**

$$= \left(\boxed{}\frac{\boxed{}}{\boxed{}}, \boxed{}\frac{\boxed{}}{\boxed{}}\right)$$ **Write the fractions in simplest form.**

The coordinates of the midpoint of $\overline{TV}$ are $\left(\boxed{}, \boxed{}\right)$.

Quick Check

2. Find the midpoint of each segment.

a.
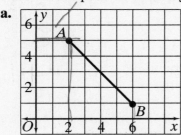

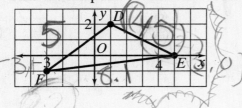

b.
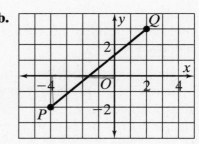

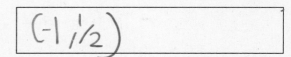

c. Find the midpoint of each side of $\triangle DEF$.

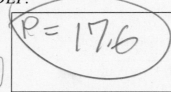

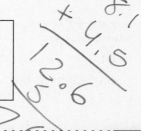

Lesson 11-4

Write a Proportion

Lesson Objective	NAEP 2005 Strand: Number Sense
▼ Write a proportion from similar triangles	**Topic:** Ratios and Proportional Reasoning
	Local Standards: _____

Example

1 At a given time of day, a building of unknown height casts a shadow that is 24 feet long. At the same time of day, a post that is 8 feet tall casts a shadow that is 4 feet long. What is the height x of the building?

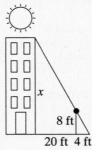

Understand the Problem

1. What information is given?

2. What are you asked to find?

Make and Carry Out a Plan

Since the triangles are similar, and you know three lengths, writing and solving a proportion is a good strategy to use. It is helpful to draw the triangles as separate figures.

Write a proportion using the legs of the similar triangles.

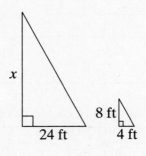

$\dfrac{4}{24} = \dfrac{\square}{\square}$ **Write a proportion.**

$\square x = \boxed{}\left(\boxed{}\right)$ **Write cross products.**

$4x = \boxed{}$ **Simplify.**

$x = \boxed{}$ **Divide each side by 4.**

The height of the building is $\boxed{}$ ft.

Daily Notetaking Guide

Name_____ Class_____ Date _____

(Check the Answer)

Solving problems that involve indirect measurement often makes use of figures that overlap.

Quick Check

1. Use the diagram of the building in Example 1 to answer the following questions.

   a. Which segments overlap?

   b. A common error students make is to use part of a side in a proportion. For example, some students might think $\frac{4}{20}$ is equal to $\frac{8}{x}$. How does drawing the triangles as separate figures help you avoid this error?

Lesson 11-5

Lesson Objectives	NAEP 2005 Strand: Geometry
▼1 Use the relationships in 45°-45°-90° triangles	**Topic:** Relationships Among Geometric Figures
▼2 Use the relationships in 30°-60°-90° triangles	**Local Standards:** _____

Vocabulary and Key Concepts

Multiplying Square Roots

For nonnegative numbers, the square root of a product equals the _____

_____

Arithmetic	**Algebra**
$\sqrt{9 \cdot 2} = \sqrt{\boxed{}} \cdot \sqrt{\boxed{}}$	If $a \geq 0$ and $b \geq 0$, then $\sqrt{ab} = \sqrt{\boxed{}} \cdot \sqrt{\boxed{}}$

45°-45°-90° Triangles

In a 45°-45°-90° triangle, the legs are $\boxed{}$ and the length of the

hypotenuse is the length of a leg times $\boxed{}$.

hypotenuse = leg · $\boxed{}$

30°-60°-90° Triangles

In a 30°-60°-90° triangle, the length of the hypotenuse is $\boxed{}$ times the

length of the shorter leg. The length of the longer leg is the length of the

shorter leg times $\boxed{}$.

hypotenuse = $\boxed{}$ · shorter leg

longer leg = shorter leg · $\boxed{}$

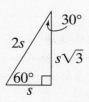

Examples

❶ Finding Length of the Hypotenuse Find the length of the hypotenuse
in the triangle.

hypotenuse = leg · $\boxed{}$ **Use the 45°–45°–90° relationship.**

$y = \boxed{} \cdot \boxed{}$ **The length of the leg is $\boxed{}$ cm.**

$\approx \boxed{}$ **Use a calculator.**

The length of the hypotenuse is about $\boxed{}$ cm.

❷ Finding the Length of a Diagonal Patrice folds square napkins diagonally to put on a table. The side length of each napkin is 20 in. How long is the diagonal?

hypotenuse = leg · [ ]   **Use the 45°–45°–90° relationship.**

y = [ ] · [ ]   **The length of the leg is [ ] in.**

≈ [ ]   **Use a calculator.**

The diagonal is about [ ] in. long.

❸ Finding Lengths in a 30°-60°-90° Triangle Find the missing lengths in the triangle.

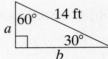

hypotenuse = [ ] · shorter leg

[ ] = [ ] · a   **The length of the hypotenuse is [ ] ft.**

$\frac{14}{[\ ]} = \frac{2b}{[\ ]}$ **Divide each side by [ ].**

[ ] = a   **Simplify.**

longer leg = shorter leg · [ ]

b = [ ] · [ ]   **The length of the shorter leg is [ ].**

b ≈ [ ]   **Use a calculator.**

The length of the shorter leg is [ ] ft. The length of the longer leg is about [ ] ft.

Quick Check

1. The length of each leg of an isosceles right triangle is 4.2 cm. Find the length of the hypotenuse. Round to the nearest tenth.

[ ]

2. Gymnasts use mats that are 12 m by 12 m for floor exercises. A gymnast does cartwheels across the diagonal of a mat. What is the length of the diagonal to the nearest meter?

[ ]

3. Find the missing lengths in each 30°-60°-90° triangle.

a.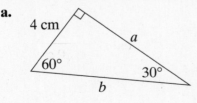

b.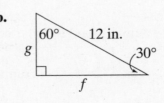

Lesson 11-6

Sine, Cosine, and Tangent Ratios

Lesson Objectives

▼ Find trigonometric ratios in right triangles

▼ Use trigonometric ratios to solve problems

Local Standards: _____

Vocabulary and Key Concepts

Trigonometric Ratios

sine $\angle A = \dfrac{\text{length of }\boxed{}}{\text{length of }\boxed{}}$; cosine $\angle A = \dfrac{\text{length of }\boxed{}}{\text{length of }\boxed{}}$

tangent $\angle A = \dfrac{\text{length of }\boxed{}}{\text{length of }\boxed{}}$

Trigonometry means _____

A trigonometric ratio is _____

_____

Example

❶ **Writing Trigonometric Ratios** Find the sine, cosine, and tangent of $\angle A$.

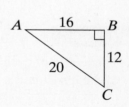

$\sin \angle A = \dfrac{\boxed{}}{\text{hypotenuse}} = \dfrac{\boxed{}}{\boxed{}} = \dfrac{\boxed{}}{\boxed{}}$

$\cos \angle A = \dfrac{\boxed{}}{\text{hypotenuse}} = \dfrac{\boxed{}}{\boxed{}} = \dfrac{\boxed{}}{\boxed{}}$

$\tan \angle A = \dfrac{\boxed{}}{\boxed{}} = \dfrac{\boxed{}}{\boxed{}} = \dfrac{\boxed{}}{\boxed{}}$

Quick Check

1. For $\triangle ABC$ in Example 1, find the sine, cosine, and tangent of $\angle C$.

$\sin \angle C = \boxed{}$; $\cos \angle C = \boxed{}$; $\tan \angle C = \boxed{}$

Name_____ Class_____ Date _____

Examples

❷ Using a Calculator Find the trigonometric ratios of 18° using a scientific calculator or the table on page 801. Round to four decimal places.

sin 18° ≈ [ ]   **Scientific calculator: Enter 18 and press the key labeled SIN, COS, or TAN.**

cos 18° ≈ [ ]

tan 18° ≈ [ ]   **Table: Find 18° in the first column. Look across to find the appropriate ratio.**

❸ Applying Trigonometric Ratios The diagram shows a doorstop in the shape of a wedge. What is the length of the hypotenuse of the doorstop?

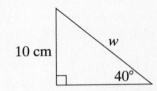
10 cm w 40°

You know the angle and the side opposite the angle.
You want to find w, the length of the hypotenuse.

$$\sin \angle A = \frac{\boxed{}}{\boxed{}}$$ **Use the sine ratio.**

$$\sin \boxed{} = \frac{\boxed{}}{\boxed{}}$$ **Substitute** [ ] **for the angle,** [ ] **for the opposite side, and** [ ] **for the hypotenuse.**

$w(\sin 40°) = 10$ **Multiply each side by w.**

$$w = \frac{10}{\boxed{}}$$ **Divide each side by** [ ].

$w \approx$ [ ]   **Use a calculator.**

The hypotenuse is about [ ] cm long.

Quick Check

2. Find each value. Round to four decimal places.

   a. sin 10° [ ]   **b.** cos 75° [ ]   **c.** tan 53° [ ]   **d.** cos 22° [ ]

3. How long is the bottom leg of the doorstop in Example 3?

Lesson 11-7

Angles of Elevation and Depression

Lesson Objectives	**Local Standards:** _____
▼ Use trigonometry for finding angles of elevation	
▼ Use trigonometry for finding angles of depression	

Vocabulary

An angle of elevation is _____

_____

An angle of depression is _____

_____

Example

① Using Angles of Elevation Janine is flying a kite. She lets out 30 yd of string and anchors it to the ground. She determines that the angle of elevation of the kite is 52°. What is the height *h* of the kite from the ground?

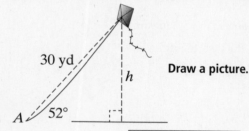

Draw a picture.

$$\sin \angle A = \frac{\boxed{}}{\boxed{}}$$

Choose an appropriate trigonometric ratio.

$$\sin 52° = \frac{h}{\boxed{}}$$

Substitute $\boxed{}$ **for the angle measure and** $\boxed{}$ **for the hypotenuse.**

$$\boxed{}(\sin 52°) = h$$

Multiply each side by $\boxed{}$.

$$\boxed{} \approx h$$

Simplify.

The kite is about $\boxed{}$ yd from the ground.

Quick Check

1a. The angle of elevation from a ship to the top of a lighthouse is 12°. The lighthouse is known to be 30 m tall. How far is the ship from the base of the lighthouse?

Name_____ Class_____ Date _____

Quick Check

1b. A rock climber looks at the top of a vertical rock wall at an angle of elevation of 74°. He is standing 4.2 m from the base of the wall and his eyes are 1.5 m from the ground. How high is the wall, to the nearest tenth of a meter?

Example

② **Using Angles of Depression** An airplane is flying 1.5 mi above the ground. If the pilot must begin a 3° descent to an airport runway at that altitude, how far is the airplane from the beginning of the runway (in ground distance)?

Draw a picture.
(not to scale)

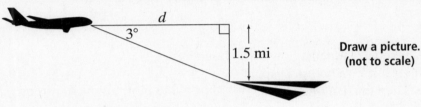

$$\tan 3° = \frac{\boxed{}}{d}$$ **Choose an appropriate trigonometric ratio.**

$$\boxed{} \cdot \tan 3° = 1.5$$ **Multiply each side by $\boxed{}$.**

$$d = \frac{1.5}{\boxed{}}$$ **Divide each side by $\boxed{}$.**

$$d \approx \boxed{}$$ **Use a calculator or table.**

The airplane is about $\boxed{}$ mi from the airport.

Quick Check

2. A group of people in a hang-gliding class are standing on top of a cliff 70 m high. They spot a hang glider landing on the beach below them. The angle of depression from the top of the cliff to the hang glider is 72°. How far is the hang glider from the base of the cliff?

Lesson 12-1

Frequency Tables, Line Plots, and Histograms

Lesson Objectives	NAEP 2005 Strand: Data Analysis and Probability
▼ Display data in frequency tables and line plots	Topic: Data Representation
▼ Display data in histograms	Local Standards: _____

Vocabulary

A frequency table is a data display that _____

_____

A line plot is a data display that _____

_____

The range of the data is _____

_____

Example

❶ Using a Line Plot A survey asked 22 students how many hours of TV they watched daily. The results are below. Display the data in a frequency table. Then make a line plot.

1	3	4	3	1	1	2	3	4	1	3
2	2	1	4	2	1	2	3	2	4	3

List the numbers of hours in order.   Use a tally mark for each result.   Count the tally marks and record the frequency.

Number	Tally	Frequency
1	‖‖‖ l	6

For a line plot, follow the steps ①, ②, and ③.

③ Write a title that describes the data.

[   ]

② Mark an **X** for each response.

1 2 3 4

① Draw a number line with the choices below it.

Quick Check

1. Display the data below in a frequency table. Then make a line plot.

10 12 13 15 10 11 14 13 10 11 11 12 10 10 15

Number	Tally	Frequency

Example

2 **Displaying Data in a Histogram** Twenty-one judges were asked how many cases they were trying on Monday. The frequency table below shows their responses. Display the data in a histogram. Then find the range.

"How many cases are you trying?"

Number	Frequency
0	3
1	5
2	4
3	5
4	4

For a histogram, follow the steps ①, ②, and ③.

③ Write a title.

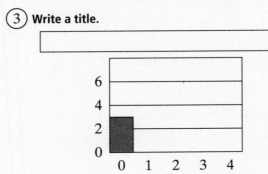

② Draw bars equal in height to the frequency.

① Label each axis.

The greatest value in the data set is [ ] and the least value is [ ].
The range is [ ] − [ ] or [ ].

Quick Check

2. **a.** Display the data below in a histogram. Then find the range.
   Miles from home to the mall:
   2, 4, 3, 7, 3, 1, 4, 2, 2, 6, 3, 5, 1, 8, 3

   b. What is the range of the data below?
   Prices of a gallon of regular gas at different gas stations:
   $1.48, $1.32, $1.30, $1.35, $1.41, $1.29, $1.32, $1.43, $1.36

Lesson 12-2

Box-and-Whisker Plots

Lesson Objectives	NAEP 2005 Strand: Data Analysis and Probability
V Make box-and-whisker plots	**Topic:** Characteristics of Data Sets
V Analyze data in box-and-whisker plots	**Local Standards:** _____

Vocabulary

A box-and-whisker plot is a data display that _____

_____

Quartiles _____

The median is _____

Example

1 **Making a Box-and-Whisker Plot** The data below represent the wingspans in centimeters of captured birds. Make a box-and-whisker plot.

61 35 61 22 33 29 40 62 21 49 72 75 28 21 54

Step 1 Arrange the data in order from least to greatest. Find the median.

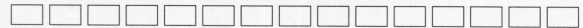

Step 2 Find the lower quartile and upper quartile, which are the medians of the lower and upper halves.

lower quartile [ ]   upper quartile [ ]

Step 3 Draw a number line. Mark the least and greatest values, the median, and the quartiles. Draw a box from the first to the third quartile. Mark the median with a vertical segment. Draw whiskers from the box to the least and greatest values.

Wingspans of Captured Birds

```
   +--+--+--+--+--+--+--+--+--+--+--+--+--+--+-->
  10   20   30   40   50   60   70   80
```

Quick Check

1. Draw a box-and-whisker plot for the distances of migration of birds (thousands of miles): 5, 2.5, 6, 8, 9, 2, 1, 4, 6.2, 18, 7.

Example

❷ **Using a Box-and-Whisker Plot to Draw Conclusions** The plots below compare the percents of students who were eligible to those who participated in extracurricular activities in one school from 1992 to 2002. What conclusions can you draw?

**Percents of Students Who Were Eligible and
Participated in Activities from 1992 to 2002**

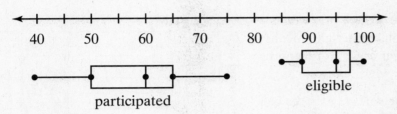

About [   ] of the students were eligible to participate in extracurricular

activities. Around [   ] of the students did participate. A little less than

[   ] of the eligible students participated in extracurricular activities.

Quick Check

2. Use the box-and-whisker plots below. What conclusions can you draw about the heights of Olympic basketball players?

Olympic Basketball Players' Heights (in.)

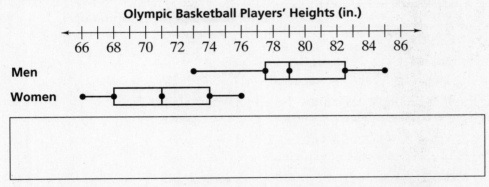

[   ]

3. Compare annual video sales and CD sales by making two box-and-whisker plots below one number line.

videos (millions of units): 28, 24, 15, 21, 22, 16, 22, 30, 24, 17
CDs (millions of units) 16, 17, 22, 16, 18, 24, 15 16, 25, 18

[   ]

Lesson 12-3

Using Graphs to Persuade

Lesson Objectives	NAEP 2005 Strand: Data Analysis and Probability
▼ Recognize the use of breaks in the scales of graphs ▼ Recognize the use of different scales	Topic: Data Representation Local Standards: _____

Example

❶ **Choosing an Appropriate Title** Which title would be more appropriate for the graph at the right: "Texas Overwhelms California" or "Areas of California and Texas"? Explain.

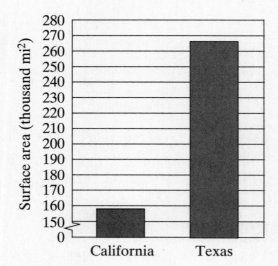

Because of the [＿＿＿＿＿] in the vertical axis, the bar for Texas appears to be more than [＿＿＿＿] times the height of the bar for California. Actually, the area of Texas is about [＿＿＿＿＿＿], which is not even [＿＿＿＿] times the area of California, which is about [＿＿＿＿＿].

The title [＿＿＿＿＿＿＿＿＿＿＿＿＿＿＿＿＿＿＿＿＿] could be misleading.

[＿＿＿＿＿＿＿＿＿＿＿＿＿＿＿＿] better describes the information in the graph.

Quick Check

1. Use the data in the graph in Example 1. Redraw the graph without a break.

Name_____ Class_____ Date _____

Example

② **Misleading Graphs** What makes this graph misleading? Explain.

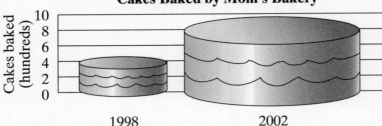

The cake on the right has much more than [   ] times the area of the cake on the left.

Quick Check

2. Use the data in the table at the right.

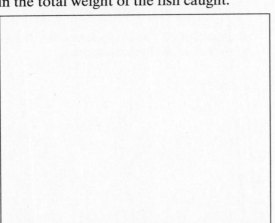

Fish Caught for Food in the U.S.

Year	Fish Caught (billions of pounds)
1993	8.2
1994	7.9
1995	7.7
1996	7.5

SOURCE: *Statistical Abstract of the United States.* Go to **www.PHSchool.com** for a data update. Web Code: adg-2041

a. Make a graph that suggests a rapid decrease in the total weight of the fish caught.

b. Make a graph that suggests a slow decrease in the total weight of the fish caught.

Lesson 12-4

Counting Outcomes and Theoretical Probability

Lesson Objectives	NAEP 2005 Strand: Data Analysis and Probability
▼ Use a tree diagram and the Counting Principle to find the number of possible choices	Topic: Probability
▼ Find the theoretical probability by counting outcomes	Local Standards: _____

Vocabulary and Key Concepts

Counting Principle

If there are m ways of making one choice and n ways of making a second choice, then there are [＿＿＿] ways of making the first choice followed by the second choice.

Theoretical Probability

$$P(\text{event}) = \frac{\text{number of } [\underline{\quad\quad}] \text{ outcomes}}{\text{number of } [\underline{\quad\quad}] \text{ outcomes}}$$

A sample space is _____

_____

Examples

❶ Drawing a Tree Diagram The school cafeteria sells sandwiches for which you can choose one item from each of the following categories: two breads (wheat or white), two meats (ham or turkey), and two condiments (mayonnaise or mustard). Draw a tree diagram to find the number of sandwich choices.

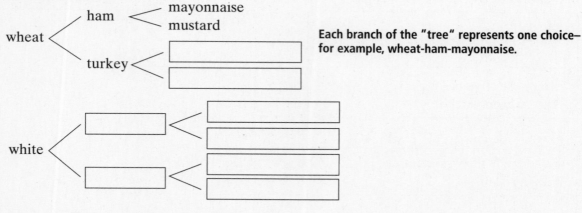

Each branch of the "tree" represents one choice—for example, wheat-ham-mayonnaise.

There are [＿] possible sandwich choices.

❷ Using the Counting Principle In some state lotteries, the winning number is made up of five digits chosen at random. Suppose a player buys 5 tickets with different numbers. What is the probability that the player has a winning number?

First find the number of possible outcomes. For each digit, there are [ ] possible outcomes, 0 through 9.

1st digit outcomes	2nd digit outcomes	3rd digit outcomes	4th digit outcomes	5th digit outcomes		total outcomes
[ ] ·	[ ] ·	[ ] ·	[ ] ·	[ ]	=	[ ]

Find the probability when there are five favorable outcomes.

$$P(\text{winning number}) = \frac{\text{number of } \boxed{} \text{ outcomes}}{\text{number of } \boxed{} \text{ outcomes}} = \frac{\boxed{}}{\boxed{}}$$

The probability is $\dfrac{\boxed{}}{\boxed{}}$, or $\dfrac{\boxed{}}{\boxed{}}$.

Quick Check

1. Suppose the cafeteria from Example 1 also offers a meat choice of salami. Draw a tree diagram. How many sandwich choices are there?

2. **a.** A lottery uses five digits chosen at random. Find the probability of buying a winning ticket.

   b. Find the probability of matching the first and second digits of the winning number.

Lesson 12-5

Independent and Dependent Events

Lesson Objectives	NAEP 2005 Strand: Data Analysis and Probability
▼ Calculate probabilities of independent events ▼ Calculate probabilities of dependent events	**Topic:** Probability **Local Standards:** _____

Vocabulary and Key Concepts

Probability of Independent Events

For two independent events A and B, the probability of both events

occurring is the [   ] of the probabilities of each event occurring.

$P(A, \text{then } B) = $ [   ] $\cdot$ [   ]

Probability of Dependent Events

For two dependent events A and B, the probability of both events

occurring is the [   ] of the probability of the first event and the

probability that, after the first event, the second event occurs.

$P(A, \text{then } B) = $ [   ] $\cdot$ [   ]

Independent events are _____

Dependent events are _____

Examples

❶ **Finding Probability for Independent Events** You roll a number cube once. Then you roll it again. What is the probability that you get 5 on the first roll and a number less than 4 on the second roll?

$P(5) = \dfrac{\boxed{}}{\boxed{}}$ **There is** $\boxed{}$ **5 among** $\boxed{}$ **numbers on a number cube.**

$P(\text{less than } 4) = \dfrac{\boxed{}}{\boxed{}}$ **There are** $\boxed{}$ **numbers less than 4 on a number cube.**

$P(5, \text{then less than } 4) = P(5) \cdot P(\text{less than } 4)$

$= \dfrac{\boxed{}}{\boxed{}} \cdot \dfrac{\boxed{}}{\boxed{}}$

$= \dfrac{\boxed{}}{\boxed{}}, \text{ or } \dfrac{\boxed{}}{\boxed{}}$ **Simplify.**

The probability of rolling 5 and then a number less than 4 is $\boxed{}$.

❷ Finding Probability for Dependent Events Three girls and two boys volunteer to represent their class at a school assembly. The teacher selects one name and then another from a bag containing the five students' names. What is the probability that both representatives will be boys?

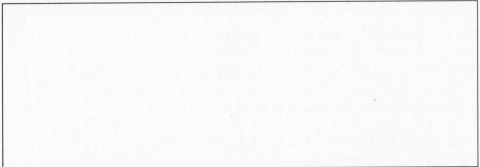

$P(\text{boy}) = \dfrac{\square}{\square}$ [   ] of [   ] students are boys.

$P(\text{boy after boy}) = \dfrac{\square}{\square}$ If a boy's name is drawn, [   ] of the [   ] remaining students is a boy.

$P(\text{boy, then boy}) = P(\text{boy}) \cdot P(\text{boy after boy})$

$= \dfrac{\square}{\square} \cdot \dfrac{\square}{\square}$ **Substitute.**

$= \dfrac{\square}{\square}$, or $\dfrac{\square}{\square}$ **Simplify.**

The probability that both representatives will be boys is [   ].

Quick Check

1. You toss a coin twice. Find the probability of getting two heads.

2. **a.** For Example 2, find $P(\text{boy, then girl})$.   **b.** Find $P(\text{girl, then boy})$.

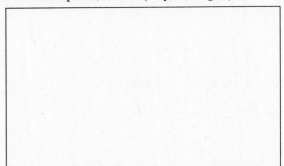

Lesson 12-6

Permutations and Combinations

Lesson Objectives	**Local Standards:** _____
▼ Use permutations	
▼ Use combinations	

Vocabulary and Key Concepts

Permutation Notation

The expression $_nP_r$ stands for the number of [_____] of [__] objects chosen [__] at a time.

Combination Notation

The expression $_nC_r$ stands for the number of [_____] of [__] objects chosen [__] at a time.

A permutation is _____

A combination is _____

Examples

1 **Counting Permutations** Find the number of permutations possible for the letters H, O, M, E, and S.

1st digit 5 choices	2nd letter 4 choices	3rd letter 3 choices	4th letter 2 choices	5th letter 1 choice		
[__] ·	[__] ·	[__] ·	[__] ·	[__] =	[_____]	

There are [_____] permutations of the letters H, O, M, E, and S.

2 **Simplify the Permutation Notation** In how many ways can you line up 3 students chosen from 7 students for a photograph?

7 students⌐ ⌐Choose 3.

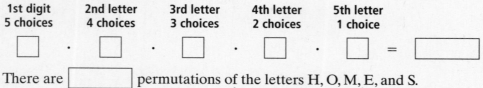

$_7P_3 = $ [__] · [__] · [__] = [_____] **Simplify.**

You can line up 3 students from 7 in [_____] ways.

Quick Check

1. Use the Counting Principle to find the number of permutations possible for the letters W, A, T, E, and R.

[_____]

❸ Counting Combinations In how many ways can you choose two states from the table when you write about the areas of states? Make an organized list of all the combinations.

State	Area (mi^2)
Alabama	50,750
Colorado	103,729
Maine	30,865
Oregon	96,003
Texas	261,914

AL, CO AL,☐ ☐,☐ ☐,☐
CO,☐ CO,☐ CO,☐
ME,☐ ☐,☐
☐,☐

Use abbreviations of each state's name. First, list all pairs including Alabama. Continue until every pair of states is listed.

There are ☐ ways to choose two states from a list of five.

❹ Simplifying Combination Notation How many different pizzas can you make if you can choose exactly 5 toppings from 9 that are available?

9 toppings ─┐ ┌─ Choose 5.

$$_9C_5 = \frac{_9P_5}{_5P_5}$$

$$= \frac{9 \cdot 8 \cdot 7 \cdot 6 \cdot 5}{5 \cdot 4 \cdot 3 \cdot 2 \cdot 1} = \boxed{}$$ **Simplify.**

You can make ☐ different pizzas.

Quick Check

2. Simplify each expression.

a. $_5P_2$

b. $_5P_3$

3. In how many ways could you choose three different items from a menu containing six items?

4. Simplify each expression.

a. $_8C_2$

b. $_8C_3$

Lesson 12-7

Lesson Objectives	**NAEP 2005 Strand:** Data Analysis and Probability
▼ Find experimental probability	**Topic:** Probability
▼ Use simulations	**Local Standards:** _____

Vocabulary and Key Concepts

Experimental Probability

$$P(\text{event}) = \frac{\text{number of times} \boxed{}}{\text{number of times} \boxed{}}$$

Experimental probability is _____

A simulation is _____

_____

Example

❶ **Finding Experimental Probability** A medical student tests a new medicine on 3,500 people. It produces side effects for 1,715 people. Find the experimental probability that the medicine will cause side effects. Then predict the number of people in a group of 3,000 for whom the medicine will have side effects.

$$P(\text{event}) = \frac{\text{number of times an event} \boxed{}}{\text{number of times experiment is} \boxed{}}$$

$$= \frac{\boxed{}}{\boxed{}} = \boxed{}$$

The experimental probability that the medicine will cause side effects is

$\boxed{}$, or $\boxed{}$%. For a group of 3,000, the number of affected

people could be $\boxed{} \cdot \boxed{} = \boxed{}$

Quick Check

1. Another medicine is effective for 1,183 of 2,275 participants. Find the experimental probability that the medicine is effective. Then predict the number of people in a group of 4,500 for whom the medicine will be effective.

Example

② **Using a Simulation** Simulate the correct guessing of answers on a multiple-choice test where each problem has four answer choices (A, B, C, and D).

Use a 4-section spinner to simulate each guess. Mark the sections as 1, 2, 3, and 4. Let 1 represent a correct choice.

Here are the results of 50 trials.

22431 13431 43121 21243 33434
32134 12224 42213 34424 32412

$P(\text{event}) = \dfrac{\text{number of times } \boxed{}}{\text{number of times } \boxed{}}$

$= \dfrac{\boxed{}}{\boxed{}}$

$= \dfrac{\boxed{}}{\boxed{}}$

The experimental probability of guessing correctly is $\dfrac{\boxed{}}{\boxed{}}$.

Quick Check

2. a. In Example 2, compare the experimental probability with the theoretical probability.

b. If you try the experiment 100 times, what is most likely to happen to the experimental probability?

Lesson 12-8

Random Samples and Surveys

Lesson Objectives	NAEP 2005 Strand: Data Analysis and Probability
▼ Choose a sample for a survey of a population ▼ Make estimates about populations	**Topic:** Experiments and Samples **Local Standards:** _____

Vocabulary

A population is _____

_____

A sample is _____

_____

For a random sample _____

_____

Example

❶ Choosing a Sample You want to find out how many people in the community use computers on a daily basis. Tell whether each survey plan describes a good sample. Explain.

a. Interview every tenth person leaving a computer store.

b. Interview people at random at the shopping center.

Quick Check

1. Explain whether each plan describes a good sample.

a. You want to know how often teens rent videos. You plan to survey teens going into the local video store.

b. You want to know the most popular breakfast cereal. You plan to survey people entering a grocery store.

❷ Using Samples to Predict From 20,000 calculators produced, a manufacturer takes a random sample of 300 calculators. The sample has 2 defective calculators. Estimate the number of defective calculators.

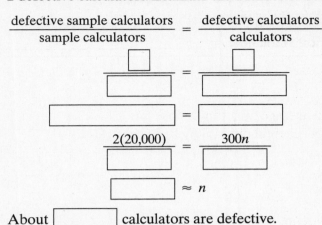

$$\frac{\text{defective sample calculators}}{\text{sample calculators}} = \frac{\text{defective calculators}}{\text{calculators}}$$ **Write a proportion.**

$$\frac{\boxed{}}{\boxed{}} = \frac{\boxed{}}{\boxed{}}$$ **Substitute.**

$$\boxed{} = \boxed{}$$ **Write cross products.**

$$\frac{2(20,000)}{\boxed{}} = \frac{300n}{\boxed{}}$$ **Divide each side by** $\boxed{}$.

$$\boxed{} \approx n$$ **Simplify.**

About $\boxed{}$ calculators are defective.

Quick Check

2. Use the data in the table at the right.

   a. Using Sample B, how many of 20,000 calculators would you estimate to be defective?

Calculator Samples

Sample	Number Sampled	Number Defective
A	500	3
B	200	2
C	50	0

   b. Reasoning Would you expect an estimate based on Sample C to be more accurate or less accurate than one based on Sample B? Explain.

3. Explain why you would take a sample rather than counting or surveying an entire population.

Lesson 12-9

Simulate the Problem

Lesson Objective ▼ Solve problems by simulation	**NAEP 2005 Strand:** Data Analysis and Probability **Topic:** Probability **Local Standards:** _____

Example

1 **Using a Simulation** A softball player has an average of getting a base hit 2 times in every 7 times at bat. What is an experimental probability that she will get a base hit the next time she is at bat?

(Understand the Problem)

Think about the problem.

1. Based on her average, what is the probability of getting a base hit?

2. What methods could you use to simulate the problem?

(Make and Carry Out a Plan)

You can use a spinner to simulate the problem. Construct a spinner with _____ congruent sections. Mark five of the sections black and two of them white. The black sections represent *not getting a base hit* and the white sections indicate *getting a base hit*.

Each spin represents _____ .

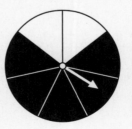

3. How many spins will you make for each experiment?

4. How many experiments will you do?

Use the results in the table at the right.
B stands for black and W stands for white.

Make a frequency table.

Makes a Base Hit	Doesn't Make a Base Hit

B	B	B	B	W	W	B	B	W	B
B	W	B	B	W	B	B	B	B	W
W	B	B	W	B	B	B	B	W	B
B	B	B	B	B	B	B	B	B	B
B	B	W	B	B	B	W	B	B	B
B	B	B	W	W	B	B	B	B	W
W	B	B	B	B	B	B	B	B	B
B	B	B	B	B	B	W	W	B	B
B	W	W	B	B	W	B	B	B	B
B	B	B	B	B	W	B	B	B	W

An experimental probability that the softball player gets a base hit

the next time she is at bat is $\dfrac{\boxed{}}{\boxed{}}$ = $\boxed{}$, or $\boxed{}$%.

(Check the Answer)

Simulations can give different results. You may find a different probability
if you do another simulation. The more experiments you do, the closer the
results of different simulations are likely to be.

Quick Check

1. a. Continue the simulation with another 100 experiments. Combine the results
with the results of the first 100 simulations. (*Hint:* Flip a coin 100 times.)

b. Based on the second simulation, what is the experimental probability
that the softball player will get a base hit the next time she is at bat?

Lesson 13-1

Patterns and Sequences

Lesson Objectives	**NAEP 2005 Strand:** Algebra
▼ Describe number patterns with arithmetic sequences	**Topic:** Patterns, Relations, and Functions
▼ Describe number patterns with geometric sequences	**Local Standards:** _____

Vocabulary

A sequence is _____

A term is _____

An arithmetic sequence is _____

_____

A common difference is _____

_____

A geometric sequence is _____

_____

A common ratio is _____

Examples

❶ **Swimming** A swimmer training for a meet swims 5 laps the first day, $6\frac{1}{2}$ laps the next day, 8 laps the third day, and so on. Find the next three terms of the sequence. Then write a rule to describe the sequence.

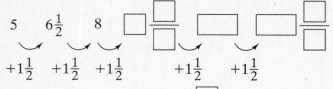

Find the common difference. Use it to find the next three terms.

The next three terms are ☐☐/☐ , ☐ , and ☐☐/☐ .

The rule for the sequence is *Start with* ☐ *and add* ☐☐/☐ *repeatedly.*

❷ **Finding the Common Ratio** Find the common ratio in the sequence 3, 9, 27, 81, ... Find the next three terms of the sequence. Then write a rule to describe the sequence.

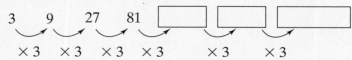

Find the common ratio. Use it to find the next three terms.

❸ **Finding the Type of Sequence** Tell whether each sequence is *arithmetic*, *geometric*, or *neither*. Find the next three terms of each sequence.

a. 3, 5, 9, 15, …

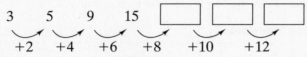

The sequence is [ ] arithmetic nor geometric. Following the pattern above, the next three terms are [ ], [ ], and [ ].

b. 2, −4, 8, −16, …

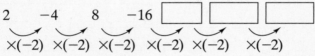

The ratios for the first four terms are $\frac{-4}{2}$, $\frac{8}{-4}$, and $\frac{-16}{8}$.

These equal [ ], which is the common ratio. The sequence is [ ]. The next three terms are [ ], [ ] and [ ].

Quick Check

Find the next three terms of each sequence. Then write a rule to describe the sequence. For 2c and 2d, first find the common ratio.

1a. 23, 19, 15, 11, …

1b. $-6, -4\frac{2}{3}, -3\frac{1}{3}, -2, \ldots$

2a. 4, 12, 36, 108, …

2b. 4, 2, 1, 0, 5, …

3. Tell whether each sequence is *arithmetic*, *geometric*, or *neither*. Then find the next three terms of the sequence.

a. 3, 9, 27, 81, …

b. 10, 13, 18, 25, …

c. −12, 12, −12, 12, …

d. 50, 200, 350, 500, …

Lesson 13-2

Graphing Nonlinear Functions

Lesson Objectives	NAEP 2005 Strand: Algebra
▼ Graph quadratic functions	**Topic:** Patterns, Relations, and Functions
▼ Graph absolute value functions	**Local Standards:** _____

Vocabulary

A quadratic function is _____

_____

An absolute value function is _____

_____

Examples

❶ Graphing a Quadratic Function For the function $y = -x^2 + 1$, make a table with integer values of x from -2 to 2. Then graph the function.

x	$-x^2 + 1 = y$	(x, y)
-2	$-(-2)^2 + 1 = \boxed{}$	$(-2, \boxed{})$
-1	$-(-1)^2 + 1 = 0$	$(-1, 0)$
0	$-(\boxed{})^2 + 1 = 1$	$(\boxed{}, 1)$
1	$-(1)^2 + 1 = \boxed{}$	$(1, \boxed{})$
2	$-(2)^2 + 1 = -3$	$(2, -3)$

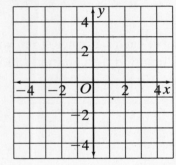

❷ Graphing an Absolute Value Function Graph the function $y = |x| - 1$.

x	$|x| - 1 = y$	(x, y)
-2	$|-2| - 1 = \boxed{}$	$(-2, \boxed{})$
-1	$|-1| - 1 = 0$	$(-1, 0)$
0	$|0| - 1 = -1$	$(0, -1)$
1	$|1| - 1 = 0$	$(1, 0)$
2	$|2| - 1 = \boxed{}$	$(2, \boxed{})$

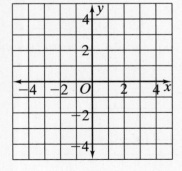

Quick Check

For each function, make a table with integer values of x from -2 to 2.
Then graph each function.

1a. $y = -2x^2$

x	$-2x^2 = y$	(x, y)
-2		
-1		
0		
1		
2		

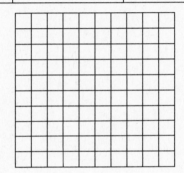

1b. $y = -x^2 + 3$

x	$-x^2 + 3 = y$	(x, y)
-2		
-1		
0		
1		
2		

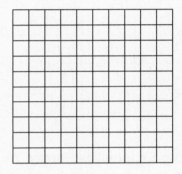

2a. $y = -|x| + 1$

x	$y = -|x| + 1$	(x, y)
-2		
-1		
0		
1		
2		

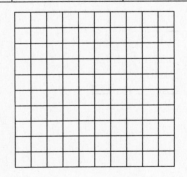

2b. $y = 2|x|$

x	$y = 2|x|$	(x, y)
-2		
-1		
0		
1		
2		

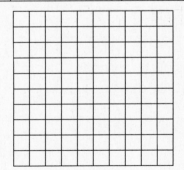

Lesson 13-3

Exponential Growth and Decay

Lesson Objectives	**NAEP 2005 Strand:** Algebra
▼ Use tables, rules, and graphs with functions modeling growth	**Topic:** Algebraic Representation
▼ Use tables, rules, and graphs with functions modeling decay	**Local Standards:** _____

Examples

❶ Graphing Exponential Growth For $y = 4(2)^x$, make a table with integer values of x from 0 to 4. Then graph the function.

x	$4(2)^x$	y	(x, y)
0	$4(2)^0$	4	$(0, 4)$
1	$4(2)^1$	8	$(1, 8)$
2	$4(2)^2$	16	$(2, 16)$
3	$4(2)^3$	☐	$(3, \boxed{})$
4	$4(2)^4$	☐	$(4, \boxed{})$

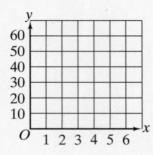

❷ Graphing Exponential Decay For the function $y = 2(0.5)^x$, make a table with integer values of x from 0 to 5. Then graph the function.

x	$2(0.5)^x$	y	(x, y)
0	$2(0.5)^0$	2	$(0, 2)$
1	$2(0.5)^1$	1	$(1, 1)$
2	$2(0.5)^2$	0.5	$(2, 0.5)$
3	$2(0.5)^3$	0.25	$(3, 0.25)$
4	$2(0.5)^4$	☐	$(4, \boxed{})$
5	$2(0.5)^5$	☐	$(5, \boxed{})$

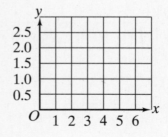

Name_____ Class_____ Date _____

Quick Check

1. For the function $y = 0.5(2)^x$, make a table with integer values of x from 0 to 5. Then graph the function.

x	0.5(2)^x	y	(x, y)
0			
1			
2			
3			
4			
5			

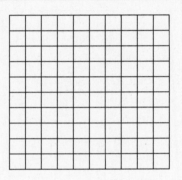

2. For the function $y = 90\left(\frac{1}{3}\right)^x$, make a table with integer values of x from 0 to 5. Then graph the function.

x	90($\frac{1}{3}$)^x	y	(x, y)
0			
1			
2			
3			
4			
5			

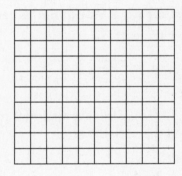

Lesson 13-4

Polynomials

Lesson Objectives	NAEP 2005 Strand: Algebra
▼ Identify polynomials	Topic: Variables, Expressions, and Operations
▼ Evaluate polynomials	Local Standards: _____

Vocabulary

A monomial is _____

_____

A polynomial is _____

_____

A binomial is _____

A trinomial is _____

Examples

❶ Recognizing a Monomial Is each expression a monomial? Explain.

a. $5 + c$

[_____] ; the expression is a [_____] .

b. $\frac{7z}{3}$

[_____] ; the expression is the [_____] of the real number $\frac{7}{3}$ and the variable z.

c. $6ab^2$

[_____] ; the expression is the [_____] of the real number 6 and the variables a, b, and b.

d. $\frac{4g}{h}$

[_____] ; the denominator contains a variable.

❷ Naming a Polynomial State whether the polynomial is a *monomial*, a *binomial*, or a *trinomial*.

a. $14x^2 + 2xy - 7y^2$

[_____]

b. $\frac{11a^2bc}{3}$

[_____]

c. $z + 10$

[_____]

❸ **Evaluating a Polynomial** Evaluate each polynomial for $r = 2$ and $s = 7$.

a. $5r^2 - s$ **b.** $\dfrac{6rs}{3}$

$5r^2 - s = 5(2)^2 - 7$ **Replace r with 2 and s with 7.** $\dfrac{6rs}{3} = \dfrac{6(2)(7)}{3}$

$= \boxed{}$ **Simplify.** $= \boxed{}$

❹ **Using a Polynomial** The polynomial $-16r^2 + 100t$ gives the height, in feet, reached by a fireworks shell in t seconds. If the shell explodes 5 seconds after launch, at what height did it explode?

$-16t^2 + 100t$

$-16\left(\boxed{}\right)^2 + 100\left(\boxed{}\right)$ **Replace t with $\boxed{}$.**

$\boxed{}$ **Simplify.**

The shell will explode at $\boxed{}$ feet.

Quick Check

1. Is the expression a monomial? Explain.

a. $\dfrac{6}{m}$ **b.** $\dfrac{m}{6}$ **c.** 45   **d.** $mx + b$

2. Is the polynomial a monomial, a binomial, or a trinomial?

a. 10   **b.** $9x^2 + xy$ **c.** $8 - y$ **d.** $5 + x - 3y$

3. Evaluate each polynomial for $x = -2$ and $y = 5$.

a. $5xy$ **b.** $x + 3y$ **c.** $y^2 - 2y + x$

4. Fireworks are set to explode 4 seconds after launch. Using the polynomial in Example 4, at what height will they explode?

Lesson 13-5

Adding and Subtracting Polynomials

Lesson Objectives	NAEP 2005 Strand: Algebra
▼ Add polynomials	Topic: Variables, Expressions, and Operations
▼ Subtract polynomials	Local Standards: _____

Examples

❶ Adding Polynomials Simplify $(4b^2 + 2b + 1) + (7b^2 + b - 3)$.

Method 1 Add using tiles.

$$\boxed{}b^2 + \boxed{}b - \boxed{}$$

Method 2 Add by combining like terms.

$$(4b^2 + 2b + 1) + (7b^2 + b - 3)$$

$$= (4b^2 + 7b^2) + (2b + b) + (1 - 3)$$

Use the ⬜ and ⬜ Properties of Addition to group like terms.

$$= \left(4 + \boxed{}\right)b^2 + \left(\boxed{} + 1\right)b + \left(\boxed{} - 3\right)$$

Use the ⬜ Property to combine like terms.

$$= \boxed{}b^2 + \boxed{}b - \boxed{}$$

Simplify.

❷ Aligning Like Terms Find the sum of $2z^2 - 9z - 15$ and $8z + 11$.

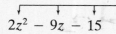 Align like terms.

$$\begin{array}{r} 2z^2 - 9z - 15 \\ + 8z + 11 \\ \hline 2z^2 - \boxed{} - \boxed{} \end{array}$$

Add the terms in each column.

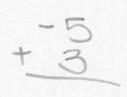

Name_____ Class_____ Date _____

❸ Subtracting Polynomials Simplify $(12y^2 + 10y - 5) - (6y^2 + 8y - 11)$.

$(12y^2 + 10y - 5) - (6y^2 + 8y - 11)$

$= 12y^2 + 10y - 5 - 6y^2 \;\boxed{}\; 8y \;\boxed{}\; 11$ **Write the opposite of each term in the second polynomial.**

$= \left(12y^2 - \boxed{}\right) + \left(\boxed{} - 8y\right) + (-5 + 11)$ **Group like terms.**

$= (12 - 6)y^2 + (10 - 8)y + (-5 + 11)$ **Use the** $\boxed{}$ **Property.**

$= \boxed{}y^2 + \boxed{}y + \boxed{}$ **Simplify.**

Quick Check

1. Simplify.

  a. $(7d^2 + 7d) + (2d^2 + 3d)$ **b.** $(x^2 + 2x + 5) + (3x^2 + x + 12)$

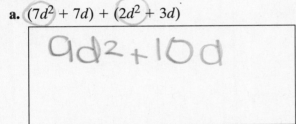

$9d^2 + 10d$

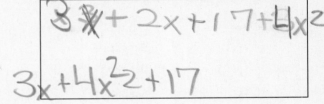

$3x + 2x + 17 + 4x^2$

$3x + 4x^2 + 17$

2. Simplify each sum.

  a. $(4g^2 - 2g + 2) + (2g^2 - 3)$ **b.** $(-2t^2 + t + 5) + (2t + 4)$

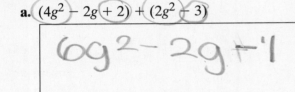

$6g^2 - 2g + 1$

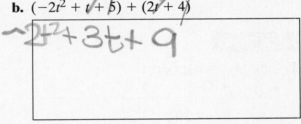

$-2t^2 + 3t + 9$

3. Simplify each difference.

  a. $(7a^2 - 2a) - (5a^2 + 3a)$ **b.** $(10z^2 + 6z + 5) - (z^2 - 8z + 7)$

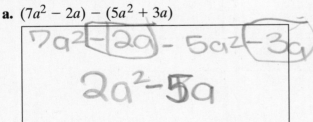

$7a^2 - 2a - 5a^2 - 3a$

$2a^2 - 5a$

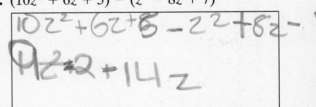

$10z^2 + 6z + 5 - z^2 + 8z - 7$

$9z^2 + 14z$

  c. $(3w^2 + 8 + v) - (5w^2 - 3 - 7v)$

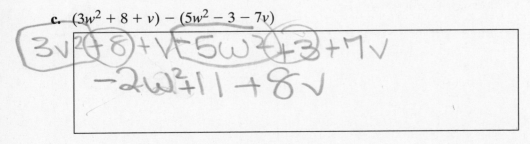

$3v^2 + 8 + v - 5w^2 + 3 + 7v$

$-2w^2 + 11 + 8v$

Lesson 13-6

Multiplying a Polynomial by a Monomial

Lesson Objectives	**NAEP 2005 Strand:** Algebra
▼ Use an area model for multiplication	**Topic:** Variables, Expressions, and Operations
▼ Write a polynomial as the product of a monomial and a polynomial	**Local Standards:** _____

Example

❶ **Finding Area** Find the area of the rectangle. All measurements are in meters.

$v + 7$

$4v$

$A = \ell w$

$\quad = 4v(v + 7)$ **Substitute.**

$\quad = 4v(v) + 4v(7)$ **Use the** [_____] **Property.**

$\quad = 4v^2 + 28v$ **Simplify.**

The area of the rectangle is [_____] m^2.

Quick Check

1. Simplify each product.

   a. $3x(x + 4)$

   $3x^2 + 12x$

   b. $x(2x - 3)$

   $2x^2 - 3x$

Name_____ Class_____ Date _____

Examples

❷ **Simplifying a Product** Simplify $5n^2(2n^3 - 4n^2 + n)$.

$5n^2(2n^3 - 4n^2 + n)$

$= 5n^2(2n^3) + 5n^2(-4n^2) + 5n^2(n)$ Use the [distributive] Property.

$= (5)(2)n^{2+}\boxed{n^3} + (5)(-4)n^{2+}\boxed{n^2} + (5)n^{2+}\boxed{n}$ Use the [____] Property of Multiplication.

$= (5)(2)n^5 + (5)(-4)n^4 + (5)n^3$ Add exponents.

$= \boxed{10}n^5 - \boxed{20}n^4 + 5n^3$ Simplify.

❸ **Finding Factors of a Polynomial** Write $6r^4 + 10r^3 - 14r^2$ as a product of two factors.

$\left.\begin{array}{l} 6r^4 = 2 \cdot 3 \cdot r \cdot r \cdot r \cdot r \\ 10r^3 = 2 \cdot 5 \cdot r \cdot r \cdot r \\ -14r^2 = -1 \cdot 2 \cdot 7 \cdot r \cdot r \end{array}\right\}$ Write prime factorizations.

$\text{GCF} = \boxed{2}$

$6r^4 = \boxed{}r^2 \cdot 3r^{\boxed{}}$

$10r^3 = 2r^{\boxed{}} \cdot \boxed{}r$ Write each term as the product of $2r^2$ and another factor.

$-14r^2 = 2r^{\boxed{}} \cdot \boxed{}$ Use the [_____] Property.

$6r^4 + 10r^3 - 14r^2 = \boxed{}(3r^2 + 5r - 7)$

Quick Check

2. Simplify each product.

   a. $x(x^2 + 2x + 4)$ **b.** $2a^2(2a^3 - 3a^2 + 3)$

   $x^3 + 2x^2 + 4x$ $4a^5 - 6a^4 + 6a^2$

3. Use the GCF of the terms to write each polynomial as the product of two factors.

   a. $2x^2 + x$

   $2x + 1$ ⊗

   b. $2b^2 + 6b^2 - 12b$

   $b + 3b^2 - 6$
   ②b

Lesson 13-7

Multiplying Binomials

Lesson Objectives	NAEP 2005 Strand: Algebra
▼ Use models in multiplying binomials	**Topic:** Variables, Expressions, and Operations
❷ Multiply two binomials	**Local Standards:** _____

Examples

❶ Using a Model Simplify $(x + 3)(x + 5)$.

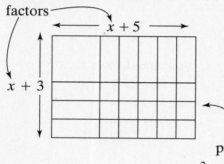

factors

$x + 5$

$x + 3$

product
$x^2 + 8x + 15$

The area is [   ].

❷ Multiplying Two Binomials Simplify $(b + 2)(3b - 1)$.

$(b + 2)(3b - 1)$

$= b(3b - 1) + 2(3b - 1)$ **Use the** [   ] **Property.**

$= \boxed{}b^2 - \boxed{} + 6b - 2$ **Use the** [   ] **Property again.**

$= 3b^2 + \boxed{}b - 2$ **Simplify.**

Quick Check

1. Simplify each product using models.

  a. $(x + 2)(x + 3)$ **b.** $(y + 1)(y + 4)$

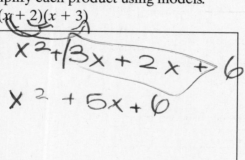

$x^2 + 3x + 2x + 6$

$x^2 + 5x + 6$

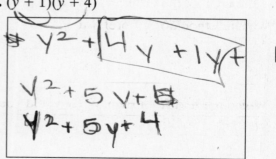

$y^2 + 4y + 1y + 4$

$y^2 + 5y + 5$

$y^2 + 5y + 4$

Name_____ Class_____ Date _____

❸ Multiplying Binomials Write a polynomial to express the area of the square at the right.

$(2x + 1)$ in.

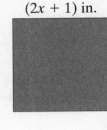

Method 1 Use a model.

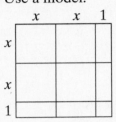

The area of the square is ⬚ + ⬚ + ⬚ in.^{2}.

Method 2 Use the formula for the area of a square and the Distributive Property.

Area = side^2

$A = (2x + 1)^2$

$= (2x + 1)(2x + 1)$

$= \boxed{}(2x + 1) + \boxed{}(2x + 1)$

$= \boxed{}(2x) + \boxed{}(1) + \boxed{}(2x) + \boxed{}(1)$

$= \boxed{}x^2 + \boxed{}x + \boxed{}x + \boxed{}$

$= \boxed{}x^2 + \boxed{}x + \boxed{}$

The area of a square is ⬚ + ⬚ + ⬚ in.^{2}.

(handwritten: $4x + 2 \oslash$ $2x \times 1$ $6x^2 + 3$ $4x^2 + 4x + 1$ *)*

Quick Check

2. Simplify each product.

  a. $(x + 2)(x - 5)$

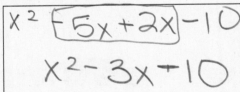

(handwritten: $x^2 \boxed{-5x + 2x} - 10$ $x^2 - 3x - 10$ *)*

  b. $(m + 2)(2m + 3)$

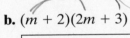

(handwritten: $2m^2 + 3m + 4m + 6$ $2m^2 + 7m + 6$ *)*

3. a. Which method do you prefer to use in Example 3? Explain.

b. Which method from Example 3 would you use to simplify $(3x + 4)(3x + 4)$?

Name_____ Class_____ Date_____

Lesson 13-8

Use Multiple Strategies

Lesson Objective	Local Standards: _____
▼ Solve problems by combining strategies	

Example

❶ Apple Display A grocer stacks apples in the shape of a square pyramid. He wants to make the pyramid have six "layers." How many apples does the grocer need?

(Understand the Problem)

Read the problem carefully.

1. What do you want to find?

2. What is the relationship between the pyramid layers and the number of apples needed?

(Make and Carry Out a Plan)

Draw a diagram of each layer of the pyramid of apples.

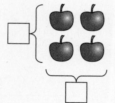

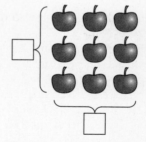

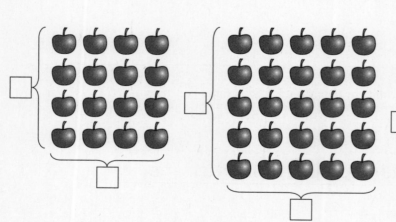

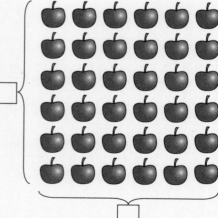

Daily Notetaking Guide

Make a table.

Layer (from top down)	No. of apples on edge of layer	No. of apples in layer	Total no. of apples
1	1	$1^2 = 1$	1
☐	☐	$2^2 =$ ☐	☐
☐	☐	☐$^2 =$ ☐	☐
☐	☐	☐$^2 =$ ☐	☐
☐	☐	☐$^2 =$ ☐	☐
☐	☐	☐$^2 =$ ☐	☐

The grocer needs ☐ apples.

Check the Answer

The original problem states that the stack of apples is in the shape of a square pyramid. This means that the number of apples in each layer should be a perfect square. In this solution, 4, 9, 16, 25, and 36 are each perfect squares. So the result fits the context of the original problem.

Quick Check

1. Suppose that the pyramid must have 9 layers. Find the number of apples the grocer will need.

Pre-Algebra Lesson 13-8

A Note to the Student:

This section of your workbook contains a series of pages that support your mathematics understandings for each chapter and lesson presented in your student edition.

- Practice pages provide additional practice for every lesson.

- Guided Problem Solving pages lead you through a step-by-step solution to an application problem in each lesson.

- Vocabulary pages contain a variety of activities to increase your reading and math understanding, ranging from graphic organizers to vocabulary review puzzles.

Practice • Guided Problem Solving • Vocabulary

Practice 1-1

Write an expression for each quantity.

1. the value in cents of 5 quarters _____

2. the value in cents of q quarters _____

3. the number of months in 7 years _____

4. the number of months in y years _____

5. the number of gallons in 21 quarts _____

6. the number of gallons in q quarts _____

Write a variable expression for each word phrase.

7. 9 less than k

_____

8. m divided by 6

_____

9. twice x

_____

10. 4 more than twice x

_____

11. the sum of eighteen and b

_____

12. three times the quantity 2 plus a

_____

Tell whether each expression is a numerical expression or a variable expression. For a variable expression, name the variable.

13. $4d$ _____

14. $74 + 8$ _____

15. $\frac{4(9)}{6}$ _____

16. $14 - p$ _____

17. $5k - 9$ _____

18. $3 + 3 + 3 + 3$ _____

19. $19 + 3(12)$ _____

20. $25 - 9 + x$ _____

The room temperature is c degrees centigrade. Write a word phrase for each expression.

21. $c + 15$

_____

22. $c - 7$

_____

1-1 • Guided Problem Solving

GPS **Student Page 6, Exercise 33**

Mia has $20 less than Brandi. Brandi has d dollars. Write a variable expression for the amount of money Mia has.

Understand the Problem

1. Who has more money, Brandi or Mia? _____

2. What operation do you think of when you hear the phrase *less than*? _____

3. Describe how much money Mia has, compared to how much Brandi has. _____

4. What does the variable d represent? _____

5. The problem asks you to write an expression for what? _____

Make and Carry Out a Plan

6. You are given two pieces of information in the problem: the amount of money that Brandi has and the fact that Mia has $20 less than Brandi.
To write an expression for the amount Mia has, start by writing the amount that Brandi has. _____

7. To complete the expression, show the subtraction of $20 from the amount that Brandi has. _____

Check the Answer

8. You know that Brandi has $20 more than Mia. To check that your expression for this amount is correct, add $20 to it to see whether you get Brandi's amount.

_____

Solve Another Problem

9. Deena has 5 more marbles than Jonna. Jonna has m marbles.
Write an expression to represent the number of marbles Deena has. _____

Practice 1-2

The Order of Operations

Simplify each expression.

1. $3 + 15 - 5 \cdot 2$ _____

2. $5 \cdot 6 + 2 \cdot 4$ _____

3. $48 \div 8 - 1$ _____

4. $68 - 12 \div 2 \div 3$ _____

5. $6(2 + 7)$ _____

6. $25 - (6 \cdot 4)$ _____

7. $3[9 - (6 - 3)] - 10$ _____

8. $60 \div (3 + 12)$ _____

9. $4 - 2 + 6 \cdot 2$ _____

10. $18 \div (5 - 2)$ _____

11. $\frac{16 + 24}{30 - 22}$ _____

12. $2[4(9 - 7) + 1]$ _____

13. $(8 \div 8 + 2 + 11) \div 2$ _____

14. $9 + 3 \cdot 4$ _____

15. $18 \div 3 \cdot 5 - 4$ _____

16. $10 + 28 \div 14 - 5$ _____

Insert grouping symbols to make each number sentence true.

17. $3 + 5 \cdot 8 = 64$

18. $4 \cdot 6 - 2 + 7 = 23$

19. $10 \div 3 + 2 \cdot 4 = 8$

20. $3 + 6 \cdot 2 = 18$

A city park has two walkways with a grassy area in the center, as shown in the diagram.

21. Write an expression for the area of the sidewalks, using subtraction.

_____

22. Write an expression for the area of the sidewalks, using addition.

_____

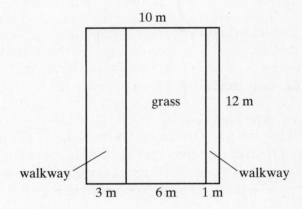

Compare. Use >, <, or = to complete each statement.

23. $(24 - 8) \div 4 \; \square \; 24 - 8 \div 4$

24. $3 \cdot (4 - 2) \cdot 5 \; \square \; 3 \cdot 4 - 2 \cdot 5$

25. $(22 + 8) \div 2 \; \square \; 22 + 8 \div 2$

26. $20 \div 2 + 8 \cdot 2 \; \square \; 20 \div (2 + 8) \cdot 2$

27. $11 \cdot 4 - 2 \; \square \; 11 \cdot (4 - 2)$

28. $(7 \cdot 3) - (4 \cdot 2) \; \square \; 7 \cdot 3 - 4 \cdot 2$

1-2 • Guided Problem Solving

GPS Student Page 12, Exercise 46

On the Job A part-time employee worked 4 hours on Monday and 7 hours each day for the next 3 days. Write and simplify an expression that shows the total number of hours worked.

Understand the Problem

1. How many hours did the employee work on Monday? _____

2. How many hours did the employee work each day on Tuesday, Wednesday, and Thursday? _____

3. For how many days did the employee work 7 hours? _____

Make and Carry Out a Plan

4. What operation should you use to find the total number of hours worked in the 3 days that the employee worked 7 hours each day? _____

5. Write an expression to find the total number of hours worked during those 3 days. _____

6. What operation should you use to combine the hours the employee worked on Monday with the hours worked in the next 3 days? _____

7. Write an expression for the total number of hours worked on Monday and the number of hours worked in the next 3 days. _____

8. Simplify the expression you wrote for Step 7 to find the total number of hours worked. Remember to use the correct order of operations. _____

Check the Answer

9. You can check your work by writing an expression that adds the number of hours worked on each day. This expression should simplify to the number of hours you found in Step 8 above.

   _____

Solve Another Problem

10. Carter bought 4 books for $8 each and another book for $5. Write and simplify an expression to find the total cost of the books he bought.

   _____

Practice 1-3

Writing and Evaluating Expressions

Evaluate each expression.

1. xy, for $x = 3$ and $y = 5$ _____

2. $24 - p \cdot 5$, for $p = 4$ _____

3. $5a + b$, for $a = 6$ and $b = 3$ _____

4. $6x$, for $x = 3$ _____

5. $9 - k$, for $k = 2$ _____

6. $63 \div p$, for $p = 7$ _____

7. $2 + n$, for $n = 3$ _____

8. $3m$, for $m = 11$ _____

9. $10 - r + 5$, for $r = 9$ _____

10. $m + n \div 6$, for $m = 12$ and $n = 18$ _____

11. $1{,}221 \div x$, for $x = 37$ _____

12. $10 - x$, for $x = 3$ _____

13. $4m + 3$, for $m = 5$ _____

14. $35 - 3x$, for $x = 10$ _____

15. $851 - p$, for $p = 215$ _____

16. $18a - 9b$, for $a = 12$ and $b = 15$ _____

17. $3ab - c$, for $a = 4$, $b = 2$, and $c = 5$ _____

18. $\frac{ab}{2} + 4c$, for $a = 6$, $b = 5$, and $c = 3$ _____

19. $\frac{rst}{3}$, for $r = 9$, $s = 2$, and $t = 4$ _____

20. $x(y + 5) - z$, for $x = 3$, $y = 2$, and $z = 7$ _____

21. Elliot is 58 years old.

    a. Write an expression for the number of years by which Elliot's age

    exceeds that of his daughter, who is y years old. _____

    b. If his daughter is 25, how much older is Elliot? _____

22. A tree grows 5 in. each year.

    a. Write an expression for the tree's height after x years. _____

    b. When the tree is 36 years old, how tall will it be? _____

1-3 • Guided Problem Solving

GPS **Student Page 17, Exercise 31**

A fitness club requires a $100 initiation fee and dues of $25 each
month. Write an expression for the cost of membership for
n months. Then find the cost of membership for one year.

Understand the Problem

1. What is the initiation fee for the club? _____

2. What are the monthly dues for the club? _____

3. What does the variable n represent? _____

4. You are asked to write an expression.
   What does this expression represent? _____

5. What are you asked to find? _____

Make and Carry Out a Plan

6. What operation must you use to find the amount of dues for n months? _____

7. Write an expression to represent the cost of dues for n months. _____

8. The total cost of membership for n months includes the
   initiation fee and the cost of monthly dues for n months.
   What operation must you use to find the total cost of membership? _____

9. Write an expression for the total cost of
   membership for n months, including the initiation fee. _____

10. Evaluate the expression in Step 9 for
    $n = 12$, the number of months in a year. _____

11. Simplify the expression to find the cost of membership for one year. _____

Check the Answer

12. Look at the expression you found in
    Step 11. Which operation do you perform first? _____

Solve Another Problem

13. Carly belongs to a book-of-the-month club. She paid $10
    to sign up and then pays $5 for a new book each month.
    Write an expression for the cost of belonging to the club
    for n months. Then find the cost of belonging to the club for 8 months. _____

Practice 1-4

Integers and Absolute Value

Graph each set of numbers on a number line. Then order the numbers from least to greatest.

1. $-4, -8, 5$

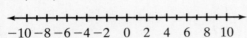

_____

2. $3, -3, -2$

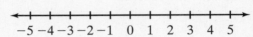

_____

3. $0, -9, -5$

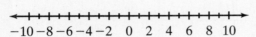

_____

4. $-7, -1, -6$

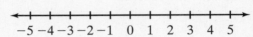

_____

Write an integer to represent each quantity.

5. 5 degrees below zero _____

6. 2,000 ft above sea level _____

7. a loss of 12 yd _____

8. 7 strokes under par _____

Simplify each expression.

9. the opposite of -15 _____

10. $|-9|$ _____

11. $-|-25|$ _____

12. the opposite of $|-8|$ _____

13. $-|-31|$ _____

14. $|847|$ _____

Write the integer represented by each point on the number line.

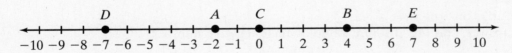

15. A _____

16. B _____

17. C _____

18. D _____

19. E _____

Compare. Use >, <, or = to complete each statement.

20. -3 ☐ 4

21. 5 ☐ 1

22. -2 ☐ -6

23. 7 ☐ $|8|$

24. $|-2|$ ☐ $|2|$

25. $|-1|$ ☐ -6

26. $|4|$ ☐ $|-5|$

27. 0 ☐ $|-7|$

1-4 • Guided Problem Solving
•••

GPS **Student Page 20, Exercise 13**

**Graph the set of numbers on a number line. Then order the
numbers from least to greatest.**

$-2, 8, -9$

Understand the Problem
••••••••••••••••••••••••••••

1. What are you asked to do? _____

2. What are the three numbers? _____

Make and Carry Out a Plan
••••••••••••••••••••••••••••••••

3. Draw a number line from -10 to 10 in the space below.

4. Negative numbers are to the left of zero and positive
   numbers are to the right of zero. Plot $-2, 8,$ and -9 on
   the number line.

5. Numbers on a number line increase in value from left to
   right. Which number is farthest to the left on the number line? _____

6. Order the numbers from least to greatest. _____

Check the Answer
•••••••••••••••••••••••

7. To check your answer, find the absolute value of each negative number.

   _____

   The negative number with the greatest absolute value
   comes first when ordering numbers from least to greatest.

Solve Another Problem

**Graph the set of numbers on a number line. Then order the
numbers from least to greatest.**

8. $4, -3, -8$ _____

Practice 1-5

Adding Integers

Write a numerical expression for each of the following. Then find the sum.

1. climb up 26 steps, then climb down 9 steps

_____

2. earn $100, spend $62, earn $35, spend $72

_____

Find each sum.

3. $-8 + (-3)$ **4.** $6 + (-6)$ **5.** $-12 + (-17)$

_____   _____   _____

6. $9 + (-11)$ **7.** $-4 + (-6)$ **8.** $18 + (-17)$

_____   _____   _____

9. $-8 + 8 + (-11)$ **10.** $12 + (-7) + 3 + (-8)$ **11.** $-15 + 7 + 15$

_____   _____   _____

12. $0 + (-11)$ **13.** $6 + (-5) + (-4)$ **14.** $-5 + (-16) + 5 + 8 + 16$

_____   _____   _____

Without adding, tell whether each sum is positive, negative, or zero.

15. $192 + (-129)$ **16.** $-417 + (-296)$ **17.** $-175 + 87$

_____   _____   _____

Evaluate each expression for $n = -12$.

18. $n + 8$ **19.** $n + (-5)$ **20.** $12 + n$

_____   _____   _____

Compare. Write >, <, or = to complete each statement.

21. $-7 + 5$ ☐ $3 + (-6)$ **22.** $4 + (-9)$ ☐ $6 + (-7) + (-4)$

23. An elevator went up 15 floors, down 9 floors, up 11 floors, and down 19

floors. Find the net change. _____

24. The price of a share of stock started the day at $37. During the day it
went down $3, up $1, down $7, and up $4. What was the price of a share
at the end of the day?

_____

1-5 • Guided Problem Solving

GPS **Student Page 28, Exercise 53**

Finance Maria had $123. She spent $35, loaned $20 to a friend, and received her $90 paycheck. How much does she have now?

Understand the Problem

1. How much money did Maria start with? _____

2. What amount did she spend? _____

3. How much money did she loan to a friend? _____

4. What was the amount of Maria's paycheck? _____

Make and Carry Out a Plan

5. Look at the amounts below. Tell whether each amount should be added to or subtracted from Maria's $123.

   a. $35 _____

   b. $20 _____

   c. $90 _____

6. Write an expression to show the original amount of $123 and the amounts that should be added or subtracted. _____

7. Simplify the expression to find the amount of money Maria has now. _____

Check the Answer

8. To check your work, start with the amount you found in Step 7 and work backward. Subtract 90, add 20, and add 35. Is your result the same as the amount Maria started with?

   _____

   _____

Solve Another Problem

9. Alec had $55. He earned $25 mowing lawns in his neighborhood. He spent $10 on a new baseball card for his collection. Then he spent $6 on lunch with a friend. How much money does Alec have now? _____

Practice 1-6

Use rules to find each difference.

1. 8 − 12

2. 13 − 6

3. 9 − (−12)

4. 57 − 39

5. −173 − 162

6. 71 − (123)

7. 51 − 89

8. −222 − (−117)

9. 843 − 677

10. −98 − 183

11. 366 − (−429)

12. −83 − (−48) − 65

Find each difference.

13. 6 − 9

14. 14 − 8

15. −15 − 3

16. −25 − 25

17. −16 − (−16)

18. 32 − (−17) − 32

Round each number. Then estimate each sum or difference.

19. −57 + (−98)

20. 448 − 52

21. −191 + (−511)

22. −361 − (−58)

23. 888 + 1,177

24. −484 − 1,695

Write a numerical expression for each phrase. Then simplify.

25. A balloon goes up 2,300 ft, then goes down 600 ft.

_____

26. You lose $50, then spend $35.

_____

27. The Glasers had $317 in their checking account. They wrote checks for $74, $132, and $48. What is their checking account balance?

_____

1-6 • Guided Problem Solving

GPS **Student Page 32, Exercise 31**

Scores Suppose you have a score of 35 in a game. You get a
50-point penalty. What is your new score?

Understand the Problem

1. What is your original score? _____

2. How many points is your penalty? _____

3. What are you asked to find? _____

Make and Carry Out a Plan

4. Is your original score positive or negative? _____

5. Should you add or subtract your penalty from your original score?

   _____

6. Write an expression to show how to combine
   a 50-point penalty with the original 35-point score.

   _____

7. Simplify the expression from Step 6 to find your new score.

   _____

Check the Answer

8. Write the expression from Step 6 as a sum.

   _____

9. Find the sum. _____

Solve Another Problem

10. Trevor has a score of 55 in a game.
    He gets a 75-point penalty. What is his new score? _____

Practice 1-7

Inductive Reasoning

Write a rule for each pattern. Find the next three numbers in each pattern.

1. 3, 6, 9, 12, 15, _____ , _____ , _____

Rule: _____

_____

2. 1, 2, 4, 8, 16, _____ , _____ , _____

Rule: _____

_____

3. 6, 7, 14, 15, 30, 31, _____ , _____ , _____

Rule: _____

_____

4. 34, 27, 20, 13, 6, _____ , _____ , _____

Rule: _____

_____

Is each statement correct or incorrect? If it is incorrect, give a counterexample.

5. All roses are red.

_____

6. A number is divisible by 4 if its last two digits are divisible by 4.

_____

7. The difference of two numbers is always less than at least one of the numbers.

_____

Describe the next figure in each pattern. Then draw the figure.

8.

_____

9.

_____

10.

_____

_____

11.

_____

_____

1-7 • Guided Problem Solving

GPS **Student Page 39, Exercise 20**

Reasoning Is the conjecture correct or incorrect? If incorrect, give a counterexample.

A whole number is divisible by 3 if the sum of its digits is divisible by 3.

Understand the Problem

1. Write the conjecture in your own words. _____

_____

Make and Carry Out a Plan

2. An example of a whole number whose digits have a sum that is divisible by 3 is 27. List three other such whole numbers. _____

3. Show that each whole number you found in Step 2 is divisible by 3.

_____

4. The sum of the digits of 102 is divisible by 3. Also, 102 is divisible by 3. What are two other three-digit numbers for which the sum of the digits is divisible by 3? _____

5. Is each number you named in Step 4 also divisible by 3? _____

6. Based on your trials, does the conjecture seem correct or incorrect? Explain. _____

_____

Check the Answer

7. Test the conjecture using the number 5,112. Is the sum of the digits divisible by 3? Is 5,112 divisible by 3? _____

Solve Another Problem

8. **Is the conjecture correct or incorrect? If it is incorrect, give a counterexample.**
   A whole number is divisible by 2 if the sum of its digits is divisible by 2.

_____

_____

Practice 1-8

Solve by looking for a pattern.

1. Each row in a window display of floppy disk cartons contains two more boxes than the row above. The first row has one box.
   a. Complete the table.

Row Number	1	2	3	4	5	6
Boxes in the Row						
Total Boxes in the Display						

   b. Describe the pattern in the numbers you wrote.

   _____

   _____

   c. Find the number of rows in a display containing the given number of boxes.

   81 _____   144 _____   400 _____

   d. Describe how you can use the number of boxes in the display to calculate the number of rows.

   _____

   _____

2. A computer multiplied 100 nines. You can use patterns to find the ones digit of the product.

   $$9 \times 9 \times 9 \times 9 \times \cdots \times 9$$

   100 times

   a. Find the ones digit for the product of:

   1 nine _____   2 nines _____   3 nines _____   4 nines _____

   b. Describe the pattern. _____

   _____

   _____

   _____

   c. What is the ones digit of the computer's product? _____

3. Use the method of Exercise 2 to find the ones digit of the product when 4 is multiplied by itself 100 times. _____

1-8 • Guided Problem Solving

....

GPS Student Page 42, Exercise 2

Solve by looking for a pattern.

Students are to march in a parade. There will be one first grader, two second graders, three third graders, and so on, through the twelfth grade. How many students will march in the parade?

Understand the Problem

1. How many first graders will march in the parade? _____

2. How many second graders will march in the parade? Third graders? _____

3. What are you asked to find? _____

Make and Carry Out a Plan

4. Make a table to organize the information. Complete the table with the information you know about the number of first, second, and third graders.

Grade	1	2	3	4	5	6	7	8	9	10	11	12
Number of Students in the Parade												

5. Look for a pattern in the number of students. What pattern do you see? _____

6. Use the pattern to complete the table above.

7. Add the number of students from each grade who will march in the parade. How many students will march in the parade? _____

Check the Answer

8. To check your answer, draw a diagram on a separate piece of paper. Use a dot to represent each student. In the first row of your diagram, draw the number of first graders, in the second row the number of second graders, and so on. The number of dots should be equal to the number of students from Question 7. _____

Solve Another Problem

9. At Highland Elementary School, one first grader, three second graders, five third graders and so on through the sixth grade are crossing guards. How many students are crossing guards? _____

Guided Problem Solving

Practice 1-9

Multiplying and Dividing Integers

Use repeated addition, patterns, or rules to find each product or quotient.

1. $23 \cdot 16$

2. $8 \cdot 7(-6)$

3. $-17 \cdot 3$

4. $-24 \div 4$

5. $-65 \div 5$

6. $117 \div (-1)$

7. $-30 \div (-6)$

8. $-21 \div (-3)$

9. $63 \div (-21)$

10. $5(-1)(-9)$

11. $-6(-3) \cdot 2$

12. $-3 \cdot 7(-2)$

13. $\dfrac{1,512}{-42}$

14. $\dfrac{-4,875}{-65}$

15. $\dfrac{-15(-3)}{-9}$

Compare. Use $>$, $<$, or $=$ to complete each statement.

16. $-7(5)$ ☐ $-6 \cdot (-6)$

17. $-20 \cdot (-5)$ ☐ $10 \cdot |-10|$

18. $3(-6)$ ☐ $-3(6)$

19. $121 \div (-11)$ ☐ $-45 \div (-6)$

20. $-40 \div 8$ ☐ $40 \div (-8)$

21. $-54 \div 9$ ☐ $21 \div (-3)$

For each group, find the average.

22. temperatures: $6°, -15°, -24°, 3°, -25°$ _____

23. bank balances: $52, -$7, $20, -$63, -$82 _____

24. stock price changes: $6, -$6, -$9, $1, $3 _____

25. golf scores: $-2, 0, 3, -2, -3, 1, -4$ _____

26. elevations (ft): $-120, 168, -60, -42, -36$ _____

Write a multiplication or division sentence to answer the question.

27. The temperature dropped $4°$ each hour for 3 hours. What was the total change in temperature?

_____

1-9 • Guided Problem Solving

GPS Student Page 47, Exercise 4

Weather The temperature dropped 5 degrees each hour for 7 h.
Use an integer to represent the total change in temperature.

Understand the Problem

1. How many degrees did the temperature drop each hour? _____

2. For how many hours did the temperature drop? _____

3. What are you asked to do? _____

Make and Carry Out a Plan

4. Use repeated subtraction to solve the problem.
   How many times will you subtract 5 degrees? _____

5. Use a number line to show your repeated subtraction. Continue on the
   number line below until you have subtracted −5 the correct number of times.

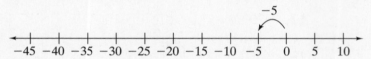

6. What integer represents the total change in temperature? _____

Check the Answer

7. To check your answer, multiply the number of degrees
   the temperature dropped each hour by the number of hours. _____
   Your answer should be the same as your answer to Question 6.

Solve Another Problem

8. A scuba diver descends 10 ft every 10 seconds. Use an integer
   to represent the position of the diver after 1 min (60 seconds). _____

Practice 1-10

The Coordinate Plane

Graph each point.

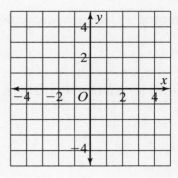

1. $A(-2, 2)$ 2. $B(0, 3)$
3. $C(-3, 0)$ 4. $D(2, 3)$
5. $E(-1, -2)$ 6. $F(4, -2)$

Write the coordinates of each point.

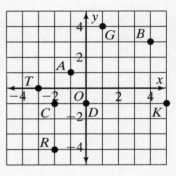

7. A _____   8. B _____

9. C _____   10. D _____

In which quadrant or on what axis does each point fall?

11. A _____   12. B _____

13. C _____   14. D _____

Name the point with the given coordinates.

15. $(1, 4)$ _____   16. $(-3, 0)$ _____

17. $(5, -1)$ _____   18. $(-2, -4)$ _____

Complete using *positive*, or *negative*, or *zero*.

19. In Quadrant II, x is _____ and y is _____.

20. In Quadrant III, x is _____ and y is _____.

21. On the y-axis x is _____.

22. On the x-axis y is _____.

1-10 • Guided Problem Solving

GPS **Student Page 55, Exercise 55**

Geometry *PQRS* is a square. Find the coordinates of *S*.

$P(-5, 0), Q(0, 5), R(5, 0), S(\blacksquare, \blacksquare)$

Understand the Problem

1. What shape is *PQRS*? _____

2. What information are you given about points *P*, *Q*, and *R*? _____

3. What are you asked to find? _____

Make and Carry Out a Plan

4. Graph *P*, *Q*, and *R* on the graph below.

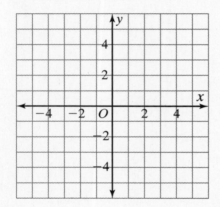

5. Draw lines to connect *P* to *Q* and *Q* to *R*. These are two sides of the square.

6. What is true about the four sides of a square? _____

7. Draw the two missing sides of the square.

8. *S* is the point where the two new
sides meet. What are the coordinates of *S*? _____

Check the Answer

9. To check your answer, use a ruler to measure each side. _____
Since *PQRS* is a square, all four sides should have the same length.

Solve Another Problem

10. *JKLM* is a rectangle. Find the coordinates of *M*.
$J(-4, 2), K(-4, -2), L(4, -2), M(\blacksquare, \blacksquare)$ _____

1A: Graphic Organizer

For use before Lesson 1-1

Study Skill Take a few minutes to explore the general contents of this text. Begin by looking at the cover. What does the cover art say about mathematics? What do the pages before the first page of Chapter 1 tell you? What special pages are in the back of the book to help you?

Write your answers. Use the Table of Contents page for this chapter at the front of the book.

1. What is the title of this chapter? _____

2. Name four topics that you will study in this chapter.

   _____   _____

   _____   _____

3. What is the topic of the Problem Solving lesson? _____

4. Complete the graphic organizer below as you work through the chapter.
   1. Write the title of the chapter in the center oval.
   2. When you begin a lesson, write the name of the lesson in a rectangle.
   3. When you complete that lesson, write a skill or key concept from that lesson in the outer oval linked to that rectangle.
   Continue with steps 2 and 3 clockwise around the graphic organizer.

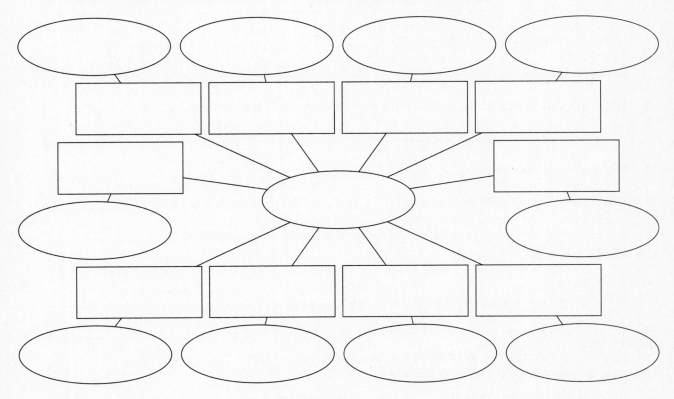

1B: Reading Comprehension

For use after Lesson 1-4

Study Skill When you read a paragraph in mathematics, read it twice. Read it the first time to get an overview of the content. Read it a second time to find the essential details and information. Write down key words that tell you the topic for each paragraph.

Read the passage below and answer the questions that follow.

Algebra is a part of mathematics that uses variables as well as the operations that combine variables. Some operations in algebra are the ones you learned in arithmetic $(+, -, \times, \div)$. In algebra, however, you might add two variables such as a and b. Then you could substitute different values for these variables. So, for example, $a + b$ can represent $3 + 4$ or $13.5 + 24.7$ or any other numbers you choose.

Two different people have commonly been called "the father of algebra." One is Diophantus, a Greek mathematician who lived in the third century. He was the first to use symbols to represent frequently used words. The other is the Arab mathematician Al-Khowarizmi. In the ninth century, he published a clear and complete explanation of how to solve an equation. Our word "algebra" comes from the word, *al-jabr*, which appears in the title of his work.

1. What is the subject of the first paragraph? What is the subject of the second paragraph?

_____

2. How are numbers used in the passage? _____

_____

3. What are the names of the mathematicians mentioned in the passage?

_____

4. What title do they share? _____

5. How much time passed between the lives of these two mathematicians? _____

6. According to this passage, what is the same in arithmetic and algebra? _____

_____

7. Which operations are named in this passage? _____

8. What was the origin of the word *algebra*? _____

9. High-Use Academic Words In the first paragraph of the passage, what does it mean to *substitute*?

    a. to use in place of another   **b.** to prove

1C: Reading/Writing Math Symbols   For use after Lesson 1-9

Study Skill Plan your time, whether you are studying or taking a test. Look at the entire amount of time you have and divide it into portions that you allocate to each task. Keep track of whether you are on schedule.

Write an explanation in words for the meaning of each mathematical expression or statement.

1. $2 \div p$ _____

2. $|x|$ _____

3. -10 _____

4. $y < -2$ _____

5. $7a$ _____

Write each expression or statement with math symbols.

6. the sum of a and b _____

7. 3 divided by 15 _____

8. 2 times the sum of x and y _____

9. The opposite of m is less than 2. _____

10. 6 less than p _____

11. the quotient of 12 and t _____

12. the absolute value of 3 _____

1D: Visual Vocabulary Practice

For use after Lesson 1-10

Study Skill The Glossary contains the key vocabulary for this course.

Concept List

opposites	ordered pair	origin
quadrants	variable	variable expression
x-axis	y-axis	y-coordinate

Write the concept that best describes each exercise. Choose from the concept list above.

1. The letter "c" in $24c + 8$	**2.** $10d - 3 + a$	**3.** -9 and 9
4. 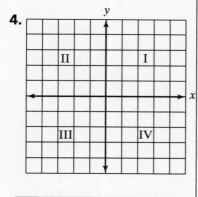	**5.** 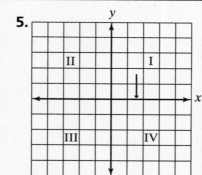	**6.** 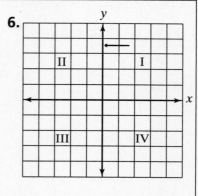
7. $(2, -3)$	**8.** 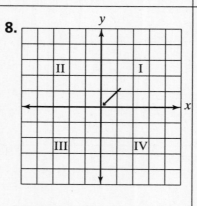	**9.** The number 8 in $(5, 8)$

1E: Vocabulary Check

Study Skill Strengthen your vocabulary. Use these pages and add cues and summaries by applying the Cornell Notetaking style.

Write the definition for each word at the right. To check your work, fold the paper back along the dotted line to see the correct answers.

_____   Integers

_____

_____

_____   Absolute value

_____

_____   Inductive reasoning

_____

_____

_____   Conjecture

_____

_____

_____   Counterexample

_____

_____

1E: Vocabulary Check (continued)

Write the vocabulary word for each definition. To check your work, fold the paper forward along the dotted line to see the correct answers.

The whole numbers and their opposites.

_____

The distance of a number from zero on a number line.

_____

Making conclusions based on patterns you observe.

_____

A conclusion reached through inductive reasoning.

_____

An example that proves a statement false.

_____

1F: Vocabulary Review Puzzle

For use with Chapter Review

Study Skill The language of mathematics has precise definitions for each vocabulary word or phrase. To help you learn these definitions, keep a list of the new words in each chapter, along with their definitions and an example.

Write the vocabulary word for each description. Complete the word search puzzle by finding and circling each vocabulary word. For help, use the glossary in your textbook. Remember that a word may go right to left, left to right, or it may go up as well as down.

1. a conclusion reached by observing patterns _____

2. the plane formed by the intersection of two number lines _____

3. a whole number or its opposite _____

4. reasoning that makes conclusions based on patterns _____

5. the horizontal or vertical number line on the coordinate plane _____

6. a letter that stands for a number _____

7. one of the four parts of the coordinate plane _____

8. point of intersection for the axes _____

9. kind of value that gives the distance of a number from zero _____

10. replacing each variable with a number in an expression and simplifying

   the result _____

```
I N T E G E R O T E U D Q
E T E E E A G V A T C L O
E N I E T R N D E A E I I
R A R U A B D J L U A E A
U R T U N O N B B L I E N
T D E A I V E T A A C T N
C A I N D U C T I V E U U
E U U T R B N O R E B L E
J Q A A O R I E A L S O I
N E D O O T T A V U X S I
O G A O C O R I G I N B N
C A X I S U T T I V E A N
```

Practice 2-1

Simplify each expression using mental math.

1. $4 \cdot 13 \cdot 25$

2. $700 + 127 + 300$

3. $68 + 85 + 32$

4. $2 \cdot 3 \cdot 4 \cdot 5$

5. $-14 + 71 + 29 + (-86)$

6. $125 \cdot 9 \cdot 8$

7. $20 \cdot 7 \cdot 5$

8. $217 + 545 - 17$

9. $39 + 27 + 11$

10. $4 \cdot 12 \cdot 250$

11. $19 + 0 + (-9)$

12. $-6 \cdot 1 \cdot 30$

Write the letter of the property shown.

13. $14(mn) = (14m)n$ _____

a. commutative property of addition
b. associative property of addition
c. commutative property of multiplication
d. associative property of multiplication
e. additive identity
f. multiplicative identity

14. $19 + 11 = 11 + 19$ _____

15. $k \cdot 1 = k$ _____

16. $(x + y) + z = x + (y + z)$ _____

17. $65t = t(65)$ _____

18. $p = 0 + p$ _____

19. $n = 1 \cdot n$ _____

20. $(x + p) + (r + t) = (r + t) + (x + p)$ _____

21. $(h + 0) + 4 = h + 4$ _____

22. $x + yz = x + zy$ _____

Evaluate each expression using mental math.

23. $x(yz)$, for $x = 8, y = -9, z = 5$ _____

24. $q + r + s$, for $q = 46, r = 19, s = 54$ _____

25. $a(b)(-c)$, for $a = 7, b = -2, c = 15$ _____

2-1 • Guided Problem Solving
. . . .

GPS Student Page 71, Exercise 22

Mental Math Loryn is flying roundtrip from Dallas, Texas, to Minneapolis, Minnesota. The fare for her ticket is $308. Each airport charges a $16 airport fee. There is also a tax of $12 on the fare. What is the total cost of Loryn's ticket?

Understand the Problem
. . . .

1. What is the fare for Loryn's flight? _____

2. What is the tax on the fare? _____

3. What are the airport fees for each airport? _____

4. How many airports will charge airport fees? _____

5. What are you asked to find? _____

Make and Carry Out a Plan
. . . .

6. Write an expression to find the total
   cost of airport fees for Loryn's flight. _____

7. Write an expression to add the cost of the fare,
   the total cost of airport fees, and the tax on the fare. _____

8. Which operation should you perform first to simplify the expression? _____

9. Write the simplified expression. _____

10. Use the Commutative Property of Addition to rewrite
    the expression so it is easier to simplify using mental math. _____

11. Use the Associative Property of Addition to group
    the two terms in the expression that are easiest to add. _____

12. What is the total cost of Loryn's ticket? _____

Check the Answer
. . . .

13. How do the Commutative and Associative
    Properties help you use mental math to solve the problem? _____

    _____

Solve Another Problem

14. Terry purchased a new seat for his bicycle for $24. He also bought a new
    helmet for $35 and two new reflectors for $3 each. How much did Terry spend? _____

Name _____ Class _____ Date _____

Practice 2-2

The Distributive Property

Write an expression using parentheses for each model. Then multiply.

1.  **2.**

_____ _____

Multiply each expression.

3. $6(h - 4)$ _____ **4.** $(p + 3)5$ _____

5. $-3(x + 8)$ _____ **6.** $(4 - y)(-9)$ _____

7. $2(7n - 11)$ _____ **8.** $-10(-a + 5)$ _____

Use the distributive property to simplify.

9. $98 \cdot 7$ _____

10. $9 \cdot 28$ _____

11. $78 \cdot 8$ _____

12. $7(2{,}009)$ _____

13. $899 \cdot 5$ _____

14. $30 \cdot 105$ _____

15. $8 \cdot 5 - 12 \cdot 5$ _____

16. $7 \cdot 10 + 7(-3)$ _____

17. $-4(3) + (-4)(6)$ _____

18. $6(8) + 6(-2)$ _____

Solve using mental math.

19. A shipping container holds 144 boxes. How many boxes can be shipped

in 4 containers? _____

2-2 • Guided Problem Solving

GPS **Student Page 76, Exercise 9**

Solve using mental math.

Ticket Sales A theater sold out its evening performances four nights in a row. The theater has 294 seats. How many people attended the theater in the four nights?

Understand the Problem

1. How many seats does the theater have? _____

2. How many nights in a row did the theater sell all of its seats? _____

3. What are you asked to find? _____

Make and Carry Out a Plan

4. Write an expression to find the number of people that attended the theater in the four nights. _____

5. In what other way can you write 294 so it will be easier to simplify the expression using mental math? _____

6. Rewrite the expression from Step 4 using your new way to write 294. _____

7. Use the Distributive Property to simplify the expression. _____

8. How many people attended the theater in the four nights? _____

Check the Answer

9. How can the Distributive Property help you find the answer mentally? _____

_____

_____

Solve Another Problem

10. Forty-eight people visited the information booth at a town fair on each day of the fair. If the fair was open for three days, how many people visited the information booth in all? _____

Guided Problem Solving

Name _____ Class _____ Date _____

Practice 2-3

Simplifying Variable Expressions

· ·

Simplify each expression.

1. $16 + 7y - 8$

_____

2. $18m - 7 + 12m$

_____

3. $5(3t) - 7(2t)$

_____

4. $2x - 9y + 7x + 20y$

_____

5. $3(9k - 4) - 4(5n - 3)$

_____

6. $6(g - h) - 6(g - h)$

_____

7. $-21(a + 2b) + 14a - 9b$

_____

8. $-7a + 3(a - c) + 5c$

_____

9. $-2(-5)q + (-72)(-q)$

_____

Name the coefficients, any like terms, and any constants.

	Coefficients	Like Terms	Constants
10. $3x + 7$	_____	_____	_____
11. $4m + (-3n) + n$	_____	_____	_____
12. $6kp + 9k + kp - 14$	_____	_____	_____
13. $-8y + 6ab + 7 - 3ba$	_____	_____	_____
14. $c + 2c + c - 5c + 1$	_____	_____	_____

Write an expression for each model. Simplify the expression.

15.

_____

16.

_____

Justify each step.

17. $5(n + 4) + 9n = (5n + 20) + 9n$ _____

$\qquad = 5n + (20 + 9n)$ _____

$\qquad = 5n + (9n + 20)$ _____

$\qquad = (5n + 9n) + 20$ _____

$\qquad = (5 + 9)n + 20$ _____

$\qquad = 14n + 20$ _____

· ·

Practice

Pre-Algebra Lesson 2-3 **267**

2-3 • Guided Problem Solving

GPS Student Page 80, Exercise 32

Pet Supplies Juan bought supplies for his new gecko. He bought four plants for p dollars each. He also bought a 10-gallon tank for $10 and a water dish for $3. Write an expression Juan could use to find the total cost of the supplies.

Understand the Problem

1. What does the variable p represent? _____

2. How much did Juan spend on the 10-gallon tank? _____

3. How much did Juan spend on the water dish? _____

4. For what situation are you asked to write an expression? _____

_____

Make and Carry Out a Plan

5. Write an expression to represent the
amount Juan paid for the four plants. _____

6. Write an expression to represent the amount Juan paid in
all for the plants, the 10-gallon tank, and the water dish. _____

7. Simplify the expression by
combining like terms and any constants. _____

Check the Answer

8. How do you know the expression is simplified? _____

_____

Solve Another Problem

9. Josie bought new school supplies. She bought three
notebooks for n dollars each. She also bought a new
calculator for $12 and a new pen for $2. Write an expression
Josie could use to find the total cost of the school supplies. _____

Practice 2-4

Is the given number a solution of the equation?

1. $9k = 10 - k; -1$ _____

2. $-7r - 15 = -2r; -3$ _____

3. $3g \div (-6) = 5 - g; -10$ _____

4. $-3p = 4p + 35; -5$ _____

5. $8 - e = 2e - 16; 8$ _____

6. $5 - 15s = 8 - 16s; 3$ _____

7. $2(x - 2) - 5x = 5(2 - x); 7$ _____

8. $6a + 3 = 3(3a - 2); 4$ _____

Is each equation true, false, or an open sentence?

9. $14 = x - 9$

10. $8 + 7 = 10$

11. $4 - 15 = 22 - 33$

12. $5 + x = 90 \div 9 + 4$

13. $-7(5 - 9) = 19 - 3(-3)$

14. $6(5 - 8) = 2(10 - 1)$

Write an equation for each sentence. Is each equation true, false, or an open sentence?

15. One fifth of a number n is equal to -7.

16. The product of 13 and -7 is -91.

17. Fifty-four divided by six equals negative nine.

18. Seven less than the product of a number z and 3 is equal to 4.

Write an equation. Is the given value a solution?

19. A truck driver drove 468 miles on Tuesday. That was 132 miles farther than she drove on Monday. Let d represent the distance she drove on Monday. Did she drive 600 miles on Monday?

Name_____ Class_____ Date_____

2-4 • Guided Problem Solving

GPS **Student Page 84, Exercise 21**

Write an equation. Is the given value a solution?

Weight A veterinarian weighs 140 lb. When she steps on a scale while holding a dog, the scale shows 192 lb. Let d represent the weight of the dog. Does the dog weigh 52 lb?

Understand the Problem

1. How much does the veterinarian weigh? _____

2. What does the variable d represent? _____

3. How much do the dog and veterinarian weigh together? _____

4. What are you asked to do? _____

Make and Carry Out a Plan

5. Write a variable expression to represent
   the total weight of the veterinarian and dog. _____

6. Write an equation in which the variable expression
   is equal to the scale weight of the veterinarian and dog. _____

7. Is the equation you wrote true, false, or an open sentence? _____

8. Substitute 52 for d in the equation. _____

9. Is the equation true or false? _____

10. Does the dog weigh 52 lb? _____

Check the Answer

11. Subtract 52 lb from 192 lb. _____
    If the dog weighs 52 lb, the difference will be equal to the weight of
    the veterinarian.

Solve Another Problem

12. Drew has 32 trading cards. Together, Beth and Drew have
    56 trading cards. Let b represent the number of trading cards Beth
    has. Write an equation to find out whether Beth has 25 trading cards.

_____

Practice 2-5

Solving Equations by Adding or Subtracting

Use mental math to solve each equation.

1. $-52 = -52 + k$ _____

2. $837 = p + 37$ _____

3. $x - 155 = 15$ _____

4. $180 = 80 + n$ _____

5. $2{,}000 + y = 9{,}500$ _____

6. $81 = x - 19$ _____

7. $111 + f = 100$ _____

8. $w - 6 = -16$ _____

Solve each equation.

9. $m - 17 = -8$ _____

10. $k - 55 = 67$ _____

11. $-44 + n = 36$ _____

12. $-36 = p - 91$ _____

13. $x - 255 = 671$ _____

14. $19 = c - (-12)$ _____

15. $x + 14 = 21$ _____

16. $31 = p + 17$ _____

17. $-19 = k + 9$ _____

18. $87 + y = 19$ _____

19. $36 + n = 75$ _____

20. $-176 = h + (-219)$ _____

21. $41 + k = 7$ _____

22. $1{,}523 + c = 2{,}766$ _____

23. $-88 + z = 0$ _____

24. $-33 + (-7) = 29 + m$ _____

25. $t + (-2) = -66$ _____

26. $-390 + x = 11 - 67$ _____

27. The combined enrollment in the three grades at Jefferson Middle School is 977. There are 356 students in the seventh grade and 365 in the eighth grade. Write and solve an equation to find how many students are in the ninth grade.

Equation _____

Solution _____

2-5 • Guided Problem Solving

GPS Student Page 91, Exercise 33

Multiple Choice In 1996, 487 million people across the world spoke English. This was 512 million people fewer than the number who spoke Mandarin Chinese. Which equation could you use to find the number of people n who spoke Mandarin Chinese.

A. $487 = n - 512$ **B.** $487 = n \times 512$
C. $487 = 512 - n$ **D.** $487 = 512 \div n$

Understand the Problem

1. How many people in the world spoke English in 1996? _____

2. What information are you given about the number of people who spoke Mandarin Chinese in 1996? _____

   _____

3. What are you asked to do? _____

   _____

Make and Carry Out a Plan

4. Each of the equation choices uses the variable n to represent an unknown quantity. What is the unknown quantity in the problem statement?

   _____

5. What mathematical operation is implied by the phrase "512 fewer than n"? Explain.

   _____

6. Which equation represents 487 is 512 fewer than n? _____

Check the Answer

7. According to the problem statement, fewer people spoke English than Mandarin Chinese. Check the reasonableness of your answer by determining whether the equation you chose makes n bigger or smaller than 487.

   _____

Solve Another Problem

8. There are 32 students taking physical science. This is 119 fewer than the number of students taking Earth science. Write an equation to find the number of students s taking Earth science.

   _____

Practice 2-6

Solving Equations by Multiplying or Dividing

Solve each equation.

1. $\frac{k}{-5} = -5$ _____

2. $-3 = \frac{n}{7}$ _____

3. $\frac{x}{12} = 0$ _____

4. $-6 = \frac{m}{-2}$ _____

5. $\frac{y}{-4} = -12$ _____

6. $\frac{s}{30} = 6$ _____

7. $\frac{1}{9}z = 0$ _____

8. $-\frac{m}{55} = 1$ _____

9. $-3x = 18$ _____

10. $-56 = 8y$ _____

11. $8p = -8$ _____

12. $-4s = -32$ _____

13. $14h = 42$ _____

14. $-175 = 25g$ _____

15. $-42 = 6m$ _____

16. $-2x = 34$ _____

17. $\frac{x}{-9} = -11$ _____

18. $216 = 9w$ _____

19. $-17v = -17$ _____

20. $-161 = 23t$ _____

21. $56h = 3,136$ _____

22. $20 = \frac{e}{-25}$ _____

23. $4,200 = 30x$ _____

24. $\frac{y}{-21} = -21$ _____

25. $\frac{m}{-3} = 21$ _____

26. $4,000 = \frac{x}{-40}$ _____

27. A bamboo tree grew 3 in. per day. Write and solve an equation to find how many days d it took the tree to grow 144 in.

Equation: _____ Solution: _____

28. Carl drove 561 miles. His car averages 33 miles per gallon of gas. Write and solve an equation to find how much gas Carl's car used. Let g represent the amount of gas Carl's car used.

Equation: _____ Solution: _____

For what values of y is each equation true?

29. $-5|y| = -25$

30. $\frac{|y|}{2} = 28$

31. $9|y| = 27$

_____ _____ _____

2-6 • Guided Problem Solving

GPS **Student Page 96, Exercise 44**

Multiple Choice One of the world's tallest office buildings is in Malaysia. The building has 88 stories. The height of the 88 stories is 1,232 ft. What is the height of one story?

A. 9 ft high   **B.** 11 ft high

C. 14 ft high   **D.** 88 ft high

Understand the Problem

1. How many stories does the building have? _____

2. How tall is the building? _____

3. What are you asked to find? _____

Make and Carry Out a Plan

4. Choose a variable to represent the height of one story. _____

5. Use the sentence "The 1,232-ft height of the building is equal to 88 stories times the height of one story," and your variable for the height of one story, to write an equation. _____

6. What should you do to get the variable alone on one side of the equation? _____

7. Solve the equation for h. _____

8. What is the height of one story? _____

Check the Answer

9. Multiply the height of one story by the number of stories. _____ The result should be equal to the height of the building.

Solve Another Problem

10. You have 34 sections of fencing, all of equal length. You put them together to build a fence 136 ft long. Write an equation and solve to find the length of one section. _____

Practice 2-7

Use the guess, check, revise strategy to solve each problem.

1. The length of a rectangle is 9 in. greater than the width. The area is
   36 in.^{2} Find the dimensions. _____

Width						
Length						
Area						

2. Shari Williams, a basketball player, scored 30 points on 2-point and
   3-point goals. She hit 5 more 2-pointers than 3-pointers. How many of

   each did she score? _____

3-Pointers						
2-Pointers						
Points						

3. The sums and products of pairs of integers are given. Find each pair of
   integers.

   a. sum = −12, product = 36 _____

   b. sum = −12, product = 35 _____

   c. sum = −12, product = 32 _____

   d. sum = −12, product = 11 _____

   e. sum = −12, product = 0 _____

4. Jess had 3 more nickels than dimes for a total of $1.50. How many of
   each coin did he have?

   _____

5. A brush cost $2 more than a comb. The brush and a comb together cost
   $3.78. Find the cost of each.

   _____

6. The hard-cover edition of a book cost 3 times as much as the paperback
   edition. Both editions together cost $26.60. Find the cost of each.

   _____

2-7 • Guided Problem Solving

GPS **Student Page 100, Exercise 9**

Coin Collections In a group of quarters and nickels, there are four more nickels than quarters. How many nickels and quarters are there if the coins are worth $2.30?

Understand the Problem

1. What two types of coins are in the group? _____

2. How many more nickels are there than quarters? _____

3. How much are the coins worth altogether? _____

4. What are you asked to find? _____

Make and Carry Out a Plan

5. To find their worth, by what number must you multiply the number of nickels? The number of quarters? _____

6. Copy the table at right. Record your conjectures about the number of quarters and nickels, adding rows as necessary.

Quarters	Nickels	Total Worth
1	5	1(.25) + 5(.05) = 0.50

7. **a.** Test the first conjecture. Are the numbers of quarters and nickels too high or too low? _____

   b. How should you revise your conjecture? _____

8. Continue until you find the correct numbers of nickels and quarters. How many nickels and quarters are worth $2.30? _____

Check the Answer

9. How did you know whether to increase or decrease the numbers of nickels and quarters in each conjecture? _____

_____

_____

Solve Another Problem

10. Kai has nickels and dimes in his pocket. The coins are worth $1.85. He has five fewer nickels than dimes. How many dimes and nickels does he have? _____

Practice 2-8

Inequalities and Their Graphs

· ·

Write an inequality for each sentence.

1. The total t is less than sixteen. _____

2. A number h is not less than 7. _____

3. The price p is less than or equal to \$25. _____

4. A number n is negative. _____

Write an inequality for each graph.

5.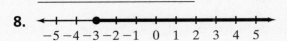
$-8\,-7\,-6\,-5\,-4\,-3\,-2\,-1\quad 0\quad 1\quad 2$

_____

6.
$-16\quad -12\quad -8\quad -4\quad 0\quad 4$

_____

7.
$-5\,-4\,-3\,-2\,-1\quad 0\quad 1\quad 2\quad 3\quad 4\quad 5$

_____

8.
$-5\,-4\,-3\,-2\,-1\quad 0\quad 1\quad 2\quad 3\quad 4\quad 5$

_____

Graph the solutions of each inequality on a number line.

9. $x < -2$

$-5\,-4\,-3\,-2\,-1\quad 0\quad 1\quad 2\quad 3\quad 4\quad 5$

10. $y \geq -1$

$-5\,-4\,-3\,-2\,-1\quad 0\quad 1\quad 2\quad 3\quad 4\quad 5$

11. $k > 1$

$-5\,-4\,-3\,-2\,-1\quad 0\quad 1\quad 2\quad 3\quad 4\quad 5$

12. $p \leq 4$

$-5\,-4\,-3\,-2\,-1\quad 0\quad 1\quad 2\quad 3\quad 4\quad 5$

Write an inequality for each situation.

13. Everyone in the class is under 13 years old. Let x be the age of a person in the class.

_____

14. The speed limit is 60 miles per hour. Let s be the speed of a car driving within the limit.

_____

15. You have \$4.50 to spend on lunch. Let c be the cost of your lunch.

_____

· ·

2-8 • Guided Problem Solving

GPS **Student Page 107, Exercise 35**

Movie Tickets Write an inequality to describe this situation.
A student pays for three movie tickets with a twenty-dollar bill
and gets change back. Let t be the cost of a movie ticket.

Understand the Problem

1. How many movie tickets did the student buy? _____

2. How did the student pay for the movie tickets? _____

3. What does the variable t represent? _____

Make and Carry Out a Plan

4. Write an expression to represent the cost of three movie tickets. _____

5. What information tells you that the
   three movie tickets cost less than twenty dollars? _____

   _____

6. Write the inequality using the expression from Step 4. _____

Check the Answer

7. How would the problem read differently if
   the three tickets cost more than twenty dollars? _____

   _____

Solve Another Problem

8. Write an inequality for this situation. Katrina bought four
   greeting cards. She gave the clerk a five-dollar bill plus some
   change to pay for the cards. Let g be the cost of a greeting card. _____

Practice 2-9

Solving One-Step Inequalities by Adding or Subtracting

Write an inequality for each sentence. Then solve the inequality.

1. Six less than n is less than -4.

   _____

2. The sum of a number k and five is greater than or equal to two.

   _____

3. Nine more than a number b is greater than negative three.

   _____

4. You must be at least 48 inches tall to ride an amusement park ride, and your little sister is 39 inches tall. How many inches i must she grow before she may ride the ride?

   _____

5. You need no more than 3,000 calories in a day. You consumed 840 calories at breakfast and 1,150 calories at lunch. How many calories c can you eat for dinner?

   _____

Solve each inequality. Graph the solutions.

6. $7 + x \geq 9$ _____

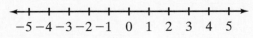

7. $-5 \leq x - 6$ _____

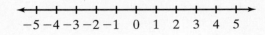

8. $0 \geq x + 12$ _____

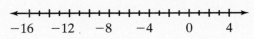

9. $x - 15 \leq -8$ _____

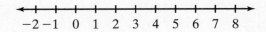

10. $13 + x \geq 13$ _____

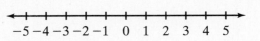

11. $x - 8 > -5$ _____

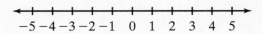

12. $4 + x < -2$ _____

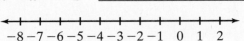

13. $x - 9 > -11$ _____

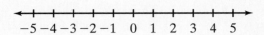

14. $x - 6 \leq -1$ _____

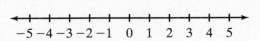

15. $-4 + x < -4$ _____

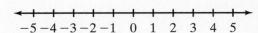

2-9 • Guided Problem Solving

GPS Student Page 110, Exercise 10

Budgeting You are saving to buy a bicycle that will cost at least $120. Your parents give you $45 toward the bicycle. How much money will you have to save?

Understand the Problem

1. How much money will the bicycle cost? _____

2. How much money did your parents give you? _____

3. What are you asked to find? _____

Make and Carry Out a Plan

4. Write an inequality to represent the situation
   "The amount of money my parents gave me,
   plus m, the amount of money I will have to
   save, is at least $120." _____

5. What number must you subtract from
   each side of the inequality to solve for m? _____

6. Solve the inequality for m. _____

7. How much money will you have to save to buy the bicycle? _____

Check the Answer

8. Subtract from $120 the amount of money
   stated in your answer to Step 7. _____
   The result should be equal to the amount of money your parents
   gave you.

Solve Another Problem

9. Shana is saving money to buy a CD player that will cost at
   least $65. She has $27. How much money will she have to save? _____

Practice 2-10

Solving One-Step Inequalities by Multiplying or Dividing

Write an inequality for each sentence. Then solve the inequality.

1. The product of k and -5 is no more than 30.

   _____

2. Half of p is at least -7.

   _____

3. The product of k and 9 is no more than 18.

   _____

4. One-third of p is at least -17.

   _____

5. The opposite of g is at least -5.

   _____

Solve each inequality.

6. $-5x < 10$ _____

7. $\frac{x}{4} > 1$ _____

8. $-8 < -8x$ _____

9. $\frac{1}{3}x > -2$ _____

10. $48 \geq -12x$ _____

11. $\frac{1}{3}x < -6$ _____

12. $\frac{x}{5} < -4$ _____

13. $-x \leq 2$ _____

Determine whether each number is a solution of $7 \geq -3k$.

14. 2 _____

15. -2 _____

16. 0 _____

17. -3 _____

Justify each step.

18. $-5n \geq 45$

   $\frac{-5n}{-5} \leq \frac{45}{-5}$ _____

   $n \leq -9$ _____

2-10 • Guided Problem Solving

GPS **Student Page 115, Exercise 38**

Budgeting Marnie pays $.06 per kilowatt-hour for electricity. She
has budgeted $72 for her electricity. What is the greatest number
of kilowatt-hours Marnie can use and stay within her budget?

Understand the Problem

1. How much does Marnie pay per kilowatt-hour of electricity? _____

2. How much has Marnie budgeted for her electricity? _____

3. What are you asked to do? _____

_____

Make and Carry Out a Plan

4. Let *k* represent the number of kilowatt-hours. Use the
sentence "$.06 per kilowatt-hour multiplied by the number of
kilowatt-hours is less than or equal to $72" to write an inequality. _____

5. What number should you divide each side of the
inequality by to get the variable *k* alone on one side? _____

6. Solve the inequality for *k*. _____

7. What is the greatest number of kilowatt-hours
of electricity Marnie can use and stay in budget? _____

Check the Answer

8. To check your answer, multiply your answer by
the price per kilowatt-hour Marnie pays for electricity. _____
The product should be less than or equal to $72.

Solve Another Problem

9. Derek enjoys going to movies. He budgets $30 a month for
movies. Admission for one movie costs $7.25. How many
movies can he see in one month and stay within budget? _____

2A: Graphic Organizer

For use before Lesson 2-1

Study Skill As you begin each new chapter, ask yourself: *What is the main idea of this chapter?* and *How is the material divided?*

Write your answers. Use the Table of Contents page for this chapter at the front of the book.

1. What is the title of this chapter? _____

2. Name four topics that you will study in this chapter.

   _____   _____

   _____   _____

3. What is the topic of the Problem Solving lesson? _____

4. Complete the graphic organizer as you work through the chapter.
   1. Write the title of the chapter in the center oval.
   2. When you begin a lesson, write the name of the lesson in a rectangle.
   3. When you complete that lesson, write a skill or key concept from that lesson in the outer oval linked to that rectangle.
   Continue with steps 2 and 3 clockwise around the graphic organizer.

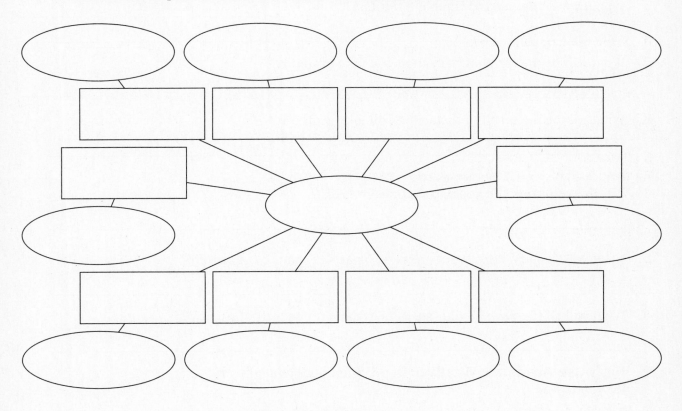

Name_____ Class_____ Date_____

2B: Reading Comprehension
For use after Lesson 2-8

Study Skill When you take notes, either as you read or as you listen to a class discussion or the teacher, you can write more quickly if you use shortcuts. Make a list of the abbreviations and symbols that you use in your notes so that you can remember the meanings of these shortcuts when you review your notes later.

Read the instructions in the box and then answer the questions about steps I–V. You do not have to do the activity in the box.

I. Write an inequality that shows that Carlos has more than 15 books.
II. List these numbers on your paper: 20, 18, 15, 12, 6, 5.
III. Look at the numbers in the list.
    a. Draw a red circle around every number in the list that is a solution.
    b. Make a blue line through every number in the list that is not a solution.
IV. a. How many red circles did you draw?
    b. How many blue lines did you make?
    c. Are there any numbers that have two color marks?
    d. Are there any numbers that have no color marks?
V. Graph the solutions of your inequality.

---

1. Read quickly through ALL the steps in the instructions. What supplies will you need to complete this task?

2. What will be the result of the action you take in step I?

3. What will be the result of the action you take in step II?

4. Notice that step III has two parts.
List the verbs that tell you what actions to take.

5. What will be the *form* of your answers to parts (a) and (b) of step IV?

6. What will be the *form* of your answers to parts (c) and (d) of step IV?

7. **High-Use Academic Words** In step V, what does *graph* mean for you to do?
    a. make a picture   **b.** make a table

2C: Reading/Writing Math Symbols   For use after Lesson 2-3

Study Skill Taking notes in class, or while you study, helps you remember the content. Your notes also help you to review what you have learned. Write your notes clearly so that you will be able to read them accurately later, when you may have forgotten some of the words.

Write the symbol(s), letter(s), or number(s) described in each of the following. The first one is done for you.

1. the constant term in $5x + 6$

_____**6**_____

2. the number of like terms in $3a + 4b - 7a + 9d$

_____

3. the identity element for multiplication

_____

4. the number of the quadrant that contains $(-1, 2)$

_____

5. the variable to be distributed in $a(b + c)$

_____

6. the identity element for addition

_____

7. the number of terms in $3x + 2y$

_____

8. the coefficient of b in $12a + 13b + 14$

_____

9. the like terms in $2x - 2y + 3x$

_____

10. the coefficient of p in $-5p - 2q$

_____

2D: Visual Vocabulary Practice

For use after Lesson 2-5

Study Skill Mathematics builds on itself so build a strong foundation.

Concept List

coefficient	constant	equation
expression	graph	inverse operations
open sentence	solution of equation	terms

Write the concept that best describes each exercise. Choose from the concept list shown above.

1. $4x$ and 9 in $4x + 9$	**2.** $-4 \ -2 \ \ 0 \ \ 2 \ \ 4 \ \ 6$	**3.** 9 in $2n - 6m + 9$
_____	_____	_____
4. The 3 and 6 in $3a + 6b - 10$	**5.** The number 3 if $y + 19 = 22$	**6.** $4c - 6 = c$
_____	_____	_____
7. $5(4 - 3) = 10$	**8.** addition and subtraction	**9.** $-8x + 6xy + 7y$
_____	_____	_____

Vocabulary and Study Skills

2E: Vocabulary Check

Study Skill Strengthen your vocabulary. Use these pages and add cues and summaries by applying the Cornell Notetaking style.

Write the definition for each word at the right. To check your work, fold the paper back along the dotted line to see the correct answers.

_____

_____

_____ Constant

_____

_____

_____ Like terms

_____

_____

_____ Deductive reasoning

_____

_____

_____ Equation

_____

_____

_____ Inequality

_____

_____

2E: Vocabulary Check (continued) For use after Lesson 2-9

Write the vocabulary word for each definition. To check your work, fold the paper forward along the dotted line to see the correct answers.

A term that has no variable.

Terms with the same variable(s) raised to the same power(s).

The process of reasoning logically from given facts to a conclusion.

A mathematical sentence with an equal sign, $=$.

_____

A sentence that uses one or more of the symbols $<$, $>$, $\geq$, $\leq$, or $\neq$.

_____

2F: Vocabulary Review

Study Skill To succeed in mathematics, you need to understand the language and the words. Learn the new math terms one at a time by drawing a diagram or by writing a sentence to make the meaning clear.

Match each word or phrase in the left column with the best example in the right column. Some words or phrases may have more than one example, but only one example is the best match.

Word or Phrase	**Example or Definition**
1. Addition Property of Equality _____	**A.** $w + 0 = w$
2. Additive Identity _____	**B.** $n \cdot 1 = n$
3. Associative Property _____	**C.** $(pq)r = p(qr)$
4. Commutative Property _____	**D.** If $a = c$, then $a + b = c + b$.
5. Multiplicative Identity _____	**E.** $x \cdot y = y \cdot x$

Word or Phrase	**Example or Definition**
6. constant _____	**A.** $6 + 22 = 28$
7. open sentence _____	**B.** $13y$
8. equation _____	**C.** $17 + b = 47$
9. solution _____	**D.** 75
10. term _____	**E.** When $x + 37 = 62$, $x = 25$.

Name _____ Class _____ Date _____

Practice 3-1

Estimate using front-end estimation.

1. 6.3 + 8.55

_____

2. 345 + 682

_____

3. 4.60 + 5.53

_____

4. $6.14 + $9.38

_____

5. $39.65 + $25.84

_____

6. 9.71 + 3.94

_____

Estimate by clustering.

7. $7.04 + $5.95 + $6.08 + $5.06 + $6.12

_____

8. 9.3 + 8.7 + 8.91 + 9.052

_____

9. 37.6 + 44.91 + 41 + 39.1

_____

10. 2.357 + 1.874 + 1.956

_____

Estimate by rounding each number to the same place value.

11. 14.66 + 25.19 _____

12. 8.7 + 3.21 + 3.899 _____

13. 194.78 − 12.31 _____

14. $289 − $67.20 _____

15. 800 − 301.47 _____

16. 0.06 + 19.41 _____

Round to the underlined place value.

17. 6.739 _____

18. 52.192 _____

19. 0.61 _____

20. 348.508 _____

Estimate. State your method (rounding, front-end, or clustering).

21. 91.7 + 88.6 + 89.1 + 92.5 + 90.6 _____

22. 3.9 + 8.1 + 2.06 _____

23. $1.08 + $.95 + $.89 + $1.14 _____

24. 11.56 + 19.43 + 13.40 + 14.39 _____

25. 0.015 + 0.039 + 0.0266 _____

3-1 • Guided Problem Solving

GPS **Student Page 133, Exercise 40**

Weather Mobile, Alabama, has an average annual rainfall of 63.96 in. The average annual rainfall in San Francisco, California, is 19.70 in. About how much more rain falls each year in Mobile than in San Francisco?

Understand the Problem

1. What is the average annual rainfall in Mobile, Alabama? _____

2. What is the average annual rainfall in San Francisco, California? _____

3. What are you asked to find? _____

_____

Make and Carry Out a Plan

4. Round the average annual rainfall in Mobile to the nearest inch. _____

5. Round the average annual rainfall
   in San Francisco to the nearest inch. _____

6. Write an expression, using your estimates, to find about
   how much more rain falls annually in Mobile than in San Francisco. _____

7. Simplify the expression. _____

8. About how many more inches of
   rain fall each year in Mobile than in San Francisco? _____

Check the Answer

9. Round the average annual rainfalls in Mobile
   and San Francisco to the tens place. Then subtract
   to find about how many more inches of rain
   fall in Mobile than in San Francisco each year. _____
   The result should be close to your answer to Question 8.

Solve Another Problem

10. A snowstorm dropped 13.88 inches of snow
    on Minneapolis, Minnesota. Only 8.12 inches
    of snow fell in Chicago, Illinois from the same storm.
    About how much more snow fell in Minneapolis than in Chicago? _____

Practice 3-2

Estimating Decimal Products and Quotients

Determine whether each product or quotient is reasonable. If it is not reasonable, find a reasonable result.

1. $62.77(29.8) = 187.0546$

_____

2. $16.132 \div 2.96 = 54.5$

_____

3. $(47.89)(6.193) = 296.5828$

_____

4. $318.274 \div 4.07 = 78.2$

_____

5. $2.65(-0.84) = -0.2226$

_____

6. $-38.6(-1.89) = 7.2954$

_____

7. $6,355 \div 775 = 8.2$

_____

8. $1,444.14 \div 67.8 = 213$

_____

9. $1.839(6.3) = 115.857$

_____

10. $3.276 \div 0.63 = 5.2$

_____

Estimate each product or quotient.

11. $8.73 \cdot 6.01$ _____

12. $11.042(4.56)$ _____

13. $197.4 \cdot 2.85$ _____

14. $675.1 \cdot 0.051$ _____

15. $479.2(3.2)$ _____

16. $712.9 \cdot 0.41$ _____

17. $11.57 \div 3.09$ _____

18. $43.68 \div 8.7$ _____

19. $29.5 \div 5.1$ _____

20. $\$41.09 \div \$6.88$ _____

21. $148.8 \div 9.8$ _____

22. $\$76.77 \div \$24.19$ _____

23. Apples cost $.89 per lb. Estimate the cost of three 5-lb bags. _____

24. You buy 3 dinners that are $6.85 each. Before tax and tip, the total is $25.42. Is this total correct? Explain.

_____

25. You worked 18 hours last week and received $92.70 in your paycheck. Estimate your hourly pay.

_____

3-2 • Guided Problem Solving

GPS **Student Page 137, Exercise 30**

Gas Mileage Shari is planning a 450-mi car trip. Her car can travel about 39 mi on a gallon of gasoline. Gasoline costs $1.89/gal. About how much will the gas cost for her trip?

Understand the Problem

1. How many miles is the car trip Shari is planning? _____

2. About how many miles can Shari's car travel on a gallon of gasoline? _____

3. How much does gasoline cost per gallon? _____

4. What are you asked to find? _____

Make and Carry Out a Plan

5. Write an expression using the total number of miles in the trip and the number of miles Shari can drive on one gallon of gasoline to find how many gallons of gasoline Shari will need to complete her trip. _____

6. Since the question says "about," round the divisor to the nearest ten. _____

7. Round the dividend to a multiple of the rounded divisor. Keep the rounded dividend close to 450. _____

8. Rewrite your expression from Step 5 using your rounded values from Steps 6 and 7. Simplify. _____

9. Round $1.89 to the nearest dollar. _____

10. Write an expression to find the approximate cost of the gasoline for Shari's trip. _____

11. About how much will the gas cost for Shari's trip? _____

Check the Answer

12. Use a calculator to simplify your expression from Step 5 and multiply by 1.89 to find the exact answer to the problem. _____ The result should be close to your answer to Question 11.

Solve Another Problem

13. Julia is planning to drive to see her sister, who lives 285 mi away. Her car can travel about 32 mi on a gallon of gasoline. Gasoline costs $1.85 a gallon. About how much will gasoline cost for her trip? _____

Practice 3-3

1. There were 8 judges at a gymnastics competition. Kathleen received these scores for her performance on the uneven parallel bars:

    8.9, 8.7, 8.9, 9.2, 8.8, 8.2, 8.9, 8.8

   a. Find these statistics: mean _____ median _____ mode _____

   b. Which measure of central tendency best describes the data? Explain.

   _____

   _____

   _____

   c. Why do you think that the highest and lowest judge's scores are disregarded in tallying the total score in a gymnastics competition?

   _____

   _____

Find the mean, median, and mode. Round to the nearest tenth where necessary. Identify any outliers.

Data	Mean	Median	Mode	Outliers
2. 8, 15, 9, 7, 4, 5, 9, 11	_____	_____	_____	_____
3. 70, 61, 28, 40, 60, 72, 25, 31, 64, 63	_____	_____	_____	_____
4. 4.9, 5.7, 6.0, 5.3, 4.8, 4.9, 5.3, 4.7, 4.9, 5.6, 5.1	_____	_____	_____	_____
5. 271, 221, 234, 240, 271, 234, 213, 253, 155	_____	_____	_____	_____
6. 0, 2, 3, 3, 3, 4, 4, 5	_____	_____	_____	_____

Use the data in the table. Round to the nearest tenth where necessary.

Peak	Height (ft)
Mont Blanc	15,771
Monte Rosa	15,203
Dom	14,911
Liskamm	14,852
Weisshom	14,780

7. What is the mean height of the five highest European mountains? _____

8. What is the median height? _____

9. Are any of the heights an outlier? Explain.

   _____

3-3 • Guided Problem Solving

GPS **Student Page 142, Exercise 22**

Find the mean, median, and mode of the data below. Which measure of central tendency best describes the data? Explain.

resting heart rate in beats per minute: 79 72 80 81 40 72

Understand the Problem

1. What values are you asked to find? _____

2. What are you asked to decide? _____

Make and Carry Out a Plan

3. How many data items are there? _____

4. Is the number of data items even or odd? _____

5. Write the data items in numerical order. _____

6. Add the data items and divide by the
   number of data items to find the mean. _____

7. Find the mean of the two middle data items to find the median. _____

8. Find the data item that occurs most often to find the mode. _____

9. Are there any outliers in the data? If so, what are they? _____

10. Compare the mean, median, and mode to the data to find which best
    describes the data. Which is the best measure of central tendency? Explain. _____

    _____

Check the Answer

11. Why does knowing whether there are any outliers in the
    data help you determine the best measure of central tendency? _____

    _____

Solve Another Problem

12. Find the mean, median, and mode. Which measure
    of central tendency best describes the data? Explain.
    scores on a quiz: 14 15 9 10 11 9 12 _____

    _____

Practice 3-4

Use the formula $P = 2l + 2w$. Find the perimeter of each rectangle.

1. _____

9 m

4.5 m

2. _____

5.2 ft

1.3 ft

3. _____

12.9 cm

4.7 cm

Use the formula $A = lw$. Find the area of each rectangle above.

4. _____ **5.** _____ **6.** _____

7. Use the formula $d = rt$ to find how far each animal in the table can travel in 5 seconds.

Animal	Speed (ft/s)	Distance in 5 s (ft)
Pronghorn antelope	89.5	
Wildebeest	73.3	
Gray fox	61.6	
Wart hog	44.0	
Wild turkey	22.0	
Chicken	13.2	

8. While vacationing on the Mediterranean Sea, Angie recorded the temperature several times during a 24-hour period. She used a thermometer in the lobby of her hotel. It was a beautiful day. Use the formula $F = 1.8C + 32$ to change the temperatures Angie recorded from Celsius to Fahrenheit.

Time	Temperature (°C)	Temperature (°F)
4:00 A.M.	19	
8:00 A.M.	22	
12:00 P.M.	30	
4:00 P.M.	28	
8:00 P.M.	24	
12:00 A.M.	20	

3-4 • Guided Problem Solving

GPS **Student Page 147, Exercise 16**

Geometry Use the formula $P = 2\ell + 2w$. Find the perimeter of the rectangle. Then use the formula $A = \ell w$ to find the area.

3.7 m

7.3 m

Understand the Problem

1. What is the width of the rectangle? _____

2. What is the length of the rectangle? _____

3. What are you asked to find? _____

Make and Carry Out a Plan

4. Replace ℓ with 7.3 and w with 3.7 in the formula $P = 2\ell + 2w$. _____

5. Simplify by multiplying. _____

6. Add. What is the perimeter of the rectangle? _____

7. Replace ℓ with 7.3 and w with 3.7 in the formula $A = \ell w$. _____

8. Multiply. What is the area of the rectangle? _____

Check the Answer

9. To check your answer to Question 6, add
the measurements of the 4 sides together. _____
Your answer should be the same as your answer to Question 6.

10. To check your answer to Question 7, divide
your answer by the length of the rectangle. _____
Your answer should be the width of the rectangle.

Solve Another Problem

11. Use the formula $P = 2\ell + 2w$. Find the perimeter of the
rectangle. Then use the formula $A = \ell w$ to find the area. _____

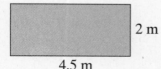

2 m

4.5 m

Guided Problem Solving

Practice 3-5

Solving Equations by Adding or Subtracting Decimals

Solve each equation.

1. $3.8 = n - 3.62$

_____

2. $x - 19.7 = -17.48$

_____

3. $12.5 = t - 3.55$

_____

4. $k - 263.48 = -381.09$

_____

5. $9.36 + k = 14.8$

_____

6. $-22 = p + 13.7$

_____

7. $y + 3.85 = 2.46$

_____

8. $-13.8 = h + 15.603$

_____

9. $y - 48.763 = 0$

_____

10. $6.21 = e + (-3.48)$

_____

11. $x + (-0.0025) = 0.0024$

_____

12. $-58.109 = v - 47.736$

_____

13. $x + 82.7 = 63.5$

_____

14. $-0.08 = f + 0.07$

_____

15. $0 = a + 27.98$

_____

16. $117.345 + m = 200$

_____

17. $z - 81.6 = -81.6$

_____

18. $5.4 = t + (-6.1)$

_____

19. $-4.095 + b = 18.665$

_____

20. $4.87 = n + 0.87$

_____

Use mental math to solve each equation.

21. $k + 23.7 = 23.7$

_____

22. $5.63 = n + 1.63$

_____

23. $x - 3.2 = 4.1$

_____

24. $p - 0.7 = 9.3$

_____

25. $6.75 + c = 12.95$

_____

26. $-1.09 = j - 4.99$

_____

3-5 • Guided Problem Solving

GPS Student Page 152, Exercise 19

Running Michael Johnson's world record in the 200-m sprint is
19.32 s. His 400-m world record is 23.86 s slower than his
200-m record. Write and solve an equation to find
Johnson's 400-m record.

Understand the Problem

1. What is Michael Johnson's world record in the 200-m sprint? _____

2. How much slower is his 400-m world
   record than his 200-m world record? _____

3. What are you asked to do? _____

   _____

Make and Carry Out a Plan

4. Let r represent Michael Johnson's 400-m world
   record. Use the sentence "Michael Johnson's
   400-m record minus 23.86 s is equal to his 200-m
   world record" to write an equation to represent the situation. _____

5. For your equation from Question 4, what number
   must you add to both sides to get r alone on one side? _____

6. Solve the equation for r. _____

7. What is Michael Johnson's 400-m world record? _____

Check the Answer

8. To check your answer, subtract
   23.86 from your answer to Question 7. _____
   The result should be Michael Johnson's 200-m world record.

Solve Another Problem

9. Karin's best time in the 50-yd freestyle is 25.68 s. Her
   best time in the 100-yd freestyle is 32.85 s slower. Write
   and solve an equation to find Karin's best time in the 100-yd freestyle. _____

Practice 3-6

Solving Equations by Multiplying or Dividing Decimals

Use mental math to solve each equation.

1. $0.7h = 4.2$ _____

2. $\frac{x}{2.5} = -3$ _____

3. $38.7 = -100k$ _____

4. $-45.6e = -4.56$ _____

Solve each equation.

5. $\frac{p}{2.9} = 0.55$ _____

6. $9.1 = \frac{x}{-0.7}$ _____

7. $-6.4 = \frac{y}{8.5}$ _____

8. $\frac{k}{-1.2} = -0.07$ _____

9. $277.4 = \frac{n}{3.5}$ _____

10. $\frac{e}{-0.76} = 2{,}809$ _____

11. $\frac{a}{27} = -32.3$ _____

12. $\frac{p}{-1.52} = -3{,}600$ _____

13. $-9k = 2.34$ _____

14. $-12.42 = 0.03p$ _____

15. $-7.2y = 61.2$ _____

16. $-0.1035 = 0.23n$ _____

17. $1.5m = 3.03$ _____

18. $-0.007h = 0.2002$ _____

19. $8.13t = -100.812$ _____

20. $0.546 = 0.42y$ _____

Write an equation for each sentence. Solve for the variable.

21. The opposite of seventy-five hundredths times some number n equals twenty-four thousandths. Find the value of n.

_____

22. A number n divided by -3.88 equals negative two thousand. Find the value of n.

_____

23. Four hundredths times some number n equals thirty-three and four tenths. Find the value of n.

_____

24. The product of some number n and -0.26 equals 169.39. Find the value of n.

_____

3-6 • Guided Problem Solving

GPS **Student Page 157, Exercise 34**

Number Sense The weight of a record-setting onion was 12.25 lb. An average-sized onion weighs 0.5 lb. About how many average-sized onions have a total weight equal to the record-setting onion?

Understand the Problem

1. How much did the record-setting onion weigh? _____

2. How much does an average-sized onion weigh? _____

3. What are you asked to find? _____

_____

Make and Carry Out a Plan

4. Let *n* represent the number of average-sized onions. Use the sentence "The number of average-sized onions times the weight of an average-sized onion equals the weight of the record-setting onion" to write a multiplication equation to represent the situation. _____

5. For your equation from Question 4, by what number must you divide each side to get *n* alone on one side? _____

6. Solve the equation for *n*. _____

7. About how many average-sized onions have a total weight equal to the record-setting onion? Round your answer to the nearest integer. _____

Check the Answer

8. Find the total weight of the number of onions you found in Question 7. _____
It should be equal to the weight of the record-setting onion.

Solve Another Problem

9. Doug has a marble collection. Altogether, his marbles weigh 232.8 g. Each marble weighs about 9 g. About how many marbles does Doug have? _____

Practice 3-7

Write the metric unit that makes each statement true.

1. 7.84 cm = 78.4 _____

2. 423 m = 0.423 _____

3. 2.8 m = 280 _____

4. 6.5 km = 650,000 _____

Complete each statement.

5. 3.4 cm = _____ mm

6. 197.5 cm = _____ m

7. 7 L = _____ mL

8. 5,247 mg = _____ g

9. 87 g = _____ kg

10. 9,246 mL = _____ L

Choose a reasonable estimate. Explain your choice.

11. the amount of water a cup would hold: 250 mL   250 L

_____

12. the mass of a bag of apples: 2 g   2 kg

_____

13. the height of your kitchen table: 68 cm   68 m

_____

Choose an appropriate metric unit. Explain your choice.

14. distance between two cities

_____

15. the mass of a pencil

_____

16. the capacity of an automobile's gas tank

_____

17. One Olympic event is the 1,500-meter run. How many kilometers is this?

_____

18. A fish pond holds 2,500 liters of water. How many kiloliters is this?

_____

3-7 • Guided Problem Solving

GPS **Student Page 162, Exercise 46**

Zoology A hippopotamus is so large that it has a stomach
304.8 cm long, yet it is agile enough to outrun a human.
How long is the stomach of a hippopotamus in meters?

Understand the Problem

1. How long is the stomach of a hippopotamus in centimeters? _____

2. What are you asked to find? _____

   _____

Make and Carry Out a Plan

3. How many centimeters are in a meter? _____

4. Use the sentence "Length in centimeters
   divided by number of centimeters per meter
   equals length in meters" to write an equation to find
   the length of the hippopotamus's stomach in meters. _____

5. Calculate to find the length
   in meters of the stomach of a hippopotamus. _____

Check the Answer

6. Convert the length of a hippopotamus's stomach
   in meters (from Question 5) back to centimeters. _____

Solve Another Problem

7. Grace is 143.7 cm tall. What is her height in meters? _____

Practice 3-8

Act It Out

Solve by acting out the problem.

1. A house-number manufacturer sold numbers to retail stores for $.09 per digit. A hardware store bought enough digits for two of every house number from 1 to 999. How many digits did the store purchase for house numbers:

   a. 1–9 _____   **b.** 10–99 _____   **c.** 100–999 _____

   d. Find the total cost of the house numbers. _____

2. A tic-tac-toe diagram uses 2 vertical lines and 2 horizontal lines to create 9 spaces. How many spaces can you create using:

   a. 1 vertical line and 1 horizontal line _____

   b. 2 vertical lines and 1 horizontal line _____

   c. 3 vertical lines and 3 horizontal lines _____

   d. 4 vertical lines and 5 horizontal lines _____

   e. 17 vertical lines and 29 horizontal lines _____

3. Each side of each triangle in the figure has length 1 cm. The perimeter (the distance around) the first triangle is 3 cm. Find the perimeter of the figure formed by connecting:

   a. 2 triangles _____   **b.** 3 triangles _____

   c. 4 triangles _____   **d.** 50 triangles _____

Solve using any strategy.

4. At the inauguration, the President was honored with a 21-gun salute. The report from each gunshot lasted 1 s. Four seconds elapsed between shots. How long did the salute last?

   _____

5. Bernie began building a model airplane on day 7 of his summer vacation and finished building it on day 65. He worked on the plane each day. How many days did it take?

   _____

3-8 • Guided Problem Solving

The school store buys pencils for $.20 each. It sells the pencils for $.25 each. How much profit does the store make if it sells five dozen pencils?

Understand the Problem

1. How much does the school store pay for pencils? _____

2. For how much does the school store sell the pencils? _____

3. What are you asked to find? _____

_____

Make and Carry Out a Plan

4. Write an expression to find the amount
   of profit the store makes on one pencil. Simplify. _____

5. How many pencils are in one dozen? _____

6. How many pencils are in five dozen? _____

7. Write an expression to find the amount
   of profit the store makes on five dozen pencils. _____

8. How much profit does the store make if it sells five dozen pencils? _____

Check the Answer

9. Solve the problem another way to check
   your answer. First, find the amount of
   money the store pays for five dozen pencils. _____

10. Next, find the amount of money
    for which the store sells five dozen pencils. _____

11. Finally, subtract the amount you found in
    Question 9 from the amount in Question 10
    to find the store's profit on the five dozen pencils. _____
    Compare with your answer to Question 8.

Solve Another Problem

12. A store sells watchbands for $4.25 each. It buys the
    watchbands for $2.10 each. If the store sells
    20 watchbands, how much profit does the store make? _____

3A: Graphic Organizer

For use before Lesson 3-1

Study Skill Keep notes as you work through each chapter to help you organize your thinking and to make it easier to review the material when you complete the chapter.

Write your answers. Use the Table of Contents page for this chapter at the front of the book.

1. What is the title of this chapter? _____

2. Name four topics that you will study in this chapter.

   _____   _____

   _____   _____

3. What is the topic of the Problem Solving lesson? _____

4. Complete the graphic organizer as you work through the chapter.
   1. Write the title of the chapter in the center oval.
   2. When you begin a lesson, write the name of the lesson in a rectangle.
   3. When you complete that lesson, write a skill or key concept from that lesson in the outer oval linked to that rectangle.
   Continue with steps 2 and 3 clockwise around the graphic organizer.

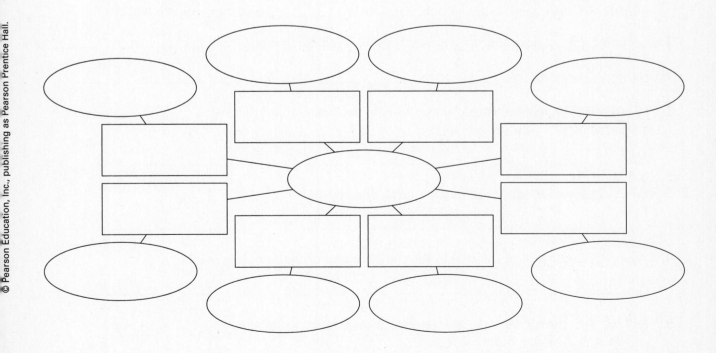

3B: Reading Comprehension

Study Skill If you cannot identify the meaning of unfamiliar words from the context of the sentence, list the word and its page number on a piece of paper. After you finish reading, use a dictionary to look up and record the meanings of the unfamiliar words on your list. Then look back at the pages where you found the unfamiliar words and read the passages again.

Read the entries from this sample glossary. Then answer the questions about how to read glossary entries.

Compatible numbers (p. 135)	Compatible numbers are numbers that are close in value to the numbers you want to add, subtract, multiply, or divide, and for which the computation is easy to perform mentally.	Estimate $151 \div 14.6$. $151 \approx 150$ $14.6 \approx 15$ $150 \div 15 = 10$ $151 \div 14.6 \approx 10$
Composite number (p. 186)	A composite number is an integer greater than 1 with more than two factors.	24 is a composite number that has 1, 2, 3, 4, 6, 8, 12, and 24 as factors.
Counterexample (p. 37)	A counterexample is an example that proves a statement false.	Statement: Motor vehicles have four wheels. Counterexample: A motorcycle is a motor vehicle with two wheels.

1. What does the page number after the glossary entry most likely tell you?

   _____

2. How could you use the page number to help you understand the glossary entry?

   _____

3. What does the first sentence of each definition repeat?

   _____

4. What is the purpose of the text in the third column of the sample glossary?

   _____

5. **Hi-Use Academic Words** What does *Estimate* mean in the glossary entry for compatible numbers?

   a. approximate   **b.** calculate

3C: Reading/Writing Math Symbols

For use after Lesson 3-7

Study Skill You may want to save time as you take notes in any subject by using abbreviations and symbols. Here are some common symbols: @ (at); # (number); w/ (with); w/o (without); & (and).

On the blank, rewrite the expression or statement using symbols in place of words.

1. p divided by 0.7

_____

2. b is less than or equal to -23.

_____

3. 7 meters

_____

4. $t + 5$ is less than 28.

_____

5. 3 more than h

_____

6. 56.9 centimeters

_____

7. 7 is greater than or equal to g.

_____

8. two thirds plus three fourths

_____

9. eleven less than four and five tenths

_____

10. negative seven twelfths

_____

11. fifteen times a number

_____

3D: Visual Vocabulary Practice
High-Use Academic Words

For use after Lesson 3-4

Study Skill If a word is not in the Glossary, use a dictionary to find its meaning.

Concept List

compare	convert	define
describe	estimate	evaluate
explain	identify	model

Write the concept that best describes each exercise. Choose from the concept list above.

1. Let n = number of CDs.	**2.** $3a + 4$ for $a = -5$ $3 \cdot a + 4 = 3 \cdot (-5) + 4$ $\qquad = -15 + 4$ $\qquad = -11$	**3.** $4.72 \cdot 1.8 \approx 10$
4. $3, 2, 3, 4, 2, 13, 4, 1, 2$ 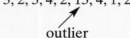 outlier	**5.** $2 + (-5)$  -3 $2 + (-5) = -3$	**6.** The outlier 15 raises the mean by 1.25.
7. $-6 < 5$	**8.** To plot (x, y), start at the origin. Move horizontally x units. Then move vertically y units.	**9.** The length of the table is 72 inches, or 6 feet.

3E: Vocabulary Check

Study Skill Strengthen your vocabulary. Use these pages and add cues and summaries by applying the Cornell Notetaking style.

Write the definition for each word at the right. To check your work, fold the paper back along the dotted line to see the correct answers.

_____

_____

_____

_____   Mean

_____

_____

_____   Mode

_____

_____

_____   Range

_____

_____

_____   Outlier

_____

_____

_____   Significant digits

_____

_____

3E: Vocabulary Check (continued)

For use after Lesson 3-8

Write the vocabulary word for each definition. To check your work, fold
the paper forward along the dotted line to see the correct answers.

The sum of a collection
of data divided by the
number of data items.

_____

The data item that occurs
most often.

_____

The difference between
the greatest and least
values in a set of data.

_____

A data value that is much
higher or lower than the
other data values in a
collection of data.

_____

The digits that represent
the actual measurement.

_____

3F: Vocabulary Review Puzzle

For use with Chapter Review

Study Skill When you are learning a new skill or new vocabulary words, stay alert so that you will store what you read or hear in your memory. If your mind wanders, take written notes to help you stay focused.

Use words from the list to complete the crossword puzzle. For help, use the Glossary in your textbook.

formula	mean	median
metric	mode	outlier
perimeter		

ACROSS

2. sum of data items divided by number of data items
3. middle number when data items are written in order
6. system of measurement units based on 10
7. data value much higher or lower than the others

DOWN

1. distance around a figure
4. equation that relates quantities represented by variables
5. data item that occurs most often

Practice 4-1

List all the factors of each number.

1. 12 _____

2. 45 _____

3. 41 _____

4. 54 _____

5. 48 _____

6. 100 _____

7. 117 _____

Test whether each number is divisible by 2, 3, 5, 9, and 10.

8. 215 _____   **9.** 432 _____

10. 770 _____   **11.** 1,011 _____

12 975 _____   **13.** 2,070 _____

14. 3,707 _____   **15.** 5,715 _____

Write the missing digit to make each number divisible by 9.

16. 7⬜1   **17.** 2,2⬜2   **18.** 88,⬜12

19. There are four different digits which, when inserted in the blank space in the number 4⬜5, make the number divisible by 3. Write them.

_____

20. There are two different digits which, when inserted in the blank space in the number 7,16⬜, make the number divisible by 5. Write them.

_____

21. There are five different digits which, when inserted in the blank space in the number 99,99⬜, make the number divisible by 2. Write them.

_____

4-1 • Guided Problem Solving

GPS **Student Page 182, Exercise 44**

Reasoning John made oatmeal cookies for a class bake sale. The cookies
need to be distributed equally on 2 or more plates. If each plate gets at
least 7 cookies, what are the possible combinations for the totals below?

a. 42 cookies   **b.** 56 cookies   **c.** 60 cookies   **d.** 144 cookies

Understand the Problem

1. At least how many plates must John use to distribute the cookies? _____

2. At least how many cookies must be on each plate? _____

Make and Carry Out a Plan

3. List the different ways that 42 can
   be written as the product of two factors. _____

4. What are the possible combinations of plates and cookies
   for 42 cookies? (Remember, the number of plates must
   be 2 or greater and the number of cookies must be 7 or greater.) _____

   _____

5. What are the possible combinations for 56 cookies? _____

   _____

6. What are the possible combinations for 60 cookies? _____

   _____

7. What are the possible combinations for 144 cookies? _____

   _____

Check the Answer

8. Why do the combinations of plates and
   cookies need to be factors of the number of cookies? _____

   _____

Solve Another Problem

9. Jenna is looking at ways to seat the guests at her wedding.
   There will be at least 8 tables and each table must have at
   least 4 guests. What are the possible combinations for 64 guests? _____

Name _____ Class _____ Date _____

Practice 4-2 $5 \times 5 \times 5 \times 5$ **Exponents**

Evaluate each expression.

1. m^4, for $m = 5$ _____625_____

2. $(5a)^3$, for $a = -1$ _____−125_____

3. $-(2p)^2$, for $p = 7$ _____−196_____

4. $-n^6$, for $n = 2$ _____−64_____

5. b^6, for $b = -1$ _____1_____

6. $(e - 2)^3$, for $e = 11$ _____729_____

7. $(6 + h^2)^2$, for $h = 3$ _____225_____

8. $x^2 + 3x - 7$, for $x = -4$ _____−3_____

9. $y^3 - 2y^2 + 3y - 4$, for $y = 5$ _____86_____

$(-4)^2 + 3(-4) - 7$

$16 - 12 - 7$

$4 - 7$

-3

$125 - 65$
$50 + 15 - 4$

Write using exponents.

10. $3 \cdot 3 \cdot 3 \cdot 3$ _____3^4_____

11. $k \cdot k \cdot k \cdot k \cdot k$ _____k^5_____

12. $(-9)(-9)(-9)m \cdot m \cdot m$ _____$(-9)m^3$_____

13. $g \cdot g \cdot g \cdot g \cdot h$ _____g^4h_____

14. $7 \cdot a \cdot a \cdot b \cdot b \cdot b$ _____$7a^2b^3$_____

15. $-8 \cdot m \cdot n \cdot n \cdot 2 \cdot m \cdot m$ _____$-16m^3n^2$_____

16. $d \cdot (-3) \cdot e \cdot e \cdot d \cdot (-3) \cdot e$ _____$(-3)^2d^2e^3$_____

$2 \times 2 \times 2 \times 2$ 316
$2 \times 2 \times 2 \times 16$ $\frac{16}{96}$
256

Simplify each expression.

17. $(-2)^3$ and -2^3 _____−8_____

18. 0^{12} _____0_____

19. 2^8 and 4^4 _____256_____

20. $-5^2 + 4 \cdot 2^3$ _____7_____
$-25 + 4$

21. $3(8 - 6)^2$ _____12_____

22. $-6^2 + 2 \cdot 3^2$ _____−18_____
$36 + 2 \times 9$

23. $(-2)(-5)^2(3)$ _____−150_____
(-25) 5×9

24. $24 + (11 - 3)^2 \div 4$ _____40_____
64

25. $(17 - 3)^2 \div (4^2 - 3^2)$ _____28_____

26. $(5 + 10)^2 \div 5^2$ _____9_____
$225 \div 25$

27. $4^3 \div (2^5 - 4^2)$ _____4_____

28. $(-1)^5 \cdot (2^4 - 13)^2$ _____−9_____
$-1 \cdot 9$

Practice   *Pre-Algebra Lesson 4-2* **317**

4-2 • Guided Problem Solving

GPS **Student Page 188, Exercise 27**

Error Analysis A student gives ab^3 as an answer when asked to write the expression $ab \cdot ab \cdot ab$ using exponents. What is the student's error?

Understand the Problem

1. What expression was the student asked to write using exponents? _____

2. What was the answer the student gave? _____

3. What are you asked to do? _____

Make and Carry Out a Plan

4. Rewrite $ab \cdot ab \cdot ab$ so that the like terms are grouped together. _____

5. Rewrite your expression from Step 4 using exponents. _____

6. How is what you wrote in Step 5 different from the answer the student gave, ab^3? _____
_____

7. What is the student's error? _____
_____

Check the Answer

8. Evaluate $ab \cdot ab \cdot ab$ for $a = 1$ and $b = 2$. _____

9. Evaluate your answer to Step 5 for $a = 1$ and $b = 2$. If you wrote $ab \cdot ab \cdot ab$ using exponents correctly, your answers for Steps 8 and 9 will be the same. _____

Solve Another Problem

10. When asked to write the expression $(-4)(-4)(-4)(-4)$ using exponents, Jeremiah wrote -4^4. What error did he make? _____
_____

Guided Problem Solving

Practice 4-3

Prime Factorization and Greatest Common Factor

Find each GCF.

1. 8, 12 ___4___

2. 36, 54 ___18___

3. 63, 81 ___9___

4. 69, 92 ___23___

5. 15, 28 ___1___

6. 21, 35 ___7___

7. $30m, 36n$ ___6___

8. $75x^3y^2, 100xy$ ___25xy___

9. 15, 24, 30 ___3___

10. 48, 80, 128 ___16___

11. $36hk^3, 60k^2m, 84k^4n$ ___12k²___

12. $2mn, 4m^2n^2$ ___2mn___

Is each number prime, composite, or neither? For each composite, write the prime factorization.

13. 75 ___Composite___

14. 152 ___Composite 2³×19___

15. 432 ___Composite___

16. 588 ___Composite 2³×3×17²___

17. 160 _____

18. 108 ___Composite 2²×3³___

19. 19 _____

20. 143 ___Prime___ Composite 11×13

21. 531 _____

22. 369 ___Composite 3²×41___

23. 83 _____

24. 137 ___Prime___

25. The numbers 3, 5, and 7 are factors of n. Find four other factors of n besides 1.

_____

26. For which expressions is the GCF $8x$?

   A. $2xy$ and $4x^2$ **B.** $16x^2$ and $24xy$ **C.** $8x^3$ and $4x$ **D.** $24x^2$ and $48x^3$

4-3 • Guided Problem Solving

GPS **Student Page 193, Exercise 29**

Organization A math teacher and a science teacher combine their first-period classes for a group activity. The math class has 24 students and the science class has 16 students. The teachers need to divide the students into groups of the same size. Each group must have the same number of math students. Find the greatest number of groups possible.

Understand the Problem

1. How many students are in the math class? _____

2. How many students are in the science class? _____

3. What must be true about the groups
   into which the students are divided? _____

   _____

4. What are you asked to find? _____

Make and Carry Out a Plan

5. The 24 math students are divided equally. List the factors of 24. _____

6. For the groups to have the same size, the science
   students must also be divided equally. List the factors of 16. _____

7. What factors do 24 and 16 have in common? _____

8. What is the greatest common factor of 24 and 16? _____

9. What is the greatest number possible of groups that
   are the same size with the same number of math students? _____

Check the Answer

10. Explain why the greatest common factor of
    24 and 16 is the greatest number of possible groups. _____

    _____

Solve Another Problem

11. Derek and Trevor are planning a treasure hunt for a group of
    friends. There are 12 adults and 18 children. They need to divide
    their friends into groups of the same size. Each group must have
    the same number of adults. Find the greatest number of groups possible. _____

Name _____ Class _____ Date _____

Practice 4-4

Simplifying Fractions

Write in simplest form.

1. $\frac{10}{15}$ _____ ~~2/3~~

2. $\frac{18}{36}$ _____ ~~1/2~~

3. $\frac{27}{36}$ _____

4. $\frac{12}{15}$ _____ ~~4/5~~

5. $\frac{26}{39}$ _____

6. $\frac{7b}{9b}$ _____ ~~7/9~~

7. $\frac{16y^3}{20y^4}$ _____ ~~4/5y~~

8. $\frac{8x}{10y}$ _____ ~~4x/5y~~

9. $\frac{6xy}{16y}$ _____ ~~3x/8~~

10. $\frac{24n^2}{28n}$ _____ ~~6n/7~~

11. $\frac{abc}{10abc}$ _____ ~~1/10~~

12. $\frac{30hxy}{54kxy}$ _____ ~~5h/9k~~

13. $\frac{mn^2}{pm^5n}$ _____ ~~n/pm^4~~

14. $\frac{5jh}{15jh^3}$ _____ ~~1/3h^2~~

15. $\frac{12h^3k}{16h^2k^2}$ _____ ~~3h/4k~~

16. $\frac{20s^2t^3}{16st^5}$ _____ ~~5s/4t^2~~

Find two fractions equivalent to each fraction.

17. $\frac{1}{4}$ _____ ~~2/8 & 3/12~~

18. $\frac{2}{3}$ _____ ~~6/9 & 4/6~~

19. $\frac{3}{5}$ _____ ~~9/15 & 12/20~~

20. $\frac{3}{18}$ _____ ~~1/6 & 9/~~

21. $\frac{8k}{16k}$ _____ ~~1/2~~

22. $\frac{3m}{8n}$ _____ ~~6m/16n & 9m/24n~~

23. $\frac{5pq}{10p^2q^3}$ _____ ~~1/2pq^2 & 25/50pq^2~~

24. $\frac{3s^2t^2}{7r}$ _____ ~~6s^2t^2/14r & 9s^2t^2/21r~~

25. Monty completed 18 passes in 30 attempts. What fraction of his passes did Monty complete? Write in simplest form.

~~3/5~~
_____

26. Five new state quarters will be issued by the United States mint this year. What fraction of the states will have quarters issued this year?

~~1/10~~
_____

4-4 • Guided Problem Solving

GPS **Student Page 198, Exercise 13**

Health Doctors suggest that most people need about 8 hours of sleep each night to stay healthy. What fraction of the day is this? Write your answer in simplest form.

Understand the Problem

1. How many hours of sleep do doctors
    suggest people need each night to stay healthy? _____

2. What are you asked to find? _____

3. How should you write your answer? _____

Make and Carry Out a Plan

4. What will be the numerator of the fraction? _____

5. What will be the denominator of the fraction? _____

6. Write the fraction that represents 8 hours of a day. _____

7. What is the greatest common factor
    of the numerator and denominator? _____

8. Divide the numerator and the denominator
    by the greatest common factor and simplify. _____

9. What fraction of the day do
    doctors recommend people sleep? _____

Check the Answer

10. How many hours are in the fraction
    of the day you found in Step 9? _____

Solve Another Problem

11. Marnie practices piano 2 hours every day
    in the summer. What fraction of the day
    is this? Write your answer in simplest form. _____

Practice 4-5

Solve each problem by solving a simpler problem.

1. A baseball team has 4 pitchers and 3 catchers. How many different pitcher-catcher combinations are possible? One way to solve this problem is to make a list like the one started below. Finish the list.

P1-C1   P2-C1
P1-C2   P2-C2

_____   _____

_____   _____

_____   _____

_____   _____

2. The baseball team has 2 first basemen, 3 second basemen, and 2 third basemen. How many combinations of the three positions are possible?

_____

3. A quarter is tossed 3 times. In how many different orders can heads and tails be tossed?

_____

4. A quarter is tossed 4 times. In how many different orders can heads and tails be tossed?

_____

5. Curtains are manufactured in 3 different styles and 5 different colors.
   a. How many different style-color combinations are possible?

   _____

   b. The curtains are produced in 2 different fabrics. How many different style-color-fabric combinations are possible?

   _____

4-5 • Guided Problem Solving

GPS **Student Page 203, Exercise 3**

You have pepperoni, mushrooms, onions, and green peppers.
How many different pizzas can you make by using one,
two, three, or four of the toppings?

Understand the Problem

1. What toppings do you have? _____

2. What are you asked to find? _____

Make and Carry Out a Plan

3. How many different pizzas can you make with only one topping each? _____

4. Complete the organized list of different pizzas with two toppings.

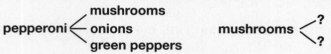

5. How many different pizzas can you make with two toppings? _____

6. How many different pizzas can you make with three
toppings? (Hint: Think about a pizza with all four toppings.
How many different ways could you remove one topping?) _____

7. How many different pizzas can you make with four toppings? _____

8. Find the sum of your answers to Steps 3, 5, 6,
and 7. How many different pizzas can you make? _____

Check the Answer

9. Use a diagram to find the number of two-topping pizzas you can make.
Draw line segments connecting the toppings to show all possible pizzas.

   pepperoni   **mushrooms**

   onions   **green peppers**

Solve Another Problem

10. Caleb has salami, cheese, and turkey to put on a sandwich
for lunch. How many different sandwiches could he
make by using one, two, or three of the sandwich fixings? _____

Practice 4-6

Rational Numbers

•••

Graph the rational numbers below on the same number line.

1. $\frac{3}{4}$

2. $-\frac{1}{4}$

3. -0.5

4. 0.3

$$\xleftarrow{\hspace{1cm}} \underset{-1.0}{|} \quad \underset{-0.5}{|} \quad \underset{0}{|} \quad \underset{0.5}{|} \quad \underset{1.0}{|} \xrightarrow{\hspace{1cm}}$$

Evaluate. Write in simplest form.

5. $\frac{x}{y}$, for $x = 12$, $y = 21$ _____

6. $\frac{n}{n + p}$, for $n = 9$, $p = 6$ _____

7. $\frac{k}{k^2 + 4}$, for $k = 6$ _____

8. $\frac{x - y}{-21}$, for $x = -2$, $y = 5$ _____

9. $\frac{m}{-n}$, for $m = 6$, $n = 7$ _____

10. $\frac{x(xy - 8)}{60}$, for $x = 3$, $y = 9$ _____

Write three fractions equivalent to each fraction.

11. $\frac{5}{7}$ _____

12. $\frac{22}{33}$ _____

13. $\frac{24}{30}$ _____

14. $\frac{6}{16}$ _____

15. Which of the following rational numbers are equal to $-\frac{17}{10}$?

$-17, -1.7, -\frac{34}{20}, 0.17$ _____

16. Which of the following rational numbers are equal to $\frac{3}{5}$?

$\frac{12}{20}, \frac{-3}{-5}, 0.3, \frac{6}{10}$ _____

17. Which of the following rational numbers are equal to $\frac{12}{15}$?

$\frac{4}{5}, \frac{40}{50}, -\frac{8}{10}, \frac{8}{10}$ _____

18. The weight w of an object in pounds is related to its distance d from the center of Earth by the equation $w = \frac{320}{d^2}$, where d is in thousands of miles. How much does the object weigh at sea level which is about 4,000 miles from the center of Earth?

_____

4-6 • Guided Problem Solving

GPS Student Page 207, Exercise 40

Science The formula $s = \dfrac{1{,}600}{d^2}$ gives the strength s of a radio signal at a distance d miles from the transmitter. What is the strength at 5 mi? Write your answer in simplest form.

Understand the Problem

1. What does the variable s represent? _____

2. What does the variable d represent? _____

3. What does the formula give? _____

   _____

4. What are you asked to find? _____

Make and Carry Out a Plan

5. Substitute 5 for d in the formula. _____

6. Simplify the denominator of the fraction. _____

7. Write the fraction in simplest form. _____

8. What is the strength of the radio signal 5 mi from the transmitter? _____

Check the Answer

9. In simplifying the answer, why
   did you simplify the denominator first? _____

10. Substitute your answer for s in the formula and solve for d. What is the distance? _____

Solve Another Problem

11. The acceleration in meters per second per second (m/s^2) of a
    racing car at 100 meters after it starts moving is given by $a = \dfrac{200}{t^2}$,
    where a is acceleration and t is time in seconds. What is the
    acceleration of the car if it takes 4 seconds to travel 100 meters? _____

Practice 4-7

Exponents and Multiplication

Complete each equation.

1. $9^3 \cdot 9^{\underline{4}} = 9^7$

2. $6^8 \cdot 6^{\underline{9}} = 6^{17}$

3. $n^{\underline{10}} \cdot n^5 = n^{15}$

4. $(a^{\underline{3}})^8 = a^{24}$

5. $(c^4)^{\underline{3}} = c^{12}$

6. $r^{\underline{8}} \cdot r^{12} = r^{20}$

Simplify each expression.

7. $(z^3)^5$ ___2^{15}___

8. $-(m^4)^3$ ___$-m^{12}$___

9. $(-3^2)^3$ ___-729___

10. $(x^3)(x^4)$ ___x^7___

11. $y^4 \cdot y^5$ ___y^9___

12. $(-y^5)(y^2)$ ___$-y^7$___

13. $(3y^2)(2y^3)$ ___$6y^5$___

14. $3x^{12} \cdot 2x^3$ ___$6x^{15}$___

15. $m^{30} \cdot m^{12}$ ___$m42$___

16. $(x^4)(y^2)(x^2)$ ___$y^2 \cdot x^6$___

17. $(-6x^7)(-9x^{12})$ ___$-54x^{19}$___

18. $(h^4)^4$ ___h^{16}___

Find the area of each rectangle.

19.

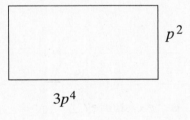

p^2

$3p^4$

___$3p^6$___

20.

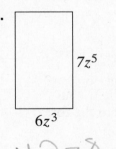

$7z^5$

$6z^3$

___$42z^8$___

Compare. Use >, <, or = to complete each statement.

21. $(4^3)^2 \boxed{=} (4^2)^3$

22. $5^3 \cdot 5^4 \boxed{<} 5^{10}$

23. $(3^5)^4 \boxed{>} 3^{10}$

24. $3^4 \boxed{=} 9^2$

25. $(9^7)^9 \boxed{<} (9^8)^8$

26. $4^2 \cdot 4^3 \boxed{=} 4^5$

27. $(6^2)^2 \boxed{=} 3^4 \cdot 2^4$

28. $5^2 \cdot 5^6 \boxed{>} 5^7$

29. $(8^2)^2 \boxed{<} (8^2)^3$

4-7 • Guided Problem Solving

GPS Student Page 211, Exercise 38

Writing in Math Explain why $x^8 \cdot x^2$ has the same value as $x^5 \cdot x^5$.

Understand the Problem

1. What are the two expressions? _____

2. What are you asked to do? _____

Make and Carry Out a Plan

3. Simplify the expression $x^8 \cdot x^2$ by adding the exponents of powers with the same base. _____

4. Simplify the expression $x^5 \cdot x^5$ by adding the exponents of powers with the same base. _____

5. Explain why $x^8 \cdot x^2$ and $x^5 \cdot x^5$ are equivalent. _____
_____

Check the Answer

6. Write another product that is equivalent to $x^8 \cdot x^2$ and $x^5 \cdot x^5$. _____

Solve Another Problem

7. Explain why $(x^2)^4$ is equivalent to $(x^4)^2$. _____
_____

Name _____ Class _____ Date _____

Practice 4-8

Exponents and Division

Complete each equation.

1. $\frac{8^n}{8^7} = 8^2$, $n =$ __9__

2. $\frac{12x^5}{4x} = 3x^n$, $n =$ __4__

3. $\frac{1}{h^5} = h^n$, $n =$ __-5__

4. $\frac{p^n}{p^8} = p^{-6}$, $n =$ __2__

5. $\frac{1}{81} = 3^n$, $n =$ __=4__

6. $\frac{12^4}{12^n} = 1$, $n =$ __4__

Simplify each expression.

7. $\frac{a^3}{a^7}$ ___$\frac{1}{a^4}$___

8. $\frac{j^5}{j^{-6}}$ ___$\frac{1}{j}$___

9. $\frac{x^7}{x^7}$ ___1___

10. $\frac{k^5}{k^9}$ ___$\frac{1}{k^4}$___

11. $\frac{9x^8}{12x^5}$ ___$\frac{3}{4x^3}$___

12. $\frac{2f^{10}}{f^5}$ ___$\frac{2f^5}{1}$___

13. $\frac{3y^4}{6y^{-4}}$ ___$\frac{y^8}{2}$___

14. $n^{-5} =$ ___$\frac{n^5}{n^{10}}$___

15. $\frac{3xy^4}{9xy}$ ___$\frac{y^3}{3}$___

16. $(-15)^0$ ___1___

17. $\frac{15h^6k^3}{5hk^2}$ ___$3h^5k$___

18. $4b^{-6}$ ___$\frac{8b^2}{2b^8}$___

Write each expression without a fraction bar.

19. $\frac{a^7}{a^{10}}$ ___a^{-3}___

20. $\frac{4x^2y}{2x^3}$ ___$2xy$___

21. $\frac{x^3y^4}{x^9y^2}$ ___$x^{-6} \cdot y^2$___

22. $\frac{12mn}{12m^3n^5}$ ___m^2n^4___

23. $\frac{16s^2t^4}{8s^5t^3}$ ___$2s^{-3}t^1$___

24. $\frac{21e^4f^2}{7e^2}$ ___$3e^2f^2$___

25. Write three different quotients that equal 4^{-5}.

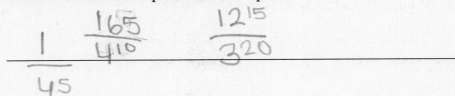

$\frac{1}{4^5}$ $\frac{16^5}{4^{10}}$ $\frac{12^{15}}{3^{20}}$

4-8 • Guided Problem Solving

GPS **Student Page 217, Exercise 35**

Earthquakes The *magnitude* of an earthquake is a measure of the amount of energy released. An earthquake of magnitude 6 releases about 30 times as much energy as an earthquake of magnitude 5. The magnitude of the 1989 earthquake in Loma Prieta, California, was about 7. The magnitude of the 1933 earthquake in Sanriku, Japan, was about 9. Simplify $\frac{30^9}{30^7}$ to find how many times as much energy was released in the Sanriku earthquake.

Understand the Problem

1. What is the magnitude of an earthquake? _____
   _____

2. What was the magnitude of the Loma Prieta earthquake? _____

3. What was the magnitude of the Sanriku earthquake? _____

4. What are you asked to do? _____
   _____

Make and Carry Out a Plan

5. Start simplifying $\frac{30^9}{30^7}$ by subtracting exponents. _____

6. Simplify your result from Step 5. _____

7. How many times as much energy was released in the Sanriku earthquake as in the Loma Prieta earthquake? _____

Check the Answer

8. What rule did you follow to simplify the expression? _____

9. Explain how using this rule makes simplifying the expression easier._____
   _____

Solve Another Problem

10. A video game is set up so that each level is 10 times more difficult than the previous level. Simplify $\frac{10^6}{10^3}$ to find how many times more difficult Level 6 is than Level 3. _____

Name _____ Class _____ Date _____

Practice 4-9

Scientific Notation

Write each number in standard notation.

1. 3.77×10^4 $\quad$ 37,700

2. 8.5×10^3 $\quad$ 8,500

3. 9.002×10^{-5} $\quad$ 9.0020000$$ .00002009

4. 1.91×10^{-3} $\quad$ 1.91000$$ .00191

Write each number in scientific notation.

5. Pluto is about 3,653,000,000 mi from the sun. $\quad$ 3.653×10^9

6. There are 63,360 in. in a mile. $\quad$ 6.336×10^4

7. At its closest, Mercury is about 46,000,000 km from the sun. $\quad$ 4.6×10^7

8. 77,250,000 $\quad$ 7.725×10^7

9. 526,000 $\quad$ 5.26×10^5

10. 8 billion $\quad$ 8×10^9

11. 8,100,000 $\quad$ 8.1×10^6

12. 0.00000073 $\quad$ 7.3×10^{-7}

13. 0.000903 $\quad$ 9.03×10^{-4}

Multiply. Express each result in scientific notation.

14. $(2 \times 10^5)(3 \times 10^2)$ $\quad$ 6×10^7

15. $(1.5 \times 10^5)(4 \times 10^9)$ $\quad$ 6×10^{14}

16. $(6 \times 10^{-4})(1.2 \times 10^{-3})$ $\quad$ 7.2×10^{-7}

17. $(5 \times 10^3)(1.7 \times 10^{-5})$ $\quad$ 8.5×10^{-2}

Order from least to greatest.

18. $72 \times 10^5, 6.9 \times 10^6, 23 \times 10^5$ $\quad$ $6.9 \times 10^6, 23 \times 10^5, 72 \times 10^5$

19. $19 \times 10^{-3}, 2.5 \times 10^{-4}, 1.89 \times 10^{-4}$ $\quad$ $1.89 \times 10^{-4}, 2.5 \times 10^{-4}, 19 \times 10^{-3}$

20. An ounce is 0.00003125 tons. Write this number in scientific notation. $\quad$ 3.125×10^{-5}

21. A century is 3,153,600,000 seconds. Write this number in scientific notation. $\quad$ 3.1536×10^9

4-9 • Guided Problem Solving

GPS Student Page 223, Exercise 25

Zoology An ant weighs about 2×10^{-5} lb. There are about 10^{15} ants on Earth. How many pounds of ants are on Earth?

Understand the Problem

1. About how much does an ant weigh? _____

2. About how many ants are on Earth? _____

3. What are you asked to find? _____

Make and Carry Out a Plan

4. Write an expression to multiply the number of ants on Earth by the weight of each ant. (Write 10^{15} as 1×10^{15}.) _____

5. Rewrite the expression using the Commutative Property of Multiplication. _____

6. Simplify by multiplying 2 and 1. _____

7. Simplify by adding the exponents. _____

8. How many pounds of ants are on Earth? _____

Check the Answer

9. To check your answer, divide it by the number of ants on Earth. Remember to subtract the exponents when you divide. _____
Your answer should be equal to the approximate weight of one ant.

Solve Another Problem

10. Marcella has a large jar of beads she uses for making bracelets and necklaces. She has about 10^3 beads in her jar right now. All of her beads are the same size, and each one weighs about 4×10^{-4} lb. About how much do all of the beads in her jar weigh? _____

4A: Graphic Organizer

For use before Lesson 4-1

Study Skill You can get a general idea about what you will learn in a chapter when you preview the chapter. Look at the titles of the lessons in this chapter. From reading these titles, what do you predict you might learn in each lesson? Write notes about your predictions and then, as you finish a lesson, compare your notes with what you actually learned. Then change and add to your notes.

Write your answers. Use the Table of Contents page for this chapter at the front of the book.

1. What is the title of this chapter? _____

2. Name four topics that you will study in this chapter:

   _____   _____

   _____   _____

3. What is the topic of the Problem Solving lesson? _____

4. Complete the graphic organizer as you work through the chapter.
   1. Write the title of the chapter in the center oval.
   2. When you begin a lesson, write the name of the lesson in a rectangle.
   3. When you complete that lesson, write a skill or key concept from that lesson in the outer oval linked to that rectangle.

   Continue with steps 2 and 3 clockwise around the graphic organizer.

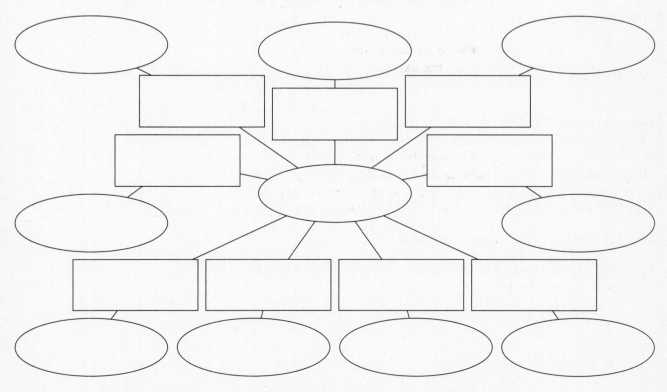

Name _____ Class _____ Date _____

4B: Reading Comprehension

Study Skill When you have several assignments to do, try starting with the one that you find the most challenging, so that you are doing it while you are at your best. Save the one that is most familiar and easiest for last, when you may be tired.

When you read exponents, the positions of the exponent and parentheses tell you what the base is for that exponent.

Use these expressions to answer the questions about reading exponents.

$$a + b^2 \qquad (a + b)^3 \qquad -a^4$$

$$(-a)^6 \qquad a^{-1} \qquad a - b^5$$

1. Identify the base for the exponent 2. _____

2. Identify the base for the exponent 3. _____

3. Identify the base for the exponent 4. _____

4. Identify the base for the exponent 6. _____

5. Identify the base for the exponent −1. _____

6. Identify the base for the exponent 5. _____

Write your answers.

7. How can you simplify an expression in which a base has exponent −1?

   _____

8. In the expression ab^0, what is the base for the exponent 0? _____

9. What is the value of the expression ab^0? _____

10. In the expression $(ab)^0$, what is the base for the exponent 0? _____

11. What is the value of the expression $(ab)^0$? _____

12. **High-Use Academic Words** In questions 1–6, what does *identify* mean for you to do?

    a. evaluate   **b.** name

4C: Reading/Writing Math Symbols

For use after Lesson 4-2

Study Skill After you take notes in class or while studying, take the time to go back and highlight what you have written. Mark key words or phrases in color to indicate the separate topics in your notes. In this way, you can quickly find the information you need as you review for a test.

Write a brief answer to each of these questions.

1. What effect does 2 have when you evaluate $2x$ for a given value of x?

   _____

   _____

2. What effect does 2 have when you evaluate x^2 for a given value of x?

   _____

   _____

3. What effect does 7 have when you evaluate $7(x + y)$ for given values of x and y?

   _____

   _____

4. What effect does 3 have when you evaluate $\frac{p}{3}$ for a given value of p?

   _____

   _____

5. What effect does 2 have when you evaluate ab^2 for given values of a and b?

   _____

   _____

6. What effect does 3 have when you evaluate x^3 for a given value of x?

   _____

   _____

4D: Visual Vocabulary Practice

For use after Lesson 4-9

Study Skill When a math exercise is difficult, try to determine what makes it difficult. Is it a word that you don't understand? Are the numbers difficult to use?

Concept List

base	equivalent fractions	exponent
greatest common factor	prime numbers	rational number
scientific notation	simplest form	standard notation

Write the concept that best describes each exercise. Choose from the concept list above.

1. 2 in 9^2 _____	**2.** 7 in 7^3 _____	**3.** relationship of 5 to the numbers 25 and 30 _____
4. 3, 7, and 13 _____	**5.** $\frac{2}{3}$ for the fraction $\frac{10}{15}$ _____	**6.** $\frac{8}{16}$ and $\frac{2}{4}$ _____
7. $\frac{a}{b}$ where a and b are integers and b is not 0 _____	**8.** 42,000,000 _____	**9.** 2.5×10^5 _____

Name _____ Class _____ Date _____

4E: Vocabulary Check

For use after Lesson 4-3

Study Skill Strengthen your vocabulary. Use these pages and add cues and summaries by applying the Cornell Notetaking style.

Write the definition for each word at the right. To check your work, fold the paper back along the dotted line to see the correct answers.

Divisible

Factor

Composite number

Prime factorization

Greatest common factor

Vocabulary and Study Skills

Pre-Algebra Chapter 4

© Pearson Education, Inc., publishing as Pearson Prentice Hall. All rights reserved.

4E: Vocabulary Check (continued)

For use after Lesson 4-3

Write the vocabulary word for each definition. To check your work, fold the paper back along the dotted line to see the correct answers.

When one integer can be divided by another integer with a remainder of zero.

_____

An integer that can divide another nonzero integer with a remainder of zero.

_____

An integer greater than 1 with more than two positive factors.

_____

The expression of a number as the product of its prime factors.

_____

The greatest factor two or more numbers have in common.

_____

4F: Vocabulary Review

Study Skill Many words in English have more than one meaning. You can often figure out which meaning to use by looking at the sentence that contains the word. To help you decide what a word means, consider the surroundings, or context, in which you see the word.

Match each word or phrase in the left column with the best example in the right column. Some words or phrases may have more than one example, but only one example is the best match.

Word or Phrase	Example
1. exponent _____	**A.** the 5 in 5^2
2. base _____	**B.** 4.06×10^3
3. factors _____	**C.** $\frac{3}{4} = \frac{6}{8}$
4. scientific notation _____	**D.** both the 3 and the 5 in $3 \cdot 5$
5. standard notation _____	**E.** 4,060
6. prime factorization _____	**F.** the 2 in 5^2
7. equivalent fractions _____	**G.** $60 = 2 \cdot 2 \cdot 3 \cdot 5$

Word or Phrase	Example
8. formula _____	**A.** the 4 in $4x$
9. outlier _____	**B.** the $5x$ in $5x - 2$
10. like terms _____	**C.** the 21 in the data set 68 68 65 21 69 72
11. coefficient _____	**D.** $3x$ and $7x$
12. term _____	**E.** 11
13. prime number _____	**F.** $P = 2l + 2w$
14. rational number _____	**G.** $\frac{2}{3}$

Practice 5-1

Comparing and Ordering Rational Numbers

Compare. Use $>$, $<$, or $=$ to complete each statement.

1. $\frac{2}{3}$ ☐ $\frac{7}{9}$

2. $\frac{3}{5}$ ☐ $\frac{7}{10}$

3. $-\frac{3}{4}$ ☐ $-\frac{13}{16}$

4. $\frac{9}{21}$ ☐ $\frac{6}{14}$

5. $-\frac{2}{8}$ ☐ $-\frac{7}{32}$

6. $\frac{7}{9}$ ☐ $-\frac{8}{9}$

7. $\frac{5}{8}$ ☐ $\frac{7}{12}$

8. $-\frac{4}{5}$ ☐ $-\frac{7}{8}$

9. $-\frac{4}{18}$ ☐ $-\frac{6}{27}$

10. $\frac{8}{17}$ ☐ $-\frac{3}{8}$

11. $\frac{4}{7}$ ☐ $2\frac{4}{7}$

12. $\frac{-9}{-11}$ ☐ $\frac{9}{11}$

13. $\frac{1}{3}$ ☐ $-\frac{3}{9}$

14. $-\frac{12}{6}$ ☐ $-\frac{9}{3}$

15. $-\frac{5}{10}$ ☐ $\frac{-3}{-4}$

Find the LCM of each group of numbers or expressions.

16. 7, 21 _____

17. 24, 32 _____

18. 15, 50 _____

19. $9a^3b$, $18abc$ _____

20. $28xy^2$, $42x^2y$ _____

21. 9, 12, 16 _____

22. A quality control inspector in an egg factory checks every forty-eighth egg for cracks and every fifty-fourth egg for weight. What is the number of the first egg each day that the inspector checks for both qualities?

_____

23. A stock sold for $3\frac{5}{8}$ one day and $3\frac{1}{2}$ the next. Did the value of the stock go up or down? Explain.

_____

24. Marissa needs $2\frac{2}{3}$ yards of ribbon for a wall-hanging she wants to make. She has $2\frac{3}{4}$ yards. Does she have enough ribbon? Explain.

_____

Order from least to greatest.

25. $\frac{2}{3}, \frac{3}{4}, \frac{1}{2}$

26. $\frac{2}{5}, \frac{1}{3}, \frac{3}{7}, \frac{4}{9}$

27. $\frac{8}{11}, \frac{9}{10}, \frac{7}{8}, \frac{3}{4}$

_____ _____ _____

5-1 • Guided Problem Solving

GPS **Student Page 239, Exercise 40**

The manager of Frank's Snack Shop buys hot dogs in packages of
36. He buys hot dog buns in packages of 20. He cannot buy part of
a package. What is the least number of packages of each product
he can buy to have an equal number of hot dogs and buns?

Understand the Problem

1. How many hot dogs are there in one package? _____

2. How many hot dog buns are there in one package? _____

3. What are you asked to find? _____

Make and Carry Out a Plan

4. List the first 10 multiples of 36. _____

5. List the first 10 multiples of 20. _____

6. Circle the common multiples of 36 and 20. _____

7. What is the least common multiple of 36 and 20? _____
   This is the smallest number of hot dogs with buns that can be made
   from packages of 36 hot dog buns and packages of 20 hot dogs.

8. To find the number of packages of hot dogs the
   manager should buy, divide the least common multiple by 36. _____

9. To find the number of packages of buns the manager
   should buy, divide the lowest common multiple by 20. _____

Check the Answer

10. To check your answer, find the least common
    multiple of 36 and 20 using prime factorization. _____
    It should be the same as your answer to question 7.

Solve Another Problem

11. An office manager buys company letterhead in boxes of 40 sheets
    and envelopes in boxes of 32. He cannot buy part of a box.
    What is the least number of boxes of each he can buy to
    have an equal number of sheets of letterhead and envelopes? _____

Practice 5-2

Fractions and Decimals

Write as a fraction or mixed number in simplest form.

1. 0.4 _____   **2.** 0.75 _____   **3.** 0.16 _____

4. 2.34 _____   **5.** 0.09 _____   **6.** 8.8 _____

Write each fraction or mixed number as a decimal.

7. $\frac{17}{20}$ _____   **8.** $\frac{7}{8}$ _____   **9.** $-\frac{9}{16}$ _____

10. $3\frac{1}{8}$ _____   **11.** $6\frac{9}{32}$ _____   **12.** $2\frac{87}{125}$ _____

13. $\frac{13}{25}$ _____   **14.** $4\frac{31}{50}$ _____   **15.** $-\frac{7}{12}$ _____

16. $\frac{4}{9}$ _____   **17.** $\frac{5}{18}$ _____   **18.** $\frac{15}{11}$ _____

Order from least to greatest.

19. $0.4, \frac{3}{5}, \frac{1}{2}, \frac{3}{10}$ _____

20. $-\frac{3}{8}, -\frac{3}{4}, -0.38, -0.6$ _____

21. $\frac{1}{4}, -\frac{1}{5}, 0.2, \frac{2}{5}$ _____

22. Write an improper fraction with the greatest possible value using each of the digits 5, 7, and 9 once. Write this as a mixed number and as a decimal.

_____

Write each decimal as a fraction or mixed number in simplest form.

23. $10.0\overline{7}$ _____   **24.** 3.44 _____   **25.** $-4.\overline{27}$ _____

26. 0.09 _____   **27.** 0.375 _____   **28.** $0.2\overline{43}$ _____

Compare. Use <, >, or = to complete each statement.

29. $\frac{5}{6}$ ☐ 0.8   **30.** $\frac{7}{11}$ ☐ 0.65   **31.** $4.\overline{2}$ ☐ $4\frac{2}{9}$

32. $-\frac{3}{11}$ ☐ -0.25 **33.** $0.\overline{80}$ ☐ $\frac{80}{99}$ **34.** -0.43 ☐ $-\frac{7}{16}$

5-2 • Guided Problem Solving

GPS Student Page 244, Exercise 32

Number Sense A carpenter has a bolt with diameter $\frac{5}{32}$ in. Will the bolt fit in a hole made by a drill bit with diameter 0.2 in.? Explain.

Understand the Problem

1. What is the diameter of the carpenter's bolt? _____

2. What is the diameter of the drill bit? _____

3. What is the diameter of a hole made by the drill bit? _____

4. What are you asked to do? _____

Make and Carry Out a Plan

5. The diameter of the bolt is given as a fraction. Change it to a decimal. _____

6. Compare the decimal diameter of the bolt to the diameter of the hole made by the drill bit. Which is greater? _____

7. Will the bolt fit into the hole? Justify your reasoning. _____

_____

Check the Answer

8. Check your answer by writing 0.2 in., the diameter of the drill bit, as a fraction and comparing it to $\frac{5}{32}$, the diameter of the bolt. _____

Solve Another Problem

9. A wooden peg has a diameter of 0.5 in. Will the peg fit into a hole that has a diameter of $\frac{7}{16}$ in.? Justify your reasoning. _____

_____

Practice 5-3

Adding and Subtracting Fractions

Find each sum or difference.

1. $\frac{2}{3} + \frac{1}{6}$ _____

2. $\frac{5}{8} - \frac{1}{4}$ _____

3. $2 - \frac{5}{7}$ _____

4. $1\frac{1}{2} - 2\frac{4}{5}$ _____

5. $\frac{1}{4} - \frac{1}{3}$ _____

6. $5\frac{7}{8} + 3\frac{5}{12}$ _____

7. $\frac{x}{3} + \frac{x}{5}$ _____

8. $\frac{2n}{5} + \left(-\frac{n}{6}\right)$ _____

9. $\frac{7}{12} - \frac{3}{12}$ _____

10. $3\frac{1}{5} + 2\frac{2}{5}$ _____

11. $1\frac{5}{8} - 1\frac{1}{8}$ _____

12. $\frac{3}{5y} + \frac{1}{5y}$ _____

13. $\frac{9}{16} + \frac{3}{4}$ _____

14. $2\frac{7}{10} - 3\frac{7}{20}$ _____

15. $3\frac{5}{6} + 2\frac{3}{4}$ _____

16. $-1\frac{2}{3} + \left(-2\frac{1}{4}\right)$ _____

Find each sum using mental math.

17. $3\frac{3}{8} + 2\frac{1}{8} + 1\frac{3}{8}$ _____

18. $6\frac{7}{12} + 4\frac{5}{12}$ _____

19. $8\frac{3}{16} + 2\frac{5}{16} + 4\frac{7}{16}$ _____

20. $7\frac{9}{10} + 3\frac{3}{10}$ _____

Estimate each sum or difference.

21. $13\frac{4}{5} - 2\frac{9}{10}$ _____

22. $18\frac{3}{8} + 11\frac{6}{7}$ _____

23. $23\frac{6}{13} + 32\frac{7}{8}$ _____

24. $26\frac{9}{10} + 72\frac{5}{6}$ _____

Use prime factors to simplify each expression.

25. $\frac{7}{30} - \frac{29}{75}$ _____

26. $\frac{3}{14} + \frac{17}{63}$ _____

27. $\frac{5}{42} + \frac{5}{12}$ _____

28. $2\frac{5}{6} - 2\frac{5}{22}$ _____

29. $4\frac{4}{15} + 2\frac{4}{39}$ _____

30. $3\frac{5}{9} - 2\frac{11}{12}$ _____

5-3 • Guided Problem Solving

GPS **Student Page 250, Exercise 35**

Weather There were three snowstorms last winter. The storms dropped $3\frac{1}{2}$ in., $6\frac{1}{2}$ in., and $10\frac{3}{4}$ in. of snow. What was the combined snowfall of the three storms?

Understand the Problem

1. How much snow did each of the three storms drop? _____

2. What are you asked to find? _____

Make and Carry Out a Plan

3. Write an expression to find the combined snowfall of the three storms. _____

4. Rewrite $3\frac{1}{2}$, $6\frac{1}{2}$, and $10\frac{3}{4}$ as improper fractions. _____

5. Rewrite the expression using a common denominator. _____

6. Simplify the expression. _____

7. Rewrite the improper fraction as a mixed number. _____

8. What was the combined snowfall of the three storms? _____

Check the Answer

9. What steps do you follow to write a mixed number as an improper fraction? _____

_____

10. What steps do you follow to write an improper fraction as a mixed number? _____

_____

Solve Another Problem

11. Alexis has three pieces of ribbon. Their lengths are $4\frac{1}{3}$ in., $8\frac{5}{6}$ in., and $12\frac{1}{2}$ in. How many inches of ribbon does she have in all? _____

Practice 5-4

Multiplying and Dividing Fractions

Find each quotient.

1. $\frac{1}{2} \div \frac{5}{8}$ _____

2. $-\frac{5}{24} \div \frac{7}{12}$ _____

3. $\frac{3}{8} \div \frac{6}{7}$ _____

4. $\frac{15}{19} \div \frac{15}{19}$ _____

5. $8 \div \frac{4}{5}$ _____

6. $6\frac{1}{4} \div 2\frac{1}{2}$ _____

7. $5\frac{5}{8} \div 1\frac{1}{4}$ _____

8. $2\frac{1}{3} \div \frac{7}{10}$ _____

9. $\frac{6}{35t} \div \frac{3}{7t}$ _____

10. $1\frac{3}{7} \div \left(-2\frac{1}{7}\right)$ _____

Find each product.

11. $\frac{2}{5} \cdot \frac{3}{7}$ _____

12. $\frac{5}{9} \cdot \frac{3}{5}$ _____

13. $\frac{7}{9} \cdot \frac{6}{13}$ _____

14. $\frac{5}{6} \cdot \left(-1\frac{3}{10}\right)$ _____

15. $-4\frac{2}{3}\left(-5\frac{1}{6}\right)$ _____

16. $2\frac{5}{6}\left(-\frac{2}{5}\right)$ _____

17. $4\frac{7}{8} \cdot 6$ _____

18. $\frac{5x}{7} \cdot \frac{3}{10}$ _____

19. $\frac{9a}{10} \cdot \frac{5}{12a}$ _____

20. $\frac{9t}{16} \cdot \frac{12}{17}$ _____

21. You are making cookies for a bake sale. The recipe calls for $2\frac{3}{4}$ cups of flour. How much flour will you need if you triple the recipe?

_____

22. It took you 1 hour to read $1\frac{3}{8}$ chapters of a novel. At this rate, how many chapters can you read in three hours?

_____

23. A teacher wants to tape sheets of paper together to make a science banner. He wants the banner to be $127\frac{1}{2}$ inches long, and each sheet of paper is $8\frac{1}{2}$ inches wide. How many sheets of paper will he need?

_____

5-4 • Guided Problem Solving

GPS **Student Page 256, Exercise 58**

You are hiking along a trail that is $13\frac{1}{2}$ mi long. You plan to rest every $2\frac{1}{4}$ mi. How many rest stops will you make?

Understand the Problem

1. How long is the trail you are hiking? _____

2. How often do you plan to rest? _____

3. What are you asked to find? _____

Make and Carry Out a Plan

4. Write an expression to divide the length of the trail into $2\frac{1}{4}$-mi sections. _____

5. Change the fractions in the expression to improper fractions. _____

6. What is the reciprocal of the divisor? _____

7. Rewrite the division as multiplication by the reciprocal. _____

8. Divide the common factors and simplify. _____

9. How many $2\frac{1}{4}$-mi sections are there in the $13\frac{1}{2}$-mi trail? _____

10. How many rest stops will you make? Note that the last $2\frac{1}{4}$-mi section will not have a rest stop because you will be finished. _____

Check the Answer

11. If you divide the $13\frac{1}{2}$-mi trail by your answer to Step 9, what result would show that your work is correct? _____

Solve Another Problem

12. You have a piece of fabric that is $8\frac{1}{4}$ yd long. You want to cut the fabric into pieces that are $\frac{3}{8}$ yd long. How many pieces of fabric will you have? _____

Practice 5-5

Using Customary Units of Measurement

Use estimation, mental math, or paper and pencil to convert from one unit to the other.

1. 2 gal 2 qt = _____ qt

2. 3 yd = _____ ft

3. 1 ft 8 in. = _____ in.

4. $\frac{3}{5}$ t = _____ lb

5. 30 in. = _____ ft

6. 20 fl oz = _____ c

7. 20 oz = _____ lb

8. $2\frac{1}{2}$ pt = _____ c

9. $1\frac{1}{8}$ lb = _____ oz

10. 7920 ft = _____ mi

Is each measurement reasonable? If not, give a reasonable measurement.

11. A glass of milk holds about 8 pt.

_____

12. A newborn baby weighs about $7\frac{1}{2}$ oz.

_____

13. A phonebook is $\frac{3}{4}$ ft wide.

_____

Choose an appropriate unit of measure. Explain your choice.

14. weight of a whale

_____

15. sugar in a cookie recipe

_____

16. length of a mouse

_____

Should each item be measured by *length*, *weight*, or *capacity*?

17. amount of soup in a can

_____

18. height of a can

_____

19. heaviness of a can

_____

20. diameter of a can

_____

5-5 • Guided Problem Solving

GPS Student Page 260, Exercise 37

Hiking You are hiking a 2-mi-long trail. You pass by a sign showing that you have hiked 1,000 ft. How many feet are left?

Understand the Problem

1. How long is the trail you are hiking? _____

2. How far have you hiked? _____

3. What are you asked to find? _____

Make and Carry Out a Plan

4. How many feet are in a mile? _____

5. What is the conversion factor for converting miles to feet? _____

6. Multiply 2 mi by the conversion
   factor to find the number of feet in 2 mi. _____

7. Write an expression to find the number
   of feet you still have to hike on the 2-mi trail. _____

8. How many feet are left to hike? _____

Check the Answer

9. To check your work, add 1,000 to your
   answer. Then convert the sum to miles. _____

Solve Another Problem

10. You are in-line skating around a 3-mi loop. You just passed a
    marker showing you have skated 5,000 ft. How many feet are left? _____

Practice 5-6

● ●

Work backward to solve each problem.

1. Manuel's term paper is due on March 31. He began doing research on March 1. He intends to continue doing research for 3 times as long as he has done already. Then he will spend a week writing the paper and the remaining 3 days typing. What day is it? (Assume he will finish typing on March 30.)

_____

2. A disc jockey must allow time for 24 minutes of commercials every hour, along with 4 minutes for news, 3 minutes for weather, and 2 minutes for public-service announcements. If each record lasts an average of 3 minutes, how many records per hour can the DJ play?

_____

3. Margaret is reading the 713-page novel *War and Peace*. When she has read twice as many pages as she has read already, she will be 119 pages from the end. What page is she on now?

_____

4. On Monday the low temperature at the South Pole dropped 9°F from Sunday's low. On Tuesday it fell another 7°, then rose 13° on Wednesday and 17° more on Thursday. Friday it dropped 8° to −50°F. What was Sunday's low temperature?

_____

5. Each problem lists the operations performed on *n* to produce the given result. Find *n*.
   a. Multiply by 3, add 4, divide by 5, subtract 6; result, −1.

   _____

   b. Add 2, divide by 3, subtract 4, multiply by 5; result, 35.

   _____

   c. Multiply by 2, add 7, divide by 17; result, 1.

   _____

   d. Divide by 3, add 9, multiply by 2, subtract 12; result, 4.

   _____

   e. Subtract 2, divide by 5, add 7, multiply by 3; result, 30.

   _____

● ●

5-6 • Guided Problem Solving

GPS Student Page 265, Exercise 7

You spent half of your money at the amusement park and had $15 left. How much money did you have originally?

Understand the Problem

1. What fraction of your money did you spend at the amusement park? _____

2. How many dollars did you have left after you had spent money at the amusement park? _____

3. What are you asked to find? _____

Make and Carry Out a Plan

4. If you spent half of your money at the amusement park, what fraction of the original amount of money do you have left? _____

5. Use the variable m to represent your original amount of money. Write a variable expression for the amount of money you have left. _____

6. Set the expression you wrote in Step 5 equal to $15, the dollar amount of money you have left. Solve for m to find the original amount of money you had. _____

Check the Answer

7. How did you decide what fraction of money you had left? _____

_____

8. Divide your answer in half. Then subtract the quotient from the original amount. The result should be the amount of money you have left. _____

Solve Another Problem

9. Two-thirds of the students in Tristan's class chose to participate in choir. If 8 students from Tristan's class do not participate in choir, how many students are in Tristan's class? _____

Practice 5-7

Solving Equations by Adding or Subtracting Fractions

Solve each equation.

1. $m - \left(-\frac{7}{10}\right) = -1\frac{1}{5}$ _____

2. $k - \frac{3}{4} = \frac{2}{5}$ _____

3. $x - \frac{5}{6} = \frac{1}{10}$ _____

4. $t - \left(-3\frac{1}{6}\right) = 7\frac{2}{3}$ _____

5. $x + \frac{5}{8} = \frac{7}{8}$ _____

6. $k + \frac{4}{5} = 1\frac{3}{5}$ _____

7. $4 = \frac{4}{9} + y$ _____

8. $h + \left(-\frac{5}{8}\right) = -\frac{5}{12}$ _____

9. $n + \frac{2}{3} = \frac{1}{9}$ _____

10. $e - \frac{11}{16} = -\frac{7}{8}$ _____

11. $w - 14\frac{1}{12} = -2\frac{3}{4}$ _____

12. $v + \left(-4\frac{5}{6}\right) = 2\frac{1}{3}$ _____

13. $a - 9\frac{1}{6} = -3\frac{19}{24}$ _____

14. $f + \left|-3\frac{11}{12}\right| = 18$ _____

15. $z + \left(-3\frac{2}{5}\right) = -4\frac{1}{10}$ _____

16. $x - \frac{7}{15} = \frac{7}{60}$ _____

17. $h - \left(-6\frac{1}{2}\right) = 14\frac{1}{4}$ _____

18. $p - 5\frac{3}{8} = -\frac{11}{24}$ _____

Solve each equation using mental math.

19. $x + \frac{3}{7} = \frac{5}{7}$ _____

20. $k - \frac{8}{9} = -\frac{1}{9}$ _____

21. $a + \frac{1}{9} = \frac{3}{9}$ _____

22. $g - \frac{4}{5} = -\frac{2}{5}$ _____

Write an equation to solve each problem.

23. Pete's papaya tree grew $3\frac{7}{12}$ ft during the year. If its height at the end of the year was $21\frac{1}{6}$ ft, what was its height at the beginning of the year?

_____

24. Lee is $1\frac{3}{4}$ ft taller than Jay. If Lee is $6\frac{1}{4}$ ft tall, how tall is Jay?

_____

5-7 • Guided Problem Solving

GPS **Student Page 270, Exercise 33**

Seafood A restaurant chef needs $8\frac{1}{2}$ lb of salmon. To get a good price, he buys more than he needs. He ends up with $4\frac{7}{8}$ lb too much. How much salmon did he buy?

Understand the Problem

1. How much salmon does the chef need? _____

2. How much extra salmon did the chef buy? _____

3. What are you asked to find? _____

Make and Carry Out a Plan

4. Use the sentence "The amount of salmon the chef bought minus the amount of salmon he needs equals the amount of extra salmon he has" to write an equation to represent the situation. Let s represent the amount of salmon he bought. _____

5. Write the mixed numbers in the equation as improper fractions. _____

6. What fraction must you add to each side to solve for s? _____

7. Rewrite the equation using a common denominator. _____

8. Simplify to solve the equation for s. _____

9. Change the result to a mixed number. _____

10. How much salmon did the chef buy? _____

Check the Answer

11. Add the amount of extra salmon the chef had to the amount he needed. _____
    The result should be the amount of salmon he bought.

Solve Another Problem

12. Each month, Sally buys a $37\frac{1}{2}$ lb bag of food for her dog. This month, she bought $5\frac{1}{4}$ lb more than she needed because the larger bag was on sale. How many pounds of dog food are in the larger bag? _____

Name _____ Class _____ Date _____

Practice 5-8

Solving Equations by Multiplying Fractions

Solve each equation.

1. $\frac{3}{4}x = \frac{9}{16}$ _____

2. $-\frac{1}{3}p = \frac{1}{4}$ _____

3. $\frac{-3}{8}k = \frac{1}{2}$ _____

4. $\frac{1}{8}h = \frac{1}{10}$ _____

5. $2\frac{2}{3}e = \frac{1}{18}$ _____

6. $-1\frac{2}{7}m = 6$ _____

7. $-\frac{1}{4}p = \frac{1}{18}$ _____

8. $\frac{11}{-12}w = -1$ _____

9. $-3\frac{4}{7}x = 0$ _____

10. $\frac{2}{3}m = 2\frac{2}{9}$ _____

11. $5c = \frac{2}{3}$ _____

12. $-8k = \frac{4}{5}$ _____

13. $\frac{4}{7}y = 4$ _____

14. $2\frac{1}{4}f = \frac{6}{5}$ _____

15. $\frac{10}{11}n = \frac{2}{11}$ _____

16. $\frac{7}{8}c = \frac{7}{6}$ _____

Solve each equation using mental math.

17. $7d = 42$ _____

18. $\frac{1}{4}y = 5$ _____

19. $-3h = \frac{3}{8}$ _____

20. $\frac{1}{5}k = -\frac{1}{3}$ _____

Write an equation to solve each problem.

21. It takes Nancy $1\frac{2}{3}$ min to read 1 page in her social studies book. It took her $22\frac{1}{2}$ min to complete her reading assignment. How long was the assignment? Let m represent the number of pages she read.

_____

22. It takes Gary three hours to drive to Boston. If the trip is 156 miles, what is Gary's average number of miles per hour? Let x represent the miles per hour.

_____

5-8 • Guided Problem Solving

GPS Student Page 274, Exercise 35

Biology In ideal conditions, the kudzu plant can grow at least $1\frac{3}{20}$ ft per week. At this rate, how many weeks would it take a kudzu plant to grow 23 ft?

Understand the Problem

1. How many feet can a kudzu plant grow each week in ideal conditions? _____

2. What are you asked to find? _____

   _____

Make and Carry Out a Plan

3. Use the sentence "Feet per week times number of weeks is 23 feet" to write an equation to represent the situation. Let w represent number of weeks. _____

4. Write $1\frac{3}{20}$ as an improper fraction in the equation. _____

5. By what number must you multiply each side of the equation to get w alone on one side? _____

6. Divide common factors and simplify the equation. _____

7. How many weeks would it take a kudzu plant to grow 23 feet? _____

Check the Answer

8. Divide 23 feet by the number of weeks you found. _____
   The result should be the number of feet per week a kudzu plant grows.

Solve Another Problem

9. A Jersey cow produces an average of $3\frac{1}{2}$ gallons of milk per day. How many days will it take a Jersey cow to produce 21 gallons of milk? _____

Practice 5-9

Powers of Products and Quotients

Simplify each expression.

1. $\left(\frac{5}{6}\right)^2$ _____

2. $\left(-\frac{4}{9}\right)^2$ _____

3. $\left(\frac{x^2}{5}\right)^3$ _____

4. $(2x)^3$ _____

5. $(-3y^2)^2$ _____

6. $(5ab^2)^3$ _____

7. $(12mn)^2$ _____

8. $(-10xy^3)^3$ _____

9. $(9qrs^4)^3$ _____

10. $\left(\frac{2x}{9y}\right)^2$ _____

11. $-(a^2b^2)^3$ _____

12. $(2a^3b^2)^4$ _____

13. $\left(\frac{2x}{y}\right)^2$ _____

14. $\left(-\frac{3x}{8y}\right)^2$ _____

15. $\left(\frac{3y^2}{x}\right)^3$ _____

16. $\left(\frac{2x^2y}{xy^3}\right)^5$ _____

Evaluate for $a = 2$, $b = -1$, and $c = \frac{1}{3}$.

17. $(a^2)^3$ _____

18. $2b^3$ _____

19. $(-9c^2)^3$ _____

20. $(a^2b)^2$ _____

21. $(ac)^2$ _____

22. $(b^3)^7$ _____

Complete each equation.

23. $(3b^{-\!\!-\!\!-})^2 = 9b^{10}$

24. $(m^2n)^{-\!\!-\!\!-} = m^8n^4$

25. $(xy^{-\!\!-\!\!-})^2 = x^2y^6$

26. $\left(\frac{3s^2t}{r}\right)^{-\!\!-\!\!-} = \frac{9s^4t^2}{r^2}$

27. Write an expression for the area of a square with a side of length $4a^2$. Simplify your expression.

_____

28. Write an expression for the volume of a cube with a side of length $3z^5$. Simplify your expression.

_____

5-9 • Guided Problem Solving

GPS **Student Page 280, Exercise 43**

Furniture A table has sides that measure $3x^2$ ft. Write an expression for the area of the tabletop. Simplify your expression.

Understand the Problem

1. What is the length of a side of the table? _____

2. What are you asked to do? _____

Make and Carry Out a Plan

3. Let s represent the length of the side of the table. Write an expression for the area of the tabletop. _____

4. Replace s with $3x^2$ in the expression. _____

5. Use the rule for raising a product to a power to evaluate the expression you wrote for Step 4. _____

6. Simplify the expression. _____

7. What is the area of the tabletop? _____

Check the Answer

8. What rule did you use to simplify $(x^2)^2$? _____

Solve Another Problem

9. The length of the side of a square is $4x^3$. Write an expression for the area of the square. Simplify the expression. _____

5A: Graphic Organizer

For use before Lesson 5-1

Study Skill Get a general overview of the main features by skimming or surveying this chapter. Read the title, headings, and the first and last paragraphs of each lesson. This helps you outline in your mind a general framework for what you are going to study in this chapter.

Write your answers. Use the Table of Contents page for this chapter at the front of the book.

1. What is the title of this chapter? _____

2. Name four topics that you will study in this chapter:

   _____   _____

   _____   _____

3. What is the topic of the Problem Solving lesson? _____

4. Complete the graphic organizer as you work through the chapter.
   1. Write the title of the chapter in the center oval.
   2. When you begin a lesson, write the lesson name in a rectangle.
   3. When you complete that lesson, write a skill or key concept from that lesson in the outer oval linked to that rectangle.
   Continue with steps 2 and 3 clockwise around the graphic organizer.

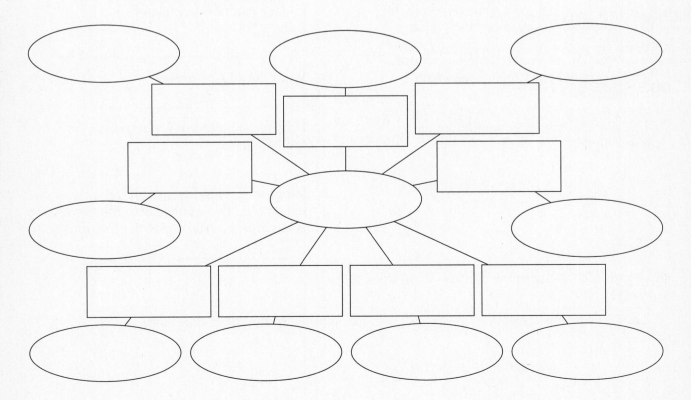

5B: Reading Comprehension

For use after Lesson 5-3

Study Skill Instead of relying on your memory, keep a special notebook where you write down your daily assignments and directions. Make notes of hints and suggestions that may be given when an assignment is explained. Check off the work as you complete it.

Read the review at the left, and then answer the questions at the right.

Summary of multiples:

An integer is a multiple of
- 2 if it ends in 0, 2, 4, 6, or 8
- 5 if it ends in 0 or 5
- 10 if it ends in 0
- 3 if the sum of its digits is divisible by 3
- 9 if the sum of its digits is divisible by 9

Summary for finding the LCM:

To find the Least Common Multiple for two integers,
- write the prime factorization for each,
- circle the greatest power of each factor,
- multiply the circled powers.

Summary for comparing nonnegative fractions:

- If two fractions have the same denominator, then the greater fraction has the greater numerator.
- If two fractions have the same numerator, then the greater fraction has the lesser denominator.
- Otherwise, rewrite both fractions using the LCM as the common denominator, and then compare.

To remember the information in this review, first look at the way the review is organized.

1. How many main parts are there in this review?

   _____

2. How many tests for finding multiples are listed?

   _____

3. Is it possible for an integer to pass more than one of the "multiples" tests?

   _____

4. According to the summary of multiples, what must be true of an integer that is a multiple of 2 and 9?

   _____

5. What does LCM mean?

   _____

6. How many steps are given to find the LCM?

   _____

7. Suppose you have to use all three steps to compare two nonnegative fractions. What must be true about the fractions?

   _____

8. **High-Use Academic Words** What does *compare* mean in Exercise 7?

   a. find which is larger   **b.** subtract to find their difference

5C: Reading/Writing Math Symbols

For use after Lesson 5-8

Study Skill When you write symbols, make them clear and complete so that you will be able to read them correctly at a later time. If you create your own symbols and abbreviations, be sure to write a key to remind you of their meanings.

On the blank on the right, write one symbol or abbreviation to complete each statement.

1. $2\frac{1}{3} = 2 \underline{\quad?\quad} \frac{1}{3}$ _____

2. $ab = a \underline{\quad?\quad} b$ _____

3. $\frac{5}{7} = 5 \underline{\quad?\quad} 7$ _____

4. The opposite of 7 is $\underline{\quad?\quad}$ 7. _____

5. 56 feet is 56 $\underline{\quad?\quad}$. _____

6. 3 cups of flour is 3 $\underline{\quad?\quad}$ of flour. _____

7. The value of 5 dimes $= 5 \underline{\quad?\quad}$ $.10. _____

8. 8 pounds is 8 $\underline{\quad?\quad}$. _____

9. $3 \div \frac{2}{3} = 3 \underline{\quad?\quad} \frac{3}{2}$ _____

10. $\frac{3}{4}$ of $p = \frac{3}{4} \underline{\quad?\quad} p$ _____

11. 15 centimeters is 15 $\underline{\quad?\quad}$. _____

12. 12 is greater than x is $12 \underline{\quad?\quad} x$. _____

13. y minus the opposite of 7 is $y \underline{\quad?\quad}$ 7. _____

14. 4 increased by b is $4 \underline{\quad?\quad} b$. _____

5D: Visual Vocabulary Practice

For use after Lesson 5-6

Study Skill When you come across something you don't understand, view it as an opportunity to increase your brain power.

Concept List

conversion factor	equivalent fractions	greatest common factor
least common denominator	least common multiple	prime factorization
reciprocals	repeating decimal	terminating decimal

Write the concept that best describes each exercise. Choose from the concept list shown above.

1. Relationship of 15 to the numbers 3 and 5 _____	**2.** Relationship of 20 to the denominators of the fractions $\frac{1}{2}, \frac{3}{4},$ and $\frac{3}{5}$ _____	**3.** 0.75 _____
4. 0.333... _____	**5.** $\frac{3}{4}$ and $\frac{4}{3}$ _____	**6.** $\frac{12 \text{ in.}}{1 \text{ ft}}$ and $\frac{4 \text{ qt}}{1 \text{ gal}}$ _____
7. Relationship of 3 to the numbers 3, 6, and 9 _____	**8.** $30 = 2 \cdot 3 \cdot 5$ _____	**9.** $\frac{6}{10}$ and $\frac{12}{20}$ _____

5E: Vocabulary Check

Study Skill Strengthen your vocabulary. Use these pages and add cues and summaries by applying the Cornell Notetaking style.

Write the definition for each word. To check your work, fold the paper back along the dotted line to see the correct answers.

_____

_____

_____

Multiple

_____

_____

Least common multiple

_____

_____

_____

Least common denominator

_____

_____

_____

Terminating decimal

_____

_____

Repeating decimal

_____

_____

_____

5E: Vocabulary Check (continued)

For use after Lesson 5-5

Write the vocabulary word for each definition. To check your work,
fold the paper forward along the dotted line to see the correct answers.

The product of a number
and any nonzero whole
number.

_____

The least number that is
a multiple of two or more
numbers.

_____

The least common
multiple of the
denominators of two
or more fractions.

_____

A decimal with a finite
number of digits.

_____

A decimal in which the
same block of digits
repeats without end.

_____

Vocabulary and Study Skills

Name _____ Class _____ Date _____

5F: Vocabulary Review Puzzle

For use with Chapter Review

Study Skill After you complete a vocabulary puzzle, word search, or game, review the list of words and say the meaning of each vocabulary term to yourself. Pay special attention to how the word is spelled.

Unscramble the UPPERCASE letters to form a math word or phrase that completes each sentence.

1. When you divide the numerator of a fraction by the denominator, and the quotient is a GATTEMINNIR decimal, then the division ends with a remainder of zero.

   _____

2. When two fractions describe the same part of a whole, the two fractions are VAQUITLEEN.

   _____

3. The PRICOLACER of 2 is one-half.

   _____

4. A fraction is in TESLIMPS form when the only common factor of the numerator and denominator is one.

   _____

5. A GREATPINE decimal is one that has the same block of digits repeating without end.

   _____

6. When you look at units to decide which conversion factors to use, you are doing LANDMINESOI analysis.

   _____

7. The SETTGEAR common factor of 24 and 36 is 12.

   _____

8. Twenty-eight is a PLLTMIUE of both 4 and 7.

   _____

9. The least NOMMOC multiple of 4 and 25 is 100.

   _____

10. SECCNTIIFI notation is a shorthand way of writing numbers using powers of 10.

    _____

Practice 6-1

Find each unit rate.

1. 78 mi on 3 gal _____

2. $52.50 in 7 h _____

3. 416 mi in 8 h _____

4. 9 bull's eyes in 117 throws _____

Write each ratio as a fraction in simplest form.

5. 7th-grade boys to 8th-grade boys _____

6. 7th-grade girls to 7th-grade boys _____

7. 7th graders to 8th graders _____

8. boys to girls _____

9. girls to all students _____

	Boys	Girls
7th Grade	26	34
8th Grade	30	22

Write three different ratios for each model.

10. ▢▢▢
    ◯◯◯◯
    _____

11. ●●●
    ◯ ◯
    _____

12.
    _____

Write each ratio as a fraction is simplest form.

13. 7 : 12 _____

14. 3 is to 6 _____

15. 10 : 45 _____

16. 32 out of 40 _____

17. 36 is to 60 _____

18. 13 out of 14 _____

19. 9 out of 21 _____

20. 45 : 63 _____

21. 24 is to 18 _____

22. 15 out of 60 _____

6-1 • Guided Problem Solving

GPS **Student Page 294, Exercise 28**

Transportation What is the rate in meters per second of a jetliner
that is traveling at a rate of 846 km/h?

Understand the Problem

1. How fast is the jetliner traveling? _____

2. What are you asked to find? _____

Make and Carry Out a Plan

3. How many meters are in 1 kilometer? _____

4. What conversion factor will you use to
   change the number of kilometers to meters? _____

5. How many seconds are in one hour? _____

6. What conversion factor will you use to
   change the number of hours to seconds? _____

7. Multiply $\frac{846 \text{ km}}{1 \text{ h}}$ by the two conversion factors. _____

8. What is the rate of the jetliner in meters per second? _____

Check the Answer

9. To check to make sure you have converted correctly,
   convert the meters per second rate back to kilometers per second. _____

Solve Another Problem

10. What is the rate in feet per minute of a car
    that is traveling 68 mi/h on an interstate freeway? _____

Name _____ Class _____ Date _____

Practice 6-2

Proportions

Write a proportion for each phrase. Then solve. When necessary, round to the nearest hundredth.

1. 420 ft² painted in 36 min; *f* ft² painted in 30 min

$$\frac{420}{36} = \frac{f}{30} \qquad f = 350$$

2. 75 points scored in 6 games; *p* points scored in 4 games

$$p = 50 \qquad \frac{75}{6} = \frac{p}{4}$$

3. 6 apples for $1.00; 15 apples for *d* dollars

$$\frac{1.00}{6} = \frac{d}{15} \qquad d\,\$2.50$$

Tell whether each pair of ratios forms a proportion.

4. $\frac{3}{4}$ and $\frac{9}{12}$ _____yes_____

5. $\frac{25}{40}$ and $\frac{5}{8}$ _____yes_____

6. $\frac{8}{12}$ and $\frac{14}{21}$ _____yes_____

7. $\frac{13}{15}$ and $\frac{4}{5}$ _____no_____

8. $\frac{4}{5}$ and $\frac{5}{6}$ _____no_____

9. $\frac{49}{21}$ and $\frac{28}{12}$ _____yes_____

Solve each proportion. Where necessary, round to the nearest tenth.

10. $\frac{3}{5} = \frac{15}{x}$ _____x = 25_____

11. $\frac{15}{30} = \frac{n}{34}$ _____14_____ 17

12. $\frac{h}{36} = \frac{21}{27}$ _____h = 28.0_____

13. $\frac{11}{6} = \frac{f}{60}$ _____f = 110_____

14. $\frac{26}{15} = \frac{130}{m}$ _____m = 75_____

15. $\frac{36}{f} = \frac{7}{20}$ _____f = 102.9_____

16. $\frac{r}{23} = \frac{17}{34}$ _____r = 105_____

17. $\frac{77}{93} = \frac{x}{24}$ _____19.9_____

18. At Discount Copy, 12 copies cost $0.66. Melissa needs 56 copies. How much should they cost?

_____3.08_____

19. You estimate that you can do 12 math problems in 45 min. How long should it take you to do 20 math problems?

_____x = 75_____

6-2 • Guided Problem Solving

GPS **Student Page 301, Exercise 51**

Quality Control A microchip inspector found three defective chips in a batch containing 750 chips. At that rate, how many defective chips would there be in 10,000 chips?

Understand the Problem

1. How many defective chips did the inspector find? _____

2. How many chips did the inspector inspect? _____

3. What are you asked to find? _____

_____

Make and Carry Out a Plan

4. Write the ratio of the number of defective chips the inspector found to the total number of chips inspected. _____

5. Let *c* represent the number of defective chips in 10,000. Write the ratio of the number of defective chips to the total number of chips, 10,000. _____

6. Use the two ratios to write a proportion. _____

7. Write the cross-product equation. _____

8. By what number must you divide each side of the equation to solve for *c?* _____

9. About how many defective chips would there be in 10,000 chips? _____

Check the Answer

10. To check your answer, use the Multiplication Property of Equality to solve the proportion from Step 6. What is the value of *c?* _____

Solve Another Problem

11. In Mr. Schulte's eighth-grade class, 17 of the 20 students participate in after-school activities. At that rate, how many of 300 eighth-grade students have after-school activities? _____

Name _____ Class _____ Date _____

Practice 6-3

Similar Figures and Scale Drawings

The scale of a map is $\frac{1}{2}$ in. : 8 mi. Find the actual distance for each map distance.

1. 2 in. _____ 32

2. 5 in. _____ 80

3. $3\frac{1}{2}$ in. _____ 56

4. 10 in. _____ 160

5. 8 in. _____ 128

6. $7\frac{1}{4}$ in. _____ 116

Each pair of figures is similar. Find the missing length. Round to the nearest tenth where necessary.

7.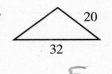

$x =$ _____ 5

8.

$p =$ _____ 67.5

9.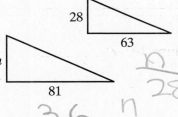

$n =$ _____ 36

10.

$e \approx$ _____ 20 $f \approx$ _____ 18

11. A meter stick casts a shadow 1.4 m long at the same time a flagpole casts a shadow 7.7 m long. The triangle formed by the meterstick and its shadow is similar to the triangle formed by the flagpole and its shadow. How tall is the flagpole?

_____ 5.5 m

A scale drawing has a scale of $\frac{1}{4}$ in. : 6 ft. Find the length on the drawing for each actual length.

12. 18 ft

 .75 in

13. 66 ft

 2.75 in

14. 204 ft

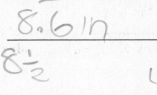 8.6 in

Practice

Pre-Algebra Lesson 6-3   **371**

6-3 • Guided Problem Solving

GPS **Student Page 305, Exercise 9**

Projection An image on a slide is similar to its projected image.
A slide is 35 mm wide and 21 mm high. Its projected image is 85 cm
wide. To the nearest centimeter, how high is the image?

Understand the Problem

1. How wide is the slide? _____

2. How high is the slide? _____

3. What is the width of the slide's projected image? _____

4. What are you asked to find? _____

Make and Carry Out a Plan

5. What is true about the lengths of corresponding sides of similar figures?. _____

_____

6. Write a ratio to compare the width
   of the slide and the width of its projected image. _____

7. Let h represent the height of the projected
   image. Write a ratio to compare the height of
   the slide to the height of its projected image. _____

8. Use the two ratios to write a proportion. _____

9. Write the cross-product equation. _____

10. By what number must you divide each side to solve for h? _____

11. How high is the projected image? _____

Check the Answer

12. To check your answer, use the Multiplication Property of
    Equality to solve the proportion in Step 8. What is the value of h? _____

Solve Another Problem

13. Marianna scans a picture into her computer so she can
    make an enlargement that is similar to the original.
    The original picture is 4 in. wide and 6 in. long. She
    wants the enlargement to be 12 in. long. How wide must it be? _____

Practice 6-4

Probability

Find each probability for choosing a letter at random from the word
PROBABILITY.

1. P(B) _____ 7/11

2. P(P) _____ 1/11

3. P(A or I) _____ 3/11

4. P(not P) _____ 10/11

A child is chosen at random from the Erb and Smith families. Find the
odds in favor of each of the following being chosen.

5. a girl _____ 1/14 ½

6. an Erb _____ 7/14 ½

7. an Erb girl _____ 2/14 = 1/6

8. a Smith girl _____ 5/14

9. not a Smith boy _____ 11/14

10. a Smith _____ 8/14

	Erb Family	Smith Family
Girls	2	5
Boys	4	3

A box contains 7 red, 14 yellow, 21 green, 42 blue, and 84 purple marbles.
A marble is drawn at random from the box. Find each probability.

11. P(red) _____ 7/168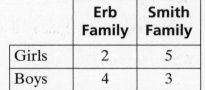

12. P(yellow) _____ 14/168 = 7/84 = 1/12

13. P(green or blue) _____ 63/168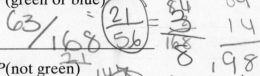

14. P(purple, yellow, or red) _____ 105/168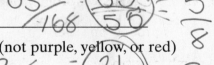

15. P(not green) _____

16. P(not purple, yellow, or red) _____ 63/168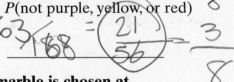

Find the odds in favor of each selection when a marble is chosen at
random from the box described above.

17. blue _____ 1/3

18. purple _____ 1/1

19. not red _____ 23/1

20. not green or blue _____ 5/3

21. yellow _____ 1/11

22. not purple or yellow _____ 5/1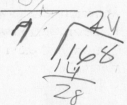

6-4 • Guided Problem Solving

GPS **Student Page 312, Exercise 24**

Reasoning The table at the right describes the loose socks in Lola's drawer. One morning Lola pulls a sock from the drawer without looking. It is white. She pulls out another sock without looking. Find the probability that it also is white.

Lola's Socks

Color	Number of Socks
Pink	6
White	4
Green	3
Purple	2

Understand the Problem

1. Look at the table. How many loose socks are in Lola's drawer? _____

2. What color is the first sock Lola pulls from her drawer? _____

3. What are you asked to find? _____

_____

Make and Carry Out a Plan

4. After Lola pulls out a white sock, how
   many white socks are left in the drawer? _____

5. How many socks are left in the drawer after Lola pulls out one white sock? _____

6. What is the number of favorable outcomes for pulling out a second white sock? _____

7. What is the number of possible outcomes
   for pulling out a second sock of any color? _____

8. Write the number of favorable outcomes over the number of possible
   outcomes to find the probability that the second sock Lola pulls out is also white. _____

Check the Answer

9. To check your answer, find the probability
   that the second sock Lola pulls out is not white. _____
   The probability that Lola pulls out a second white sock plus the
   probability of pulling out a second sock that is not white should
   equal 1.

Solve Another Problem

10. Sadie randomly pulls out a red golf ball from a bag with 5 orange,
    3 red, 2 blue, and 6 green golf balls. What is the probability that
    the second golf ball she pulls randomly from the bag will also be red? _____

Practice 6-5

Fractions, Decimals, and Percents

Write each decimal or fraction as a percent. Round to the nearest tenth of a percent where necessary.

1. 0.16 ___16%___

2. 0.72 ___72%___

3. $\frac{24}{25}$ ___96%___

4. $\frac{31}{40}$ ___77.5%___

5. $\frac{111}{200}$ ___55.5%___

6. $\frac{403}{1,000}$ ___40.3%___

7. 3.04 ___304%___

8. 5.009 ___500.9%___

9. 0.0004 ___.04%___

10. $\frac{40}{13}$ ___307.7%___

11. $\frac{4}{7}$ ___57.1%___

12. $\frac{57}{99}$ ___58%___
   ___57.6%___

Write each percent as a decimal.

13. 8% ___.68___

14. 12.4% ___.124___

15. 145% ___1.45___

16. 0.07% ___.0007___

17. $7\frac{1}{2}$% ___.0007___
   ___.075___

18. $15\frac{1}{4}$% ___.1525___

Write each percent as a fraction or mixed number in simplest form.

19. 60% $\frac{12}{20} = \frac{6}{10} = \frac{3}{5}$

20. 5% $\frac{1}{20}$

21. 35% $\frac{7}{20}$

22. 32% $\frac{8}{25}$

23. 140% $1\frac{2}{5}$

24. 0.8% $\frac{1}{125}$

Use >, <, or = to complete each statement.

25. 0.7 ☒ 7%

26. 80% $=$ $\frac{4}{5}$

27. $\frac{1}{3}$ □ 33%

28. In the United States in 1990, about one person in twenty was 75 years old or older. Write this fraction as a percent.

_____ 1/20 ____ 5% ____ 5% ____

6-5 • Guided Problem Solving

GPS **Student Page 317, Exercise 72**

Jeanette answered 32 questions correctly on a 45-question test.
The passing grade was 70%. Did Jeanette pass? Justify your answer.

Understand the Problem

1. How many questions did Jeanette answer correctly? _____

2. How many questions were on the test? _____

3. What was a passing grade for the test? _____

4. What are you asked to do? _____

Make and Carry Out a Plan

5. What fraction of the questions on the test did Jeanette answer correctly? _____

6. Write the fraction as a decimal. Divide the numerator
    by the denominator and round to two decimal places. _____

7. Write the decimal as a percent. (Move
    the decimal point two places to the right.) _____

8. Is your answer greater than, equal to, or less than 70%? _____

9. Did Jeanette pass? Explain your answer. _____

    _____

Check the Answer

10. To check your answer, find Jeanette's incorrect answer rate.
    An incorrect answer rate greater than 30% is a failing grade.
    How does her incorrect answer rate support your answer to Step 9? _____

    _____

Solve Another Problem

11. Ms. Martinez's class is voting on whether to take its science quiz
    a day early. Of 26 students, 19 vote yes. A yes vote of 70% or better
    is needed to change the quiz day. Will the class take the quiz early? Explain. _____

    _____

Practice 6-6

Proportions and Percents

Write a proportion. Then solve. Where necessary, round to the nearest tenth or tenth of a percent.

1. $62\frac{1}{2}$% of *t* is 35. What is *t*? _____56_____

2. 38% of *n* is 33.44. What is *n*? _____12.7____

3. 120% of *y* is 42. What is *y*? _____35_____

4. 300% of *m* is 600. What is *m*? ____200____

5. 1.5% of *h* is 12. What is *h*? ____800_____

6. What percent of 40 is 12? ____3.3%_____

7. What percent of 48 is 18? ____37.5%____

8. What percent is 54 of 60? ____90%_____

9. What percent is 39 of 50? ____78%_____

10. Find 80% of 25. ____20_____

11. Find 150% of 74. ____111_____

12. Find 44% of 375. ____165_____

13. Find 65% of 180. ____117_____

14. The Eagles won 70% of the 40 games that they played. How many games did they win?
_____28 wins_____

15. Thirty-five of 40 students surveyed said that they favored recycling. What percent of those surveyed favored recycling?
_____87.5%_____

16. Candidate Carson received 2,310 votes, 55% of the total. How many total votes were cast?
_____4,200_____

Name _____ Class _____ Date _____

6-6 • Guided Problem Solving

gps **Student Page 323, Exercise 33**

Profit You invested some money and made a profit of $55. Your profit was 11% of your investment. How much did you invest?

Understand the Problem

1. What was the profit on the money you invested? _____

2. What percent of the investment was the profit? _____

3. What are you asked to find? _____

Make and Carry Out a Plan

4. Write 11% as a fraction. _____

5. Let *n* represent the amount of money invested. Write the amount of profit as a fraction of the amount of money invested. _____

6. Use the two fractions to write a proportion. _____

7. Write the cross-product equation. _____

8. By what number must you divide each side to solve for *n*? _____

9. Simplify to find how much money you invested. _____

Check the Answer

10. To check your answer, multiply it by 11%. _____
The result should be the amount of profit you made.

Solve Another Problem

11. Simon puts 15% of his monthly allowance into his savings account. If he saves $9 each month, what is his monthly allowance? _____

Practice 6-7

Percents and Equations

**Write and solve an equation. Where necessary, round to the nearest tenth
or tenth of a percent.**

1. What percent of 25 is 17? _68%_____

2. What percent is 10 of 8? _8%_____

3. What percent is 63 of 84? _80%_____

4. What percent is 3 of 600? _2%_____

5. Find 45% of 60. _____

6. Find 325% of 52. _169_____

7. Find $66\frac{2}{3}$% of 87. _____

8. Find 1% of 3,620. _36.2_____

9. $62\frac{1}{2}$% of x is 5. What is x? _____

10. 300% of k is 42. What is k? _?14_____

11. $33\frac{1}{3}$% of p is 19. What is p? _____

12. 70% of c is 49. What is c? _?17_____

13. 15% of n is 1,050. What is n? _____

14. 38% of y is 494. What is y? _?1300_____

15. A camera regularly priced at $295 was placed on sale at $236. What
percent of the regular price was the sale price?

    _____

16. Nine hundred thirty-six students, 65% of the entire student body,
attended the football game. Find the size of the student body.

    _____

$$\frac{325\%}{100} \cdot \frac{x}{52}$$

$$\frac{300}{100} = \frac{4}{5}$$

1440

6-7 • Guided Problem Solving

GPS Student Page 326, Exercise 29

Commission A salesperson receives 5.4% commission. On one sale, she received $6.48. What was the amount of the sale?

Understand the Problem

1. What percent commission does the salesperson receive? _____

2. What cash commission did she receive on one sale? _____

3. What are you asked to find? _____

Make and Carry Out a Plan

4. Use the sentence "$6.48 is 5.4% of the amount of the sale" to write an equation. Let *s* represent the amount of the sale, and write 5.4% as a decimal. _____

5. By what number must you divide each side of the equation to solve for *s*? _____

6. Solve the equation to find the amount of the sale. _____

Check the Answer

7. To check your answer, multiply it by 5.4%. _____
The product should be equal to the amount of commission the salesperson received.

Solve Another Problem

8. Tasha works in a bicycle shop. She receives 3.5% commission on each bicycle she sells. She received a $28 commission on one bicycle. What was the selling price of the bicycle? _____

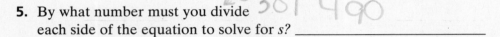

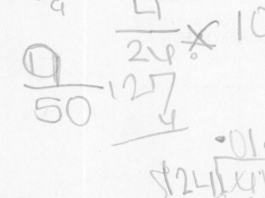

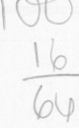

Practice 6-8

formula: amount more/less (handwritten)

original amount × 100 (handwritten)

Percent of Change

Find each percent of change. Round to the nearest tenth of a percent. Tell whether the change is an increase or a decrease.

1. 24 to 21 _____

2. 64 to 80 _25%_____

3. 100 to 113 _____

4. 50 to 41 _18%_____

5. 63 to 105 _____

6. 42 to 168 _80%_____

7. 80 to 24 _70%_____

8. 200 to 158 _21%_____

9. 56 to 71 _____

10. 127 to 84 _____

11. 20 to 24 _20%_____

12. 44 to 22 _50%_____

13. 16 to 12 _38.3%_____

14. 10 to 100 _10%_____

15. 20 to 40 _50%_____

16. 10 to 50 _20%_____

17. 12 to 16 _____

18. 80 to 100 _80%_____

19. 69 to 117 _____

20. 19 to 9 _____

21. 95 to 145 _____

22. 88 to 26 _____

23. Mark weighed 110 pounds last year. He weighs 119 pounds this year. What is the percent of increase in his weight, to the nearest tenth of a percent?

_____

24. Susan had $140 in her savings account last month. She added $20 this month and earned $.50 interest. What is the percent of increase in the amount in her savings account to the nearest tenth of a percent?

_____

25. The population density of California was 151.4 people per square mile in 1980. By 1990 it had increased to 190.8 people per square mile. Find the percent increase to the nearest percent.

_____

6-8 • Guided Problem Solving

GPS Student Page 331, Exercise 32

Economics The average cost of a gallon of gasoline was $1.29 in 1997 and $1.12 in 1998. Find the percent of decrease.

Understand the Problem

1. What was the average cost of a gallon of gasoline in 1997? _____

2. What was the average cost of a gallon of gasoline in 1998? _____

3. What are you asked to find? _____

Make and Carry Out a Plan

4. Write an expression to find the amount of decrease in the average price of a gallon of gasoline from 1997 to 1998. _____

5. What is the amount of decrease? _____

6. Write the formula for percent of change. _____

7. Replace the amount of change with the amount of decrease you found in Step 5. Replace the original amount with the gallon cost for 1997. _____

8. Write the fraction as a decimal. Divide the numerator by the denominator and round to three decimal places. _____

9. Write the decimal as a percent. Multiply by 100 and write a percent sign. _____

10. What is the percent of decrease to the nearest percent? (Round to the nearest tenth.) _____

Check the Answer

11. To check your answer, multiply it by $1.29. _____
    The product should be the same as the difference between $1.29 and $1.12.

Solve Another Problem

12. A store usually sells a particular game for $21.95. The game is now on sale for $18.05. Find the percent of decrease to the nearest percent. _____

Name _____ Class _____ Date _____

Practice 6-9 **Markup and Discount**

Find each sale price. Round to the nearest cent where necessary.

	Regular Price	Percent of Discount	Sale Price
1.	$46	25%	$34.50
2.	$35.45	15%	$30.13
3.	$174	40%	$104.10
4.	$1.40	30%	$.98
5.	$87	50%	$43.5
6.	$675	20%	$540

Find each selling price. Round to the nearest cent where necessary.

	Cost	Percent Markup	Selling Price
7.	$5.50	75%	9.63
8.	$25	50%	37.50
9.	$170	85%	314.50
10.	$159.99	70%	271.98
11.	$12.65	90%	24.04
12.	$739	20%	886.80

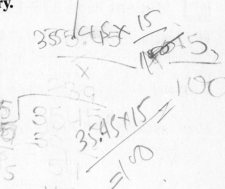
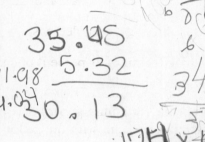

13. A company buys a sweater for $14 and marks it up 90%. It later discounts the sweater 25%.

a. Find the selling price of the sweater after markup.

_____ $26.

b. How much was the discount?

_____ 6.68

c. Find the sale price after the discount.

_____ 19.95

d. The company's profit on the sweater can be found by subtracting the final selling price minus the cost. What was the company's profit on the sweater?

_____ 5.95

e. The profit was what percent of the cost?

_____ 42.5%

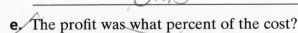
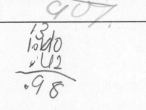
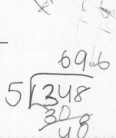

6-9 • Guided Problem Solving

Student Page 335, Exercise 21

Video Sales Store A is selling a video for 20% off the store's regular price of $25.95. Store B is selling the same video for 30% off the store's regular price of $29.50. Which store's sale price is lower? How much lower is it?

Understand the Problem

1. What is the regular price of the video at Store A? _____

2. What is the percent of discount on the video at Store A? _____

3. What is the regular price of the video at Store B? _____

4. What is the percent of discount on the video at Store B? _____

5. What are you asked to find? _____

Make and Carry Out a Plan

6. Write 20% as a decimal. _____

7. Multiply the original price of the video at Store A by the decimal from Step 6 to find the discount. _____

8. Subtract the discount from the original price to find the sale price of the video at Store A. _____

9. Repeat Steps 6–8 to find the sale price of the video at Store B. _____

10. Which store has the lower sale price? Subtract the lower sale price from the higher sale price to find out how much lower it is. _____

Check the Answer

11. To check your answer, find the sale price of each video directly.

    For Store A, find 80% of $25.95. _____

    For Store B, find 70% of $29.50. _____

    Which store has the lower sale price? _____

Solve Another Problem

12. Sherry bought a CD that was on sale for 25% off the regular price of $15.99. Tate bought a CD that was on sale for 30% off the regular price of $16.99. Who paid less for the CD? How much less? _____

Practice 6-10

Make a table to solve each problem.

1. A car was worth $12,500 in 2005. Its value depreciates, or decreases, 15% per year. Find its value in 2009.

Year	2005	2006	2007	2008	2009
Car's Value	$12,500				

2. Marcus spent $105 on 6 items at a sale. Videotapes were on sale for $15 each and music CDs were on sale for $20 each. How many of each item did Marcus buy?

Number of Videotapes	1	2	3	4	5
Number of CDs	5	4	3	2	1
Total Cost					

_____

3. Karina likes to mix either apple, orange, or grape juice with either lemon-lime soft drink or sparkling water to make a fizz. How many different fizzes can she make?

_____

4. How many ways can you have 25 cents in change?

_____

5. The deer population of a state park has increased 8% a year for the last 4 years. If there are 308 deer in the park this year, find how large the population was 4 years ago by completing the table.

Year		1	2	3	4
Deer Population					308

6. How many different sandwiches can you make from 3 types of bread, 2 types of cheese, and 2 types of meat? Assume that only one type of each item is used per sandwich.

_____

7. A bus leaves a station at 8:00 A.M. and averages 30 mi/h. Another bus leaves the same station following the same route two hours after the first and averages 50 mi/h. When will the second bus catch up with the first bus?

_____

6-10 • Guided Problem Solving

Ticket Sales A family went to the movies. Tickets cost $4 for each child and $6 for each adult. The total admission charge for the family was $26. List all the possible numbers of adults and children in the family.

Understand the Problem

1. What was the price of a movie ticket for a child? _____

2. What was the price of a movie ticket for an adult? _____

3. What was the total admission charge for the family? _____

4. What are you asked to find? _____

Make and Carry Out a Plan

5. On a separate piece of paper, make a table to list all of the possible combinations. Begin with one adult and one child. Continue increasing the number of children with one adult until the total admission charge reaches $26 or more. Then increase the number of adults by one and repeat the process. Continue the table until the total admission price for the adults is greater than $26.

Number of Adults $6 Each	Number of Children $4 Each	Total Admission Charge
1	1	$10
1	2	$14

6. Which combinations of adults and children have a total admission charge of $26? _____

Check the Answer

7. To check your answer, multiply $6 by the number of adults and $4 by the number of children in each of the combinations from Step 6 and add the products. What result will tell you that your answers to Step 6 are correct? _____

Solve Another Problem

8. Dane bought new hand towels and bath towels. Hand towels cost $4 each and bath towels cost $6 each. He spent a total of $22. List all the possible numbers of hand towels and bath towels he bought. _____

6A: Graphic Organizer

For use before Lesson 6-1

Study Skill Look at the pages before the first page of the first lesson in this chapter. What do they tell you about the chapter? Reading takes concentration and effort, so as you read these introductory pages, pay attention to what you are reading so that you could, for example, explain the contents to a friend. Take notes on any questions that you have about the chapter, and look back at these questions later to see if you have found the answers.

Write your answers. Use the Table of Contents page for this chapter at the front of the book.

1. What is the title of this chapter? _____

2. Name four topics that you will study in this chapter:

   _____   _____

   _____   _____

3. What is the topic of the Problem Solving lesson? _____

4. Complete the graphic organizer as you work through the chapter.
   1. Write the title of the chapter in the center oval.
   2. When you begin a lesson, write the name of the lesson in a rectangle.
   3. When you complete a lesson, write a skill or key concept from that lesson in the outer oval linked to that rectangle.

   Continue with steps 2 and 3 clockwise around the graphic organizer.

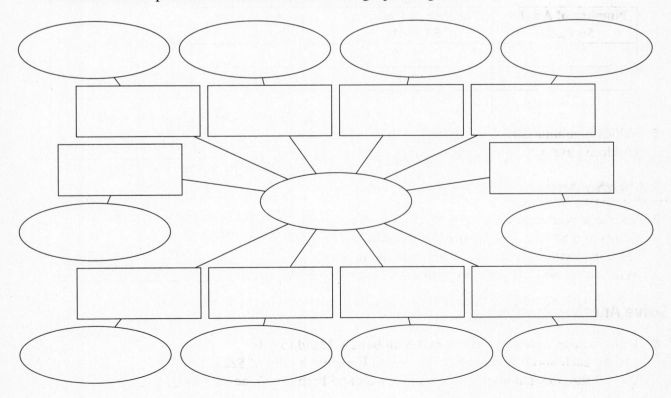

Pre-Algebra **Chapter 6**   **387**

6B: Reading Comprehension

For use after Lesson 6-9

Study Skill As you read or study, take notes that summarize the key points and information. Use these notes to help you review for a test.

Read the steps and notes in the example at the left, and answer the questions at the right.

EXAMPLE Solving With a Proportion

Seven of the twenty-three students in the class voted to have the test on Thursday. What percent of the class voted for Thursday?

Write a proportion.

- $\frac{7}{23} = \frac{c}{100}$

Write the cross products.

- $7 \cdot 100 = 23c$

Simplify.

- $700 = 23c$

Divide each side by 23.

- $\frac{700}{23} = c$

Use a calculator to simplify $700 \div 23$.

- $30.434783 \approx c$

Round to the nearest tenth.

- $30.4 \approx c$

Answer the question asked in the problem.

- Approximately 30.4% percent of the class voted for Thursday.

1. Read the title of the example. What process are you going to use to solve the problem?

   _____

2. What is a proportion?

   _____

3. What does writing the cross products mean?

   _____

   _____

4. Why do you divide both sides by 23?

   _____

   _____

5. What does the symbol $\approx$ stand for?

   _____

6. Why is the $\approx$ used in this problem?

   _____

7. Why does the answer contain the word *approximately?*

   _____

8. **High-Use Academic Words** In the last step and notes in the first column, what does *approximately* mean?
   a. about
   b. exactly

Vocabulary and Study Skills

Name_____ Class_____ Date_____

6C: Reading/Writing Math Symbols

For use after Lesson 6-4

Study Skill Whenever you work on an assignment or a test, read the instructions or direction line two times to make sure you understand what to do. Before you begin to work, think about what the final result will look like and the form it will take.

In mathematics, the order of the numerals and symbols has meaning and is important. Under each pair of math expressions, explain how changing the order changes the meaning.

1. $3 - 2$ $\qquad$ $2 - 3$

_____

2. $(2, -3)$ $\qquad$ $(-3, 2)$

_____

3. 2^3 $\qquad$ 3^2

_____

4. 3 miles per hour $\qquad$ 3 hours per mile

_____

5. $2 \div 3$ $\qquad$ $3 \div 2$

_____

6. $2 < 3$ $\qquad$ $3 < 2$

_____

7. 3 snacks for 6 people $\qquad$ 6 snacks for 3 people

_____

8. $1 : 2$ $\qquad$ $2 : 1$

_____

9. $\angle PQR$ $\qquad$ $\angle PRQ$

_____

6D: Visual Vocabulary Practice
High-Use Academic Words

For use after Lesson 6-5

Study Skill If a word is not in the Glossary, use a dictionary to find its meaning.

Concept List

analyze	common	equivalent
graph	list	order
pattern	property	rule

Write the concept that best describes each exercise. Choose from the concept list above.

1. To multiply a number or variable with the same base, add the exponents.	**2.** $\frac{3}{4}$ and $\frac{9}{12}$	**3.** | | Coin 1 | Coin 2 | | 1 | H | H | | 2 | H | T | | 3 | T | H | | 4 | T | T |
4. $2, 4, 8, 16, \ldots$	**5.** A student gives ab^3 when asked to write $ab \cdot ab \cdot ab$. What is the student's error?	**6.** $-5, \frac{1}{4}, \frac{1}{3}, \frac{1}{2}, 1$
7. The denominators in $\frac{3}{25} + \frac{9}{25} + \frac{1}{25}$	**8.** $-4 \cdot 3 = 3 \cdot -4$	**9.** $-\frac{8}{10}, -0.2, \frac{1}{2},$ and 1 on the number line 

Vocabulary and Study Skills

6E: Vocabulary Check

For use after Lesson 6-10

Study Skill Strengthen your vocabulary. Use these pages and add cues and summaries by applying the Cornell Notetaking style.

Write the definition for each word. To check your work, fold the paper back along the dotted line to see the correct answers.

_____

_____

_____   Rate

_____

_____   Unit rate

_____

_____   Commission

_____

_____   Markup

_____

_____   Discount

_____

6E: Vocabulary Check (continued)

Write the vocabulary word for each definition. To check your work, fold the paper forward along the dotted line to see the correct answers.

A ratio that compares quantities measured in different units.

_____

A rate that has a denominator of 1.

_____

Pay that is equal to a percent of sales.

_____

The amount of increase in price.

_____

The amount by which a price is decreased.

_____

6F: Vocabulary Review Puzzle

For use with Chapter Review

Study Skill You may have noticed that math tests often contain word problems for you to solve. In order to read and understand the problems, so that you can solve them, you must know the meanings of the words used to state the problems. The next time you study for a math test, be sure to begin by studying the vocabulary involved.

Write the words that are described below. Complete the word search puzzle by finding the words. For help, use the Chapter Review in your textbook. Remember that a word may go right to left, left to right, or it may go up as well as down.

1. an equality of two ratios _____

2. the possible result of an action _____

3. the amount of price decrease _____

4. the opposite of an event _____

5. ratio comparing a number to 100 _____

6. any outcome or group of outcomes _____

7. ratio comparing quantities in different units _____

8. amount you are paid based on amount you sell _____

9. ratio comparing favorable and unfavorable outcomes _____

10. comparison of two quantities by division _____

11. amount of increase over cost _____

```
E  D  I  S  C  O  U  N  T  M  O  P  E
M  M  O  E  N  R  T  R  A  M  D  T  R
S  S  R  O  A  N  E  P  M  T  D  N  I
E  C  A  D  R  A  T  E  O  O  S  E  O
C  I  T  T  P  E  R  C  E  N  T  M  U
E  C  I  P  N  O  I  A  E  U  N  E  M
P  P  O  S  O  E  A  T  T  N  T  L  N
E  P  R  O  P  O  R  T  I  O  N  P  E
C  M  S  T  R  N  M  C  P  A  E  M  C
O  T  O  U  T  C  O  M  E  R  V  O  O
C  O  M  M  I  S  S  I  O  N  E  C  E
C  N  O  V  M  A  R  K  U  P  N  C  O
R  N  T  T  U  E  U  U  C  P  P  K  T
```

$$\frac{27}{4} \times \frac{1}{2} =$$

$$\frac{27}{8} \times \frac{7}{4}$$

$$\frac{189}{32}$$

$$\frac{189}{189}$$

$$\frac{27}{4} \cdot \frac{6}{8} = \frac{27}{1}$$

$$\frac{3}{2} + \frac{7}{4} x = 6 \quad \frac{3}{4} \quad 21$$

$$x = 12$$

$$\frac{3}{4} \quad 21\frac{17}{4} = 21\frac{13}{4} = 24\frac{1}{4}$$

Practice 7-1

Solving Two-Step Equations

Solve each equation.

1. $4x - 17 = 31$ _____ x=12 _____ **2.** $15 = 2m + 3$ _____ m=6 _____

3. $\frac{k}{3} + 3 = 8$ _____ K=15 _____ **4.** $7 = 3 + \frac{h}{6}$ _____ h=24 _____

5. $9n + 18 = 81$ _____ n=7 _____ **6.** $5 = \frac{y}{3} - 9$ _____ y=42 _____

7. $14 = 5k - 31$ _____ K=9 _____ **8.** $\frac{t}{9} - 7 = -5$ _____ t=18 _____

9. $\frac{v}{8} - 9 = -13$ _____ v=-32 _____ **10.** $25 - 13f = -14$ _____ 3 _____

Solve each equation using mental math.

11. $3p + 5 = 14$ _____ p=3 _____ **12.** $\frac{k}{2} - 5 = 1$ _____ K=12 _____

13. $\frac{m}{7} - 3 = 0$ _____ m=21 _____ **14.** $10v - 6 = 24$ _____ v=3 _____

15. $8 + \frac{x}{2} = -7$ _____ x=-30 _____ **16.** $7 = 6r - 17$ _____ r=4 _____

Choose the correct equation. Solve.

17. Tehira has read 110 pages of a 290-page book. She reads 20 pages each
day. How many days will it take to finish?

    A. $20 + 110p = 290$ **B.** $20p + 290 = 110$

    C. $110 + 20p = 290$ **D.** $290 = 110 - 20p$

_____ C _____

Write an equation to describe the situation. Solve.

18. A waitress earned $73 for 6 hours of work. The total included $46 in tips.
What was her hourly wage?

    73 + 46 ÷ 60   6h + 46 = 73

    $4.50

19. You used $6\frac{3}{4}$ c of sugar while baking muffins and nutbread for a class
party. You used a total of $1\frac{1}{2}$ c of sugar for the muffins. Your nutbread
recipe calls for $1\frac{3}{4}$ c of sugar per loaf. How many loaves of nutbread did
you make?

    3 loafs

Name_____ Class_____ Date_____

7-1 • Guided Problem Solving

Carmela wants to buy a digital camera for $249. She has $24 and
is saving $15 each week. Solve the equation $15w + 24 = 249$
to find how many weeks w it will take Carmela to save enough to
buy the digital camera.

Understand the Problem

1. What does the variable w represent? _____

2. What are you asked to find? _____

Make and Carry Out a Plan

3. To solve the equation $15w + 24 = 249$, you
   must undo the addition operation first. What value
   should you subtract from each side of the equation? _____

4. Subtract the answer from Step 3 from both sides
   of the equation. What expression are you left with? _____

5. By what value must you divide each
   side of the equation to find the value of w? _____

6. Divide both sides of the equation by your answer
   to Step 5 and simplify. How many weeks will Carmela
   have to save to have enough money to buy the camera? _____

Check the Answer

7. Replace w in the original equation with your
   result from Step 6. Do you get a true statement? _____

Solve Another Problem

8. Kirk has $240 in his savings account. He
   deposits $20 in his account every week,
   working toward the goal of saving $500. Solve
   the equation $20w + 240 = 500$ to find how
   many weeks he will need to save to reach his goal. _____

Name _____ Class _____ Date _____

Practice 7-2

Solving Multi-Step Equations

· ·

Solve and check each equation.

1. $\frac{p}{3} - 7 = -2$

$p = 15$

2. $2(n - 7) + 3 = 9$

$n = 10$

3. $0 = 5(k + 9)$

$k = 9$

4. $4h + 7h - 16 = 6$

$h = 2$

$-11h - 16 = 6$

5. $3(2n - 7) = 9$

$n = 5$

6. $-27 = 8x - 5x$

$x = -9$

7. $4p + 5 - 7p = -1$

$p = -2$

8. $7 - y + 5y = 9$

$y = -\frac{1}{2}$

$7 + 4y = 9$

$4y = -2$

9. $8e + 3(5 - e) = 10$

$e = -1$

10. $-37 = 3x + 11 - 7x$

$x = 12$

$-4x + 14 = -\frac{1}{2}$

11. $9 - 3(n - 5) = 30$

$n = -2$

12. $\frac{1}{6}(y + 42) - 15 = -3$

Write and solve an equation for each situation.

13. Find three consecutive integers whose sum is 51. $x + x + 1 + x + 2$

$16 + 17 + 18$

$\frac{1}{6}x + 42$

14. Find three consecutive integers whose sum is -15.

$-6, -5, -4$

15. Find four consecutive integers whose sum is 30.

$6 + 7 + 8 + 9$

16. Jack's overtime wage is $3 per hour more than his regular hourly wage. He worked for 5 hours at his regular wage and 4 hours at the overtime wage. He earned $66. Find his regular wage.

$15.

$x + (x + 1) + (x + 2) = -15$

$3x + 3 = -15$

$3x = -18$ $x = -6$

$\frac{1}{6}y + 1 - 15 = -3$

$\frac{1}{6}y - 8 = -3$

$\frac{1}{6}y + 8$

$\frac{1}{6}y = 5$

$y = 30$

· ·

7-2 • Guided Problem Solving

GPS Student Page 359, Exercise 7

Collections Bill and Jasmine together have 94 glass marbles.
Bill has 4 more than twice as many marbles as Jasmine. If Jasmine
has m marbles, then Bill has $2m + 4$ marbles. Solve the equation
$m + 2m + 4 = 94$. Find how many glass marbles each has.

Understand the Problem

1. What does the variable m represent? _____

2. What are you asked to find? _____

Make and Carry Out a Plan

3. To solve the equation $m + 2m + 4 = 94$,
   you must combine like terms first.
   What are the like terms in the equation? _____

4. Combine the like terms. What expression are you left with? _____

5. Undo the addition operation by subtracting from both
   sides of the equation. What expression are you left with? _____

6. Divide both sides of the equation by the same
   number and simplify. Solve the equation for m. _____

7. How many marbles does Jasmine have? _____

8. How many marbles does Bill have? _____

Check the Answer

9. Check to see whether your answer is reasonable.
   Add the number of marbles Bill has and the number
   of marbles Jasmine has. Is your answer reasonable? _____

Solve Another Problem

10. Tanya and her brother, Jake, collect rare stamps.
    Together, they have 43 stamps. Tanya calculated she
    has 1 fewer than 3 times as many stamps as Jake.
    If Jake has m stamps, then Tanya has $(3m - 1)$ stamps.
    Solve the equation $m + (3m + 1) = 43$. How many
    rare stamps does Tanya have? How many does Jake have? _____

Guided Problem Solving

Name _____ Class _____ Date _____

Practice 7-3

Multi-Step Equations With Fractions and Decimals

Solve and check each equation.

1. $0.7n - 1.5 + 7.3n = 14.5$

2. $18p - 45 = 0$

3. $16.3k + 19.2 + 7.5k = -64.1$

4. $h + 3h + 4h = 100$

5. $40 - 5n = -2$

6. $14 = \frac{2}{3}(9y - 15)$

7. $\frac{2}{3}y - 6 = 2$

8. $1.2m + 7.5m + 2.1 = 63$

9. $\frac{7}{8}h - \frac{5}{8} = 2$

10. $93.96 = 4.7p + 8.7p - 2.6p$

11. $9w - 16.3 = 5.3$

12. $88.1 - 2.3f = 72.46$

13. $-15.3 = -7.5k + 55.2$

14. $26e + 891 = -71$

15. $2.3(x + 1.4) = -9.66$

16. $(x - 17.7) + 19.6 = 27.8$

Write an equation to describe each situation. Solve.

17. Jolene bought three blouses at one price and 2 blouses priced $3 below the others. The total cost was $91.50. Find the prices of the blouses.

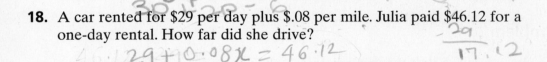

18. A car rented for $29 per day plus $.08 per mile. Julia paid $46.12 for a one-day rental. How far did she drive?

_____

By what number would you multiply each equation to clear denominators or decimals? Do not solve.

19. $\frac{1}{3}z + \frac{1}{6} = 5\frac{1}{6}$

20. $3.7 + 2.75k = 27.35$

7-3 • Guided Problem Solving

GPS **Student Page 364, Exercise 34**

Sales A pair of athletic shoes is on sale for $\frac{1}{4}$ off the original cost. The sale price is $49.95. Solve the equation $c - \frac{1}{4}c = 49.95$ to find the original cost c of the shoes.

Understand the Problem

1. What does the variable c represent? _____

2. What does $\frac{1}{4}c$ represent? _____

Make and Carry Out a Plan

3. First, combine like terms and write the new expression. _____

4. How can you use a reciprocal to solve the equation? _____

_____

5. What is the reciprocal of $\frac{3}{4}$? _____

6. Multiply both sides of the equation by your answer to step 5 to solve the equation for c. _____

7. What was the original cost of the shoes? _____

Check the Answer

8. Why is the equation $c - \frac{1}{4}c = 49.95$ used to find the original cost of the shoes? _____

_____

Solve Another Problem

9. A framed picture is on sale for $\frac{1}{5}$ off the original cost. The sale price of the picture is $63.60. Use the equation $c - \frac{1}{5}c = 63.60$ to find the original cost c of the picture. _____

Practice 7-4

Write an equation. Then solve.

1. Bill purchased 4 pens for $3.32, including $.16 sales tax. Find the cost of 1 pen.

   $4p + .16 = 3.32$

   $.79

2. Arnold had $1.70 in dimes and quarters. He had 3 more dimes than quarters. How many of each coin did he have?

   $x + 3x = 1.70$ 1.70 3 7 dime

   $7d + x = 1.70$ 4 $x = 1.70$ 4 quarters
   quarters

3. A baby weighed 3.2 kg at birth. She gained 0.17 kg per week. How old was she when she weighed 5.75 kg?

   $3.2 + .17w = 5.75$

   15 weeks

4. In the parking lot at a truck stop there were 6 more cars than 18-wheel trucks. There were 134 wheels in the parking lot. How many cars and trucks were there?

   $c + t = 13$ $c + t = 134$

   $7x = 134 = x$ $t + 6 + t = 134$

   $2t = 128$

5. The product of 6 and 3 more than k is 48.

   $6 \cdot 3 > k \cdot 6$ $k = 5$ $t = 64$

   $6(3 + k) = 48$ $t + 6 = 70$

6. A bottle and a cap together cost $1.10. The bottle costs $1 more than the cap. How much does each cost?

   $b + c = 1.10$ $c + b = 1.1$

   $1 + 1 + b = 1.6$ $b = 1.00$

   $b = 1.05$ $b = 1$ $.10$ $c + (c + 1) = 1.1$

   $c = 1.05$ $c = .10$ $2c + 1 = 1.1$

                              $-1 \quad -1.0$

7. The perimeter of a rectangular garden is 40 ft. The width is 2 ft more than one half the length. Find the length and width.

   $\left(\frac{L}{2} + 2\right) + L + \left(\frac{L}{2} + 2\right) + L = 40$ $2c = .1$

   $2L + \frac{3}{2} + L = 40$ $L = 12$ $c = .05$

                              $w = 8$

7-4 • Guided Problem Solving

GPS **Student Page 368, Exercise 5**

Lamar's summer job is mowing lawns for a landscaper. His pay is $7.50/h. Lamar also makes $11.25/h for any time over 40 h that he works in one week. He worked 40 h last week plus n overtime hours and made $339.38. How many overtime hours did he work?

Understand the Problem

1. What is Lamar's hourly pay? _____

2. What is Lamar's hourly pay for working overtime hours? _____

3. What does the variable n represent? _____

4. How much money did Lamar make last week? _____

5. What are you asked to find? _____

Make and Carry Out a Plan

6. Use the sentence "$7.50/h multiplied by 40 hours plus $11.25/h multiplied by n hours equals $339.38" to write an equation to represent the situation. _____

7. Simplify by multiplying. _____

8. What number must you subtract from each side of the equation? _____

9. By which number must you then divide each side of the equation? _____

10. Solve for n. _____

11. How many overtime hours did Lamar work last week? _____

Check the Answer

12. To check your answer, multiply your answer by 11.25 and multiply 7.5 by 40. Add the products. _____ The sum should be the amount of money Lamar made last week.

Solve Another Problem

13. Jonna works in the summer as a lifeguard. She earned $435 last week for working 40 hours plus 5 overtime hours. If she earns $15/h for overtime, what is her normal hourly pay? _____

Practice 7-5

Solving Equations With Variables on Both Sides

Solve each equation.

1. $3k + 16 = 5k$ $16 = 2k$

  $k = 8$
_____

2. $5e = 3e + 36$ $2e = 36$

  $c = 18$
_____

3. $n + 4n - 22 = 7n$

  $n = 11$
_____

4. $2(x - 7) = 3x$ $2x - 7 = 3x$

  $x = 7 - 14$ $7 = 1x$
_____

5. $8h - 10h = 3h + 25$

  $h = -5$
_____

6. $7n + 6n - 5 = 4n + 4$

  $13n - 5 = 4n + 4$

  $13n - 1 = 4n$
_____

7. $11(p - 3) = 5(p + 3)$

  $p = 8$
_____

8. $9(m + 2) = -6(m + 7)$

  $m = 8 - 4$ $9m + 18 =$

  $-6m + 42$
_____

9. $y + 2(y - 5) = 2y + 2$

_____

10. $-9x + 7 = 3x + 19$

  $x = -2 - 1$
_____

11. $k + 9 = 6(k - 11)$

  15
_____

12. $-6(4 - t) = 12t$ $3m = 24$

  -4
_____

13. $2(x + 7) = 5(x - 7)$

  $16\frac{1}{3}$
_____

14. $5m + 9 = 3(m - 5) + 7$

  $-\frac{1}{2}$
_____

15. $5x + 7 = 6x$

  $x = 7$
_____

16. $k + 12 = 3k$

  $k = -6$
_____

17. $8m = 5m + 12$ $3m = 12$

  $m = 4$
_____

18. $3p - 9 = 4p$

  $p = -9$
_____

  $-6x + 7 =$

Write an equation for each situation. Solve.

19. The difference when 7 less than a number is subtracted from twice the number is 12. What is the number?

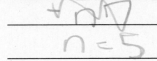 19
_____

  $n = 5$ $-24 - 6L = 12$
_____

20. Four less than three times a number is three more than two times the number. What is the number?

  7
_____

_____

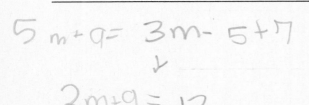

$5m + 9 = 3m - 5 + 7$

  $\downarrow$

$2m + 9 = 12$

7-5 • Guided Problem Solving

GPS Student Page 374, Exercise 28

Cell Phones A cellular phone company charges a $27.95 monthly fee and $.12/min for local calls. Another company charges $12.95 a month and $.32/min for local calls. For what number of minutes of local calls are the costs of the plans the same?

Understand the Problem

1. What information are you given? _____

   _____

2. What are you asked to find? _____

Make and Carry Out a Plan

3. Write an expression using the variable m to represent the cost of the plan with the first phone company for m minutes of local calls. _____

4. Write an expression using the variable m to represent the cost of the plan with the second phone company for m minutes of local calls. _____

5. Set the expressions from Steps 3 and 4 equal to each other and solve the resulting equation for m. _____

6. For what number of minutes of local calls are the costs of the plans the same? _____

Check the Answer

7. Why are the expressions set equal in order to find the number of local minutes for which the costs of the plans are the same? _____

   _____

Solve Another Problem

8. A DVD club charges a $15 membership fee and $3 for each DVD you rent. Another DVD club charges a $10 membership fee and $4 for each DVD rental. For what number of DVD rentals is the cost of both clubs the same? _____

Practice 7-6

Solving Two-Step Inequalities

• •

Solve each inequality. Graph the solutions on a number line.

1. $5x + 2 \le 17$ _____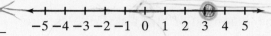

2. $7x + 2x \ge 21 - 3$ _____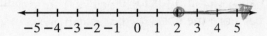

3. $9 - x \ge 10$ _____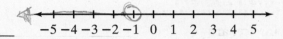

4. $19 + 8 \le 6 + 7x$ _____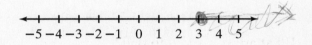

5. $-6x < 12$ _____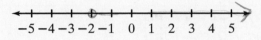

6. $\frac{x}{-4} > 0$ _____ $x < 0$ _____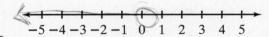

Solve each inequality.

7. $2x - 5 > 1$ ____ $x > -3$ ____

8. $9x - 7 \le 38$ ____ $x \le 5$ ____

9. $3 < \frac{1}{2}x + 1$ ____ $x > 4$ ____

10. $-12 < -12x$ ____ $x > 1$ ____

11. $-8x + 18 > -22$ ____ $x < 5$ ____

12. $50 < 8 - 6x$ ____ $x < -7$ ____

13. $\frac{1}{5}x + 6 > -3$ ____ $x > -45$ ____

14. $30 \ge -6(5 - x)$ ____ $x \ge 0$ ____

Write an inequality for each situation. Then solve the inequality.

15. Nine more than half the number n is no more than -8. Find n.

_____ $n \le 34$ _____

_____

16. Judith drove h hours at a rate of 55 mi/h. She did not reach her goal of driving 385 miles for the day. How long did she drive?

_____ $h < 7$ _____

_____

• •

7-6 • Guided Problem Solving

GPS **Student Page 379, Exercise 24**

You want to spend at most $10 for a taxi ride. Before you go anywhere, the taxi driver sets the meter at the initial charge of $2. The meter then adds $1.25 for every mile driven. If you plan on a $1 tip, what is the farthest you can go?

Understand the Problem

1. What are you asked to find? _____

2. What information is given to help you find what the cost of the taxi ride will be? _____

_____

Make and Carry Out a Plan

3. Write an expression for the cost of the taxi ride using the variable *m* for the number of miles. _____

4. Use the expression to write an inequality showing that the cost of the taxi ride is less than or equal to $10. _____

5. Solve the inequality for *m*. _____

6. How many miles can you go for at most $10? _____

Check the Answer

7. Why is the expression for the cost of the taxi ride set less than or equal to 10? _____

_____

8. To test your answer, find the cost of a taxi ride that is 5.7 miles. What does the result tell you? _____

_____

Solve Another Problem

9. You have $15 to spend on a pizza. A 16-inch pizza costs $7 plus $2 per topping. What is the greatest number of toppings you can afford to get on a 16-inch pizza? _____

Practice 7-7

Use this information to answer Exercises 1–4: Shopping City has a 6% sales tax.

1. Solve the formula $c = 1.06p$ for p, where c is the cost of an item at Shopping City, including tax, and p is the selling price.

   _____

2. Clara spent $37.10 on a pair of pants at Shopping City. What was the selling price of the pants?

   _____

3. Manuel spent $10.59 on a basketball at Shopping City. What was the selling price of the ball?

   _____

4. Clara and Manuel's parents spent $165.84 on groceries at Shopping City. How much of that amount was sales tax?

   _____

Transform the formulas.

5. The area of a triangle A can be found with the formula $A = \frac{1}{2}bh$ where b is the length of the base of the triangle and h is the height of the triangle. Solve the formula for h.

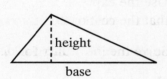

   _____

6. Solve the formula $A = \frac{1}{2}bh$ for b.

   _____

Find the missing part of each triangle.

7. $A = 27$ cm^2

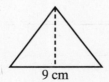

8. $A = 18$ ft^2

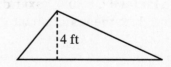

   $h =$ _____ $b =$ _____

Solve for the variable indicated.

9. $V = \frac{1}{3}lwh$, for w

10. $\frac{1}{a} + \frac{1}{b} = \frac{1}{c}$, for c

   _____   _____

7-7 • Guided Problem Solving

GPS **Student Page 384, Exercise 14**

a. **Construction** Bricklayers use the formula $N = 7LH$ to estimate the number N of bricks needed in a wall. L is the length of the wall and H is the height. Solve the formula for H.

b. If 1,134 bricks are used to build a wall that is 18 ft long, how high is the wall?

Understand the Problem

1. What does each variable stand for? _____

2. What are you asked to do in part (a)? _____

3. What are you asked to find in part (b)? _____

Make and Carry Out a Plan

4. To solve for H, by what quantity must you divide each side of $N = 7LH$? _____

5. What is the formula for H? _____

6. Replace N with 1,134 and L with 18. Simplify to find H. _____

7. What is the height of the wall? _____

Check the Answer

8. Why did part (a) ask you to solve the formula for H? _____

_____

9. Use the formula $N = 7LH$ to test your answer. Replace N with 1,134, L with 18, and H with 9, and then simplify. Is the resulting statement true? _____

_____

Solve Another Problem

10. The number of feet of fencing needed to enclose a square-shaped backyard is found by the formula $4s = P$, where s is the length of a side and P is the perimeter. Solve the formula for s. What is the length of a side of the backyard if its area is 272 square feet? _____

Practice 7-8

Simple and Compound Interest

Find each balance.

	Principal	Interest Rate	Compounded	Time (years)	Balance
1.	$400	7%	annually	3	
2.	$8,000	5%	annually	9	
3.	$1,200	4%	semi-annually	2	
4.	$50,000	6%	semi-annually	6	

Find the simple interest.

5. $900 deposited at an interest rate of 3% for 5 years

_____

6. $1,348 deposited at an interest rate of 2.5% for 18 months

_____

Complete each table. Compound the interest annually.

7. $5,000 at 6% for 4 years.

Principal at Beginning of Year	Interest	Balance
Year 1: $5,000		
Year 2:		
Year 3:		
Year 4:		

8. $7,200 at 3% for 4 years

Principal at Beginning of Year	Interest	Balance
Year 1: $7,200		
Year 2:		
Year 3:		
Year 4:		

7-8 • Guided Problem Solving

GPS **Student Page 389, Exercise 9**

Savings You deposit $600 in a savings account for 3 years.
The account pays 8% annual interest compounded quarterly.
a. What is the quarterly interest rate?
b. What is the number of payment periods?
c. Find the balance in the account.

Understand the Problem

1. How much is deposited in the savings account? _____

2. How long is the money in the savings account? _____

3. What interest does the account pay? _____

4. What are you asked to find in part (a)? _____

5. What are you asked to find in part (b)? _____

6. What are you asked to find in part (c)? _____

Make and Carry Out a Plan

7. Divide the annual interest rate by the number of
   interest periods in one year to find the quarterly interest rate. _____

8. Multiply the number of payment periods in one
   year by 3 to find the total number of payment periods. _____

9. Use the compound interest formula $B = p(1 + r)^n$.
   Replace p with 600, r with the quarterly interest
   rate, and n with the total number of payment periods. _____

10. Solve the equation for B. Round your answer to the nearest hundredth. _____

11. What is the balance in the account after 3 years? _____

Check the Answer

12. To check your answer, replace B with your answer
    in the compound interest formula and solve for p. _____
    p should be equal to the original amount deposited in the account.

Solve Another Problem

13. You deposit $500 in a savings account for 5 years. The account pays 6% annual interest
    compounded semiannually.
    a. What is the semiannual interest rate? _____
    b. What is the number of payment periods? _____
    c. Find the balance in the account. _____

7A: Graphic Organizer

For use before Lesson 7-1

Study Skill Compare the title of this chapter to the titles of the chapters before this one. Ask yourself how the contents of this chapter might connect to the contents of previous chapters. What did you learn before that you may need as you learn the topics in this chapter?

Write your answers. Use the Table of Contents page for this chapter at the front of the book.

1. What is the title of this chapter? _____

2. Name four topics that you will study in this chapter:

   _____   _____

   _____   _____

3. What is the topic of the Problem Solving lesson? _____

4. Complete the graphic organizer as you work through the chapter.
   1. Write the title of the chapter in the center oval.
   2. When you begin a lesson, write the name of the lesson in a rectangle.
   3. When you complete that lesson, write a skill or key concept from that lesson in the outer oval linked to that rectangle.
   Continue with steps 2 and 3 clockwise around the graphic organizer.

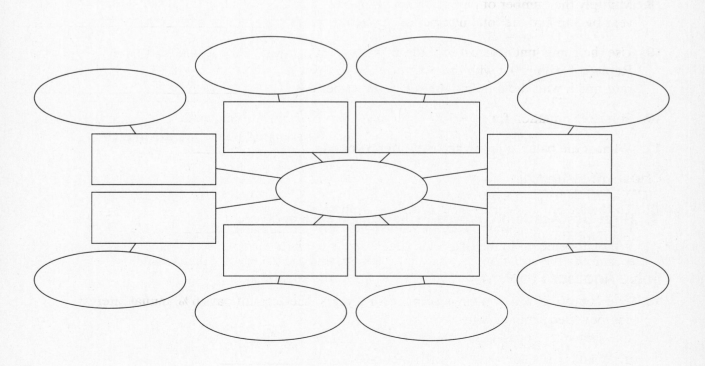

7B: Reading Comprehension

Study Skill Sometimes you can better remember what you read by forming a "picture" in your mind of what the words say. Make mental pictures of the content, like a "mind movie," to help you recall the material later.

Read the directions for the exercise below.

Solve $-2(3x - 1) + x = 27$ and check.

Read the steps in the solution below, and answer the questions at the right.

$$-2(3x - 1) + x = 27$$
$$-6x + 2 + x = 27$$
$$-6x + x + 2 = 27$$
$$-5x + 2 = 27$$
$$-5x + 2 - 2 = 27 - 2$$
$$-5x + 0 = 25$$
$$-5x = 25$$
$$x = \frac{25}{-5}$$
$$x = -5$$

Check:

$$-2(3x - 1) + x = 27$$
$$-2[3(-5) - 1] + (-5) \stackrel{?}{=} 27$$
$$-2[-16] + (-5) \stackrel{?}{=} 27$$
$$32 - 5 \stackrel{?}{=} 27$$
$$27 = 27 \text{yZ}$$

1. What is the variable in the equation?

   _____

2. When you have solved the equation, what should your result look like?

   _____

3. What are you to do after you solve the equation?

   _____

4. Refer to the solution steps. What property do you use in the first step?

   _____

5. What property simplifies $-5x + 0$ to $-5x$?

   _____

6. What operation do you use to undo multiplication by -5?

   _____

7. **High-Use Academic Words** In the exercise, what does *solve* mean for you to do?

   a. simplify the equation

   b. find the values of x that satisfy the equation

7C: Reading/Writing Math Symbols

For use after Lesson 7-6

Study Skill As you study, have a dictionary close by so that you can look up the meaning of any words or symbols that you find confusing. When you look something up, be sure to add it to your personal written vocabulary list.

Write the meaning of each symbol on the line provided.

1. $\approx$ _____

2. % _____

3. $\triangle$ used in an expression such as $\triangle ABC$ _____

4. P used in an expression such as P(odd number) or P(heads)

   _____

5. $\neq$ _____

6. $\stackrel{?}{=}$ _____

7. $\sim$ _____

8. : used in an expression such as 1 ft : 10 yd _____

9. $<$ _____

10. $\circ\!\!\longrightarrow$ used as a graph on a number line _____

11. $\geq$ _____

12. | | used in an expression such as $|z|$ _____

13. / used in a spreadsheet or calculator _____

14. $\cdot$ used in an expression such as $a \cdot b$ _____

15. $^{-}$ used in an expression such as $0.\overline{3}$ _____

7D: Visual Vocabulary Practice

For use after Lesson 7-7

Study Skill One way to check if you understand something is to try to explain it to someone else.

Concept List

area formula	compound inequality	consecutive integers
inequality	least common multiple	perimeter formula
proportion	two-step inequality	variable

Write the concept that best describes each exercise. Choose from the concept list above.

1. 181, 182, 183	**2.** $a \leq -2$ and $a > -8$	**3.** $A = lw$
_____	_____	_____
4. $P = 2l + 2w$	**5.** $3x + 4 \geq -2$	**6.** $\dfrac{a}{b} = \dfrac{c}{d}$
_____	_____	_____
7. a in $3a - 4 = 5$	**8.** 20 for the numbers 5 and 4	**9.** $5c \geq 2b + 9$
_____	_____	_____

Vocabulary and Study Skills

7E: Vocabulary Check

Study Skill Strengthen your vocabulary. Use these pages and add cues and summaries by applying the Cornell Notetaking style.

Write the definition for each word at the right. To check your work, fold the paper back along the dotted line to see the correct answers.

_____

_____

_____ Principal

_____

_____ Interest

_____

_____

_____ Interest Rate

_____

_____

_____ Simple Interest

_____

_____

_____ Compound Interest

_____

_____

7E: Vocabulary Check (continued)

Write the vocabulary word for each definition. To check your work, fold the paper forward along the dotted line to see the correct answers.

The initial amount of an investment or loan.

_____

An amount paid for the use of money.

_____

The percentage of the balance that an account or investment earns in a fixed period of time.

_____

Interest paid only on the principal.

_____

Interest paid on both the principal and the interest earned in previous interest periods.

_____

7F: Vocabulary Review

• •

Study Skill Often when you learn about a new topic in mathematics, you also learn several new words. To understand the new vocabulary, take the time to review some of the vocabulary terms from previous topics, and see how they relate to the new words. In general, you will keep adding to your active math vocabulary and reusing the terms you learned before.

Many mathematical ideas are opposites, inverses, or contrasts. For each pair, write a brief explanation of how to tell the difference between the two mathematical ideas in the pair. For help, use the Glossary in your textbook.

1. simple interest/compound interest

_____

_____

_____

2. principal /interest

_____

_____

_____

3. consecutive even integers/consecutive odd integers

_____

_____

_____

_____

4. equation/expression

_____

_____

_____

5. interest/interest rate

_____

_____

6. ratio/proportion

_____

_____

_____

Vocabulary and Study Skills

Vocabulary and Study Skills

Practice 8-1

Relations and Functions

Graph each relation. Is the relation a function? Explain.

1.

x	y
−1	4
2	3
4	−1
−1	−2

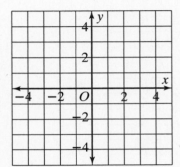

_____

_____

_____

2.

x	y
2	−4
−4	0
−2	3
3	−1

_____

_____

_____

For each relation, list the members of the domain. List the members of the range. Is the relation a function? Explain.

3. $\{(7, -2), (8, -2), (-5, 7), (-9, 1)\}$

Domain: _____   Range: _____

Function? _____

4. $\{(-8, 0), (10, 6), (10, -2), (-5, 7)\}$

Domain: _____   Range: _____

Function? _____

5. $\{(9.2, 4.7), (-3.6, 4.8), (5.2, 4.7)\}$

Domain: _____   Range: _____

Function? _____

6. Is the time is takes you to run a 100-meter race a function of the speed you run? Explain.

_____

8-1 • Guided Problem Solving

GPS **Student Page 407, Exercise 19**

Graph the relation shown at right. Is the relation a function? Explain.

x	y
–5	6
–2	3
3	3
4	6

Understand the Problem

1. List the ordered pairs in the relation. _____

2. What are you asked to do? _____

Make and Carry Out a Plan

3. Graph the ordered pairs in the
relation in the coordinate plane.

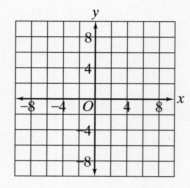

4. What test can you use to decide whether the relation is a function? _____

5. Hold a pencil parallel to the y-axis and move it across the
graph from left to right. Does the line of the pencil ever pass
through more than one point of the graph? What does this tell you? _____

_____

6. Is the relation a function? Explain. _____

_____

Check the Answer

7. To check your answer, list the domain values and the range values in
order. Draw arrows from the domain values to their range values. Is
each member of the domain paired with exactly one member of the range? _____

What does this tell you? _____

Solve Another Problem

8. Graph the relation
{(1, –4), (2, 5), (4, –1), (5, 3)}.
Is the relation a function? Explain. _____

Practice 8-2

Write each equation as a function in "y = ..." form.

1. $3y = 15x - 12$

$y = \underline{5x - 12}$ (written: 3, 2)

2. $5x + 10 = 10y$

$y = \underline{\frac{1}{2}x + 1}$

3. $3y - 21 = 12x$

$y = \underline{4x + 7}$

4. $5y + 3 = 2y - 3x + 5$

$y = \underline{-1x + \frac{2}{3}}$

5. $-2(x + 3y) = 18$

$y = \underline{-\frac{1}{3}x = -3}$

6. $5(x + y) = 20 + 3x$

$y = \underline{-\frac{2}{5}x + 4}$

$5x + y = 20 + 3x$

Graph each equation.

7. $y = -0.5x + 4$

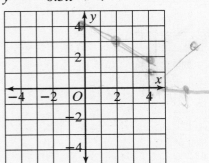

8. $y = 4$

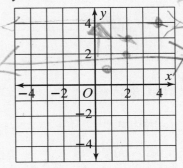

9. $2x - 3y = 6$

$y = \underline{\frac{2}{3}x - 2}$

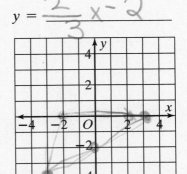

10. $-10x = 5y$

$y = \underline{-2x}$

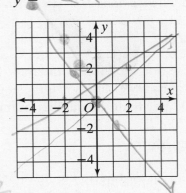

Is each ordered pair a solution of $3x - 2y = 12$? Write *yes* or *no*.

11. $(0, 4)$ ___no___

12. $(6, 3)$ ___yes___

13. $(4, 0)$ ___yes___

Is each ordered pair a solution of $-2x + 5y = 10$? Write *yes* or *no*.

14. $(-3, 2)$ ___no___

15. $(-10, -2)$ ___no___

16. $(5, 4)$ ___yes___

8-2 • Guided Problem Solving

GPS **Student Page 412, Exercise 36**

José is driving on a highway. The equation $d = 55t$ relates the number of miles d and the amount of time in hours t. About how many hours does José spend driving 100 mi?

Understand the Problem

1. What does the variable d represent? _____

2. What does the variable t represent? _____

3. What equation relates d and t? _____

4. What are you asked to find? _____

_____

Make and Carry Out a Plan

5. Replace d in the equation with 100. _____

6. By what number must you divide
   each side of the equation to solve for t? _____

7. Solve the equation for t. _____

8. About how many hours does José spend driving 100 mi? _____

Check the Answer

9. To check your answer, replace t in the
   equation with your answer and solve the equation for d. _____
   The result should be about the number of miles José will drive.

Solve Another Problem

10. The equation $c = \$6.50t$ relates the number of
    tickets t purchased for a baseball game and the total
    cost c of the tickets. What is the total cost of 15 tickets? _____

Name _____ Class _____ Date _____

Practice 8-3

Slope and *y*-intercept

Find the slope of the line through each pair of points.

1. $A(1, 1), B(6, 3)$ $\dfrac{3-1}{6-1} = \dfrac{2}{5}$

$\dfrac{2}{5}$

2. $J(-4, 6), K(-4, 2)$ $\dfrac{6-2}{-4+4}$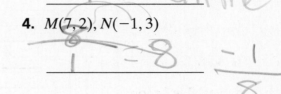

4 undtfine $\dfrac{4}{0}$

3. $P(3, -7), Q(-1, -7)$ $\dfrac{3+(-1)}{-7\cdot(-7)}$

0   4

4. $M(7, 2), N(-1, 3)$ $\dfrac{-1}{8}$

Complete the table.

Equation	Equation in Slope-Intercept Form	Slope	*y*-intercept
5. $5x - y = 6$	$\dfrac{y_1 + y_2}{x_1 + x_2}$	$m = 5$	-6
6. $7x + 2y = 10$	$\dfrac{y_1 - y_2}{x_1 + x_2}$	$m = \dfrac{-7}{2}$	5

Find the slope of each line.

7. ____0____

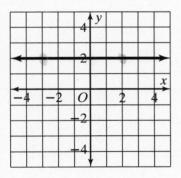

8. $\dfrac{4}{3}$

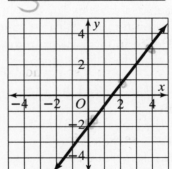

Graph each equation.

9. $y = -2x + 3$

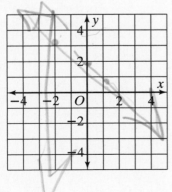

10. $y = \frac{1}{3}x - 1$

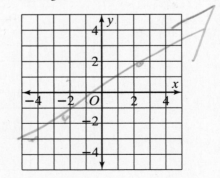

Practice

Pre-Algebra Lesson 8-3

423

8-3 • Guided Problem Solving

GPS **Student Page 419, Exercise 23**

Find the slope of the line.

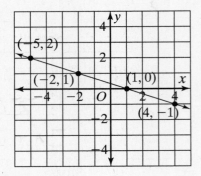

Understand the Problem

1. What are you asked to find? _____

2. What four points are given on the line? _____

Make and Carry Out a Plan

3. What is the formula for finding slope of a line
   using the coordinates of two points on the line? _____

4. Choose two points on the line. Write a ratio
   to show the difference in the *y*-coordinates
   over the difference in the *x*-coordinates. _____

5. Subtract the *y*-coordinates and the *x*-coordinates. _____

6. Simplify. What is the slope of the line? _____

Check the Answer

7. To check your answer, find the slope of the line
   by using the other two points labeled on the line. _____

Solve Another Problem

8. Find the slope of the line.

   _____

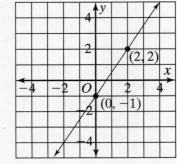

Practice 8-4

mx +b

Writing Rules for Linear Functions

Write a rule for each function.

1. *y = 1¼x + 2* ~~EASY~~

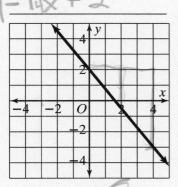

2. *y = 2x + (−4)*   *y = 2x − 4*

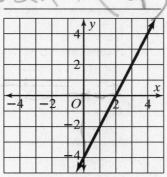

3. ~~*y = +6x*~~   *y = −16x*

x	$f(x)$
−3	18
−1	6
1	−6
3	−18

+2, +2, +2, +2   −12, −12, −12

4. *y = 7x + 0*   *x − 7*

x	$f(x)$
5	−2
7	0
9	2
11	4

+2, +2, +2   +2, +2, +2

$-\frac{2}{2} = 1$ slope

5. *y = 3x − 8*

x	$f(x)$
−3	−17
−1	−11
1	−5
3	1

6. *4x + 6*

x	$f(x)$
−4	4
0	6
2	7
4	8

+2, +1, +1

$y = \frac{1}{2}x + 6$

Write a function rule to describe each situation.

7. The number of pounds $p(z)$ as a function of the number of ounces z.

_____ $p(z) = \frac{z}{16}$ _____

8. The selling price $s(c)$ after a 45% markup of an item as a function of the stores' cost c.

_____ $45 - s(c)$ _____

9. The total number of miles $m(r)$ covered when you walk 7 miles before lunch, and you walk for 2 hours at r mi/hr after lunch.

_____ $m(r) = 2r + 7$ _____

8-4 • Guided Problem Solving

GPS **Student Page 424, Exercise 12**

a. Geometry Write a rule that expresses the perimeter $p(s)$ of a square as a function of the length s of one side.

b. Use your function to find the perimeter of a square with side length 7 cm.

Understand the Problem

1. What does the variable $p(s)$ represent? _____

2. What does the variable s represent? _____

3. What are you asked to do in part (a)? _____

4. What are you asked to do in part (b)? _____

   _____

Make and Carry Out a Plan

5. What is the definition of perimeter? _____

6. How many sides with length s does a square have? _____

7. Use the sentence "The perimeter of a square is four times the length of one side" to write a rule for the function. _____

8. To find the perimeter of a square with side length 7 cm, replace s with 7 in the function rule. _____

9. Simplify. _____

10. What is the perimeter of a square with side length 7 cm? _____

Check the Answer

11. To check your answer, add the lengths of the four sides of a square with side length 7 cm. _____ The sum should be the perimeter you found in Question 10.

Solve Another Problem

12. Write a rule that expresses the area $a(s)$ of a square as a function of the length s of one side. Use your function to find the area of a square with side length 4 cm. _____

Guided Problem Solving

Practice 8-5

• •

Use the data in the table.

1. Make a (year, units of CD's) scatter plot.

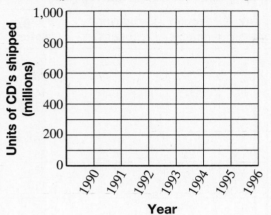

Sales of Recorded Music			
Year	Millions of Units Shipped		
	CD's	Cassettes	LP's
1990	287	442	12
1991	333	360	5
1992	408	366	2
1993	495	340	1
1994	662	345	2
1995	723	273	2
1996	779	225	3

2. Make a (year, units of cassettes) scatter plot.

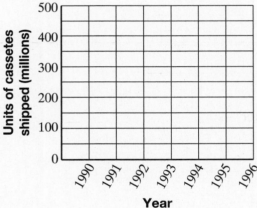

3. Make a (year, units of LP's) scatter plot.

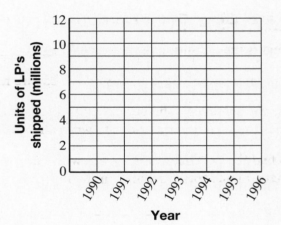

Is there a *positive correlation*, a *negative correlation*, or *no correlation* between the data sets in each scatter plot?

4. (year, units of CD's) scatter plot _____

5. (year, units of cassettes) scatter plot _____

6. (year, units of LP's) scatter plot _____

• •

8-5 • Guided Problem Solving

GPS **Student Page 430, Exercise 4**

Use the table at right. Make a scatter plot for calories and grams of protein. Graph calories on the horizontal axis.

Nutritional Values for 100 Grams of Food

Food	Fat (grams)	Protein (grams)	Carbohydrates (grams)	Energy (calories)
Bread	4	8	50	267
Cheese	33	25	1	403
Chicken	4	31	0	165
Eggs	11	13	1	155
Ground beef	19	27	0	292
Milk	3	3	5	61
Peanuts	49	26	16	567
Pizza	5	12	33	223
Tuna	1	26	0	116

Understand the Problem

1. What are you asked to do? _____

2. What will you graph on the horizontal axis? _____

3. What will you graph on the vertical axis? _____

Make and Carry Out a Plan

4. Make your scatter plot on the graph to the right. Label the horizontal axis (1 unit = 50 calories).

5. Label the vertical axis (1 unit = 5 grams of protein).

6. Plot the data for each food on the scatter plot. Find the number of calories for each food on the horizontal axis and its corresponding number of grams of protein on the vertical axis. Make a dot for each (calories, grams) ordered pair.

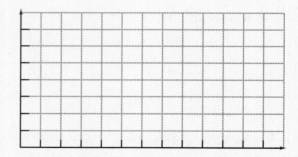

Check the Answer

7. To make sure you have plotted the graph correctly, check each point to make sure its location corresponds to its coordinates in the data table.

Solve Another Problem

8. Make a scatter plot for the data.

Minutes Studied	28	38	15	75	46	55	87	28
Score on Test	65	70	58	86	70	72	97	55

Practice 8-6

Solve by Graphing

A giraffe was 1 ft tall at birth, 7 ft tall at the age of 4, and $11\frac{1}{2}$ ft tall at the age of 7.

1. Use the data to make a (age, height) scatter plot.

2. Draw a trend line.

3. Write an equation for your trend line in slope-intercept form.

4. Use your equation to find the following information.

   a. the giraffe's height at the age of 5

   _____

   b. the age at which the giraffe was 16 ft tall

   _____

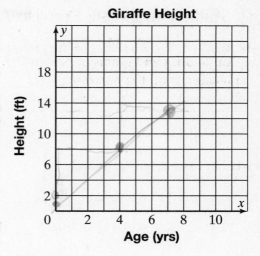

Giraffe Height

A hippopotamus weighed 700 lb at the age of 1 and 1,900 lb at the age of 3, and 2,500 lb at the age of 4.

5. Use the data to make a (age, weight) scatter plot.

6. Draw a trend line.

7. Write an equation for your trend line.

_____

8. Use the equation to predict the following information.

   a. the hippo's weight at the age of 8

   _____

   b. the age at which the hippo weighed 7,900 lb

   _____

Hippopotamus Weight

9. Can this equation be used to predict the hippo's weight at any age? Explain.

_____

_____

8-6 • Guided Problem Solving

Data Analysis Use the data in the table below. Predict the number of gallons bought for $15.

Dollars Spent	12	14	11	12	10	6	10	8
Gallons Bought	7.3	8.0	5.9	6.5	5.7	3.5	5.1	4.4

Understand the Problem

1. What are the two variables? _____

2. What are you asked to predict? _____

Make and Carry Out a Plan

3. Graph the data in a scatter plot. Use the horizontal axis for dollars spent and the vertical axis for gallons bought. Then graph the (dollars, gallons) ordered pairs.

4. Sketch a trend line. Remember that the line should be as close as possible to each data point, and there should be about as many points above the line as there are below.

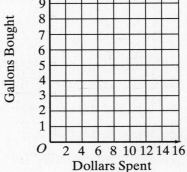

5. Find the point on your trend line that corresponds to 15 on the horizontal axis. To what value does this point correspond on the vertical axis? _____

6. About how many gallons can be bought for $15? _____

Check the Answer

7. To check your answer, solve the proportion $\frac{11}{5.9} = \frac{15}{x}$. _____

   This should be close to the answer you got for Step 6.

Solve Another Problem

8. Use the data in the table below.
   Predict the cost of making a 25-minute call. _____

Length of Phone Call (min)	2	4.5	20	13.25	8	4.5	17.75	10.5
Cost of Phone Call	$0.18	$0.25	$1.01	$0.76	$0.40	$0.23	$0.96	$0.60

Guided Problem Solving

Practice 8-7

Solving Systems of Linear Equations

Is each ordered pair a solution of the given system? Write *yes* or *no*.

1. $y = 6x + 12$
$2x - y = 4$

$(-4, -12)$ _____

2. $y = -3x$
$x = 4y + \frac{1}{2}$

$\left(-\frac{1}{2}, \frac{3}{2}\right)$ _____

3. $x + 2y = 2$
$2x + 5y = 2$

$(6, -2)$ _____

Solve each system by graphing. Check your solution.

4. $x + y = 3$
$x - y = -1$
Solution:

_____

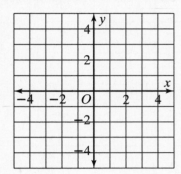

5. $2x + y = 1$
$x - 2y = 3$
Solution:

_____

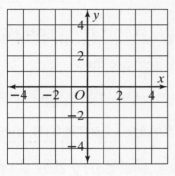

6. $y + 2 = 0$
$2x + y = 0$
Solution:

_____

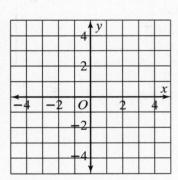

7. $3x + 2y = -6$
$x + 3y = -2$
Solution:

_____

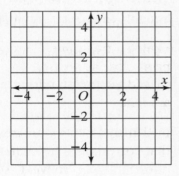

Write a system of linear equations. Solve by graphing.

8. The sum of two numbers is 3. Their difference is 1. Find the numbers.

_____

_____

_____

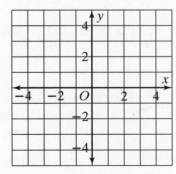

8-7 • Guided Problem Solving

GPS **Student Page 443, Exercise 28**

There are 11 animals in a barnyard. Some are chickens and some are cows. There are 38 legs in all. Let x be the number of chickens and y be the number of cows. How many of each kind of animal are in the barnyard?

Understand the Problem

1. How many animals are in the barnyard? _____

2. How many legs are in the barnyard? _____

3. What does the variable x represent? _____

4. What does the variable y represent? _____

5. What are you asked to do? _____

Make and Carry Out a Plan

6. How many legs does a chicken have? A cow? _____

7. Write an expression to represent the number of chicken legs in the barnyard. _____

8. Write an expression to represent the number of cow legs in the barnyard. _____

9. Use the two expressions to write an equation for the total number of legs in the barnyard. _____

10. Use x and y to write an equation for the number of animals in the barnyard. _____

11. Use graph paper. Graph the two equations.

12. At what point do the two lines intersect? _____

13. How many chickens and cows are in the barnyard? _____

Check the Answer

14. To check your answer, replace x and y in the two equations with the values you found for Question 12. Do the values make both equations true? _____

Solve Another Problem

15. There are seven vehicles parked in a garage. Some are bicycles and some are cars. There are 18 wheels in all. Let x be the number of bicycles and y be the number of cars. How many bicycles are in the garage? How many cars are in the garage? _____

Guided Problem Solving

Practice 8-8

Graphing Linear Inequalities

Graph each inequality.

1. $y < x$

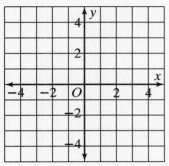

2. $x + y \leq 2$

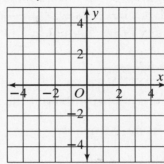

3. $x + 2y \geq 4$

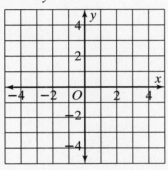

4. $x > -2$

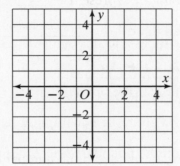

Solve each system by graphing.

5. $y \geq -x - 2$
$x - 2y < 4$

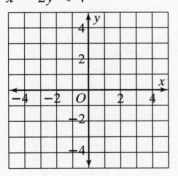

6. $x + y < 3$
$y \geq 3x - 2$

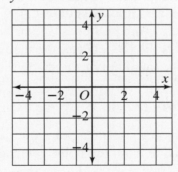

7. Is the origin a solution to the system in Exercise 5? _____

8. Is $(4, 0)$ a solution to the system in Exercise 5? _____

9. Is $(1, 0)$ a solution to the system in Exercise 6? _____

10. Is $(-1, 0)$ a solution to the system in Exercise 6? _____

8-8 • Guided Problem Solving

•••

GPS **Student Page 448, Exercise 14**

A number is greater than or equal to three times another
number. What are the numbers? Show all the solutions
by writing and graphing a linear inequality.

Understand the Problem

1. What information are you given about the two numbers? _____

2. What are you asked to do? _____

Make and Carry Out a Plan

3. Let *y* represent a number and *x* represent another
   number. Use the sentence "A number is greater than
   or equal to three times another number" to write an inequality. _____

4. Write an equation for the inequality.
   This is the equation of the boundary line. _____

5. Use graph paper. Graph the equation of the boundary line.

6. Choose a point on the boundary line. Does the point
   make the inequality you wrote in Step 3 true or false? _____
   If the point makes the equation true, make the boundary line solid. If the
   point does not make the inequality true, make the boundary line dashed.

7. Choose a point not on the boundary line to
   test in the inequality. Does the point make
   the inequality you wrote in Step 3 true or false? _____
   If the point makes the inequality true, shade the region containing the point. If the point
   does not make the inequality true, shade the region that does not contain the point.

Check the Answer

8. To check your answer, choose a point on the
   other side of the line from the point you chose in
   Question 7. Does this point make the inequality true or false? _____

   How does this support how you shaded your graph? _____

Solve Another Problem

9. A number is greater than three more than two times another number.
   Show all the solutions by writing and graphing a linear inequality. Use
   graph paper.

8A: Graphic Organizer

Study Skill Look at the title of this chapter. Do you already know the meaning of the words *linear functions* in the title? Look at the titles of the lessons in this chapter. Do they give you any clues about the meaning of *linear functions*? Write notes to record your thoughts about the meaning of the words in these titles. As you finish a lesson, review your notes and update them to contain what you have learned about linear functions.

Write your answers. Use the Table of Contents page for this chapter at the front of the book.

1. What is the title of this chapter? _____

2. Name four topics that you will study in this chapter:

   _____   _____

   _____   _____

3. What is the topic of the Problem Solving lesson? _____

4. Complete the graphic organizer as you work through the chapter.
   1. Write the title of the chapter in the center oval.
   2. When you begin a lesson, write the name of the lesson in a rectangle.
   3. When you complete that lesson, write a skill or key concept from that lesson in the outer oval linked to that rectangle.
   Continue with steps 2 and 3 clockwise around the graphic organizer.

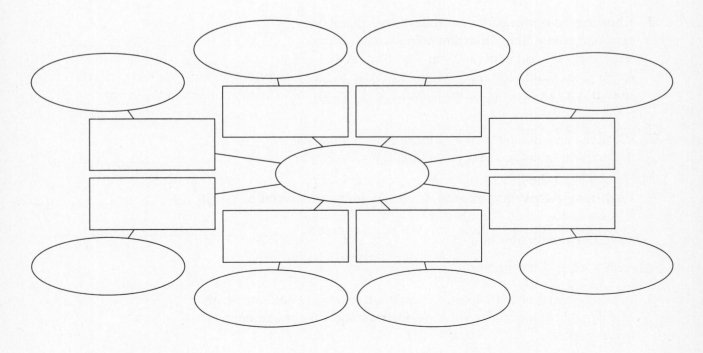

8B: Reading Comprehension

Study Skill The notes you take in class should contain all of the important information. In general, anything your teacher writes on the board or overhead projector should go into your notes. Other signals that information is important are repetition and emphasis. If your teacher presents a math idea more than once, then it belongs in your written notes.

Answer the questions below about how to read this graph.

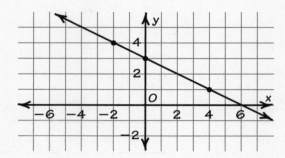

1. What is the label on the horizontal axis? _____

2. What is the label on the vertical axis? _____

3. What marks on the horizontal and vertical axes
   show that these lines extend without ending? _____

4. Write the coordinates of the ordered pair that names
   the point where the graphed line crosses the *y*-axis. _____

5. Write the coordinates of the ordered pair that names
   the point where the graphed line crosses the *x*-axis. _____

6. Write the coordinates of the ordered pair that names
   the point in Quadrant II that is marked on the graphed line. _____

7. **High-Use Academic Words** In questions 1 and 2, you are asked
   to identify the *label*. What is a label?

   a. writing that names something   **b.** the key feature

8C: Reading/Writing Math Symbols

For use after Lesson 8-4

Study Skill As you listen and take notes in class, bear in mind that you will probably want to use your notes to do your homework and study for tests. Take time to make your notes clear, using full sentences or phrases instead of isolated words. Write an example whenever you can.

Answer the following questions about math symbols in the space provided.

1. Complete the sentence that describes this expression: $\{(2, 3), (2, 4), (4, 3)\}$.

   These symbols show a relation consisting of _____

   _____

2. Describe this expression: $\{(0, 1), (1, 2), (2, 2), (3, 4)\}$.

   _____

   _____

3. On a coordinate system, both the x-axis and the y-axis have arrowheads at the ends. The graph of a line also has arrowheads drawn at both ends. Write a sentence that explains what these arrowhead symbols mean.

   _____

   _____

4. For the expression $f(x) = 3x + 7$, write how to say $f(x)$ and what it means.

   _____

   _____

5. In the slope-intercept form of a linear equation, $y = mx + b$, describe the meaning of m.

   _____

   _____

6. In the slope-intercept form of a linear equation, $y = mx + b$, what does b represent?

   _____

   _____

8D: Visual Vocabulary Practice

For use after Lesson 8-8

Study Skill When learning about a new concept, try to draw a picture to illustrate it.

Concept List

function notation	linear equation	linear inequality
negative correlation	positive correlation	scatter plot
slope	slope-intercept form	trend line

Write the concept that best describes each exercise. Choose from the concept list shown above.

1. $f(x)$	**2.** $\dfrac{\text{rise}}{\text{run}}$	**3.** $y = mx + b$
_____	_____	_____
4. 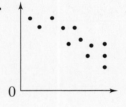	**5.** 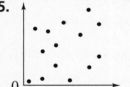	**6.** 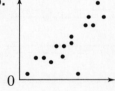
_____	_____	_____
7. 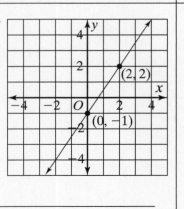	**8.** 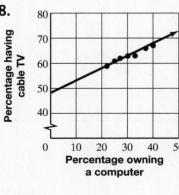	**9.** 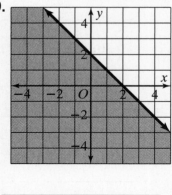
_____	_____	_____

8E: Vocabulary Check

Study Skill Strengthen your vocabulary. Use these pages and add cues and summaries by applying the Cornell Notetaking style.

Write the definition for each word at the right. To check your work, fold the paper back along the dotted line to see the correct answers.

_____

_____

Domain

_____

_____

Range

_____

_____

Function

_____

_____

Slope

_____

_____

Correlation

8E: Vocabulary Check (continued)

For use after Lesson 8-5

Write the vocabulary word for each definition. To check your work, fold
the paper forward along the dotted line to see the correct answers.

The set of first coordinates
of the ordered pairs of
the relation.

_____

The set of second
coordinates of the ordered
pairs of a relation.

_____

A relationship in which
each member of the
domain is paired with
exactly one member
of the range.

_____

A ratio that describes the
tilt of a line.

_____

A relation between two
sets of data.

_____

8F: Vocabulary Review Puzzle

For use with Chapter Review

Study Skill As you study the new words in a chapter, you may see familiar words that have unexpected new meanings when they are used mathematically. Write notes about the new mathematical meaning and compare it to the familiar one.

Use the words below to complete the crossword puzzle. For help, use the Glossary in your textbook.

domain	function	negative
positive	range	relation
solution	trend	

ACROSS

1. the second coordinates
2. an ordered pair that makes an equation true
5. line that closely fits the data points of a scatter plot
6. the first coordinates
7. correlation where one set of values increases as the other decreases

DOWN

1. a set of ordered pairs
3. each member of the domain is paired with exactly one member of the range
4. correlation where one set of values increases as the other increases

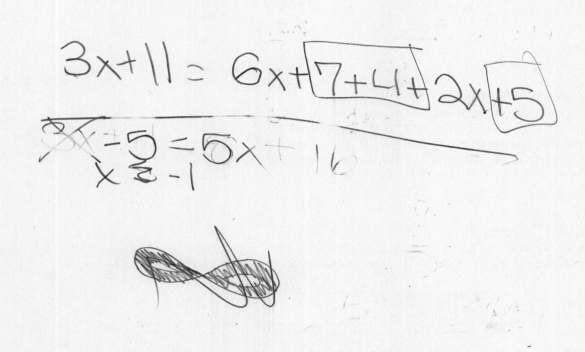

$$3x + 11 = 6x + \boxed{7 + 4 +} 2x \boxed{+5}$$

$$3x + 5 = 5x + 16$$

$$x = -1$$

Name _____ Class _____ Date _____

Practice 9-1

Introduction to Geometry: Points, Lines, and Planes

Use the figures at the right. Name each of the following.

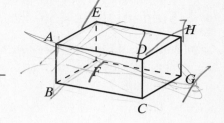

1. Four segments that intersect $\overline{AB}$. ___bf___ ___EA___ ___bc___ ___da___

2. Three segments parallel to $\overline{AB}$. ___EF___ ___cd___ ___hg___

3. Four segments skew to $\overline{AB}$. ___gf___ ___dh___ ___cg___ ___he___

Use the figure at the right. Find each of the following.

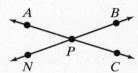

4. all points shown ___•A___ ___•P___ ___•B___ ___•C___ ___•N___

5. all segments shown ___NP___ ___PB___ ___ap___ ___ac___ ___nb___ ___cp___

6. five different rays ___PB___ ___PA___ ___ac___ ___PN___ ___PC___

7. all lines shown ___nb___ ___ac___

8. all names for $\overleftrightarrow{NB}$ ___bN___ ___PN___ ___bp___ ___pb___

Write an equation. Then find the length of each segment. $-3+11 \ -2+5$

9.

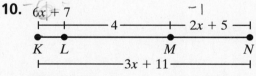

equation: ___$3n+5 = 5n-3$___

$n =$ ___4___

$AB =$ ___12___ $AC =$ ___17___

10. $6x + 7$ -1

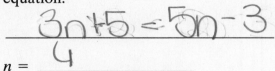

equation: ___$6x+7+4+(2x)+5 = 3x+11$___

$x =$ ___-1___

$MN =$ ___3___ $KN =$ ___8___

9-1 • Guided Problem Solving

GPS **Student Page 466, Exercise 42**

City Planning Use the map. Tell whether the streets in each pair appear to be parallel or intersecting.

a. N.W. Highway and Fifth Avenue

b. N.W. Highway and B Street

c. A and C Streets   **d.** B and C Streets   **e.** C and Main Streets

Understand the Problem

1. What are you asked to do? _____

Make and Carry Out a Plan

2. How do you know whether two lines are intersecting? _____

3. How do you know whether two lines are parallel? _____

4. Find N.W. Highway and Fifth Avenue on the map. Do they share exactly one point? _____

   Are they parallel or intersecting? _____

5. Find each pair of streets in parts (b) through (e) and tell whether they are parallel or intersecting.

   b. _____   **c.** _____

   d. _____   **e.** _____

Check the Answer

6. If a pair of streets do not intersect on the map, does that mean they do not intersect? Explain. _____
   _____

Solve Another Problem

7. Look at the picture of the side of a barn. Tell whether each pair of lines appears to be parallel or intersecting.

   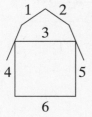

   a. 1 and 2 _____

   b. 3 and 6 _____

   c. 3 and 4 _____

Guided Problem Solving

Name _____ Class _____ Date _____

Practice 9-2

Angle Relationships and Parallel Lines

Find the measure of each angle in the figure at the right.

1. $m\angle1$ ___34___°   2. $m\angle2$ ___56___°

3. $m\angle3$ ___56___   4. $m\angle VWR$ ___180___ 146

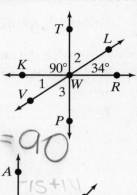

Use the figure at the right for Exercises 5-8.

5. Write an equation. ___$(3x-14)+(2x+9)=90$___

6. Find the value of x. ___19___

7. Find $m\angle ABD$. ___43___

8. Find $m\angle DBC$. ___47___

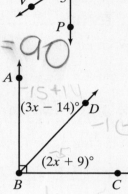

Use the figure at the right for Exercises 9-12.

9. Write an equation. ___$5x-18=4x+7$___

10. Find the value of x. ___25___°

11. Find $m\angle MNQ$. ___107___°

12. Find $m\angle MNR$. ___73___°

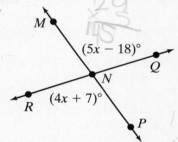

In each figure, find the measures of $\angle1$ and $\angle2$.

13. Given $p \parallel q$.

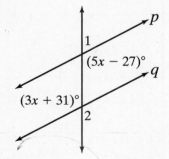

$m\angle1 =$ ___62___ $m\angle2 =$ ___118___

14. Given $a \parallel b$.

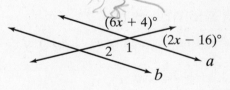

$m\angle1 =$ ___148___ $m\angle2 =$ ___32___

15. Find a pair of complementary angles such that the difference of their
measures is 12°.

___51° 39°___

9-2 • Guided Problem Solving

GPS Student Page 473, Exercise 16

Algebra Given $a \parallel b$ at the right, find the measures of $\angle 1$ and $\angle 2$.

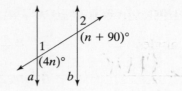

Understand the Problem

1. What information are you given? _____

2. What are you asked to find? _____

Make and Carry Out a Plan

3. What is a name for the line that intersects a and b? _____

4. Since $a \parallel b$, how are $\angle 1$ and $\angle 2$ related to each other? _____

5. How are the angles measuring $4n$ and $n + 90$ related to each other? _____

6. What is true about angles that are related in this way? _____

7. Use $4n$ and $n + 90$ to write an equation to solve for n. _____

8. Solve for n. _____

9. Substitute the value into each expression to find the measures of the two angles. _____

10. How is the angle that measures $4n$ related to $\angle 1$? _____

11. How can this help you find $m\angle 1$? _____

12. How is the angle that measures $n + 90$ related to $\angle 2$? _____

13. How can this help you find $m\angle 2$? _____

14. What are the measures of $\angle 1$ and $\angle 2$? _____

Check the Answer

15. To check your answer, find the measures of the angles a different way. Use the fact that $\angle 1$ and the angle that measures $4n$ are supplementary to write an equation and solve for n. What is the value of n? _____

Solve Another Problem

16. Given $a \parallel b$, find the measures of $\angle 1$ and $\angle 2$.

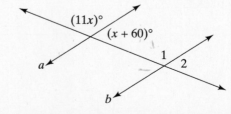

_____

Practice 9-3

Classifying Polygons

Name all quadrilaterals that have each of the named properties.

1. four 90° angles

   __sqaure__

2. opposite sides congruent and parallel

   __trapezoid__  parallelogram/rhombus

3. at least one pair of parallel sides

   __trapezoid, sqaure, rectangle /sqaure__

Judging by appearances, classify each triangle by its sides and angles.

4.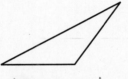

   Icoseles obtuse

5.

   right angle

6.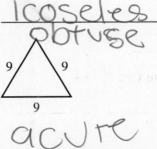

   acute

7.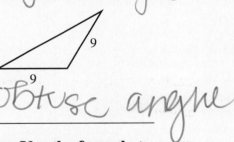

   obtuse angle

Write a formula to find the perimeter of each figure. Use the formula to find the perimeter.

8. a regular dodecagon (12-gon); one side is 9.25 cm

   $P =$ __120 2x__ $P =$ __111.00__

9. a rhombus; one side is $1\frac{3}{4}$ yd

   $P =$ __4x__ $P =$ __7__

10. a parallelogram; the sides are 10.4 m and 5.6 m

    $P =$ __20.8__ $P =$ __11.2__

    2x + 2x

    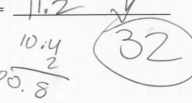

9-3 • Guided Problem Solving

GPS **Student Page 477, Exercise 13**

Architecture The Pentagon is a pentagonal-shaped building near Washington, D.C., that is home to the United States Department of Defense. Write a formula for the perimeter of a regular pentagon in terms of the length of a side. Evaluate the formula to find the perimeter of the Pentagon, which has a side length of 921 ft.

Understand the Problem

1. What shape is the Pentagon? _____

2. What is the side length of the Pentagon? _____

3. What are you asked to do? _____

Make and Carry Out a Plan

4. How many equal sides does a pentagon have? _____

5. Let *x* equal the length of a side of a regular pentagon.
   Use *x* to write a formula for the perimeter of a pentagon. _____

6. Replace *x* with 921 in the formula. _____

7. What is the perimeter of the Pentagon? _____

Check the Answer

8. To check your answer, add the lengths
   of the sides of the Pentagon together. _____
   Your answer should be the same as your answer to Question 7.

Solve Another Problem

9. Maggie is digging a hexagonal-shaped flower garden.
   Write a formula for the perimeter of a regular hexagon
   in terms of the length of a side. Evaluate the formula to find
   the perimeter of the flower garden, which has a side length of 8 ft. _____

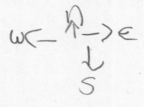

Guided Problem Solving

Name _____ *(handwritten: (9-2)180 11)* Class _____ Date _____

(handwritten top: n= # of sides)

Practice 9-4

Solve by drawing a diagram.

1. How many diagonals does a quadrilateral have?

   (handwritten: 2)

2. Which quadrilaterals always have congruent diagonals?

   (handwritten: squart isoscles trapezoids)

3. Find a formula for the number of diagonals *d* in a polygon with *n* sides. Complete the table to help you. Look for a pattern.

Figure	Number of sides	Number of vertices	Number of diagonals from each vertex	Total number of diagonals
triangle	3	*3*	*0*	*0*
quadrilateral	4	*4*	*1*	*2*
pentagon	5	*5*	*8 2*	*5*
hexagon	6	*6*	*8 3*	*9*
octagon	8	*8*	*5*	*20*
n-gon	*n*	*9*	*27 6 (n-3)*	*20*

(handwritten right column: 180, 360, 540, 720, 1060, 1260)

$d = $ *(handwritten: (n-2)180)*

4. One day in the lunch line, Maurice was ahead of Aquia and behind Rochelle. Rochelle was ahead of Shequille and behind Whitney. Shequille was ahead of Maurice. Who was last?

   (handwritten: Shequille)

5. A mail carrier leaves the post office at 10:00 A.M. and travels 4 miles south, then 7 miles east, then 5 miles south, then 10 miles west, and 9 miles north. At the end of her route, how far and in which direction is the mail carrier from the post office?

   (handwritten: 3 m. west)

9-4 • Guided Problem Solving

GPS **Student Page 482, Exercise 5**

Solve by drawing a diagram.

There are 25 students in a math class. Ten students are in the math club. Twelve students are in the band. Five students are in both. How many students in the math class are members of neither club?

Understand the Problem

1. How many students are in the math class? _____

2. How many students are members of the math club? _____

3. How many students are in the band? _____

4. How many students are in both the math club and band? _____

5. What are you asked to find? _____

Make and Carry Out a Plan

6. The numbers 1–25 in the diagram below represent the students.
   Circle the numbers 1–10 to represent the students in the math club.
   1 2 3 4 5 6 7 8 9 10 11 12 13 14 15 16 17 18 19 20 21 22 23 24 25

7. Underline five of the numbers already circled to represent the students who are in both the math club and band. Then underline numbers without circles until you have a total of 12 underlined numbers, representing the 12 students in the band.

8. The numbers that are not circled or underlined represent students who belong to neither group. How many students are not connected to either math club or band? _____

Check the Answer

9. To check your answer, add the numbers of students in math club and band. Next subtract the number of students who are in both. This tells you how many students are in band, math club, or both. Subtract this result from 25, the total number of students in the math class. _____ The result should be the same as your answer to Question 8.

Solve Another Problem

Solve by drawing a diagram.

10. There are 18 students in a class. Eight of the students are in soccer. Seven of the students are in the science club. Two of the students are in both. How many students in the class are not in soccer or the science club? _____

Guided Problem Solving

Practice 9-5
Congruence

Given that $\triangle GHM \cong \triangle RSA$, **complete the following.**

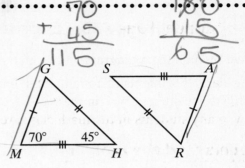

1. $\overline{GH} \cong$ ___SR___

2. $\overline{AS} \cong$ ___MH___

3. $\angle S \cong$ ___∠H___

4. $\angle M \cong$ ___∠A___

5. $\overline{AR} \cong$ ___GM___

6. $\angle R \cong$ ___G___

7. $m\angle A =$ ___70°___

8. $m\angle G =$ ___65___

List the congruent corresponding parts of each pair of triangles. Write a congruence statement for the triangles.

9. _abc ≅ dec_
   _∠b ≅ ∠d_
   _a ≅ e_
   cba ≅ ced by ___ASA___

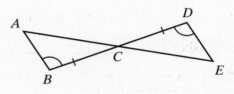

10. _JK ≅ JM_
    _JL ≅ JL_
    _KL ≅ ML_
    JKl ≅ JML by ___SSS___

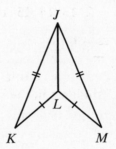

Given that $HPKT \cong BEWL$, **complete the following.**

11. $\overline{PK} \cong$ ___EW___

12. $\angle L \cong$ ___T___

13. $\angle KPH \cong$ ___WEB___

14. $\overline{LB} \cong$ ___TH___

15. $\overline{EB} \cong$ ___PH___

16. $\angle PHT \cong$ ___EBL___

17. Explain why the pair of triangles is congruent.
    Then, find the missing measures.
    ___ASA___
    $X = 24$
    $Y = 30$
    $z = 97°$

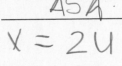

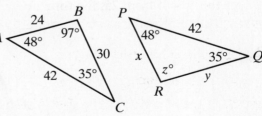

9-5 • Guided Problem Solving

GPS **Student Page 487, Exercise 25**

List the congruent corresponding parts for the pair of triangles.
Write a congruence statement (and reason) for the triangles.

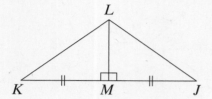

Understand the Problem

1. What are you asked to do? _____

Make and Carry Out a Plan

2. Name the corresponding congruent sides of the two triangles. _____

3. Name the corresponding congruent angles. _____

4. Write a congruence statement for the two triangles. _____

5. By which way do you know the two triangles are
congruent—Side-Side-Side, Side-Angle-Side, or Angle-Side-Angle? _____

Check the Answer

6. To check your answer, look at the triangles again. Make sure
you have listed the congruent corresponding parts correctly. Check
your congruence statement and reason to make sure it is true of
the triangles.

Solve Another Problem

7. List the congruent corresponding parts for the pair of triangles.
Write a congruence statement (and reason) for the triangles.

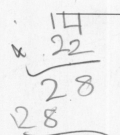

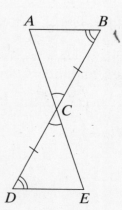

Guided Problem Solving

Practice 9-6

Circles

Find the measures of the central angles that you would draw to represent each percent in a circle graph. Round to the nearest degree.

Voter Preference for Senator		Central Angle
1. Peterson	40%	X 60 144°
2. Washington	30%	X 70 108°
3. Gomez	15%	X 85 54°
4. Thomson	10%	X 90 36°
5. Miller	5%	X 95 18°

Proportions
$$\frac{?}{100} = \frac{X}{360}$$

6. Draw a circle graph for the data on voter preference.

Voter Preference for Senator

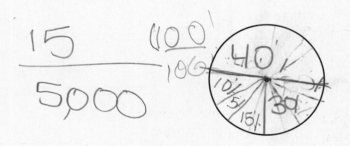

$\frac{15}{5000}$ $\frac{100}{100}$

$\frac{.15}{50} = \frac{.30}{100}$

7. The total number of voters surveyed was 5,000. How many voters preferred Gomez?

30 people

Find the circumference of each circle with the given radius or diameter. Use 3.14 for π.

8. $d = 25.8$ m

$C =$ _80.07M_

9. $r = 9.1$ cm

$C =$ _57.574_

$C = d\pi$ or $C = 2\pi r$

10. $r = 0.28$ km

$C =$ _1.7584 km_

11. $d = 14$ ft

$C =$ _43.96 ft_

12. $d = 5$ in.

$C =$ _15.7 in_

13. $r = \frac{7}{8}$ in.

$C =$ _____

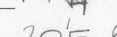
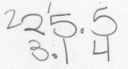

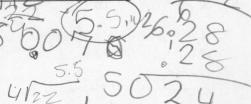

9-6 • Guided Problem Solving

GPS **Student Page 493, Exercise 21**

The data below show how a group of students travel to school each day. Make a circle graph for the data.

How Students Travel to School

Transportation	Walk	Bicycle	Bus	Car	Other
Number of Students	55	80	110	40	15

Understand the Problem

1. What do the data show? _____

2. What are you asked to do? _____

Make and Carry Out a Plan

3. Find the total number of students by adding the numbers of students in all five categories. _____

4. Write the number of students in each category as a fraction of the total number of students. _____

5. Use the fractions to write proportions to find the measure of each central angle. For example, solve $\frac{55}{300} = \frac{w}{360}$ to find w, the measure of the central angle for the number of students who walk to school.

walk _____ bicycle _____ bus _____

car _____ other _____

6. Use a compass to draw a circle. Draw each central angle with a protractor. Label each section with a title and the measure of the central angle.

Check the Answer

7. To check your answer, compare the data in the table and your circle graph. Do the sizes of the sections of the circle graph correspond to the data in the table? Explain. _____

Solve Another Problem

8. Alex surveyed his classmates about their favorite subjects. Draw a circle graph for the data at right.

Favorite Subjects of Students

Subject	Math	Science	Reading	History	Art
Number of Students	4	6	5	3	7

Guided Problem Solving

Practice 9-7

Construct each figure using the diagram at the right.

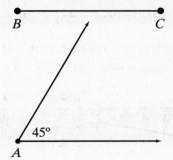

1. $\overline{MP}$ congruent to $\overline{BC}$

●————————————————▶
M

2. $\overline{JK}$ twice as long as $\overline{BC}$

●————————————————————————▶
J

3. ∠D congruent to ∠A

4. ∠PQR half the measure of ∠A

●————————————————▶
D

Q   R

5. ∠STU with measure 135°

6. $\overline{EF}$ half as long as $\overline{BC}$

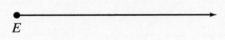
E

◀————————————●
          U

7. Construct △WXY so that ∠W is congruent to ∠A, $\overline{WY}$ is congruent to $\overline{BC}$, and ∠Y is half the measure of ∠A.

8. What seems to be true about ∠X in △WXY you constructed?

_____

●————————————————▶
W

9-7 • Guided Problem Solving

GPS **Student Page 499, Exercise 19**

The bisector of $\angle XYZ$ is $\overrightarrow{YN}$. If the measure of $\angle XYN$ is 55°, what is the measure of $\angle XYZ$?

Understand the Problem

1. What is the bisector of $\angle XYZ$? _____

2. What is the measure of $\angle XYN$? _____

3. What are you asked to find? _____

Make and Carry Out a Plan

4. Sketch $\angle XYZ$ and its bisector $\overrightarrow{YN}$ to help you visualize the problem.

5. What does an angle bisector do to an angle? _____

_____

6. What is the measure of $\angle ZYN$? _____

7. Add the measures of $\angle XYN$ and $\angle ZYN$ to find the measure of $\angle XYZ$. _____

Check the Answer

8. To check your answer, subtract the measure of $\angle ZYN$ from your answer. _____ The result should be the measure of $\angle XYN$.

Solve Another Problem

9. The perpendicular bisector of $\overline{QR}$ is $\overline{ST}$. $\overline{ST}$ crosses $\overline{QR}$ at point P. If the measure of $\overline{QP}$ is 4 mm, what is the measure of $\overline{QR}$? _____

Name _____ Class _____ Date _____

Practice 9-8

Translations

Write a rule to describe each translation.

1. $(x, y) \rightarrow$ _____

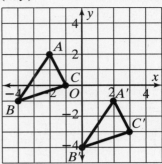

2. $(x, y) \rightarrow$ _____

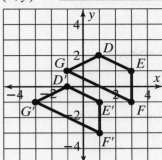

3. $(x, y) \rightarrow$ _____

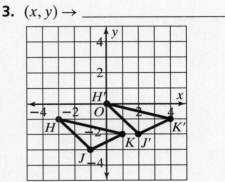

4. $(x, y) \rightarrow$ _____

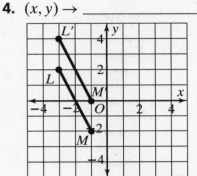

The vertices of a triangle and a translation are given. Graph each triangle and its image.

5. $G(-4, 4)$, $H(-2, 3)$,
$J(-3, 0)$; right 5 and down 2

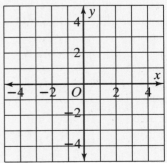

6. $K(0, -1)$, $L(4, 2)$, $M(3, -3)$;
left 4 units and up 3 units

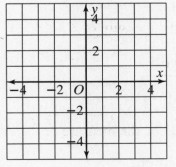

A point and its image after a translation are given. Write a rule to describe the translation.

7. $A(9, -4)$, $A'(2, -1)$ $(x, y) \rightarrow$ _____

8. $B(-3, 5)$, $B'(-5, -3)$ $(x, y) \rightarrow$ _____

9-8 • Guided Problem Solving

GPS **Student Page 504, Exercise 37**

Translate point $T(2, 5)$ 2 units to the right and 6 units up.
Translate its image, point T', 4 units to the left and 1 unit down.
What are the coordinates of the image of point T'?

Understand the Problem

1. What are the coordinates of point T? _____

2. Describe the translation of point T to T'. _____

3. Describe the translation of point T' to its image. _____

4. What are you asked to find? _____

Make and Carry Out a Plan

5. Plot point $T(2, 5)$ on the graph at right.

6. Start at point T. Move 2 units to the right and 6 units up.
   Label this point T'.

7. Start at point T'. Move 4 units to the left and 1 unit down.
   This is the image of point T'.

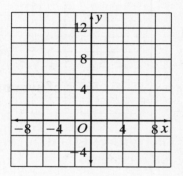

8. What are the coordinates of the image of point T'? _____

Check the Answer

9. Use mental math and combine
   (2 units right, 6 units up) with (4 units left, 1 unit down). _____

10. What is the result of translating
    $T(2, 5)$ 2 units to the left and 5 units up? _____
    The result should be the coordinates of the image of point T'.

Solve Another Problem

11. Translate point $B(4, 5)$ 3 units to the left
    and 4 units down. Translate its image,
    point B', 2 units to the right and 5 units up.
    What are the coordinates of the image of B'? _____

Practice 9-9

The vertices of a polygon are listed. Graph each polygon and its image after a reflection over the given line. Name the coordinates of the image.

1. $A(1, 3), B(4, 1), C(3, -2),$
   $D(2, -4); x = 0$

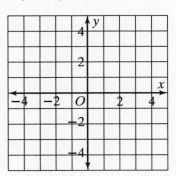

2. $J(-2, 1), K(1, 3), L(4, 2);$
   $y = -1$

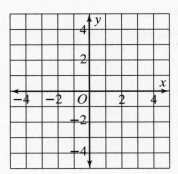

A' _____ B' _____

C' _____ D' _____

J' _____ K' _____

L' _____

Draw all the lines of symmetry for each figure.

3.

4.

5.

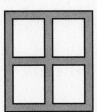

Is the dashed line a line of symmetry? Write yes or no.

6. _____

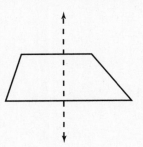

7. _____

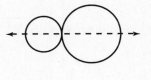

8. _____

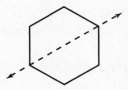

9-9 • Guided Problem Solving

GPS **Student Page 509, Exercise 8**

$\triangle WXY$ has vertices $W(-1, -1)$, $X(0, 0)$, $Y(-5, 0)$. Graph $\triangle WXY$
and its image after a reflection over $y = 2$.

Understand the Problem

1. What is the first thing you are asked to do? _____

2. Over what line are you asked to graph the reflection? _____

Make and Carry Out a Plan

3. Graph figure $\triangle WXY$ on the graph below.

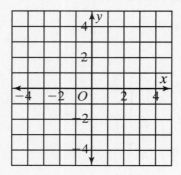

4. Draw a dashed line on the graph at $y = 2$.

5. When you reflect the triangle over the line $y = 2$, the x-coordinates
   of each point will remain the same. To determine the y-coordinate
   for each point, count the number of units to each point from $y = 2$.
   For example, if a point is 2 units below $y = 2$, its reflection will be
   2 units above $y = 2$. Plot W', X', and Y' and connect the points to
   form $\triangle W'X'Y'$.

Check the Answer

6. To check your answer, draw the image of $\triangle W'X'Y'$ after a reflection
   over $y = 2$. The reflected image should be the same as $\triangle WXY$.

Solve Another Problem

7. $\triangle JKL$ has vertices $J(-2, 0)$, $K(0, 1)$, $L(2, 0)$. On a separate sheet of
   paper, graph $\triangle JKL$ and its image after a reflection over $y = -2$.

Practice 9-10

Rotations

• •

Judging from appearances, does each figure have rotational symmetry? If yes, what is the angle of rotation?

1. _____

2. _____

3. _____

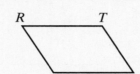

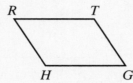

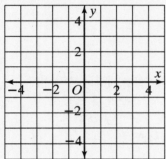

The vertices of a triangle are given. Graph each triangle and its image after a rotation of (a) 90° and (b) 180° about the origin. Name the coordinates of the vertices of the images.

4. $A(1, 4), B(1, 1), C(4, 2)$

5. $S(2, 3), T(-2, 4), U(-4, 2)$

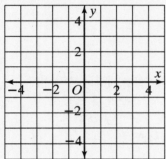

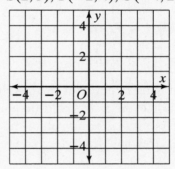

90°   180°

90°   180°

A' _____ A'' _____

S' _____ S'' _____

B' _____ B'' _____

T' _____ T'' _____

C' _____ C'' _____

U' _____ U'' _____

Look for a pattern in Exercises 4 and 5 to complete the following.

6. In a 90° rotation, $(x, y) \rightarrow$ _____

7. In a 180° rotation, $(x, y) \rightarrow$ _____

• •

9-10 • Guided Problem Solving

GPS **Student Page 513, Exercise 13**

The vertices of a triangle are $V(0, 0)$, $W(2, 5)$, and $X(1, 5)$. On separate coordinate planes, graph the triangle and its image after rotations of (a) 90° and (b) 180° about $(1, 1)$.

Understand the Problem

1. What are the coordinates of the three vertices of the triangle? _____

2. What is the angle of rotation in part (a)? _____

3. What is the angle of rotation in part (b)? _____

4. What is the center of rotation in parts (a) and (b)? _____

5. What are you asked to do? _____

Make and Carry Out a Plan

6. On a sheet of graph paper, draw $\triangle VWX$.

7. Place a piece of tracing paper over the graph. Trace the vertices of the triangle, the x-axis, and the y-axis. Place your pencil at the point $(1, 1)$ and rotate the tracing paper 90° counterclockwise. How will you know you have rotated the triangle 90°? _____

   _____

8. Press through the tracing paper to mark the position of each vertex of the triangle. Then remove the tracing paper and draw $\triangle V'W'X'$ on the graph.

9. On a second coordinate plane, draw $\triangle VWX$. Place the tracing paper you used to rotate the triangle 90° over $\triangle VWX$. Place your pencil at the origin and rotate the tracing paper 180°. Press to mark the vertices, and then draw $\triangle V'W'X'$.

Check the Answer

10. To check your answers, rotate the first $\triangle V'W'X'$ 90° clockwise. Then rotate the second $\triangle V'W'X'$ 180° clockwise. The resulting triangles should be the same as $\triangle VWX$.

Solve Another Problem

11. A triangle has vertices $A(2, 0)$, $B(0, 0)$, and $C(1, 5)$. On a separate coordinate plane, graph the triangle and its image after a rotation of 90° and 180° about the origin.

9A: Graphic Organizer

For use before Lesson 9-1

Study Skill When you read mathematics, have a pencil and paper ready so you can take notes and write down any questions you may have. You may want to draw diagrams or sketches to show how the math topics relate to each other.

Write your answers. Use the Table of Contents page for this chapter at the front of the book.

1. What is the title of this chapter? _____

2. Name four topics that you will study in this chapter:

   _____   _____

   _____   _____

3. What is the topic of the Problem Solving lesson? _____

4. Complete the graphic organizer as you work through the chapter.
   1. Write the title of the chapter in the center oval.
   2. When you begin a lesson, write the name of the lesson in a rectangle.
   3. When you complete that lesson, write a skill or key concept from that lesson in the outer oval linked to that rectangle.

   Continue with steps 2 and 3 clockwise around the graphic organizer.

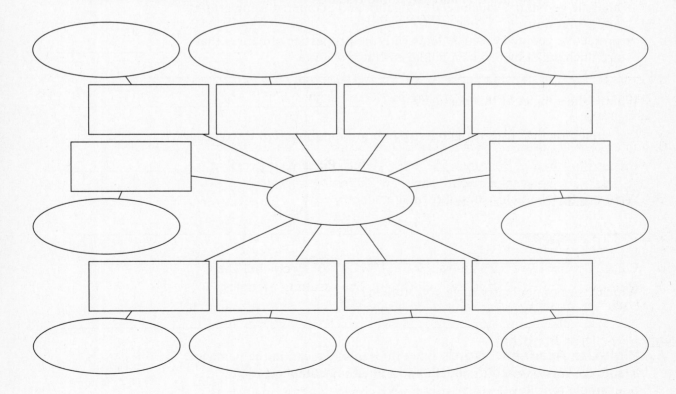

9B: Reading Comprehension

For use after Lesson 9-5

Study Skill After you read a long paragraph, pause and review the essential information in that paragraph. Remember that the first sentence of a paragraph often tells you the topic and the last sentence may summarize the content.

Read the passage below and answer the questions that follow.

The word "geometry" comes from two Greek words that mean "measuring the earth." Geometry was originally concerned with practical problems that involved measuring pieces of land. In the third century B.C., the Greek mathematician Euclid wrote a logical treatise on geometry that became the model for classical geometry. Formal geometry is based on stated assumptions that consist of a set of undefined terms and a set of statements about those terms, called postulates or axioms. Then, based on these assumptions, new terms are defined and the logical process of deduction is used to prove statements, called theorems.

There are many different types of geometry, some of which are listed here:
- plane geometry, which deals with figures in a two-dimensional plane
- solid geometry, which deals with figures in three-dimensional space
- Euclidean geometry, both plane and solid, which is based on Euclid's postulates
- non-Euclidean geometries, such as spherical and hyperbolic geometry, which change one or more of Euclid's postulates
- analytic geometry, which relates algebra and geometry, using graphs and equations
- projective geometry, which deals with the properties of figures that are unchanged by projection, like casting a shadow

1. What is the subject of this passage? _____

2. List some practical uses for geometry that are mentioned in the passage.

_____

3. What are the characteristics of formal geometry?

_____

_____

4. Which types of geometry have you studied?

_____

5. **High-Use Academic Words** What does *model* mean in the passage?
   a. simpler version used to understand something complicated
   b. example to follow

9C: Reading/Writing Math Symbols

For use after Lesson 9-8

Study Skill As you read your text, or other assignments, pause often to ask yourself questions such as these:

- What is this chapter about?

- What is the main topic of this paragraph?

- How does this connect to what I learned before?

- What is the most important idea here?

Answering your own questions helps you concentrate as you read so that you will remember the content.

Use symbols to write each expression.

1. Angle *P* is congruent to angle *Q*. _____

2. Triangle *MAN* is congruent to triangle *DOG*. _____

3. Side *MA* is congruent to side *DO*. _____

4. The point *P* with coordinates $(1, -3)$ translates to
    the point *P'* with the coordinates $(2, 1)$. _____

5. The circumference of a circle is equal to pi multiplied by the diameter. _____

Make marks or symbols on each figure to indicate the description.

6. right angle   **7.** isoceles triangle   **8.** rectangle

     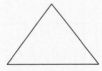   

Make marks on the two figures to show each congruence.

9. $\angle T \cong \angle R$

10. $\angle A \cong \angle U$

11. $\angle C \cong \angle F$

12. $\overline{CT} \cong \overline{RF}$

13. $\overline{TA} \cong \overline{RU}$

14. $\overline{AC} \cong \overline{UF}$

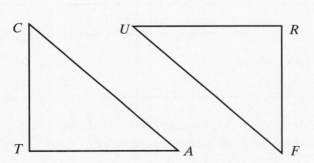

9D: Visual Vocabulary Practice
High-Use Academic Words

For use after Lesson 9-2

Study Skills Mathematics is like learning a foreign language. You have to know the vocabulary before you can speak the language correctly.

Concept List

consecutive	correlation	formula
notation	simplify	solve
strategy	table	test

Write the concept that best describes each exercise. Choose from the concept list above.

1. $I = prt$ _____	**2.** Act It Out Draw a Diagram Guess, Check, Revise Look for a Pattern Work a Simpler Problem Work Backward _____	**3.** 73 and 74 _____
4. <table><tr><td>x</td><td>y</td></tr><tr><td>−2</td><td>4</td></tr><tr><td>0</td><td>0</td></tr><tr><td>2</td><td>4</td></tr><tr><td>3</td><td>9</td></tr></table> _____	**5.** $2(c + 4) - 5c = -3c + 8$ _____	**6.** 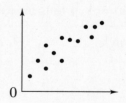 _____
7. 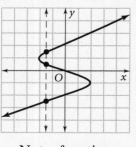 Not a function. _____	**8.** $2(5x - 3) = 14$ $10x - 6 = 14$ $10x = 20$ $x = 2$ _____	**9.** $f(x)$ for y _____

9E: Vocabulary Check

Study Skill Strengthen your vocabulary. Use these pages and add cues and summaries by applying the Cornell Notetaking style.

Write the definition for each word at the right. To check your work, fold the paper back along the dotted line to see the correct answers

_____

_____

_____

Circle

_____

_____

Radius

_____

_____

Diameter

_____

_____

_____

Circumference

_____

_____

Chord

_____

_____

9E: Vocabulary Check (continued)

For use after Lesson 9-6

Write the vocabulary word for each definition. To check your work, fold the paper forward along the dotted line to see the correct answers.

The set of all points in a plane that are equidistant from a given point, called the center.

_____

A segment that has one endpoint at the center of the circle and the other endpoint on the circle.

_____

A chord that passes the center of the circle.

_____

The distance around a circle.

_____

A segment whose endpoints are on the circle.

_____

Name _____ Class _____ Date _____

9F: Vocabulary Review

Study Skill Make your own vocabulary list for each subject you are studying. Provide a formal definition with some informal notes in your own words, and an example. Review your list when you are studying for a test.

Draw an example of your own in the box provided for each term given. Include labels. Write a sentence about your example.

1. complementary angles

_____
_____
_____

2. parallel lines

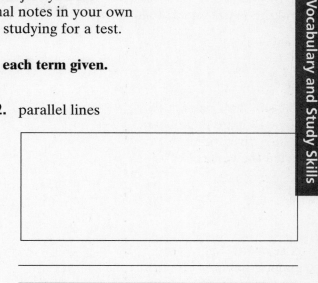

_____
_____
_____

3. perpendicular lines

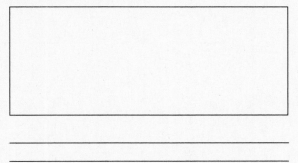

_____
_____
_____

4. vertical angles

_____
_____
_____

5. transversal

_____
_____
_____

6. supplementary angles

_____
_____
_____

$$500$$
$$+1750$$
$$\overline{6750}$$

$$25$$

$$
\begin{array}{r}
15 \\
45\cancel{6}\cancel{0}0 \\
-675 \\
\hline
\end{array}
$$

$$
\begin{array}{r}
235 \\
\times5 \\
\hline
175
\end{array}
$$

$$
\begin{array}{r}
4925 \\
-675 \\
\hline
\end{array}
$$

$$\boxed{5,600}$$

$$+750$$

$$
\begin{array}{r}
5600 \\
500 \\
\hline
6100 \\
-1750 \\
\hline
350
\end{array}
$$

Name _____ Class _____ Date _____

Practice 10-1

Area: Parallelograms

Find the area of each parallelogram.

1.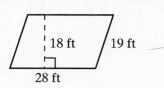

18 ft   19 ft
28 ft

$504 ft^2$

2.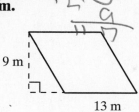

9 m   13 m

$117 m^2$

3.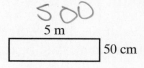

5 m   50 cm

$2,500 cm^2$

Find the area of each shaded region. Assume that all angles that appear
to be right angles are right angles.

4.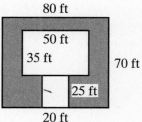

80 ft
50 ft
35 ft   70 ft
25 ft
20 ft

$3,350 ft^2$

5.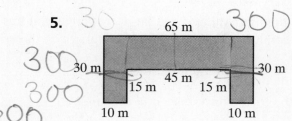

65 m
30 m   45 m   30 m
15 m   15 m
10 m   10 m

$2,275 m^2$

The vertices of a parallelogram are given. Draw each parallelogram. Find
its area.

6. $P(1, 1), Q(3, 1), R(2, 4), S(4, 4)$

$6 u^2$

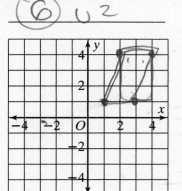

7. $J(-3, 2), K(1, 2), M(-1, -3), L(3, -3)$

$20 u^2$

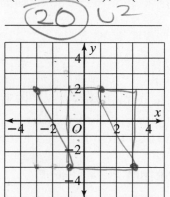

8. The perimeter of a square is 72 in. What is its area?

$324 in$

10-1 • Guided Problem Solving

GPS **Student Page 528, Exercise 18**

Find the area of the figure at the right.
Assume that all angles are right angles.

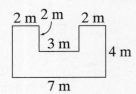

Understand the Problem

1. What are you asked to do? _____

Make and Carry Out a Plan

2. Think of the figure above as a large rectangle that has the
   missing rectangle filled in. What is the length of the large rectangle? _____

3. What is the width of the large rectangle? _____

4. What is the formula for area of a rectangle? _____

5. What is the area of the large rectangle? _____

6. What are the length and width of the small
   rectangle that has been removed from the large rectangle? _____

7. What is the area of the small rectangle? _____

8. Subtract the area of the small
   rectangle from the area of the large rectangle. _____

9. What is the area of the figure? _____

Check the Answer

10. To check your answer, find the area of the figure in another
    way. Divide the figure into three rectangles. Find the area of
    each rectangle and add them together to find the area of the figure. _____

Solve Another Problem

11. Find the area of the figure at the right.
    Assume that all angles are right angles.

    _____

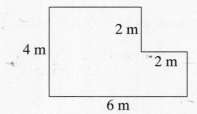

Practice 10-2

Area: Triangles and Trapezoids

Find the area of each trapezoid.

1.

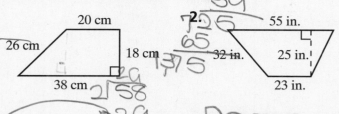

20 cm
26 cm
18 cm
38 cm

$562 cm^*$ *(circled)*

2.

55 in.
32 in. 25 in.
23 in.

$1375 in^2$ *(circled)*

3.

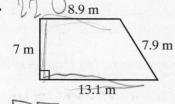

8.9 m
7 m   7.9 m
13.1 m

$77 m$

4. base₁ = 13 in.
base₂ = 8 in.
height = 5 in.

$52.5 in^2$ *(circled)*

5. base₁ = 24.6 cm
base₂ = 9.4 cm
height = 15 cm

$255 cm^2$ *(circled)*

6. base₁ = 2.25 ft
base₂ = 4.75 ft
height = 3.5 ft

$8.25 ft$ *(circled)*

Find the area of each triangle.

7.

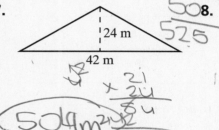

24 m
42 m

$504 m^2$ *(circled)*

8.

9 ft   12 ft
15 ft

9.

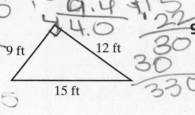

21 in.   35 in.
6 in.   22 in.

$231 in^2$

10. base = 24 in.
height = 9 in.

area = $108 in^2$

11. height = 27 cm
base = 34 cm

area = $459 cm^2$

12. base = 40 ft
height = 8.25 ft

area = $1,660$ 1650

Find the area of each shaded region.

13.

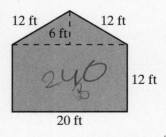

12 ft   12 ft
6 ft
12 ft
20 ft

240

$300 ft^2$

14.

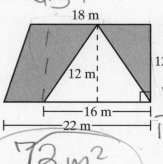

18 m
12 m   12 m
16 m
22 m

192

$72 m^2$ *(circled)*

15. A triangle has an area of 36 cm² and a base of 6 cm. What is the height of the triangle?

$12 cm^2$ *(circled)*

10-2 • Guided Problem Solving

GPS **Student Page 536, Exercise 13**

A trapezoid has area 50 in.^{2}. The two bases are 5 in. and 15 in.
What is the height of the trapezoid?

Understand the Problem

1. What is the area of the trapezoid? _____

2. What are the bases of the trapezoid? _____

3. What are you asked to find? _____

Make and Carry Out a Plan

4. What is the formula for area of a trapezoid? _____

5. Use the formula for area of a trapezoid.
   Replace b_1 with 5, b_2 with 15, and A with 50. _____

6. Evaluate the expression within the parentheses
   and then use the Commutative Property of
   Multiplication to gather the constants together and simplify. _____

7. By what number must you divide both sides of the equation to solve for h? _____

8. What is the height of the trapezoid? _____

Check the Answer

9. To check your answer, use the measurements of the bases
   and your answer to Question 8 to find the area of the trapezoid. _____
   The area should be the same as the area stated in the problem.

Solve Another Problem

10. The area of a trapezoid is 40 cm^2. The two bases
    are 8 cm and 12 cm. What is the height of the trapezoid?

Practice 10-3

Area: Circles

Find the area of each circle. Give an exact area and an approximate area to the nearest tenth.

1. $r = 7$ m

$A =$ _153.86_

$A \approx$ _49πm²_

2. $d = 18$ cm

$A =$ _____

$A \approx$ _81π cm²_

3. $d = 42$ m

$A =$ _1384.7_

$A \approx$ _441πm²_

4. $r = 35$ km

$A =$ _____

$A \approx$ _____

5. $d = 22$ cm

$A =$ _379.9_

$A \approx$ _121π cm²_

6. $r = 25$ ft

$A =$ _____

$A \approx$ _____

7. $r = 3\frac{1}{2}$ mi

$A =$ _38.5_

$A \approx$ _12.25π m²_

8. $d = 5$ in.

$A =$ _____

$A \approx$ _____

9. $d = 9.8$ mm

$A =$ _24.01_

$A \approx$ _75.4π mm_

Find the area of each shaded region to the nearest tenth.

10.

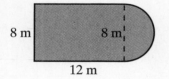

8 m, 8 m, 12 m

_____

11.

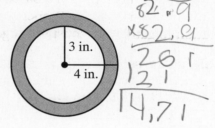

3 in., 4 in.

_____

12.

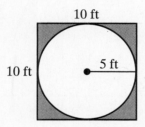

10 ft, 10 ft, 5 ft

_____

13.

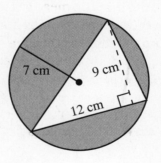

7 cm, 9 cm, 12 cm

_____

14. A goat is tethered to a stake in the ground with a 5-m rope. The goat can graze to the full length of the rope a full 360° around the stake. How much area does the goat have in which to graze?

_____

10-3 • Guided Problem Solving

GPS **Student Page 542, Exercise 23**

Which has a greater area, four circles, each with
radius 1 m, or one circle with radius 4 m? Explain.

Understand the Problem

1. What is the radius of each of the four small circles? _____

2. What is the radius of the single larger circle? _____

3. What are you asked to do? _____

Make and Carry Out a Plan

4. What is the formula for area of a circle? _____

5. Replace *r* with 1 to find the area of one small circle. _____

6. Multiply the area of one small circle by the
   number of small circles to find their total area. _____

7. In the formula, replace *r* with 4 to find the area of the large circle. _____

8. Which has the greater area, the four circles
   with radius 1 m or the circle with radius 4 m? Explain. _____

   _____

Check the Answer

9. To check your answer, use a compass to draw the large
   and small circles. Draw a circle with radius 4 cm to represent
   the large circle. Can you draw the four smaller circles so
   that they fit inside the large circle, without overlapping?
   How does the diagram support your answer to Question 8? _____

   _____

   _____

Solve Another Problem

10. Which has a greater area, three circles, each with
    radius 2 cm, or two circles, each with radius 3 cm? Explain. _____

    _____

    _____

Guided Problem Solving

Name _____ Class _____ Date _____

Practice 10-4

Space Figures

Name the space figure you can form from each net.

1.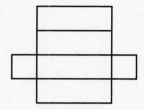

2.

3.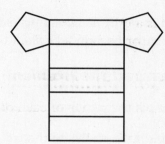

_____   _____   _____

For each figure, describe the base(s) and name the figure.

4.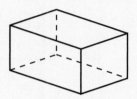

5.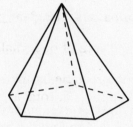

_____   _____

_____   _____

6.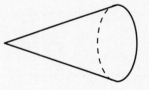

7.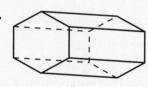

_____   _____

_____   _____

8.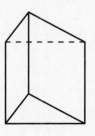

9.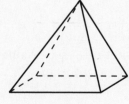

_____   _____

_____   _____

10-4 • Guided Problem Solving

GPS Student Page 548, Exercise 24

Writing in Math Suppose you see a net for a rectangular prism and a net for a rectangular pyramid. Explain how you can match each net with its name.

Understand the Problem

1. For what space figures are the two nets? _____

2. What are you asked to do? _____

Make and Carry Out a Plan

3. How many bases does a rectangular prism have? What shape are they? _____

4. How many lateral faces does a rectangular prism have? What shape are they? _____

_____

5. What shape is the base of a rectangular pyramid? _____ *450*

6. How many lateral faces does a rectangular pyramid have? What shape are they? _____

_____

7. What will the net of a rectangular prism look like? _____

_____

8. What will the net of a rectangular pyramid look like? _____

_____

9. How can you match each net with its name? _____

_____   *2 2 4*
                                                8 4
Check the Answer   *4 8*

10. To check your answer, draw a net for a
    rectangular prism and a net for a rectangular
    pyramid. Do the nets support your answer to Question 9? _____

Solve Another Problem

11. Suppose you see a net for a triangular prism and a triangular
    pyramid. Explain how you can match each net with its name. _____

_____

Guided Problem Solving

Practice 10-5

Surface Area: Prisms and Cylinders

Find the surface area of each space figure. If the answer is not a whole number, round to the nearest tenth.

1.
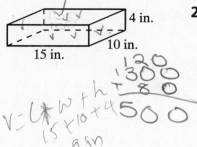
4 in.
10 in.
15 in.

120
300
80
$V = L \times w \times h + h$
15+10+4 500
= 29 in

V- 500 in²

2.
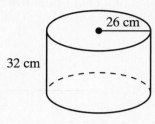
26 cm
32 cm

_____

3.
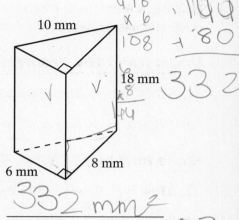
10 mm
18 mm
6 mm   8 mm

418
x 6
108   108
+ 80
332

108
.144
332

8
8
44

332 mm²

Find the surface area of the space figure represented by each net to the nearest square unit.

4.
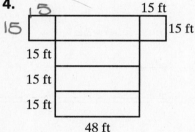
15
15   15 ft
15 ft
15 ft
15 ft
15 ft
48 ft

4,050 ft²

5.
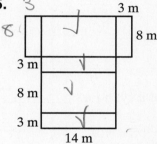
3   3 m
8   8 m
3 m
8 m
3 m
14 m

213
x27

356 m²

6.
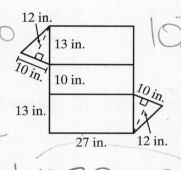
12 in.   13 in.
10 in.   10 in.
13 in.   10 in.
27 in.   12 in.

60   708
.270
60
1032
60

1,082 in²

7. A room is 18 ft long, 14 ft wide, and 8 ft high.

a. Find the cost of painting the four walls with two coats of paint costing $9.50 per gallon. Each gallon covers 256 ft² with one coat.

_____

b. Find the cost of carpeting the floor with carpet costing $5/ft².

_____

c. Find the cost of covering the ceiling with acoustic tile costing $7.50/ft².

_____

d. Find the total cost of renovating the walls, floor, and ceiling.

_____

10-5 • Guided Problem Solving

GPS **Student Page 555, Exercise 16**

Find the area of the top and lateral surfaces of a cylindrical water
tank with radius 20 ft and height 30 ft.

Understand the Problem

1. What is the radius of the water tank? _____

2. What is the height of the water tank? _____

3. What shape is the water tank? _____

4. What are you asked to find? _____

Make and Carry Out a Plan

5. Draw and label a diagram of the water tank.

6. What is the formula for lateral area of a cylinder? _____

7. Use the formula to find the lateral area
   of the water tank to the nearest square foot. _____

8. What is the formula for area of a base of a cylinder? _____

9. Use the formula to find the area of the top
   of the water tank to the nearest square foot. _____

10. Add the two areas to find the area of the
    top and lateral surfaces of the water tank. _____

Check the Answer

11. To check your answer, calculate Steps 7 and 9 in terms
    of π. Then calculate Step 10 in terms of π. Substitute 3.14
    for π and simplify to find the area of the top and lateral surface. _____
    The result should be the same as your answer to Step 10.

Solve Another Problem

12. Find the area of the top and lateral surfaces
    of a cylinder with radius 15 ft and height 40 ft. _____

Practice 10-6

Surface Area: Pyramids, Cones, and Spheres

Find the surface area of each space figure to the nearest square unit.

1.

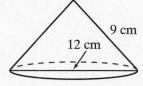

9 cm
12 cm

_____

2.

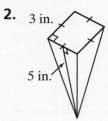

3 in.
5 in.

_____

3.

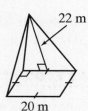

22 m
20 m

_____

4.

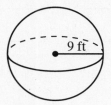

9 ft

_____

5.

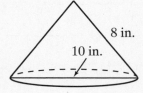

8 in.
10 in.

_____

6.

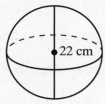

22 cm

_____

7.

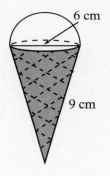

6 cm
9 cm

_____

8.

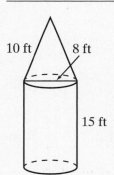

10 ft   8 ft
15 ft

_____

9.

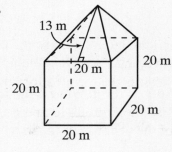

13 m
20 m
20 m
20 m
20 m
20 m

_____

10. a hemisphere with diameter 70 cm

_____

11. A cone and a square-based pyramid have slant heights of 6 in. The diameter for the cone and the base edge of the pyramid are both 8 in.

   a. Which space figure has the greater surface area?

_____

   b. By how much does the greater surface area exceed the lesser? Use 3.14 for π.

_____

10-6 • Guided Problem Solving

GPS **Student Page 561, Exercise 8**

The base of a cone has radius 3 ft. Its slant height is 8 ft. Find the surface area of the cone.

Understand the Problem

1. What is the radius of the base of the cone? _____

2. What is the slant height of the cone? _____

3. What are you asked to find? _____

Make and Carry Out a Plan

4. Draw a sketch of the cone below. Label its radius and slant height.

5. Find the lateral area of the cone. Replace r with 3 and ℓ with 8 in the formula L.A. $= \pi r \ell$. _____

6. Use 3.14 for π. What is the lateral area of the cone? _____

7. Find the base area of the cone. Replace r with 3 in the formula $B = \pi r^2$. _____

8. What is the base area of the cone? _____

9. Add the lateral area and the base area. What is the surface area of the cone? (Round to the nearest square foot.) _____

Check the Answer

10. To check your answer, find the surface area of the cone in terms of π. Then replace π with 3.14 as the final step. _____ Your answer should be the same as your answer to Question 9.

Solve Another Problem

11. The base of a cone has radius 2 m. Its slant height is 11 m. Find the surface area of the cone. _____

Practice 10-7

Volume: Prisms and Cylinders

Find the volume of each prism or cylinder to the nearest cubic unit.

1.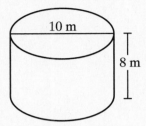

10 m
8 m

_____

2.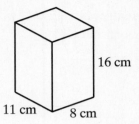

16 cm
11 cm   8 cm

_____

3.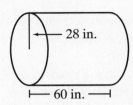

28 in.
60 in.

_____

4.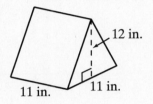

12 in.
11 in.   11 in.

_____

5.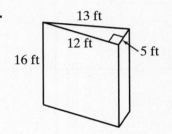

13 ft
12 ft   5 ft
16 ft

_____

6.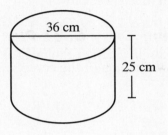

36 cm
25 cm

_____

7. prism
rectangular base:
8 in. by 6 in.
height: 7 in.

_____

8. cylinder
radius: 14 in.
height: 18 in.

_____

9. cylinder
radius: 5 cm
height: 11.2 cm

_____

10. prism
square base:
3.5 ft on a side
height: 6 ft

_____

11. cube
sides: 13 m

_____

12. cylinder
diameter: 5 ft
height: 9 ft

_____

13. A water storage tank has a cylindrical shape. The base has a diameter of
18 m and the tank is 32 m high. How much water, to the nearest cubic
unit, can the tank hold?

_____

14. A tent in the shape of a triangular prism has a square base with a side of
8 feet and a height of 6 feet. What is the volume of the tent?

_____

10-7 • Guided Problem Solving

GPS **Student Page 565, Exercise 9**

Storage An under-the-bed storage box measures 24 in. by 12 in.
by 3 in. Find its volume to the nearest cubic centimeter
(1 in. = 2.54 cm).

Understand the Problem

1. What are the dimensions of the storage box? _____

2. What are you asked to find? _____

Make and Carry Out a Plan

3. Multiply each of the measurements by 2.54 to
find the dimensions of the storage box in centimeters. _____

4. What is the formula for the volume of a prism? _____

5. Find the area of the base, *B*, in square centimeters.
Round your answer to the nearest square centimeter. _____

6. Replace *B* with your answer to Step 5 and *h* with the
height in centimeters in the formula for the volume of a prism. _____

7. What is the volume of the storage box to the nearest cubic centimeter? _____

Check the Answer

8. To check your answer, find the volume of the storage
box in cubic inches and then convert cubic inches
to cubic centimeters (1 cubic in. = 16.39 cubic cm). _____
Your answer should be close to your answer to Question 7.

Solve Another Problem

9. A small drawer measures 16 in. by 10 in. by 4 in. Find its
volume to the nearest cubic centimeter (1 in. = 2.54 cm). _____

Practice 10-8

Make a Model

Solve by making a model.

1. A narrow strip of paper is twisted once, then joined at the ends with glue or tape. The strip is then cut lengthwise along the dotted line shown.

   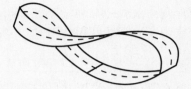

   a. Guess the results.

   _____

   b. Make and cut a model as directed. What are the results?

   _____

2. The midpoint of a segment is the point that divides the segment into two segments of equal length. A quadrilateral with unequal sides is drawn. The midpoints of the four sides are found and connected in order.

   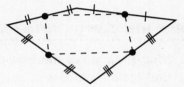

   a. Guess what kind of quadrilateral is formed.

   _____

   b. Draw four quadrilaterals with unequal sides and connect the midpoints of adjacent sides. What kind of quadrilaterals appear to have been formed?

   _____

3. A penny with Lincoln's head upright is rolled along the edge of another penny as shown in the figure.

   a. At the end, do you think Lincoln will be right-side-up or upside-down?

   _____

   b. Conduct an experiment to find out. What are your results?

   _____

4. A net for an octahedron is shown. All the sides are congruent, equilateral triangles. Cut and fold on the dotted lines. Find the surface area of the octahedron. Round to the nearest square centimeter.

   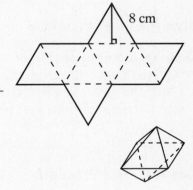

   8 cm

   _____

10-8 • Guided Problem Solving

GPS Student Page 570, Exercise 5

Pets A dog owner wants to use 200 ft of fencing to enclose the greatest possible area for his dog. He wants the fenced area to be rectangular. What dimensions should he use?

Understand the Problem

1. How many feet of fencing does the dog owner have? _____

2. What shape does he want the fenced area to be? _____

3. What are you asked to do? _____

Make and Carry Out a Plan

4. What is the formula for perimeter of a rectangle? _____

5. What will be the perimeter of the fenced area? _____

6. What is the formula for area of a rectangle? _____

7. Look at how changing the dimensions changes the area by completing the table below.

Length	Width	Area (ft²)	Perimeter
90	10	900	200 ft
80	20		
70			
60			
50			
40			
30			

8. What dimensions should the dog owner use? _____

Check the Answer

9. Using the table, how do you know when you have found the dimensions that will give the greatest area? _____

_____

Solve Another Problem

10. A sheep rancher wants to use 100 ft of fencing to make a rectangular feeding pen for lambs. He wants the pen to have the largest area possible. What should the dimensions of the pen be? _____

Practice 10-9

Volume: Pyramids, Cones, and Spheres

Find the volume of each figure to the nearest cubic unit.

1.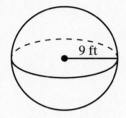

2.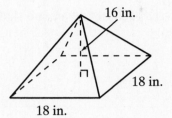

3.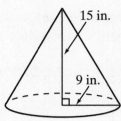

_____   _____   _____

4.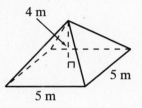

5.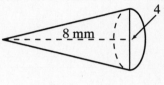

6.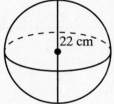

_____   _____   _____

7. square-based pyramid
$s = 9$ in.
$h = 12$ in.

8. cone
$r = 8$ cm
$h = 15$ cm

9. sphere
$r = 6$ in.

_____   _____   _____

10. You make a snow figure using three spheres with radii of 12 in., 10 in.,
and 8 in., with the biggest on the bottom and the smallest for the head.
You get snow from a rectangular area that is 6 ft by 7 ft.
  a. Find the volume of snow in your snow figure to the nearest
  hundredth of a cubic inch.

  bottom: _____   middle: _____

  head: _____   total: _____

  b. Find the area in square inches from which you get snow.

  _____

  c. How deep does the snow need to be before you have enough snow to
  make a figure? State your answer to the nearest $\frac{1}{4}$ in.

  _____

10-9 • Guided Problem Solving

GPS Student Page 574, Exercise 16

Snacks How much frozen yogurt can you pack inside a cone that is 5 in. high with a base radius of 1.25 in.?

Understand the Problem

1. How high is the cone? _____

2. What is the radius of the base of the cone? _____

3. What are you asked to find? _____

Make and Carry Out a Plan

4. What is the formula for volume of a cone? _____

5. What is the formula for B for a cone? _____

6. In the formula, replace π with 3.14, r with 1.25, and h with 5. _____

7. Simplify. Round to the nearest tenth. _____

8. How much frozen yogurt can you pack inside the cone? _____

Check the Answer

9. Explain why the volume of the cone gives the
   amount of frozen yogurt that can be packed inside the cone. _____

   _____

Solve Another Problem

10. To decorate a cake, a baker fills a decorating
    cone that is 4 in. high and has a base radius of
    1.5 in. with frosting. How much frosting is in the cone? _____

10A: Graphic Organizer

For use before Lesson 10-1

Study Skill As you begin chapters toward the end of the text, take a minute to turn back through the chapters you have already studied. Think about the math you have already learned. Which chapter was your favorite? Which was your least favorite?

Write your answers. Use the Table of Contents page for this chapter at the front of the book.

1. What is the title of this chapter? _____

2. Name four topics that you will study in this chapter:

   _____   _____

   _____   _____

3. What is the topic of the Problem Solving lesson? _____

4. Complete the graphic organizer as you work through the chapter.
   1. Write the title of the chapter in the center oval.
   2. When you begin a lesson, write the name of the lesson in a rectangle.
   3. When you complete that lesson, write a skill or key concept from that lesson in the outer oval linked to that rectangle.
   Continue with steps 2 and 3 clockwise around the graphic organizer.

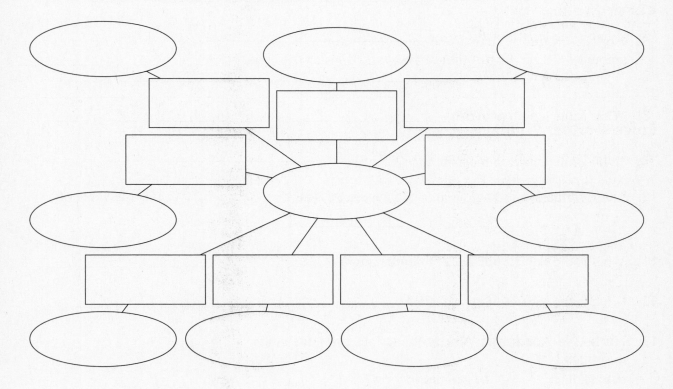

10B: Reading Comprehension

For use after Lesson 10-8

Study Skill When you first look at a paragraph, graph, or diagram, begin by taking time to read all the captions and titles. These labels tell you what this item is about and often contain important information.

Look at this geometric figure, and then answer the questions about it.

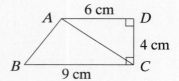

1. What is the name of the figure *ABC*? _____

2. What is the name of the figure *ADC*? _____

3. What is the name of the figure *ADCB*? _____

4. What kind of angle is ∠*ADC*? _____

5. What kind of angle is ∠*DCB*? _____

6. What is the length of $\overline{BC}$? _____

7. What is the length of $\overline{CD}$? _____

8. What is the length of $\overline{AD}$? _____

9. What is the height of the figure *ADCB*? _____

10. The formula for finding the area of figure *ADCB* is $A = \frac{1}{2}h(b_1 + b_2)$. What is the value of $(b_1 + b_2)$? _____

11. What is the unit for the area of figure *ADCB*? _____

12. What is the area of figure *ADCB*? _____

13. **High-Use Academic Words** What does *figure* mean in questions 1-3?

    a. calculate   **b.** geometric form

10C: Reading/Writing Math Symbols For use after Lesson 10-3

Study Skill When you read symbols, use the context to help you decide their meanings. Often one symbol can have more than one meaning, each depending on how it is used. Clues from the context can sometimes help you decide the meanings of symbols or terms with which you are not familiar.

Certain letters and symbols are often used with area and volume. Write the letter or symbol that is described in the blank.

1. the letter used for the area of a figure _____

2. the letter used for the base length of a figure _____

3. the letter used for the area of the base of a space figure _____

4. the abbreviation used for square feet _____

5. the expression used for the sum of the bases of a trapezoid _____

6. the letter used for the circumference of a circle _____

7. the letter used for the radius of a circle _____

8. the symbol used for ratio of the circumference of a circle to its diameter _____

Write your answers.

9. Write a brief explanation of the difference in meaning of the 2 in these expressions: b^2 $b_1 + b_2$

   _____

   _____

   _____

10. On a certain multiple choice question, you are asked to find the area of a figure. The answer choices are given below. Which ones can you immediately eliminate? Explain your reasoning.

    A. 13π ft^2 **B.** 26π ft   **C.** 36 ft^2 **D.** 42π ft^3

   _____

   _____

10D: Visual Vocabulary Practice

For use after Lesson 10-9

Study Skill Math symbols give us a way to express complex ideas in a small space.

Concept List

cylinder	prism	pyramid
surface area	sphere	surface area of a prism or cylinder
volume	volume of a cone	volume of a sphere

Write the concept that best describes each exercise. Choose from the concept list shown above.

1. $L.A. + 2B$	**2.** the amount of liquid that fills a container	**3.**
4.	**5.** $\frac{1}{3}Bh$	**6.**
7.	**8.** the amount of material needed to make a container	**9.** $\frac{4}{3}\pi r^3$

10E: Vocabulary Check

Study Skill Strengthen your vocabulary. Use these pages and add cues and summaries by applying the Cornell Notetaking style.

Write the definition for each word at the right. To check your work, fold the paper back along the dotted line to see the correct answers.

_____

_____

_____

Prism

_____

_____

_____

Pyramid

_____

_____

Cylinder

_____

_____

Cone

_____

_____

_____

Sphere

10E: Vocabulary Check (continued)   For use after Lesson 10-4

• •

Write the vocabulary word for each definition. To check your work, fold the paper forward along the dotted line to see the correct answers.

A space figure with two parallel and congruent polygonal faces, called bases, and lateral faces that are parallelograms.

_____

A space figure with triangular faces that meet at a vertex, and a base that is a polygon.

_____

A space figure with two circular, parallel, and congruent bases.

_____

A space figure with one circular base and one vertex.

_____

The set of points in space that are a given distance from a point, called a center.

_____

10F: Vocabulary Review

For use with Chapter Review

Study Skill When you make a link between something visual, such as a picture, graph, or diagram, and a new vocabulary term, that link can help you to remember the meaning of the term. Make your own drawings whenever you can to picture the meaning of a new word.

Draw an example of your own in each box for each term given here. Label important parts of each figure.

1. cone

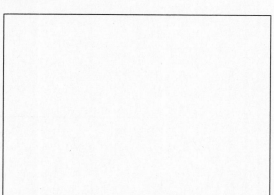

2. cylinder

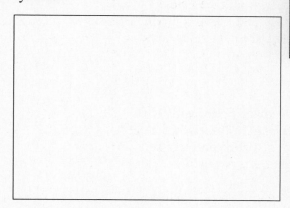

3. sphere

4. prism

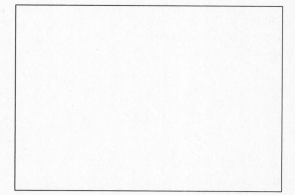

5. pyramid

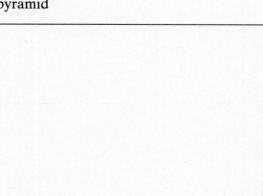

6. net for a square prism

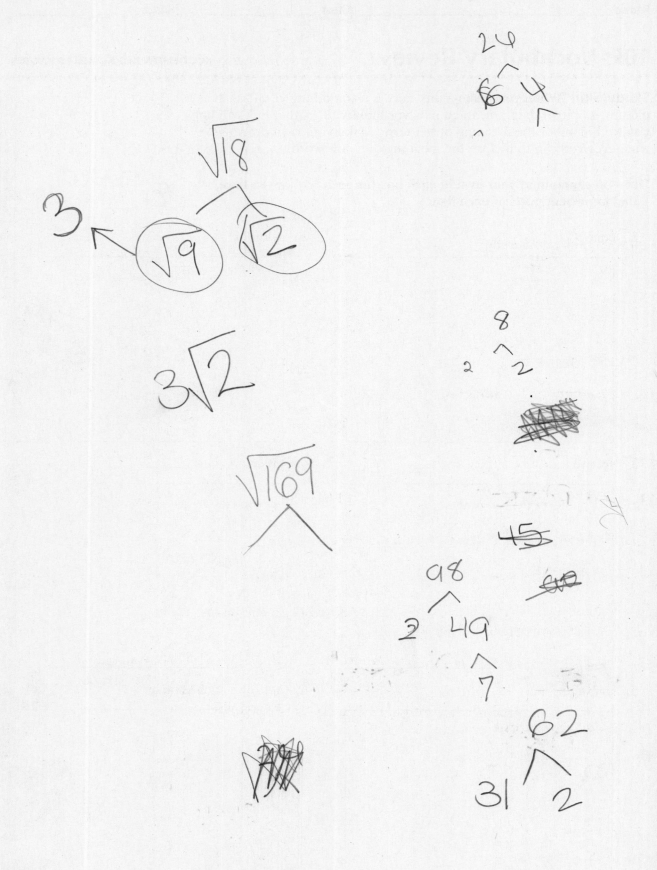

$\sqrt{18}$

$\sqrt{9}$ $\sqrt{2}$

3

$3\sqrt{2}$

$\sqrt{169}$

24

66   4

8

2   2

45

98

2   49

7

62

31   2

Name handwritten: $\frac{n6}{+9}$ over 25 Class circled: -3

Practice 11-1

Square Roots and Irrational Numbers

Estimate to the nearest integer.

1. $\sqrt{18}$ _4___

2. $\sqrt{24}$ _5___

3. $\sqrt{50}$ _7___

4. $\sqrt{8}$ _3___

5. $\sqrt{62}$ _8___

6. $\sqrt{78}$ _9___

7. $\sqrt{98}$ _10___

8. $\sqrt{46}$ _7___

9. $\sqrt{38}$ _6___

Simplify each square root.

10. $\sqrt{144}$ _√12___

11. $\sqrt{9+16}$ _5___

12. $\sqrt{900}$ _30___

13. $\sqrt{169}$ _√13___

14. $-\sqrt{100}$ _-10___

15. $\sqrt{0.16}$ _.4___

16. $\sqrt{\frac{16}{81}}$ _$\frac{4}{9}$___

17. $\sqrt{\frac{4}{25}}$ _$\frac{2}{5}$___

18. $\sqrt{\frac{121}{144}}$ _$\frac{11}{12}$___

Handwritten side work: $3\overline{)147}$, 49, $\frac{12}{24}$

Identify each number as rational or irrational.

19. $\sqrt{289}$ _rational___

20. $5.7777\ldots$ _rational___

21. $\sqrt{41}$ _ir___

22. $0.62662\ldots$ _ir___

23. $\sqrt{49}$ _rational___

24. $\sqrt{52}$ _ir___

Find two integers that make each equation true.

25. $x^2 = 16$ _x = 4___

26. $3m^2 = 147$ _m = 7___ (handwritten: 35, 49)

Use the formula $d = \sqrt{1.5h}$ to estimate the distance to the horizon d in miles for each viewer's eye height h, in feet.

27. $h = 12$ ft $\sqrt{18}$ 4

28. $h = 216$ ft $\sqrt{324}$ 18

29. $h = 412$ ft $\sqrt{620}$ 25

30. The Moon has a surface area of approximately 14,650,000 mi². Estimate its radius to the nearest mile.

_1080 mi___ na

Handwritten work: $\begin{array}{r} 115 \\ \times 12 \\ \hline 30 \\ 15 \\ \hline 180 \end{array}$

$\begin{array}{r} 216 \\ \times 1.5 \\ \hline 1080 \\ 216 \\ \hline 3\,1.5 \end{array}$ 32 4,0

$\begin{array}{r} 412 \\ \times 1.5 \\ \hline 2080 \\ 412 \\ \hline 620.0 \end{array}$

11-1 • Guided Problem Solving

GPS **Student Page 591, Exercise 44**

Geometry Find the length of a side of a square with an area of 81 cm^2.

Understand the Problem

1. What is the area of the square? _____

2. What are you asked to find? _____

Make and Carry Out a Plan

3. The length of a side of a square is the square
   root of the area of the square. Let s represent
   the length of a side. Write an equation to show
   that the side of the square equals the square root of 81. _____

4. To solve for s, find the square root of 81. _____

5. What is the length of a side of
   a square with an area of 81 cm^2? _____

Check the Answer

6. To check your answer, square it. _____
   The result should be the area of the square.

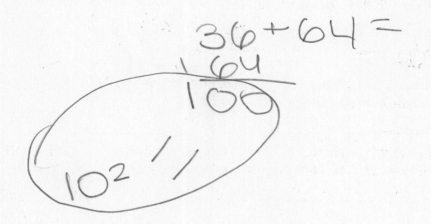

Solve Another Problem

7. Find the length of a side of a
   square with an area of 121 cm^2. _____

Guided Problem Solving

Name _____ Class _____ Date _____

Practice 11-2

The Pythagorean Theorem

Can you form a right triangle with the three lengths given? Show your work.

100 + 44 = 144

1. 20, 21, 29 _Yes_

2. 7, 11, 12 _no_

3. 10, $2\sqrt{11}$, 12 _Yes_

4. 28, 45, 53 _Yes_

5. 9, $\sqrt{10}$, 10 _no_

6. 10, 15, 20 _no_

Find each missing length to the nearest tenth of a unit.

7.
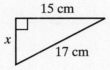
15 cm

x

17 cm

_____

8.
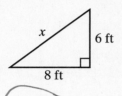
x

6 ft

8 ft

_10 ft_

9.
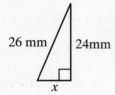
26 mm

24mm

x

_____

10.
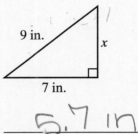
9 in.

x

7 in.

_5.7 in_

11.
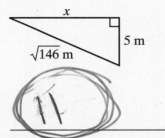
x

$\sqrt{146}$ m

5 m

_11_

12.
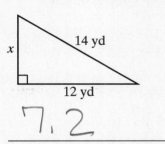
x

14 yd

12 yd

_7.2_

Use the triangle at the right. Find the missing length to the nearest tenth of a unit.

361 + 1225

13. $a = 6$ m, $b = 9$ m

$c \approx$ _10.8_

14. $a = 19$ in., $c = 35$ in.

$b \approx$ _39 29.4_

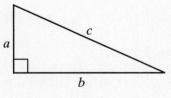

c

a

b

15. $b = 24$ cm, $c = 32$ cm

$a \approx$ _____

16. $a = 14$ ft, $c = 41$ ft

$b \approx$ _38.5_

17. A rectangular park measures 300 ft by 400 ft. A sidewalk runs diagonally from one corner to the opposite corner. Find the length of the sidewalk.

_____

Name _____ Class _____ Date _____

11-2 • Guided Problem Solving

GPS **Student Page 595, Exercise 10**

House Painting A painter places an 11-ft ladder against a house. The base of the ladder is 3 ft from the house. How high on the house does the ladder reach?

Understand the Problem

1. How long is the ladder? What part of a right triangle does the ladder represent? _____

2. How far from the house is the base of the ladder? What part of a right triangle does this represent? _____

3. What are you asked to find? What part of a right triangle is this? _____

Make and Carry Out a Plan

4. Draw a sketch of an 11-ft ladder leaning against a house. The base of the ladder is 3 ft from the house.

5. Write the Pythagorean Theorem equation. Use a and b for the legs and c for the hypotenuse. _____

6. Replace b with 3 and c with 11. _____

7. Square 3 and 11. _____

8. Subtract from each side to solve for a^2. _____

9. Find the positive square root of each side to solve for a. Round to the nearest tenth. _____

10. How high on the house does the ladder reach? _____

Check the Answer

11. To check your answer, use the Pythagorean Theorem. Replace b with 3 and a with your answer. Find the length of the ladder, c. _____

Solve Another Problem

12. A wire from the top of a telephone pole is anchored to the ground 12 ft from the base of the pole. The pole is 16 ft tall. How long is the wire? Draw a sketch and solve the problem. _____

Guided Problem Solving

Practice 11-3

Distance and Midpoint Formulas

The table has sets of endpoints of several segments. Find the distance
between each pair of points and the midpoint of each segment. Round to
the nearest tenth when necessary.

	Endpoints	Distance Between (Length of Segment)	Midpoint
1.	$A(2, 6)$ and $B(4, 10)$	4.5	(3, 8)
2.	$C(5, -3)$ and $D(7, 2)$	5.2	(6, -½)
3.	$E(0, 12)$ and $F(5, 0)$	13	(2½, 6)
4.	$G(4, 7)$ and $H(-2, -3)$	45 11.7	(1, 2)
5.	$J(-1, 5)$ and $K(2, 1)$	5	(½, 3)
6.	$L(-3, 8)$ and $M(-7, -1)$	13.5 9.8	(-5, 3½)

Find the perimeter of each figure. Round to the nearest tenth when
necessary.

7.

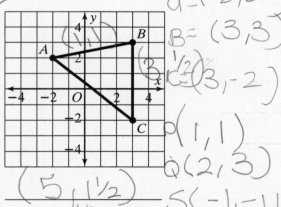

a = (-2, 2)
B = (3, 3)
C (3, -2)

(5, 1½)

8.

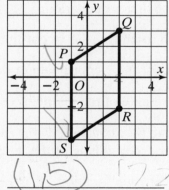

O (1, 1)
Q (2, 3)
S (-1, -4)

(1, 5) 7.2

(0, -3)
(0, 1.5)

9.

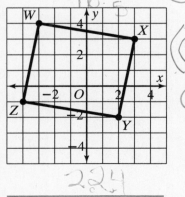

22.4

10.

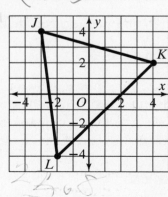

Handwritten margin notes:
$2^2 + 4^2$
$16 + 4$
20
$2^2 + -1^2$
$4 + 1$
$5^2 + 12^2$
$4 + 16$

11-3 • Guided Problem Solving

GPS **Student Page 601, Exercise 15**

Reasoning The midpoint of $\overline{AB}$ is (3, 5). The coordinates of A are $(-6, 1)$. What are the coordinates of B?

Understand the Problem

1. What is the midpoint of $\overline{AB}$? _____

2. What are the coordinates of A? _____

3. What are you asked to find? _____

Make and Carry Out a Plan

4. Write the Midpoint Formula. _____

5. Write the formula for the x-coordinate of the midpoint. _____

6. What is the x-coordinate of the midpoint of $\overline{AB}$? _____

7. Use your answers to Steps 5 and 6 to write an equation for the x-coordinate of the midpoint. _____

8. Replace x_1 with -6 in your equation. _____

9. Solve the equation to find x_2, the x-coordinate of B. _____

10. Write the formula for the y-coordinate of the midpoint. _____

11. What is the y-coordinate of the midpoint of $\overline{AB}$? _____

12. Use your answers to Steps 10 and 11 to write an equation for the y-coordinate of the midpoint. _____

13. Replace y_1 with 1 in your equation. _____

14. Solve the equation to find y_2, the y-coordinate of B. _____

15. What are the coordinates of B? _____

Check the Answer

16. To check your answer, use the coordinates of A and the coordinates of B to find the midpoint of $\overline{AB}$. _____

Solve Another Problem

17. The midpoint of $\overline{RS}$ is (1, 6). The coordinates of R are (2, 8). What are the coordinates of S? _____

Name _____ Class _____ Date _____

Practice 11-4

Write a Proportion

•••

Write a proportion and find the value of *x*.

1. $\triangle KLM \sim \triangle NPQ$

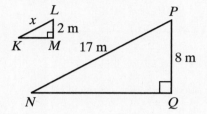

Proportion: _____

x = _____

2. $\triangle RST \sim \triangle RPQ$

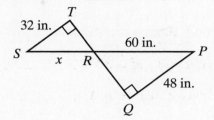

Proportion: _____

x = _____

3. $\triangle ABC \sim \triangle ADE$

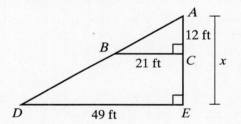

Proportion: _____

x = _____

4. $\triangle UVW \sim \triangle UYZ$

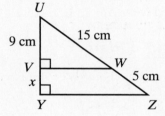

Proportion: _____

x = _____

Solve. Show the proportion you use.

5. A surveyor needs to find the distance across a canyon. She finds a tree on the edge of the canyon and a large rock on the other edge. The surveyor uses stakes to set up the similar right triangles shown. Find the distance from the tree to the other side of the canyon, *x*.

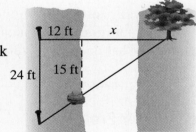

_____

6. Three cartons of juice cost $4.77. Find the cost of 8 cartons.

_____

7. If a pizza with a diameter of 12 inches costs $10.99, based on area, how much should a 15-inch pizza cost?

_____

•••

Pre-Algebra Lesson 11-4 **503**

11-4 • Guided Problem Solving

Landscaping A landscaper needs to find the distance *x* across a piece of land. He estimates the distance using the similar triangles at the right. What is the distance?

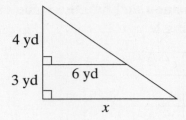

Understand the Problem

1. How many triangles are in the diagram? _____

2. What information are you given about the triangles in the problem and in the diagram? _____

3. In the smaller triangle, what are the given measurements? _____

4. In the larger triangle, what are the given measurements? _____

5. What are you asked to find? _____

Make and Carry Out a Plan

6. Write a proportion using the legs of the two triangles. _____

7. Write cross products. _____

8. By what number will you divide each side to solve for *x*? _____

9. What is the distance *x*? _____

Check the Answer

10. To check your answer, substitute your answer for *x* in the proportion you wrote in Step 6. Write cross products. What does the result tell you about your answer? _____

_____

Solve Another Problem

11. Jenna wants to find the distance *x* across a small pond. She estimates the distance using the similar triangles at the right. What is the distance?

_____

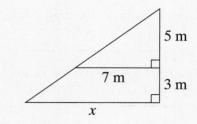

Practice 11-5

Special Right Triangles

The length of one side of the triangle is given in each row of the table.
Find the missing lengths for that triangle.

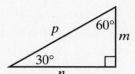

	m	n	p
1.	14		
2.			36
3.		$9\sqrt{3}$	
4.	5		

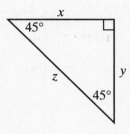

	x	y	z
5.	11		
6.		8.7	
7.			$7\sqrt{2}$
8.	17		

Tell whether a triangle with sides of the given lengths could be 45°-45°-90°
or 30°-60°-90°. Explain.

9. $3\sqrt{2}, 3\sqrt{2}, 6$

_____

10. $10, 24, 26$

_____

_____

In the figure, $BD = 6\sqrt{2}$. Find each value.

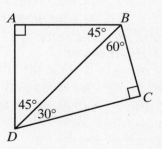

11. AB _____

12. AD _____

13. BC _____

14. CD _____

15. One leg of a 45°-45°-90° right triangle measures 14 cm.
Find the exact perimeter.

_____

11-5 • Guided Problem Solving

GPS **Student Page 611, Exercise 14**

Mrs. Fernandez wants to string a rope diagonally across her
square classroom for her students to hang their completed art
projects. If one side of the room measures 20 ft, what is the
minimum length of rope she can use?

Understand the Problem

1. What shape is Mrs. Fernandez's classroom? _____

2. What does Mrs. Fernandez want to do? _____

3. What is the measure of one of the sides of the room? _____

4. What are you asked to find? _____

Make and Carry Out a Plan

5. Draw a sketch of Mrs. Fernandez's classroom.
   Label the measure of each side. Draw the rope
   hung diagonally across the room. Label the rope *d*.

6. What is true about the measurements of the four angles of a square? _____

7. What type of special right triangle is formed
   by two sides and the diagonal of the square?_____

8. How is the length of the hypotenuse related
   to the length of a leg in this type of a triangle? _____

9. Replace the length of the hypotenuse with *d* and the
   length of a leg with 20. Use a calculator to solve for *d*. _____

10. What is the minimum length of rope Mrs. Fernandez
    can use? Round your answer to the nearest tenth. _____

Check the Answer

11. To check your answer, use the Pythagorean Theorem to solve for *d*. _____
    Your answer should be the same as your answer to Step 10.

Solve Another Problem

12. Jorge wants to string lights diagonally across his square-
    shaped outdoor patio. If one side of his patio measures 10 ft,
    what is the minimum length of the string of lights Jorge can use? _____

Name _____ Class _____ Date _____

Practice 11-6

Find each value. Round to four decimal places.

1. cos 20° _____

2. tan 64° _____

3. sin 41° _____

4. tan 8° _____

5. sin 88° _____

6. cos 53° _____

Use △MNP for Exercises 7 to 12. Find each ratio.

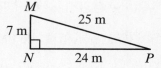

7. sine of ∠P _____

8. cosine of ∠P _____

9. tangent of ∠P _____

10. sine of ∠M _____

11. cosine of ∠M _____

12. tangent of ∠M _____

Use △RST for Exercises 13 to 18. Find each ratio in simplest form.

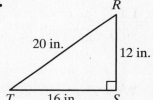

13. sine of ∠T _____

14. cosine of ∠T _____

15. tangent of ∠T _____

16. sine of ∠R _____

17. cosine of ∠R _____

18. tangent of ∠R _____

Write each ratio using square root signs. Use your knowledge of 45°-45°-90° and 30°-60°-90° right triangles.

19. tan 30° _____

20. cos 45° _____

21. sin 60° _____

22. cos 60° _____

23. tan 45° _____

24. sin 30° _____

Solve.

25. A surveyor standing 2,277 ft from the base of a building measured a 31° angle to the topmost point. To the nearest ft, how tall is the building?

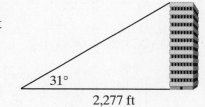

_____

11-6 • Guided Problem Solving

GPS **Student Page 617, Exercise 22**

Hot-Air Balloons A hot-air balloon climbs continuously along a 30° angle to a height of 5,000 feet. To the nearest tenth of a foot, how far has the balloon traveled to reach 5,000 feet? Draw a sketch, and then solve.

Understand the Problem

1. Along what size of angle does the hot-air balloon climb? _____

2. To what height is the balloon climbing? _____

3. What are you asked to find? _____

Make and Carry Out a Plan

4. Draw a sketch of a right triangle. One leg of the triangle will be the ground. The other leg will show the height of the balloon, 5,000 feet. Label the 30° angle. Let *x* represent the distance the balloon travels.

5. You know the angle and the side opposite the angle. What trigonometric ratio will you use to find *x?* _____

6. Substitute 30° for the angle and 5,000 for the height of the balloon. _____

7. Multiply each side by *x*. _____

8. Divide each side by sin 30°. _____

9. Use a calculator to solve for *x*. _____

10. How far does the balloon travel to reach 5,000 ft? _____

Check the Answer

11. To check your answer, use 5,000 ft and your answer to write a trigonometric ratio to find the measure of the angle. _____

Solve Another Problem

12. A pole of a circus tent is held in place by cables staked into the ground. One of the cables forms a 55° angle with the ground. It is staked 10 feet away from the base of the pole. How long is the cable to the nearest tenth of a foot? Draw a sketch and then solve. _____

Practice 11-7

Angles of Elevation and Depression

Find *x* to the nearest tenth.

1.

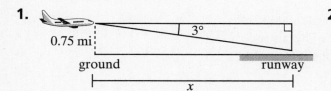

0.75 mi   3°   ground   runway   *x*

x ≈ _____

2.

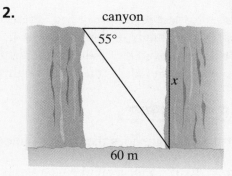

canyon   55°   *x*   60 m

x ≈ _____

3.

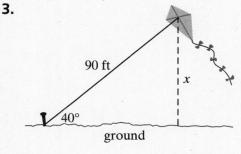

90 ft   *x*   40°   ground

x ≈ _____

4.

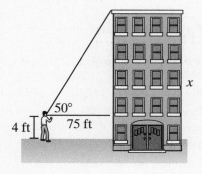

50°   4 ft   75 ft   *x*

x ≈ _____

Solve each problem. Round to the nearest unit.

5. A helicopter is rescuing a would-be mountain climber. The helicopter is hovering, so there is an angle of depression of 35° from the helicopter to the climber. The bottom of the helicopter's 12-meter ladder is hanging even with the climber. How far does the helicopter need to move horizontally to be directly above the climber?

_____

6. Kara's kite is flying at the end of 35 yards of string. Her end of the string is 1 yard off the ground. The angle of elevation of the kite is 50°. What is the height of the kite from the ground?

_____

7. Karl is standing 80 ft from the base of a tree. He sees the top of the tree from an angle of elevation of 42°. His eye is 4.5 feet off the ground. How tall is the tree?

_____

Name _____ Class _____ Date _____

11-7 • Guided Problem Solving

GPS Student Page 624, Exercise 15

Aeronautics The pilot of a helicopter at an altitude of 6,000 ft sees a second helicopter at an angle of depression of 43°. The altitude of the second helicopter is 4,000 ft. What is the distance from the first helicopter to the second along the line of sight?

Understand the Problem

1. At what altitude is the pilot of the first helicopter flying? _____

2. What is the angle of depression at which the pilot can see the second helicopter? _____

3. What is the altitude of the second helicopter? _____

4. What are you asked to find? _____

Make and Carry Out a Plan

5. Draw a sketch on a separate sheet of paper to help you visualize the situation. Label both helicopters and their altitudes and the angle of depression. Let *d* represent the distance from the first helicopter to the second helicopter.

6. What is the difference in altitude between the two helicopters? _____
   Label this on your sketch.

7. What trigonometric ratio will you use to find *d*? _____

8. Substitute 43 for the angle measure and 2,000 for the opposite side. _____

9. Multiply each side by *d*. _____

10. Divide each side by sin 43°. _____

11. Use a calculator to simplify. What is the distance from the first helicopter to the second along the line of sight? _____

Check the Answer

12. To check your answer, use the cosine of the complementary angle, 47°, to solve for *d*. _____
    The result should be the same as your answer to Step 11.

Solve Another Problem

13. The pilot of a hot-air balloon at an altitude of 1,000 ft sees the top of a building at an angle of depression of 65°. The height of the building is 40 ft. What is the distance from the hot-air balloon to the building along the line of sight? _____

Guided Problem Solving

11A: Graphic Organizer

For use before Lesson 11-1

Study Skill The title for this chapter tells you what the chapter is about. Take a moment to sketch a right triangle and write some notes about what you know about these special triangles. Then skim the chapter to see what else you are going to learn from it about right triangles.

Write your answers. Use the Table of Contents page for this chapter at the front of the book.

1. What is the title of this chapter? _____

2. Name four topics that you will study in this chapter:

   _____   _____

   _____   _____

3. What is the topic of the Problem Solving lesson? _____

4. Complete the graphic organizer as you work through the chapter.
   1. Write the title of the chapter in the center oval.
   2. When you begin a lesson, write the name of the lesson in a rectangle.
   3. When you complete that lesson, write a skill or key concept from that lesson in the outer oval linked to that rectangle.
   Continue with steps 2 and 3 clockwise around the graphic organizer.

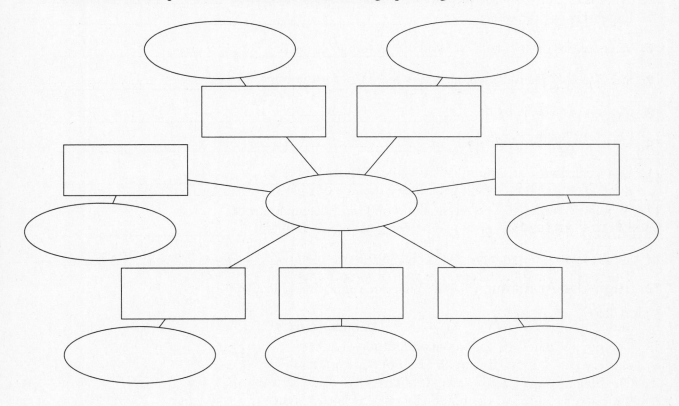

11B: Reading Comprehension

For use after Lesson 11-3

Study Skill When you have quite a few pages to read, take a break every two or three pages by looking up from the page, and reflecting on what you have just read.

Look at the formula. Then answer the questions that follow.

Distance Formula

$$d = \sqrt{(x_2 - x_1)^2 + (y_2 - y_1)^2}$$

1. What will this formula help you find? _____

   _____

2. In order to apply this formula to find d, what values do you have to know?

   _____

3. What is the difference in the meaning of the small 2 in x_2 and the small 2's that are written after the parentheses?

   _____

Use (1, 6) and (5, 9) as (x_1, y_1) and (x_2, y_2) and find the value of each expression.

4. $(x_2 - x_1)$ _____

5. $(y_2 - y_1)$ _____

6. $(x_2 - x_1)^2$ _____

7. $(y_2 - y_1)^2$ _____

8. $(x_2 - x_1)^2 + (y_2 - y_1)^2$ _____

9. $\sqrt{(x_2 - x_1)^2 + (y_2 - y_1)^2}$ _____

10. d _____

11. Would the value of d be the same if you found the square root of $(x_2 - x_1)^2$ and of $(y_2 - y_1)^2$ before you added? Explain. _____

    _____

12. **High-Use Academic Words** What does *apply* mean in Question 2?

    a. use   **b.** understand

11C: Reading/Writing Math Symbols   For use after Lesson 11-5

Study Skill The position of symbols can be very important to their meaning. Learn these whenever you come across them, and add them to your personal vocabulary list.

Find the values for each set of expressions. Use a calculator and round final answers to the nearest tenth when necessary.

1. Find the value of each expression when $x = 3$.

   a. $-x^2$ _____   **b.** $(-x)^2$ _____

2. Find the value of each expression when $x = 5$.

   a. $\sqrt{x}$ _____   **b.** $-\sqrt{x}$ _____

3. Find the value of each expression when $x = 4$.

   a. $\sqrt{x^2}$ _____   **b.** $(\sqrt{x})^2$ _____

4. Find the value of each expression when $x = 2$ and $y = 3$.

   a. $(x + y)^2$ _____   **b.** $x + y^2$ _____

5. Find the value of each expression when $x = 1$ and $y = 5$.

   a. $\sqrt{x^2 + y^2}$ _____   **b.** $\sqrt{x^2} + \sqrt{y^2}$ _____

6. Although 49 has two square roots, the square root symbol means only one of them. Write the value of the expression.

   $\sqrt{49}$ = _____

7. Write a symbol in the blank that best makes a true statement.

   π _____ 3.14

11D: Visual Vocabulary Practice

For use after Lesson 11-6

Study Skill When reading a diagram, look for any special features implied by the diagram. For instance, if the diagram is a triangle, check if it is just a 3-sided figure or a special triangle, such as a right triangle.

Concept List

cosine	distance	hypotenuse
leg	midpoint	Pythagorean Theorem
right triangle	sine	tangent

Write the concept that best describes each exercise. Choose from the concept list above.

1. the side labeled a or b in	**2.** the side labeled c in	**3.** $a^2 + b^2 = c^2$
4. $\sqrt{(x_2 - x_1)^2 + (y_2 - y_1)^2}$	**5.** $\left(\dfrac{x_1 + x_2}{2}, \dfrac{y_1 + y_2}{2}\right)$	**6.** $\dfrac{\text{opposite}}{\text{hypotenuse}}$
7. $\dfrac{\text{adjacent}}{\text{hypotenuse}}$	**8.** $\dfrac{\text{opposite}}{\text{adjacent}}$	**9.**

11E: Vocabulary Check

For use after Lesson 11-7

Study Skill Strengthen your vocabulary. Use these pages and add cues and summaries by applying the Cornell Notetaking style.

Write the definition for each word at the right. To check your work, fold the paper back along the dotted line to see the correct answers.

_____

_____

_____   Square root

_____

_____

_____   Irrational number

_____

_____

_____   Trigonometry

_____

_____

_____   Angle of elevation

_____

_____

_____   Angle of depression

_____

_____

11E: Vocabulary Check (continued)

Write the vocabulary word for each definition. To check your work, fold the paper forward along the dotted line to see the correct answers.

A number that when multiplied by itself equals the given number.

_____

A number whose decimal form neither terminates nor repeats.

_____

A branch of mathematics involving triangle measures.

_____

An angle formed by a horizontal line and a line of sight above it.

_____

An angle formed by a horizontal line and a line of sight below it.

_____

11F: Vocabulary Review Puzzle

For use with Chapter Review

Study Skill When you want to remember a new rule, definition, or formula, try saying it over and over to yourself. This repetition helps the new idea stay in your memory.

Unscramble the UPPERCASE letters to form a math word or phrase that completes the sentence.

1. A CEPTFER RAQUES is the square of an integer.

   _____

2. The longest side of a right triangle is the SOYPENTHUE.

   _____

3. In a right triangle, the TANGTEN of ∠A is the ratio of the length of the opposite leg to the length of the adjacent leg.

   _____

4. In a right triangle, the GLES form the sides of the right angle.

   _____

5. In a right triangle, the leg TENDJACA to an angle of the triangle forms one side of that angle.

   _____

6. An angle of SEPRIDNOSE is formed by a horizontal line and a line of sight below it.

   _____

7. In a right triangle, the ratio of two sides is called a ROROTTENGIMIC ratio.

   _____

8. Finding a RAQUES TORO is the inverse of squaring a number.

   _____

9. In a right triangle, the ratio of the length of the leg adjacent to ∠A to the length of the hypotenuse is the SOCENI of ∠A.

   _____

10. The word GOOTIMNERRYT means triangle measure.

    _____

11. An angle of VEEANTILO is formed by a horizontal line and a line of sight above it.

    _____

12. In a right triangle, the ratio of the length of the leg opposite ∠A to the length of the hypotenuse is the INSE of ∠A .

    _____

Practice 12-1

Frequency Tables, Line Plots, and Histograms

Display each set of data in a frequency table.

1. 5 1 4 6 2 6 4 5 1 3 2 6 4 5 4 6

Number						
Frequency						

2. 4 3 1 2 1 3 3 1 3 2 1

Number				
Frequency				

Draw a line plot and histogram for each frequency table. Find the range.

3.

Number	1	2	3	4	5	6
Frequency	2	0	4	1	2	4

range: _____

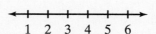

4.

Number	1	2	3	4	5	6
Frequency	4	4	0	0	3	2

range: _____

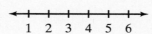

Construct a frequency table from the line plot.

5.

State Average Pupils per Teacher

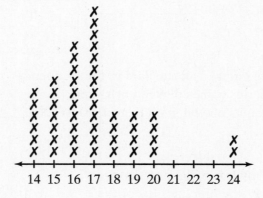

Pupils per Teacher											
Frequency											

6. What is the range in pupil-teacher ratios? _____

12-1 • Guided Problem Solving

GPS Student Page 638, Exercise 19

Baseball In the World Series, the first team to win four games is the champion. Sometimes the Series lasts for seven games, but sometimes the Series ends in fewer games. Below are data for 1970–2004. Make a frequency table and use it to find the mode. Numbers of World Series Games, 1970–2004: 5, 7, 7, 7, 5, 7, 4, 6, 6, 7, 6, 6, 7, 5, 5, 7, 7, 7, 5, 4, 4, 7, 6, 6, 0, 6, 6, 7, 4, 4, 5, 7, 7, 6, 4

Understand the Problem

1. What data are you given? _____

2. What are you asked to do? _____

Make and Carry Out a Plan

3. Look at the data. Put a tally mark in the row corresponding to the number of games played for each year.

4. When all of the tally marks have been made, count the tally marks and record the frequency for each number of games.

5. To find the mode of the data, look in the "Frequency" column. Which number of games occurred most often? _____

Number of Games	Tally	Frequency
0		
1		
2		
3		
4		
5		
6		
7		

Check the Answer

6. Check to make sure you have entered all the data in the frequency table. Use the list of World Series games played each year. Add to find the number of games played in all from 1970 to 2004. _____

Solve Another Problem

7. Angela kept track of how many hours she practiced her saxophone each week over the nine months of the school year. Make a frequency table and use it to find the mode. _____

Number of hours of practice each week: 3, 5, 5, 0, 5, 3, 2, 1, 1, 4, 2, 4, 4, 5, 3, 0, 4, 3, 4, 2, 3, 3, 0, 4, 3, 5, 5, 0, 3, 4, 5, 3, 2, 2, 1

Name _____ Class _____ Date _____

Practice 12-2

Use the box-and-whisker plot to answer each question.

Weekly Mileage Totals, 24 Runners

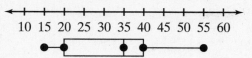

1. What is the highest weekly total? _____ the lowest? _____

2. What is the median weekly total? _____

3. What percent of runners run less than 40 miles a week? _____

4. How many runners run less than 20 miles a week? _____

Make a box-and-whisker plot for each set of data.

5. 16 20 30 15 23 11 15 21 30 29 13 16

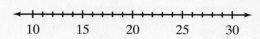

6. 9 12 10 3 2 3 9 11 5 1 10 4 7 12 3 10

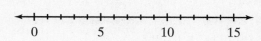

7. 70 77 67 65 79 82 70 68 75 73 69 66
70 73 89 72

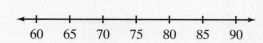

Use box-and-whisker plots to compare data sets. Use a single number line for each comparison.

8. 1st set: 7 12 25 3 1 29 30 7 15 2 5
           10 29 1 10 30 18 8 7 29
  2nd set: 37 17 14 43 27 19 32 1 8 48
           26 16 28 6 25 18

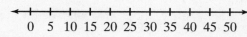

1st Set

2nd Set

9. Area in 1,000 mi^2
Midwestern states:
45 36 58 97 56 65 87 82 77
Southern states:
52 59 48 52 42 32 54 43 70 53 66

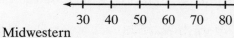

Midwestern
States

Southern
States

12-2 • Guided Problem Solving

GPS **Student Page 644, Exercise 8**

a. Olympics Compare the ages of male and female soccer players by making two box-and-whisker plots below one number line.

Ages of U.S. Olympic Soccer Team Players
men: 22, 21, 22, 26, 20, 26, 23, 21, 22, 22, 22, 22, 21, 22, 23, 21, 20, 22
women: 30, 27, 28, 25, 31, 24, 31, 24, 21, 23, 27, 18, 19, 24, 23, 20

b. Compare the two box-and-whisker plots. What can you conclude? _____

Understand the Problem

1. What data are you given? _____

2. What are you asked to do in part (a)? _____

3. What are you asked to do in part (b)? _____

Make and Carry Out a Plan

4. Arrange the ages of the men in order from least to greatest. Find the median of the data. Find the lower quartile and upper quartile, which are the medians of the lower and upper halves of the data. _____

5. Arrange the ages of the women in order from least to greatest. Find the median of the data. Find the lower quartile and upper quartile of the data. _____

6. On a separate sheet of paper, draw a number line that includes all of the ages of both the men and women soccer players.

7. Using the data you found in Step 4, draw a box-and-whisker plot for the data on the men's ages. (*Hint:* Since the upper quartile and the median are the same value, make only one mark.)

8. Below the first box-and-whisker plot, draw a box-and-whisker plot for the data on the women's ages.

9. How are the two box-and-whisker plots different? _____

Check the Answer

10. What information can you find from the two box-and-whisker plots due to the fact that they use the same number line? _____

Solve Another Problem

11. **a.** Use the data below to make two box-and-whisker plots on one number line.

    Ages of Members of the Varsity Swim Team
    boys: 16, 15, 15, 16, 17, 18, 17, 18, 17, 18, 14, 15, 15, 18, 17, 16, 18, 17
    girls: 12, 15, 15, 14, 17, 18, 18, 17, 14, 15, 14, 14, 16, 14, 13, 15

    b. Compare the two box-and-whisker plots. What can you conclude? _____

Practice 12-3

Use the graph at the right for Exercises 1–5.

1. Which group of animals appears to have more than twice as many endangered species as mammals?

_____

2. Does one group actually have twice as many endangered species as mammals?

_____

3. What gives the impression that one group has twice as many endangered species as mammals?

_____

4. Redraw the graph without a break.

5. Describe the effect the change in scale has on what the graph suggests.

_____

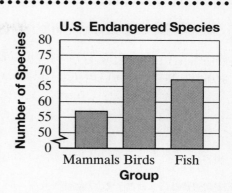

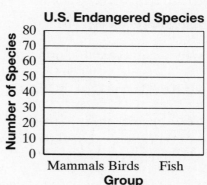

Use the data in the table for Exercises 6–8.

U.S. Union Membership							
Year	1930	1940	1950	1960	1970	1980	1990
Union members (millions)	3	9	14	17	19	20	17

6. Draw a line graph of the data using the grid below.

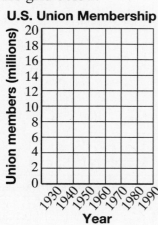

7. Draw a line graph of the data using the grid below.

8. What gives the different impressions in the two graphs?

_____

12-3 • Guided Problem Solving

Student Page 652, Exercise 15

Use the data at the right. Draw a line graph that gives the impression of a gradual increase in college tuition and fees from 1980 to 2001.

Average Annual Tuition and Fees for Four-Year Public Colleges

Year	Tuition and Fees
1980–1981	$1,647
1990–1991	$2,529
2000–2001	$3,535

Source: College Board

Understand the Problem

1. What information is given in the chart? _____

2. What are you asked to do? _____

Make and Carry Out a Plan

3. Use a separate sheet of paper. To begin your graph, draw a horizontal and vertical scale. Label the horizontal scale "Years." Label the vertical scale "Costs."

4. Begin labeling the vertical scale with $1,500. To make the costs seem to increase gradually, use large intervals. Label the axis in increments of $500.

5. Label the years on the horizontal axis. Space out the years to help make the increase look more gradual.

6. Plot the three data points on the graph and connect them to complete your line graph.

Check the Answer

7. Explain why the graph you drew gives the impression that college costs rose gradually from 1980 to 2001. _____

_____

Solve Another Problem

8. Use the data at the right. Draw a line graph that gives the impression that the number of students participating in sports increased sharply from 1990 to 1999.

Students in Sports

Year	Number of Students
1990–1991	187
1994–1995	210
1998–1999	225

Practice 12-4

Counting Outcomes and Theoretical Probability

A computer store sells 4 models of a computer (m1, m2, m3, and m4). Each model can be fitted with 3 sizes of hard drive (A, B, and C).

1. Find the sample space.

_____

_____

2. What is the probability of choosing a computer with a size C hard drive at random?

_____

3. What is the probability of choosing a model 2 computer with a size A hard drive at random?

_____

Solve each problem by drawing a tree diagram.

4. A ballot offered 3 choices for president (A, B, C) and 2 choices for vice president (M, N). How many choices for a combination of the two offices did it offer? List them.

_____

5. The Cougar baseball team has 4 pitchers (P1, P2, P3, P4) and 2 catchers (C1, C2). How many pitcher-catcher combinations are possible? List them.

_____

_____

Solve each problem by using the counting principle.

6. There are 5 roads from Allen to Baker, 7 roads from Baker to Carlson, and 4 roads from Carlson to Dodge. How many different routes from Allen to Dodge by way of Baker and Carlson are possible?

_____

7. Drapery is sold in 4 different fabrics. Each fabric comes in 13 different patterns. Each pattern is offered in 9 different colors. How many fabric-pattern-color combinations are there?

_____

12-4 • Guided Problem Solving

GPS **Student Page 660, Exercise 14**

Find the probability that you toss tails and roll an even number (when you toss a coin and roll a number cube).

Understand the Problem

1. What actions do you do? _____

2. What are you asked to find? _____

Make and Carry Out a Plan

3. What is the formula for theoretical probability? _____

4. Fill in the tree diagram to display and
   count the possible outcomes.
   Possible outcomes of coin toss:

   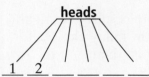 

   Possible outcomes of rolling a number cube: 1 2 __ __ __ __   1 __ __ __ __ __

5. What is the number of favorable outcomes
   (tossing tails and rolling an even number)? _____

6. What is the total number of possible outcomes? _____

7. Substitute your answers for Steps 5 and 6 into
   the probability formula and simplify if
   necessary. What is the probability of the event? _____

8. What is the probability you toss tails and roll an even number? _____

Check the Answer

9. Use the Counting Principle to find the number
   of possible outcomes of tossing a coin, m,
   and of rolling a number cube, n. Multiply m by n. _____
   The result should be the same as your answer to Step 6.

Solve Another Problem

10. You toss a coin and roll a number cube. You toss
    heads and roll a 1 or 2. Find the probability of the event. _____

Guided Problem Solving

Practice 12-5

Independent and Dependent Events

A shelf holds 3 novels, 2 biographies, and 1 history book. Two students in turn choose a book at random. What is the probability that the students choose each of the following?

1. both novels _____

2. both biographies _____

3. a history, then a novel _____

4. both history books _____

Meg flipped a penny the given number of times. What is the probability the results were as follows?

5. 2; two heads _____

6. 3; three tails _____

7. 2; a tail, then a head _____

8. 5; five tails _____

Two puppies are chosen at random from a box at the mall. What is the probability of these outcomes?

| Free Puppies for Adoption! |
| 5 black retrievers |
| 3 brown hounds |
| 4 black setters |

9. both black _____

10. both brown _____

11. a setter, then a hound _____

12. a retriever, then a setter _____

13. both setters _____

Are the events independent or dependent? Explain.

14. A guest at a party takes a sandwich from a tray. A second guest then takes a sandwich.

_____

_____

15. Sam flips a coin and gets heads. He flips again and gets tails.

_____

You can select only two cards from the right. Find the probability of selecting a T and an N for each condition.

16. You replace the first card before drawing the second.

_____

17. You do not replace the first card before drawing the second.

_____

12-5 • Guided Problem Solving

GPS Student Page 666, Exercise 25

A refrigerator contains 12 orange drinks, 4 grape drinks, and
25 apple drinks. Ann is first in the line for drinks. Mark is second.
What is the probability that Ann gets an apple drink and Mark
gets a grape drink, if they are given drinks at random?

Understand the Problem

1. How many orange, grape, and
   apple drinks are in the refrigerator? _____

2. Who is first in line? Second in line? _____

3. What are you asked to find? _____

Make and Carry Out a Plan

4. How many drinks are there in the refrigerator? _____

5. What is the probability that Ann gets an apple drink? _____

6. How many drinks are left in the refrigerator after Ann gets a drink? _____

7. Assuming that Ann gets an apple drink, what is the probability
   that, of the drinks left in the refrigerator, Mark gets a grape drink? _____

8. Are the two events, Ann getting an apple drink and Mark
   getting a grape drink, independent or dependent? Explain. _____

   _____

9. To find the probability of both events occurring, multiply the
   probability of Ann getting an apple drink and the probability
   of Mark getting a grape drink after Ann has gotten an apple drink. _____

Check the Answer

10. Explain how Ann getting an apple drink before
    Mark gets a drink affects Mark's probability of
    getting a grape drink in terms of the number of drinks he
    has to choose from and the number of grape drinks there are. _____

    _____

Solve Another Problem

11. There are 9 apples, 15 peaches, and 12 pears in a bowl.
    Jason is first in line for a piece of fruit. Tasha is second
    in line. What is the probability that Jason gets an apple
    and Tasha gets a peach, if they are given fruit at random? _____

Practice 12-6

Permutations and Combinations

Simplify each expression.

1. $_7P_2$ _____

2. $_7C_2$ _____

3. $_8P_3$ _____

4. $_9P_4$ _____

5. $_3C_2$ _____

6. $_{10}C_4$ _____

7. Art, Becky, Carl, and Denise are lined up to buy tickets.

   a. How many different permutations of the four are possible?

   _____

   b. Suppose Ed was also in line. How many permutations would there be?

   _____

   c. In how many of the permutations of the five is Becky first?

   _____

   d. What is the probability that a permutation of this five chosen at random will have Becky first?

   _____

8. Art, Becky, Carl, Denise, and Ed all want to go to the concert. However, there are only 3 tickets. How many ways can they choose the 3 who get to go to the concert?

   _____

9. A combination lock has 36 numbers on it. How many different 3-number combinations are possible if no number may be repeated?

   _____

Numbers are to be formed using the digits 1, 2, 3, 4, 5, and 6. No digit may be repeated.

10. How many two-digit numbers can be formed? _____

11. How many three-digit numbers can be formed? _____

12. How many four-digit numbers can be formed? _____

13. How many five-digit numbers can be formed? _____

14. How many six-digit numbers can be formed? _____

12-6 • Guided Problem Solving

GPS **Student Page 670, Exercise 16**

Literature Louisa May Alcott published 13 novels during her lifetime. In how many ways could you select three of these books?

Understand the Problem

1. How many novels did Louisa May Alcott publish in her lifetime? _____

2. What are you asked to find? _____

Make and Carry Out a Plan

3. Does the order in which you select the books matter? Explain. _____

_____

4. Is this a permutation or combination problem? _____

5. How many books are you choosing at a time? This is the value r in $_nC_r$. _____

6. What value is n, the number of books from which you choose? _____

7. Substitute the values for r and n in $_nC_r = \dfrac{_nP_r}{_rP_r}$. _____

8. Simplify the expression from Step 7. _____

9. In how many ways could you select three of Louisa May Alcott's books? _____

Check the Answer

10. Explain the difference between a permutation and combination and how you determined whether the problem was a permutation or combination. _____

_____

_____

Solve Another Problem

11. Terri just had her picture taken at a studio. The photographer took 12 pictures. In how many different ways could Terri choose four of the pictures to buy? _____

Practice 12-7

The table shows the colors of Rahmi's soccer shirts. For each color, find the experimental probability that a random shirt from Rahmi's collection is that color. Write the probability as a percent, to the nearest tenth of a percent.

Color	Number of shirts
red	6
white	4
orange	3
blue	2

1. red _____

2. white _____

3. orange _____

4. blue _____

5. red or blue _____

6. not white _____

7. not orange or red _____

8. green _____

Your school's basketball team has an equal chance of winning or losing the first three games of the season. You simulate the probability by tossing a coin 60 times, letting heads stand for a win and tails stand for a loss. Use the data below. Find each experimental probability as a percent.

HHH THH THT TTH THH
HTH THH THH HTH HHH
THH TTH THH HTT TTT
HTT HHT TTH HTH THH

9. P(win all 3) _____

10. P(win exactly 2) _____

11. P(win exactly 1) _____

12. P(win none) _____

13. P(win at least 2) _____

14. P(win at least 1) _____

15. P(win less than 2) _____

Students were surveyed about the number of children living in their household. The table shows the results. Write each experimental probability as a fraction in simplest form.

Number of Children	Number of Students
0	0
1	11
2	15
3	3
4 or more	4

16. P(one child) _____

17. P(2 or more children) _____

18. P(at least 3 children) _____

12-7 • Guided Problem Solving

GPS **Student Page 676, Exercise 15**

Two players played a number-cube game.
The table shows the results.
  a. Find P(A wins) and P(B wins).
  b. **Writing in Math** A *fair game* is one in which each player has
  the same chance of winning. Do you think the game that A and
  B played is fair? Explain.

Game Results

A Wins	B Wins
⁜⁜⁜⁜⁜⁜⁜⁜⁜⁜⁜⁜⁜⁜⁜⁜⁜⁜⁜⁜ ⁜⁜⁜⁜⁜ IIII	⁜⁜⁜⁜⁜⁜⁜⁜⁜⁜⁜⁜⁜⁜⁜⁜⁜⁜⁜⁜ ⁜⁜⁜⁜⁜⁜⁜⁜⁜⁜⁜⁜⁜⁜⁜⁜⁜⁜⁜⁜ ⁜⁜⁜⁜⁜⁜⁜⁜⁜⁜ II

Understand the Problem

1. What data are shown in the table? _____

2. What are you asked to do in part (a)? _____ In part (b)? _____

Make and Carry Out a Plan

3. How many times did player A win? _____ Player B? _____

4. How many times did the two players play the game? _____

5. What is the experimental probability that player A wins? _____ Player B? _____

6. How do the chances that player A wins
compare with the chances that player B wins? _____

7. Is the game that A and B played fair? Explain. _____

_____

Check the Answer

8. Why do you use experimental probability
instead of theoretical probability in this problem? _____

_____

Solve Another Problem

9. Two players played a game with a spinner several times.
The table shows the results.

  a. Find P(R wins) and P(S wins). _____

  b. Do you think the game that
  R and S played is fair? Explain. _____

Game Results

R Wins	S Wins
⁜⁜⁜⁜⁜⁜⁜⁜⁜⁜⁜⁜⁜⁜⁜⁜⁜⁜⁜⁜ ⁜⁜⁜⁜⁜⁜⁜⁜⁜⁜⁜⁜⁜⁜⁜⁜⁜⁜⁜⁜ ⁜⁜⁜⁜⁜ III	⁜⁜⁜⁜⁜⁜⁜⁜⁜⁜⁜⁜⁜⁜⁜⁜⁜⁜⁜⁜ ⁜⁜⁜⁜⁜⁜⁜⁜⁜⁜⁜⁜⁜⁜⁜⁜⁜⁜⁜⁜ ⁜⁜⁜⁜⁜

_____

_____

Practice 12-8

A school has 800 students. Two random surveys are conducted to determine students' favorite sport. Use the data in the table to estimate the total number of students who prefer each sport.

Sport Samples				
Sample	Number Sampled	Favorite sport		
		Basketball	Football	Baseball
A	40	16	14	10
B	50	22	16	12

1. basketball based on Sample A _____

2. basketball based on Sample B _____

3. baseball based on Sample A _____

4. baseball based on Sample B _____

You want to find out if a school bond issue for a new computer center is likely to pass in the next election. State whether each survey plan describes a good sample. Explain your reasoning.

5. You interview people coming out of a computer store in your town.

_____

_____

_____

6. You choose people to interview at random from the city telephone book.

_____

_____

_____

7. You interview every tenth person leaving each voting place in your school district.

_____

_____

12-8 • Guided Problem Solving

GPS **Student Page 679, Exercise 5**

Estimation Of 75 pairs of jeans, 7 have flaws. Estimate how many
of 24,000 pairs of jeans are flawed.

Understand the Problem

1. How many pairs of jeans are checked? _____

2. Of those pairs of jeans, how many have flaws? _____

3. What are you asked to estimate? _____

_____

Make and Carry Out a Plan

4. Write a ratio that compares the number of
   flawed jeans found to the number of jeans checked. _____

5. Write a ratio that compares the number n of flawed
   jeans in all compared to the total number of jeans. _____

6. Use the ratios for Steps 4 and 5 to write a proportion. _____

7. Write the cross product equation. _____

8. By what number must you divide each side to solve for n? _____

9. Simplify to estimate how many of 24,000 pairs of jeans are flawed. _____

Check the Answer

10. You can check your answer by replacing n with
    your answer in the proportion in Step 6. How
    will you know whether your answer is correct? _____

_____

Solve Another Problem

11. Of 100 students chosen at random, 42 had attended
    the school's soccer game the night before. Estimate how
    many of the school's 650 students attended the soccer game. _____

Practice 12-9

Solve by simulating the problem.

1. Twenty people seated in a circle counted to seven, beginning with the number one. The seventh person dropped out and those remaining counted to seven again. If every seventh person dropped out, what was the number of the last person remaining in the circle? Use the number circle to simulate the problem.

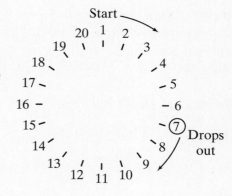

_____

2. The Rockets played their first volleyball game on Friday, October 18, and played a game every Friday thereafter.

   a. What was the date of their ninth game?

   _____

   b. What was the number of the game they played on February 7?

   _____

3. Five coins are placed side by side as shown. A move consists of sliding two adjacent coins to an open spot without changing the order of the two coins. (The move "2-3 right" is illustrated.) Find three successive moves that will leave the coins in this order: 3-1-5-2-4

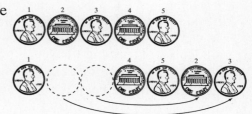

_____

_____

4. An irresponsible TV weatherperson forecasts the weather by throwing a number cube and consulting the weather key shown here. The weather during one 5-day stretch is given in the table. What is the probability that the forecaster was right at least 3 days out of 5? Use a number cube to simulate the forecaster's predictions. A successful trial occurs when you roll the correct weather three or more times out of five.

Weather Key
1–clear and warm
2–clear and cool
3–cloudy and cool
4–intermittent showers
5–continual rain
6–snow

Mon	Tue	Wed	Thu	Fri
continual rain	continual rain	clear and cool	cloudy and cool	snow

Work with a partner. Carry out 50 trials. Write the probability after the given number of trials.

a. 10 _____   **b.** 30 _____   **c.** 50 _____

12-9 • Guided Problem Solving

Thirteen of 25 students are going on a field trip. Six students are
traveling in a van. What is the theoretical probability that a
student chosen at random from those going on the trip is *not*
traveling in the van?

Understand the Problem

1. How many of the 25 students are going on a field trip? _____

2. How many students are traveling in a van? _____

3. What are you asked to find? _____

_____

Make and Carry Out a Plan

4. For traveling in the van, how many students are there to choose from? _____
   This is the number of possible outcomes.

5. If 6 students will travel in the van, how
   many students will *not* travel in the van? _____
   This is the number of favorable outcomes.

6. What is the theoretical probability that a
   student going on the field trip is *not* traveling in the van? _____

Check the Answer

7. To check your answer, find the probability that a student
   chosen at random from those going on the trip *is* traveling in the van. _____

8. How does this result support your answer? _____

_____

Solve Another Problem

9. Seventeen of 26 students in a class play instruments.
   Four of them play saxophone. What is the theoretical
   probability that a student chosen at random from
   those who play instruments does *not* play the saxophone? _____

12A: Graphic Organizer

For use before Lesson 12-1

Study Skill As you near the end of this text, begin now to start reviewing previous chapters, instead of waiting until you have completely finished. Studying for any test is much easier if you begin your review early.

Write your answers. Use the Table of Contents page for this chapter at the front of the book.

1. What is the title of this chapter? _____

2. Name four topics that you will study in this chapter:

   _____   _____

   _____   _____

3. What is the topic of the Problem Solving lesson? _____

4. Complete the graphic organizer as you work through the chapter.
   1. Write the title of the chapter in the center oval.
   2. When you begin a lesson, write the name of the lesson in a
      rectangle.
   3. When you complete that lesson, write a skill or key concept from
      that lesson in the outer oval linked to that rectangle.
   Continue with steps 2 and 3 clockwise around the graphic organizer.

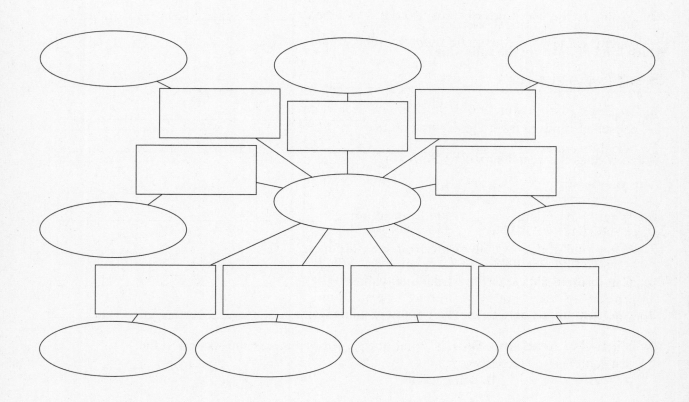

12B: Reading Comprehension

For use after Lesson 12-8

Study Skill If you will be answering questions about a passage, read the questions before you read the passage and have a notebook handy so that you can write brief notes as you read.

Read the passage below and answer the questions that follow.

The data used in statistics can be either discrete or continuous. The number of hits by a baseball player and the number of students in a class are examples of discrete data, because the data can have only certain values. Discrete data are often in the form of whole numbers—the results of counting. However, discrete data sometimes have fractional values. For example, a hat size might be 7 or $7\frac{1}{4}$ or $7\frac{1}{2}$, but there are no hat sizes between those values.

On the other hand, heights and temperatures are examples of continuous data, because these measurements can have any values, including fractional and even irrational values. A door might be 79.75 inches tall, or 79.754 inches tall (if a measuring instrument that is precise enough is used); the temperature of a liquid might be 99.8 degrees, or 99.8032 degrees, or anywhere in between. Continuous data are often the results of measurements. Continuous data are often grouped into discrete sets for the purpose of organization. For example, heights might be measured to the nearest inch or nearest half inch.

1. What is the subject of this passage? _____

2. What are the two kinds of statistical data described? _____

Which kind of data are the following?

3. basketball scores _____

4. shoe sizes _____

5. weights of coins _____

Write your answer.

6. What kind of data usually result from counting? _____

7. What kind of data usually result from measurement? _____

8. Can discrete data ever have fractional values? _____

9. Can continuous data have whole number values? _____

10. **High-Use Academic Words** What does *purpose* mean in the second to the last sentence in the passage?
   a. goal   **b.** comparison

12C: Reading/Writing Math Symbols   For use after Lesson 12-3

Study Skill Diagrams can be very useful tools if they are complete. When making a diagram, be sure it contains all the key information even if this information has been given in the text that goes with the diagram.

Use this box-and-whisker plot to answer the questions about the data set it represents.

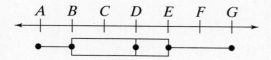

What does each dot show?

1. *A* _____

2. *G* _____

3. *B* _____

4. *D* _____

5. *E* _____

What fraction represents each of the following?

6. data contained in the box from *B* to *E* _____

7. data contained in the box from *B* to *D* _____

8. data contained in the box from *D* to *E* _____

9. data shown by the whisker from *A* to *B* _____

10. data shown by the whisker from *E* to *G* _____

11. What can you say about the number of data points
    from *B* to *D*, compared to the number from *D* to *E*? _____

12D: Visual Vocabulary Practice

For use after Lesson 12-6

Study Skill Mathematic skills are easier to understand and remember if you can apply them to your own life.

Concept List

bar graph	box-and-whisker plot	circle graph
frequency table	histogram	line graph
line plot	stem-and-leaf plot	tree diagram

Write the concept that best describes each exercise. Choose from the concept list above.

1.

Number	Frequency
0	3
1	5
2	4
3	5
4	4

_____

2.

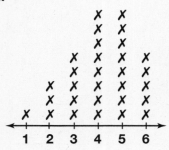

_____

3.

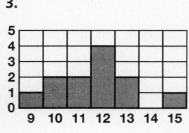

_____

4.

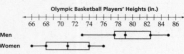

Olympic Basketball Players' Heights (in.)

_____

5.

```
4 | 1 7
5 | 3 7
6 | 0
7 | 5 6 9
8 | 1 4 5 6

7 | 5  means 75
```

_____

6.

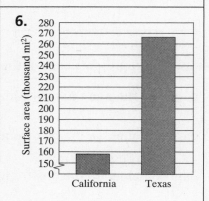

_____

7.

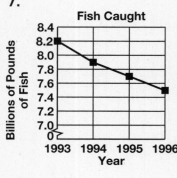

_____

8.

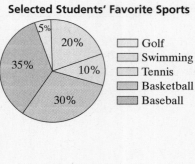

Selected Students' Favorite Sports

_____

9.

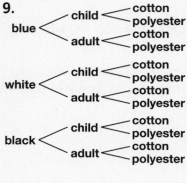

_____

12E: Vocabulary Check

Study Skill Strengthen your vocabulary. Use these pages and add cues and summaries by applying the Cornell Notetaking style.

Write the definition for each word at the right. To check your work, fold the paper back along the dotted line to see the correct answers.

_____

_____

_____

Theoretical probability

_____

_____

Independent events

_____

_____

Dependent events

_____

_____

_____

Simulation

_____

_____

_____

Experimental probability

_____

_____

Vocabulary and Study Skills

12E: Vocabulary Check (continued)

For use after Lesson 12-7

Write the vocabulary word for each definition. To check your work,
fold the paper forward along the dotted line to see the correct answers.

$P(E)$ = number of
favorable outcomes/
number of possible
outcomes.
When outcomes
are equally likely.

_____

Two events if the
occurrence of one event
does not affect the
probability of the
occurrence of the other.

_____

Two events for which
the occurrence of one
event affects the
probability of the
occurrence of the other.

_____

A model used to find
experimental probability.

_____

$P(E)$ = number of times
an event occurs/number
of times experiment
is done.

_____

12F: Vocabulary Review Puzzle

For use with Chapter Review

Study Skill When reviewing a chapter, use the Chapter Review materials that have been provided in the text. Verify that you know the definition of each word or phrase in the Vocabulary Review.

Write the words that match the descriptions below and then circle the letters that form each word in the puzzle. Remember that a word may go right to left, left to right, or it may go up as well as down.

1. difference between greatest and least values

   _____

2. the number of times a data item occurs

   _____

3. divides the data into four equal parts

   _____

4. a model used to find experimental probability

   _____

5. a part of the population used to make estimates

   _____

6. a group about which you want information

   _____

7. one member is as likely to be chosen as any other

   _____

8. events in which the first event does affect the second event

   _____

```
E  D  E  P  E  N  D  E  N  T  F  U  N
P  O  P  U  L  A  T  I  O  N  R  M  O
E  E  N  P  O  Q  R  S  U  P  E  O  I
A  T  U  N  P  U  A  U  I  E  Q  S  T
N  U  M  D  E  A  N  L  D  U  U  D  A
S  U  D  L  L  R  G  N  M  M  E  T  L
N  A  N  A  G  T  E  N  E  A  N  I  U
M  T  O  E  O  I  P  Q  U  I  C  E  M
N  A  P  O  E  L  U  E  R  L  Y  O  I
E  T  S  F  E  E  R  A  N  D  O  M  S
N  L  N  D  S  A  M  P  L  E  P  U  D
```

Practice 13-1

Tell whether each sequence is *arithmetic*, *geometric*, or *neither*. Find the
next three terms of each sequence. If the sequence is arithmetic or
geometric, write a rule to describe the sequence.

1. 7, 14, 28, 56, _____ , _____ , _____   type: _____

rule: _____

2. 5, 11, 17, 23, _____ , _____ , _____   type: _____

rule: _____

3. 32, 16, 8, 4, _____ , _____ , _____   type: _____

rule: _____

4. 25, 21, 17, 13, _____ , _____ , _____   type: _____

rule: _____

5. 9, 3, −3, −9, _____ , _____ , _____   type: _____

rule: _____

6. 8, 3, −3, −10, _____ , _____ , _____   type: _____

rule: _____

7. 2, −6, 18, −54, _____ , _____ , _____   type: _____

rule: _____

8. 1, 4, 9, 16, _____ , _____ , _____   type: _____

rule: _____

What is the common difference of each arithmetic sequence?

9. 16, 19, 22, 25, . . .   _____   **10.** 3, 5.8, 8.6, 11.4, . . .   _____

What is the common ratio of each geometric sequence?

11. 6, 24, 96, 384, . . .   _____   **12.** 12, 3, $\frac{3}{4}$, $\frac{3}{16}$, . . .   _____

13-1 • Guided Problem Solving

GPS **Student Page 699, Exercise 30**

Find the next three terms of the sequence $1, 4, 16, 64, \ldots$
Then write a rule to describe the sequence.

Understand the Problem

1. What are you asked to do? _____

Make and Carry Out a Plan

2. Look at the numbers in the sequence. Is there
a common difference, common ratio, or pattern? _____

3. What is the common difference, common ratio, or pattern? _____

4. Find the next three terms using the
common difference, common ratio, or pattern. _____

5. Write a rule for the sequence. _____

Check the Answer

6. To check your answer, work backward from the last
term you found. For example, if the rule were "Start with
2 and multiply by 3 repeatedly," then you would work
backward dividing each number by 3 until you reached 2. _____

Solve Another Problem

7. Find the next three terms in the sequence $2, 5, 8, 11, \ldots$
Then write a rule to describe the sequence.

_____

Practice 13-2

**For each function, complete the table for integer values of x from -2 to 2.
Then graph each function.**

1. $y = |x| - 2$

x	$y = |x| - 2$	(x, y)
−2		
−1		
0		
1		
2		

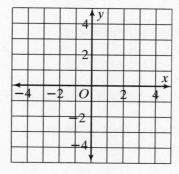

2. $y = -x^2 + 3$

x	$y = -x^2 + 3$	(x, y)
−2		
−1		
0		
1		
2		

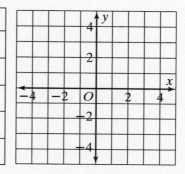

3. $y = 2x^2 - 4$

x	$y = 2x^2 - 4$	(x, y)
−2		
−1		
0		
1		
2		

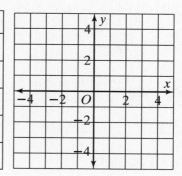

4. $y = -2|x| + 3$

x	$y = -2|x| + 3$	(x, y)
−2		
−1		
0		
1		

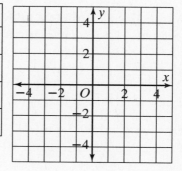

13-2 • Guided Problem Solving

GPS Student Page 704, Exercise 26

State whether the graph of the function $y = -\frac{1}{2}|x|$ has a U shape or a V shape.
Make a table with integer values of x from -2 to 2. Then graph the function.

Understand the Problem

1. What are you asked to do first? _____

2. List the integer values of x that will be included in your table. _____

Make and Carry Out a Plan

3. Is the function a quadratic function or an absolute value function?

   _____

4. What kind of shape is the function you chose in Step 3?

   _____

x	$y = -\frac{1}{2}|x|$	(x, y)
–2		
–1		
0		
1		
2		

5. Make a table like the one at right with integer values of x from -2 to 2. Use the function to find the y value for each x value.

6. Draw a coordinate plane on a sheet of graph paper.
   Label the x- and y-axes with values between -2 and 2.
   Use the ordered pairs from your table to graph the function.

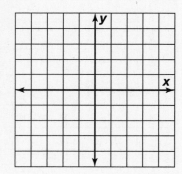

Check the Answer

7. Compare the shape of your graph with the shape you predicted in Step 4.

Solve Another Problem

8. State whether the graph of the function $y = 2x^2 - x$ has a U shape or a V shape. Make a table with integer values of x from -2 to 2. Then graph the function.

x	$y = 2x^2 - x$	(x, y)
–2		
–1		
0		
1		
2		

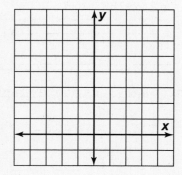

Guided Problem Solving

Practice 13-3

Exponential Growth and Decay

Complete the table for integer values of *x* from 0 to 4. Then graph each function.

1. $y = \frac{1}{3} \cdot 3^x$

x	y	(x, y)
0		
1		
2		
3		
4		

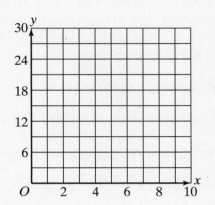

2. $y = \frac{5}{2} \cdot 2^x$

x	y	(x, y)
0		
1		
2		
3		
4		

3. $y = 50(0.2)^x$

x	y	(x, y)
0		
1		
2		
3		
4		

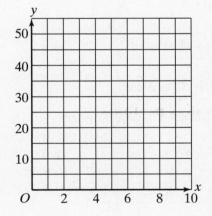

Is the point (3, 9) on the graph of each function?

4. $y = x^2$ _____

5. $y = 3^x$ _____

6. $y = \frac{1}{3} \cdot 3^x$ _____

7. $y = 3 \cdot \left(\frac{1}{3}\right)^x$ _____

8. $y = 3x$ _____

9. $y = x^3$ _____

13-3 • Guided Problem Solving

GPS Student Page 709, Exercise 7

Biology A bacteria culture starts with 10 cells and doubles every hour. The function $y = 10(2)^x$ models the number of cells y in the culture after x hours. Make a table of integer values of x from 0 to 3. Then graph the function.

Understand the Problem

1. How many cells are in the bacteria culture to start? _____

2. How often does the number of bacteria cells double? _____

3. What is the function that models the
   number of cells y in the culture after x hours? _____

4. What are you asked to do? _____

Make and Carry Out a Plan

5. Replace x with 0 in the function. Simplify to find the value of y.
   Repeat with x values of 1, 2, and 3.

6. Graph the function using the values from step 5.

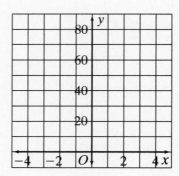

Check the Answer

7. To check your answer, multiply 10 by 2. This is the number
   of cells after 1 hour. Then multiply that number by 2. This
   is the number of cells after 2 hours. Finally, multiply again by 2. _____
   This is the number of cells after three hours. These numbers should
   match the values of y for x values of 1, 2, and 3 in your table of values.

Solve Another Problem

8. A bacteria culture starts with 20 cells and triples every hour. The
   function $y = 20(3)^x$ models the number of cells y in the culture
   after x hours. Make a table of integer values from 0 to 3. Then
   graph the function.

Practice 13-4

Evaluate each polynomial for $x = -1$, $y = 3$, and $z = 2$.

1. $x^2 + z$ _____

2. $3y + x$ _____

3. $2z + y$ _____

4. $x + y + z$ _____

5. $x^2 + y^2$ _____

6. $z - x - y$ _____

Evaluate each polynomial for $m = 21$, $n = -9$, and $p = 28$.

7. $3m - 2p$ _____

8. $2n^2 - 5m$ _____

9. $m^2 - n^2$ _____

10. $n^2 + 5n - 6$ _____

11. $5p^2 - 5p$ _____

12. $7m + 6p$ _____

Solve using the given polynomials.

13. Find the number of diagonals that can be drawn in a polygon with 24 sides.
$N = \frac{1}{2}n^2 - \frac{3}{2}n$
N = number of diagonals
n = number of sides

_____

14. A rock thrown from the top of a cliff at an initial velocity of 3 m/s takes 6.2 s to reach the bottom. To the nearest meter, how tall is the cliff?
$d = 4.9t^2 - vt$
d = distance fallen
t = time falling
v = initial velocity

_____

Tell whether each polynomial is a *monomial*, a *binomial*, or a *trinomial*.

15. $36abc$ _____

16. $10 - h^3$ _____

17. $95xy + y$ _____

18. $a^2 + b^2 + cd$ _____

19. $3k$ _____

20. $-12e + 12f^2$ _____

13-4 • Guided Problem Solving

Sports The polynomial $-16t^2 + 32t + 4$ gives the height, in feet, that a tossed ball reaches in t seconds. If the ball reaches a maximum height after one second, what is that height?

Understand the Problem

1. What does the polynomial $-16t^2 + 32t + 4$ give? _____

   _____

2. What does the variable t represent? _____

3. What are you asked to find? _____

   _____

Make and Carry Out a Plan

4. Replace t with 1 in the polynomial. _____

5. Simplify the polynomial. _____

6. What is the maximum height the ball reaches? _____

Check the Answer

7. To check your answer, replace t with $\frac{1}{2}$ and simplify the polynomial. Then replace t with $1\frac{1}{2}$ and simplify. Do these results support the statement that the maximum height is reached at one second? _____

Solve Another Problem

8. The polynomial $-16t^2 + 20t + 12$ gives the height, in feet, that a ball tossed from the top of a 12-foot ladder reaches in t seconds. What is the ball's height after one second? _____

Practice 13-5

Adding and Subtracting Polynomials

Simplify each sum or difference.

1. $(10m - 4) - (3m - 5)$ ___$7m + 1$___

2. $(k^2 - 2k + 5) - (k^2 + 5k + 3)$ ___$2k^2 + 3 + 2$___ $-7k + 2$

$2k^2$

3. $(2x^2 + 7x - 4) - (x^2 + 4)$ ___$3x^2 + 7x$___ x

4. $2x^2 + 4 + (3x^2 - 4x - 5)$ ___$5x^2 - 1 - 4x$___

5. $(-2x^2 + 4x - 5) + (8x + 5x^2 + 6)$ ___$3x^2 + 12x + 1$___

6. $(3x^2y^2 + 2xy + 5y) - (-2x^2y^2 - 4x - 5y)$ $5x^2y^2 + 2xy + 4x$

7. $(7x^3 - 5x^2 - 3x + 8) - (10x^3 - 4x^2 + 5x + 9)$ $-3x^3 - 1x^2 - 8x - 1$

8. $\begin{array}{l} 2x^3 - 5x^2 \quad\;\; - 5 \\ + 3x^3 + 7x^2 + 9x \end{array}$

___$5x^3 + 2x^2 + 9x - 5$___

9. $\begin{array}{l} -4x^2y^2 + 3xy + x^2 - 4y^2 \\ + x^2y^2 - 6xy - x^2 - 5y^2 \end{array}$

___$-3x^2y^2 - 3xy - 9y^2$___

10. $(x^2 + 2y + 5) - (4x + 4y)$

___$x^2 - 2y + 5 - 4x$___

11. $(-4a^2b + 7ab^2 - 9a - 6b + 13) - (-6a^2b + 8a + 10b - 18)$

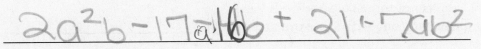

$2a^2b - 17 - 16b + 21 - 7ab^2$

Write the perimeter of each figure as a polynomial. Simplify.

12.

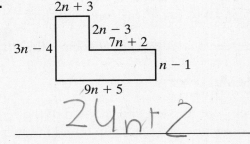

5m

$2m^2 - 2$ $2m^2 - 3$

___$4m^2 + 5m - 5$___

13.

2n + 3
2n - 3
3n - 4   7n + 2
n - 1
9n + 5

___$24n + 2$___

13-5 • Guided Problem Solving

GPS **Student Page 720, Exercise 27**

a. Write an expression for the sum of three consecutive
integers. Let x be the first integer. Then simplify the expression.

b. What three consecutive integers have the sum 108?

Understand the Problem

1. What are you asked to do in part (a)? _____

2. What does the variable x represent? _____

3. What are you asked to find in part (b)? _____

Make and Carry Out a Plan

4. Write any three consecutive integers. _____

5. If x is the first integer, write an
   expression using x to represent the second integer. _____

6. If x is the first integer, write an
   expression using x to represent the third integer. _____

7. Use x and the expressions for the second
   and third consecutive integers to write an
   expression for the sum of three consecutive integers. _____

8. Simplify the expression. _____

9. Use the sentence "The sum of three consecutive integers
   is 108" and your expression from Step 8 to write an equation. _____

10. Solve the equation for x. _____

11. Use the value of x and your expressions from
    Steps 5 and 6 to find the second and third consecutive integers. _____

12. What three consecutive integers have the sum 108? _____

Check the Answer

13. To check your answer, find the sum of the
    three consecutive integers you found in Question 12. _____

Solve Another Problem

14. **a.** Write an expression for the sum of three consecutive odd integers. _____

    b. What three consecutive odd integers have the sum 27? _____

Practice 13-6

Multiplying a Polynomial by a Monomial

Simplify each product.

1. $4x(3x - 5)$ $12x^2 - 20x$

2. $-8x(x - 7)$ $-8x^2 + 56x$

3. $7xy^2(y - 2x + x^2)$ $7xy^3 - 14x^2y^2 + 7x^3y^2$

4. $3xy(2xy + 5)$ $6x^2y^2 + 15xy$

5. $-9xyz(-2xy + 3yz - 4xz)$ $18x^2y^2z - 27xy^2z^2 + 36x^2yz^2$

6. $12ab\left(-\frac{1}{2}b + \frac{1}{4}a^3\right)$ $-6ab^2 + 3a^4b$

7. $-15a^2(a - b + 3c)$ $-15a^3 + 15ba^2 - 15a^2c$

8. $-3x^2a^2(2a^3 + ab - x)$ $-6x^2a^5 - 3a^3bx^2 + 3x^3a^2$

Write an expression for the area of each shaded region. Simplify.

9.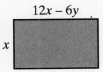

$x \cdot (12x - 6y)$

10.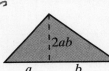

$ab(2ab)$

$\frac{1}{2}(2ab)(a+b) = a^2b + ab^2$

11.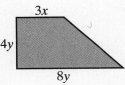

$8y(3x + 4y)$

Use the GCF of the terms to write each expression as the product of two factors.

12. $8x + 8y$ $8(x+y)$ $8x + 8y$

13. $13a - 13b$ $13(a - b)b$

14. $2x^3 + 2x^2$ $2x^2(x+1)$

15. $11a + 11b + 11c$ $11(abc)$

16. $x^3y^2 + x^2y^3 + x^4y$ $x^2y(xy + y^2 + x^2)$

17. $-12ab^2c + 18a^2bc^2 - 30ab^3c^3$ $6abc$

18. $90w^3x + 144w^2$ $18w^2(5wx + 8)$

13-6 • Guided Problem Solving

GPS Student Page 725, Exercise 11

Sports The length of an Olympic-size pool is 50 meters. If x represents the width of one lane, what is the area of a pool with five lanes?

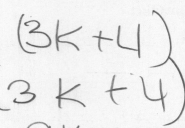

Understand the Problem

1. What is the length of the pool? _____

2. What does the variable x represent? _____

3. What are you asked to find? _____

Make and Carry Out a Plan

4. Write an expression to represent the width of the pool. _____

5. What is the formula for area of a rectangle? _____

6. Replace ℓ with 50 and w with the expression you wrote for Step 4 in the formula for area of a rectangle. _____

7. Simplify the product. _____

8. What is the area of a pool with five lanes? _____

Check the Answer

9. To check your answer, divide the area by the length of the pool. _____
   The answer should be the same as the expression you wrote for the width of the pool.

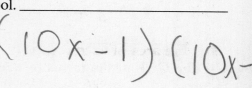

Solve Another Problem

10. One block of a city street is 100 ft long. The street has 4 lanes. If x represents the width of one lane, what is the area of this block of city street? _____

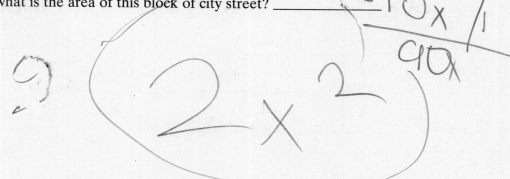

Practice 13-7

Simplify each product.

1. $(x + 2)(x + 3)$

  $x^2 + 5x + 6$

  $x^2 + 3x + 2x + 6$

2. $(x + 5)(x + 1)$

  $x^2 + x + 5x + 5$

  $x^2 + 6x + 5$

3. $(x + 4)(x + 5)$

  $x^2 + 5x + 4x + 20$

  $x^2 + 9x + 20$

4. $(x + 7)(x + 2)$

  $x^2 + 9x + 14$

5. $(x + 1)(x - 6)$

  $x^2 - 5x - 6$

6. $(x + 8)(x - 3)$

  $x^2 + 5x - 24$

7. $(2x + 5)(x + 3)$

  $11x + 15$ $2x^2 + 11x + 15$

8. $(x - 4)(x - 6)$

  $x^2 - 2x + 24$

9. $(2x - 7)(2x + 7)$

  $4x^2 - 49$

10. $(m - 15)(m - 20)$

  $m^2 - 30 + 300$

11. $(3k + 4)^2$

  $19k + 16$

12. $(x - 20)(x + 20)$

  $x^2 - 400$

13. $(5n + 4)(4n - 5)$

  $20n^2 - 9n - 20$

14. $(10x - 1)^2$

  $100x^2 - 20x + 1$

15. $(y - 7)(y - 6)$

  $y^2 - 13y + 42$

16. $(x - 9)(x - 5)$

  $x^2 - 14x + 45$

17. $(x - 10)(x + 3)$

  $x^2 - 7x + 30$

18. $(2x + 3)(3x + 2)$

  $6x^2 + 13x + 6$

Find the area of each rectangle.

19.

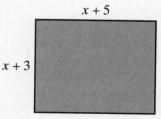

$x + 5$

$x + 3$

$x^2 + 8x + 15$

20.

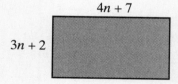

$4n + 7$

$3n + 2$

$33n + 8n + 14$

$(4n + 7)(3n + 2)$

$12n + 8n + 2n$

21.

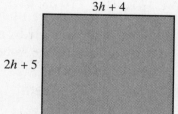

$3h + 4$

$2h + 5$

$6h^2 3h + 20$

13-7 • Guided Problem Solving

GPS **Student Page 729, Exercise 20**

Find the area of the rectangle.

$2c + 4$ ⬚
  $5c + 3$

Understand the Problem

1. What is the length of the rectangle? _____

2. What is the width of the rectangle? _____

3. What are you asked to find? _____

Make and Carry Out a Plan

4. What is the formula for area of a rectangle? _____

5. Replace ℓ with the length of the rectangle and
   w with the width of the rectangle in the formula. _____

6. Use the Distributive Property. _____

7. Use the Distributive Property again. _____

8. Add like terms together to simplify. _____

9. What is the area of the rectangle? _____

Check the Answer

10. To check your answer, use a model to multiply the
    length of the rectangle by the width of the rectangle. The
    product should be the same as your answer to Question 9. _____

Solve Another Problem

Find the area of the rectangle.

11.  _____
    $2x + 2$
    $6x + 1$

Practice 13-8

Use multiple strategies to solve each problem.

1. A rectangle has length $(x - 3)^2$ and width 4. The perimeter of the rectangle is 40. Find the length.

   _____

2. A rectangular prism has length $x + 2$, width $x + 1$, height 4, and volume 24. Find the length and the width.

   _____

3. A piece of cardboard measures 12 ft by 12 ft. Corners are to be cut from it as shown by the broken lines, and the sides folded up to make a box with an open top. What size corners should be cut from the cardboard to make a box with the greatest possible volume?

   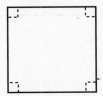

   _____

4. What size corners should be cut from a piece of cardboard that measures 30 in. by 30 in. to make an open-top box with the greatest possible volume?

   _____

5. What is the maximum number of small boxes that can fit inside the large box?

   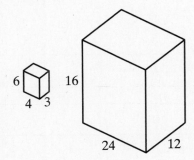

   _____

6. The perimeter of a right triangle is 24 in. Find the dimensions of the triangle if the sides are all whole-number lengths.

   _____

13-8 • Guided Problem Solving

GPS **Student Page 734, Exercise 10**

Geometry A lot measures 50 ft by 100 ft. The house on the lot measures 25 ft by 50 ft. What is the area of the lawn?

Understand the Problem

1. What are the measurements of the lot? _____

2. What are the measurements of the house? _____

3. What are you asked to find? _____

4. Draw and label a diagram of the house on the lot in the space below.

Make and Carry Out a Plan

5. Use the formula for area of a rectangle to find the area of the lot. _____

6. Find the area of the house. _____

7. Use the area of the lot and the area of the house to write an expression for the area of the lawn. _____

8. Simplify to find the area of the lawn. _____

Check the Answer

9. To check your answer, rewrite the expression, $50 \cdot 100 - 50 \cdot 25$ using the Distributive Property and simplify. _____
   The result should be the same as the area of the lawn you found in Question 8.

10. Does it make a difference where you place the house? Explain. _____

   _____

Solve Another Problem

11. A deli plate has a radius of 50 cm. The undecorated part has a radius of 17 cm. What is the area of the plate?

   _____

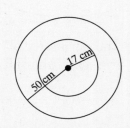

13A: Graphic Organizer

For use before Lesson 13-1

Study Skill As you complete the book, create for yourself a graphic organizer for the entire book. In the center, write the title of the book. Then write the chapter names in rectangles. Look back through each chapter and write the key ideas in circles linked to the chapter rectangles. Use your graphic organizer as you study for your final exam.

Write your answers. Use the Table of Contents page for this chapter at the front of the book.

1. What is the title of this chapter? _____

2. Name four topics that you will study in this chapter:

   _____   _____

   _____   _____

3. What is the topic of the Problem Solving lesson? _____

4. Complete the graphic organizer as you work through the chapter.
   1. Write the title of the chapter in the center oval.
   2. When you begin a lesson, write the name of the lesson in a rectangle.
   3. When you complete that lesson, write a skill or key concept from that lesson in the outer oval linked to that rectangle.

   Continue with steps 2 and 3 clockwise around the graphic organizer.

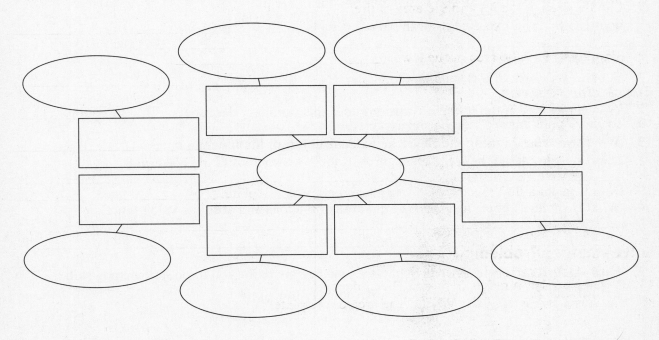

Pre-Algebra Chapter 13 **561**

13B: Reading Comprehension

Study Skill When memorizing material, read it aloud. When you involve more than one of your senses, such as both sight and hearing, as you learn, you will recall the content more easily.

Look at the summary in the box, and then answer the questions that follow.

Summary of Some Types of Nonlinear Functions

Quadratic Function—

Equation: has x^2, but y is not squared.
Example: $y = 3x^2$
Graph: a U-shaped curve called a parabola.
May open upward or downward.
Is the same on both sides of a vertical line of symmetry
that goes through the lowest or highest point of the graph.

Absolute Value Function—

Equation: has $|x|$ and y, not $|y|$.
Example: $y = -|x| + 2$
Graph: a V-shape
May open upward or downward.
Is the same on both sides of a vertical line of symmetry
that goes through the lowest or highest point of the graph.

Exponential Function—

Equation: has x as an exponent, and y with exponent 1.
Example: $y = 3(2^x)$
Graph: a curved shape that is not a U nor a V
$y = a^x$ is always increasing for $a > 1$ and always decreasing
for $0 < a < 1$.

---

1. What is the topic of this summary? _____

2. How many types of non-linear functions does this summary describe? _____

3. What two types of information are included for each of the function types? _____

_____

4. What is similiar about the graphs of quadratic functions and absolute value functions?

_____

5. **High-Use Academic Words** What does *involve* mean for you to do in the study skill?
   a. turn off   **b.** actively use

13C: Reading/Writing Math Symbols

For use after Lesson 13-7

Study Skill At the end of a lesson, chapter, or course, take time to reflect back on what you have just done and learned. Think about how your new skills relate to what you already know, and to what you will learn next.

Express each of the following equalities in a symbolic form.

1. y is four more than the square of x.

   _____

2. The absolute value of negative 3 is the opposite of negative 3.

   _____

3. y is the opposite of the absolute value of x.

   _____

4. The function of x is the absolute value of x.

   _____

5. y is the square of the quantity four more than x.

   _____

6. The square of the absolute value of x is the same as the square of x.

   _____

Express each of the following inequalities in a symbolic form.

7. The absolute value of p is always greater than or equal to p.

   _____

8. x is less than its absolute value if x is less than zero.

   _____

9. If b is between 0 and 1 (but not equal to 0 or 1), then the reciprocal of b is greater than b.

   _____

10. The product of negative 2 and the absolute value of x is less than or equal to zero.

    _____

11. The value of a is between 0 and 10.

    _____

12. The value of b is greater than 2, but less than or equal to 5.

    _____

13D: Visual Vocabulary Practice

For use after Lesson 13-4

Study Skill When interpreting an illustration, notice the information that is given and also notice what is not given. Do not make assumptions.

Concept List

absolute value graph	arithmetic sequence	binomial
exponential decay graph	exponential growth graph	geometric sequence
monomial	parabola	trinomial

Write the concept that best describes each exercise. Choose from the concept list above.

1. 2, 9, 16, 23, 30, . . . _____	**2.** 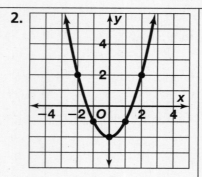 _____	**3.** 1, 2, 5, 25, 125, . . . _____
4. 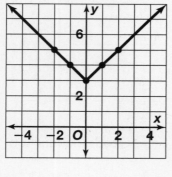 _____	**5.** $3a + 9$ _____	**6.** 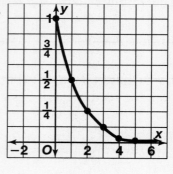 _____
7. $4c^3$ _____	**8.** 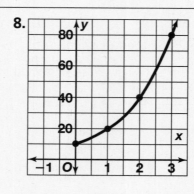 _____	**9.** $6y^2 - y + 9$ _____

13E: Vocabulary Check

Study Skill Strengthen your vocabulary. Use these pages and add cues and summaries by applying the Cornell Notetaking style.

Write the definition for each word at the right. To check your work, fold the paper back along the dotted line to see the correct answers.

_____

_____

_____   Sequence

_____

_____   Arithmetic sequence

_____

_____

_____   Geometric sequence

_____

_____

_____   Quadratic function

_____

_____

_____   Absolute value function

_____

_____

13E: Vocabulary Check (continued)   For use after Lesson 13-2

Write the vocabulary word for each definition. To check your work, fold the paper forward along the dotted line to see the correct answers.

A set of numbers that follow a pattern.

_____

A sequence of numbers in which each term after the first is the result of adding a fixed number, called a common difference, to the previous number.

_____

A sequence of numbers in which each term after the first is the result of multiplying the previous term by a fixed number, called the common ratio.

_____

A function based on squaring the input variable. The graph is a parabola.

_____

A function with a graph that is V-shaped and opens up or down.

_____

13F: Vocabulary Review

For use with Chapter Review

Study Skill Many mathematical ideas are similar. When you think two mathematical words or phrases have the same meaning, use the Glossary in your textbook to verify that you correctly understand each meaning.

For each pair below, write a brief explanation of how to tell the difference between the two mathematical ideas in the pair.

1. monomial/binomial

   _____

2. trinomial/polynomial

   _____

   _____

3. linear function/quadratic function

   _____

   _____

4. arithmetic sequence/geometric sequence

   _____

   _____

   _____

5. common difference/common ratio

   _____

   _____

   _____

   _____

6. factor/term

   _____

   _____

   _____